Further acclaim for Erik Larson's No.1 bestse"
DEAD WAKE:

'Vivid . . . Larson tells his story well'
SUNDAY TIMES

'Larson's approach to history resembles a novelist's . . .
a rattling read'
GUARDIAN

'Larson's irresistibly pacey narrative moves between the various
scenes of action, conjuring them up in vivid detail . . . remarkable'
LITERARY REVIEW

'Larson has an eye for haunting, unexploited detail . . .
illuminating . . . suspenseful'
SCOTLAND ON SUNDAY

'Enthralling . . . demonstrates that there was far more going on
beneath the surface than is generally known . . . Larson's account
is the most lucid and suspenseful yet written'
WASHINGTON POST

'Larson is a master storyteller and quickens the pace as target and
attackers hurtle towards their inevitable, deadly rendezvous. The
suspense builds because readers care about his fully-formed
characters, and it's not always clear who will live and who will die'
SALON.COM

'Larson is a superb storyteller and a relentless research hound'
Lev Grossman, *TIME*

'Gripping . . . covers the ship's ill-fated transatlantic voyage in
absorbing detail . . . it is when dealing with the aftermath of the
tragedy, along with the attendant ⌐⌐⌐⌐⌐⌐⌐⌐ ⌐ries, that Larson
breaks ne⌐⌐⌐⌐⌐⌐⌐⌐⌐⌐⌐⌐⌐⌐⌐⌐⌐⌐⌐⌐⌐⌐⌐ ⌐ut down'

Erik Larson is a prize-winning journalist and narrative historian. His books include *Isaac's Storm*, *Thunderstruck*, the number one bestseller *The Devil in the White City*, which won an Edgar Award and was shortlisted for the CWA Gold Dagger Non-Fiction Award, and the acclaimed *In the Garden of Beasts*. He divides his time between Seattle and New York. To find out more, visit www.eriklarsonbooks.com

ALSO BY ERIK LARSON

In the Garden of Beasts

Thunderstruck

The Devil in the White City

Isaac's Storm

Lethal Passage

The Naked Consumer

DEAD WAKE

THE LAST CROSSING OF THE

LUSITANIA

ERIK LARSON

BLACK SWAN

TRANSWORLD PUBLISHERS
61–63 Uxbridge Road, London W5 5SA
www.transworldbooks.co.uk

Transworld is part of the Penguin Random House group of companies
whose addresses can be found at global.penguinrandomhouse.com

First published in Great Britain in 2015 by Doubleday
an imprint of Transworld Publishers
Black Swan edition published 2015

A CIP catalogue record for this book
is available from the British Library.

ISBN
9780552779340

Book design: Lauren Dong
Maps: Jeffrey L. Ward
Frontispiece: Mary Evans/Epic/Tallandier
Typeset in Sabon by Falcon Oast Graphic Art Ltd.
Printed and bound by CPI Group (UK) Ltd, Croydon, CR0 4YY

Penguin Random House is committed to a sustainable
future for our business, our readers and our planet. This book is made from
Forest Stewardship Council® certified paper.

1 3 5 7 9 10 8 6 4 2

For Chris, Kristen, Lauren, and Erin
(and Molly and Ralphie, absent, but not forgotten)

CONTENTS

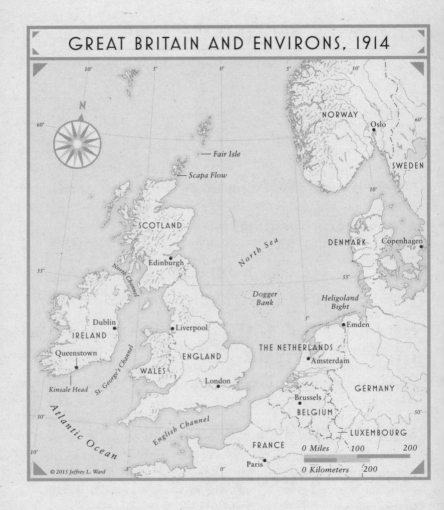

GREAT BRITAIN AND ENVIRONS, 1914

10°   5°   0°   5°   10°

N

60°

NORWAY

Oslo

60°

SWEDEN

— *Fair Isle*

— *Scapa Flow*

SCOTLAND

DENMARK

Copenhagen

North Sea

55°

Edinburgh

55°

Dogger Bank

Heligoland Bight

5°

10°

Dublin

Liverpool

Emden

IRELAND

THE NETHERLANDS

Queenstown

ENGLAND

Amsterdam

WALES

Kinsale Head

London

GERMANY

50°

Brussels

Paris

BELGIUM

50°

LUXEMBOURG

Atlantic Ocean

English Channel

FRANCE

0 Miles   100   200

0 Kilometers   200

North Channel

St. George's Channel

© 2015 Jeffrey L. Ward

MINING SUSPENSE

(A Note to Readers)

I FIRST STARTED READING about the *Lusitania* on a whim, following my between-books strategy of reading voraciously and promiscuously. What I learned both charmed and horrified me. I thought I knew everything there was to know about the incident, but, as so often happens when I do deep research on a subject, I quickly realized how wrong I was. Above all, I discovered that buried in the muddled details of the affair—deliberately muddled, in certain aspects—was something simple and satisfying: a *very* good story.

I hasten to add, as always, that this is a work of nonfiction. Anything between quotation marks comes from a memoir, letter, telegram, or other historical document. My goal was to try to marshal the many nodes of real-life suspense and, yes, romance that marked the *Lusitania* episode, in a manner that would allow readers to experience it as did people who lived through it at the time (although squeamish readers may wish to skip the details of a certain autopsy that appears late in the narrative).

In any event, I give you now the saga of the *Lusitania*, and the myriad forces, large and achingly small, that converged one lovely day in May 1915 to produce a tragedy of monumental scale, whose true character and import have long been obscured in the mists of history.

ERIK LARSON
SEATTLE

A WORD ABOUT TIME: *To avoid confusing myself and readers, I've converted German submarine time to Greenwich Mean Time. Thus an entry in Kptlt. Walther Schwieger's War Log for 3:00 P.M. becomes 2:00 P.M. instead.*

AS FOR BRITAIN'S ADMIRALTY: *It is important always to keep in mind that the Admiralty's top official was the "First Lord," who served as a kind of chief executive officer; his second-in-command was "First Sea Lord," essentially the chief operating officer, in charge of day-to-day naval operations.*

The Captains are to remember that, whilst they are expected to use every diligence to secure a speedy voyage, *they must run no risk which by any possibility might result in accident to their ships. They will ever bear in mind that the safety of the lives and property entrusted to their care is the ruling principle which should govern them in the navigation of their ships, and no supposed gain in expedition, or saving of time on the voyage, is to be purchased at the risk of accident.*

"Rules to Be Observed in the Company's Service," the Cunard Steam-Ship Company Limited, March 1913

—⚓—

The first consideration is the safety of the U-boat.

Adm. Reinhard Scheer,
Germany's High Sea Fleet in the World War, 1919

DEAD WAKE

A WORD FROM THE CAPTAIN

ON THE NIGHT OF MAY 6, 1915, AS HIS SHIP APproached the coast of Ireland, Capt. William Thomas Turner left the bridge and made his way to the first-class lounge, where passengers were taking part in a concert and talent show, a customary feature of Cunard crossings. The room was large and warm, paneled in mahogany and carpeted in green and yellow, with two fourteen-foot-tall fireplaces in the front and rear walls. Ordinarily Turner avoided events of this kind aboard ship, because he disliked the social obligations of captaincy, but tonight was no ordinary night, and he had news to convey.

There was already a good deal of tension in the room, despite the singing and piano playing and clumsy magic tricks, and this became more pronounced when Turner stepped forward at intermission. His presence had the perverse effect of affirming everything the passengers had been fearing since their departure from New York, in the way that a priest's arrival tends to undermine the cheery smile of a nurse.

It was Turner's intention, however, to provide reassurance. His looks helped. With the physique of a bank safe, he was the embodiment of quiet strength. He had blue eyes and a kind and gentle smile, and his graying hair—he was fifty-eight years old—conveyed wisdom and experience, as did the mere fact of his being a Cunard captain. In accord with Cunard's practice of rotating captains from ship to ship, this was his third stint as the *Lusitania*'s master, his first in wartime.

Turner now told his audience that the next day, Friday, May 7, the ship would enter waters off the southern coast of Ireland that were part of a "zone of war" designated by Germany. This in itself was anything but news. On the morning of the ship's departure from New York, a notice had appeared on the shipping pages of New York's newspapers. Placed by the German Embassy in Washington, it reminded readers of the existence of the war zone and cautioned that "vessels flying the flag of Great Britain, or of any of her allies, are liable to destruction" and that travelers sailing on such ships "do so at their own risk." Though the warning did not name a particular vessel, it was widely interpreted as being aimed at Turner's ship, the *Lusitania*, and indeed in at least one prominent newspaper, the *New York World*, it was positioned adjacent to Cunard's own advertisement for the ship. Ever since, about all the passengers had been doing was "thinking, dreaming, sleeping, and eating submarines," according to Oliver Bernard, a theater-set designer traveling in first class.

Turner now revealed to the audience that earlier in the evening the ship had received a warning by wireless of fresh submarine activity off the Irish coast. He assured the audience there was no need for alarm.

Coming from another man, this might have sounded like a baseless palliative, but Turner believed it. He was skeptical of the threat posed by German submarines, especially when it came to his ship, one of the great transatlantic "greyhounds," so named for the speeds they could achieve. His superiors at Cunard shared his skepticism. The company's New York manager issued an official response to the German warning. "The truth is that the *Lusitania* is the safest boat on the sea. She is too fast for any submarine. No German war vessel can get her or near her." Turner's personal experience affirmed this: on two previous occasions, while captain of a different ship, he had encountered what he believed were submarines and had successfully eluded them by ordering full speed ahead.

He said nothing about these incidents to his audience. Now he offered a different sort of reassurance: upon entering the war zone the next day, the ship would be securely in the care of the Royal Navy.

He bade the audience good night and returned to the bridge. The talent show continued. A few passengers slept fully clothed in the dining room, for fear of being trapped below decks in their cabins if an attack were to occur. One especially anxious traveler, a Greek carpet merchant, put on a life jacket and climbed into a lifeboat to spend the night. Another passenger, a New York businessman named Isaac Lehmann, took a certain comfort from the revolver that he carried with him always and that would, all too soon, bring him a measure of fame, and infamy.

With all but a few lights extinguished and all shades pulled and curtains drawn, the great liner slid forward through the sea, at times in fog, at times under a lacework of stars. But even in darkness, in moonlight and mist, the ship stood out. At one o'clock in the morning, Friday, May 7, the officers of a New York–bound vessel spotted the *Lusitania* and recognized it immediately as it passed some two miles off. "You could see the shape of the four funnels," said the captain, Thomas M. Taylor; "she was the only ship with four funnels."

Unmistakable and invulnerable, a floating village in steel, the *Lusitania* glided by in the night as a giant black shadow cast upon the sea.

PART I

"BLOODY MONKEYS"

THE OLD SAILORMAN

THE SMOKE FROM SHIPS AND THE EXHALATIONS OF THE river left a haze that blurred the world and made the big liner seem even bigger, less the product of human endeavor than an escarpment rising from a plain. The hull was black; seagulls flew past in slashes of white, pretty now, not yet the objects of horror they would become, later, for the man standing on the ship's bridge, seven stories above the wharf. The liner was edged bow-first into a slip at Pier 54, on the Hudson, off the western end of Fourteenth Street in Manhattan, one of a row of four piers operated by the Cunard Steam-Ship Company of Liverpool, England. From the two catwalks that jutted outward from the ship's bridge, its "wings," the captain could get a good look along the full length of the hull, and it was here that he would stand on Saturday, May 1, 1915, a few days hence, when the ship was to set off on yet another voyage across the Atlantic.

Despite the war in Europe, by now in its tenth month—longer than anyone had expected it to last—the ship was booked to capacity, set to carry nearly 2,000 people, or "souls," of whom 1,265 were passengers, including an unexpectedly large number of children and babies. This was, according to the *New York Times*, the greatest number of Europe-bound travelers on a single vessel since the year began. When fully loaded with crew, passengers, luggage, stores, and cargo, the ship weighed, or displaced, over

44,000 tons and could sustain a top speed of more than 25 knots, about 30 miles an hour. With many passenger ships withdrawn from service or converted to military use, this made the *Lusitania* the fastest civilian vessel afloat. Only destroyers, and Britain's latest oil-fueled *Queen Elizabeth*–class battleships, could move faster. That a ship of such size could achieve so great a speed was considered one of the miracles of the modern age. During an early trial voyage—a circumnavigation of Ireland in July 1907—a passenger from Rhode Island sought to capture the larger meaning of the ship and its place in the new century. "The *Lusitania*," he told the *Cunard Daily Bulletin*, published aboard ship, "is in itself a perfect epitome of all that man knows or has discovered or invented up to this moment of time."

The paper reported that the passengers had taken "a vote of censure" against Cunard "for two flagrant omissions from the ship. She has neither a grouse moor nor a deer forest aboard." One passenger noted that if the need for a new Noah's ark ever arose, he would skip the bit about building the boat and just charter the *Lusitania*, "for I calculate that there is room on her for two of every animal extant and more."

The *Bulletin* devoted the last paragraph to waggling Cunard's fingers at Germany, claiming that the ship had just received news, by wireless, that Kaiser Wilhelm himself had sent a telegram to the ship's builders: "Please deliver me without delay a dozen—baker's measure—*Lusitania*s."

From the first, the ship became an object of national pride and affection. In keeping with Cunard's custom of naming its ships for ancient lands, the company had selected *Lusitania*, after a Roman province on the Iberian Peninsula that occupied roughly the same ground as modern-day Portugal. "The inhabitants were warlike, and the Romans conquered them with great difficulty," said a memorandum in Cunard's files on the naming of the ship. "They lived generally upon plunder and were rude and unpolished in their manners." In popular usage, the name was foreshortened to "Lucy."

There was nothing rude or unpolished about the ship itself. As the *Lusitania* departed Liverpool on its first transatlantic run in 1907, some one hundred thousand spectators gathered at various points along the Mersey (pronounced Merzey) River to watch, many singing "Rule, Britannia!" and waving handkerchiefs. Passenger C. R. Minnitt, in a letter he wrote aboard ship, told his wife how he had climbed to the highest deck and stood near one of the ship's four towering funnels to best capture the moment. "You do not get any idea of her size till you get right on top and then it is like being on Lincoln Cathedral," Minnitt wrote. "I went over parts of the 1st class and it is really impossible to describe, it is so beautiful."

The ship's beauty belied its complexity. From the start, it needed a lot of attention. In its first winter, woodwork in the first-class writing room and dining saloon and in various passageways began to shrink and had to be rebuilt. Excess vibration forced Cunard to pull the ship from service so that extra bracing could be installed. Something was always breaking or malfunctioning. A baking oven exploded, injuring a crew member. Boilers needed to be scaled and cleaned. During crossings in winter, pipes froze and ruptured. The ship's lightbulbs failed at an alarming rate. This was no small problem: the *Lusitania* had six thousand lamps.

The ship endured. It was fast, comfortable, and beloved and, as of the end of April 1915, had completed 201 crossings of the Atlantic.

To READY the ship for its Saturday, May 1, departure, much had to be done, with speed and efficiency, and at this Capt. William Thomas Turner excelled. Within the Cunard empire, there were none better than he at handling large ships. While serving a rotation as captain of Cunard's *Aquitania*, Turner had achieved a measure of fame during an arrival in New York by fitting the ship into its slip and snugging it to its wharf in just nineteen minutes. He held the record for a "round" voyage, meaning round-trip, which he achieved in December 1910, when, as captain of the *Lusitania*'s twin, the *Mauretania*, he piloted the ship to New York and back in just fourteen days. Cunard rewarded him with a Silver Salver. He found it "very gratifying" but also surprising. "I did not expect to receive any such recognition of my part in the matter," he wrote, in a thank-you letter. "We all on board simply tried to do our duty as under any ordinary circumstances."

Complex, detailed, and messy, this process of readying the *Lusitania* involved a degree of physical labor that was masked by the ship's outward grace. Anyone looking up from the dock saw only beauty, on a monumental scale, while on the far side of the ship men turned black with dust as they shoveled coal—5,690 tons in all—into the ship through openings in the hull called "side pockets." The ship burned coal at all times. Even when docked it consumed 140 tons a day to keep furnaces hot and boilers primed and to provide electricity from the ship's dynamo to power lights, elevators, and, very important, the Marconi transmitter, whose antenna stretched between its two masts. When the *Lusitania* was under way, its appetite for coal was enormous. Its 300 stokers, trimmers, and firemen, working 100 per shift, would shovel 1,000 tons of coal a day into its 192 furnaces to heat its 25 boilers and generate enough superheated steam to spin the immense turbines of its engines. The men were called "the black gang," a reference not to their race but to the coal dust that coated their bodies. The boilers occupied the bottom deck of the ship and were gigantic, like wheelless locomotives, each 22 feet long and 18 feet in diameter. They needed close attention at all times, for when fully pressurized each stored enough explosive energy to tear a small ship in half. Fifty years earlier, exploding boilers had caused America's worst-ever maritime disaster—the destruction of the Mississippi River steamboat *Sultana* at a cost of 1,800 lives.

No matter what measures the crew took, coal dust migrated everywhere, under stateroom doors, through keyholes, and up companionways, compelling stewards to go through the ship with dust cloths to clean rails, door handles, table tops, deck chairs, plates, pans, and any other surface likely to collect falling soot. The dust posed its own hazard. In certain concentrations it was highly explosive and raised the possibility of a cataclysm within the ship's hull. Cunard barred crew members from bringing their own matches on board and provided them instead with safety matches, which ignited only when scraped against a chemically treated surface on the outside of the box. Anyone caught bringing his own matches aboard was to be reported to Captain Turner.

The ship was built to be fast. It was conceived out of hubris and anxiety, at a time—1903—when Britain feared it was losing the race for dominance of the passenger-ship industry. In America, J. P. Morgan was buying up shipping lines in hopes of creating a monopoly; in Europe, Germany had succeeded in building the world's fastest ocean liners and thereby winning the "Blue Riband," awarded to the liner that crossed the Atlantic in the shortest time. By 1903 German ships had held the Riband for six years, to the sustained mortification of Britain. With the empire's honor and Cunard's future both at stake, the British government and the company agreed to a unique deal. The Admiralty would lend Cunard up to £2.4 million, or nearly $2 billion in today's dollars, at an interest rate of only 2.75 percent, to build two gigantic liners— the *Lusitania* and *Mauretania*. In return, however, Cunard had to make certain concessions.

First and foremost, the Admiralty required that the *Lusitania* be able to maintain an average speed across the Atlantic of at least 24.5 knots. In early trials, it topped 26 knots. There were other, more problematic conditions. The Admiralty also required that the two ships be built so that in the event of war they could be readily equipped with naval artillery and brought into service as "armed auxiliary cruisers." The Admiralty went so far as to direct the *Lusitania*'s builders to install mounts, or "holding-down" rings, in its decks, capable of accepting a dozen large guns. Moreover, the *Lusitania*'s hull was to be designed to battleship specifications, which required the use of "longitudinal" coal bunkers—essentially tunnels along both sides of the hull to store the ship's coal and speed its distribution among the boiler rooms. At the time, when naval warfare took place at or above the waterline, this was considered smart warship design. To naval shipbuilders, coal was a form of armor, and longitudinal bunkers were thought to provide an additional level of protection. A naval engineering journal, in 1907, stated that the coal in these bunkers would limit how far enemy shells could penetrate the hull and thus would "counteract, as far as possible, the effect of the enemy's fire at the water line."

When the war began, the Admiralty, exercising rights granted by its deal with Cunard, took possession of the *Lusitania* but soon determined the ship would not be effective as an armed cruiser because the rate at which it consumed coal made it too expensive to operate under battle conditions. The Admiralty retained control of the *Mauretania* for conversion to a troopship, a role for which its size and speed were well suited, but restored the *Lusitania* to Cunard for commercial service. The guns were never installed, and only the most astute passenger would have noticed the mounting rings embedded in the decking.

The *Lusitania* remained a passenger liner, but with the hull of a battleship.

A STICKLER for detail and discipline, Captain Turner called himself "an old-fashioned sailorman." He had been born in 1856, in the age of sail and empire. His father had been a sea captain but had hoped his son would choose a different path and enter the church. Turner refused to become a "devil-dodger," his term, and at the age of eight somehow managed to win his parents' permission to go to sea. He wanted adventure and found it in abundance. He first served as a cabin boy on a sailing ship, the *Grasmere*, which ran aground off northern Ireland on a clear, moonlit night. Turner swam for shore. All the other crew and all passengers aboard were rescued, though one infant died of bronchitis. "Had it been stormy," one passenger wrote, "I believe not a soul could have been saved."

Turner moved from ship to ship and at one point sailed under his father's command, aboard a square-rigger. "I was the quickest man aloft in a sailing ship," Turner said. His adventures continued. While he was second mate of a clipper ship, the *Thunderbolt*, a wave knocked him into the sea. He had been fishing at the time.

A fellow crewman saw him fall and threw him a life buoy, but he floated for over an hour among circling sharks before the ship could fight its way back to his position. He joined Cunard on October 4, 1877, at a salary of £5 per month, and two weeks later sailed as third officer of the *Cherbourg*, his first steamship. He again proved himself a sailor of more than usual bravery and agility. One day in heavy fog, as the *Cherbourg* was leaving Liverpool, the ship struck a small bark, which began to sink. Four crew and a harbor pilot drowned. The *Cherbourg* dispatched a rescue party, which included Turner, who himself pulled a crewman and a boy from the rigging.

Turner served as third officer on two other Cunard ships but resigned on June 28, 1880, after learning that the company never promoted a man to captain unless he'd been master of a ship before joining the company. Turner built his credentials, earned his master's certificate, and became captain of a clipper ship, and along the way found yet another opportunity to demonstrate his courage. In February 1883, a boy of fourteen fell from a dock into Liverpool Harbor, into water so cold it could kill a man in minutes. Turner was a strong swimmer, at a time when most sailors still held the belief that there was no point in knowing how to swim, since it would only prolong your suffering. Turner leapt in and rescued the boy. The Liverpool Shipwreck and Humane Society gave him a silver medal for heroism. That same year he rejoined Cunard and married a cousin, Alice Hitching. They had two sons, the first, Percy, in 1885, and Norman eight years later.

Even now, as a certified ship's master, Turner's advance within Cunard took time. The delay, according to his best and longtime friend, George Ball, caused him great frustration, but, Ball added, "never, at any time, did he relax in devotion to duty nor waver in the loyalty he always bore to his ship and his Captain." Over the next two decades, Turner worked his way upward from third officer to chief officer, through eighteen different postings, until on March 19, 1903, Cunard at last awarded him his own command. He became master of a small steamship, the *Aleppo*, which served Mediterranean ports.

His home life did not fare as well. His wife left him, took the boys, and moved to Australia. Turner's sisters hired a young woman, Mabel Every, to care for him. Miss Every and Turner lived near each other, in a suburb of Liverpool called Great Crosby. At first she served as a housekeeper, but over time she became more of a companion. She saw a side of Turner that his officers and crew did not. He liked smoking his pipe and telling stories. He loved dogs and cats and had a fascination with bees. He liked to laugh. "On the ships he was a very strict disciplinarian," Miss Every wrote, "but at Home he was a very kind jolly man and fond of children and animals."

DESPITE THE SORROW that shaded his personal life, his career gained momentum. After two years as master of the *Aleppo*, he moved on to command the *Carpathia*, the ship that later, in April 1912, under a different captain, would become famous for rescuing survivors of the *Titanic*. Next came the *Ivernia*, the *Caronia*, and the *Umbria*. His advance was all the more remarkable given that he lacked the charm and polish that Cunard expected its commanders to display. A Cunard captain was supposed to be much more than a mere navigator. Resplendent in his uniform and cap, he was expected to exude assurance, competence, and gravitas. But a captain also served a role less easy to define. He was three parts mariner, one part club director. He was to be a willing guide for first-class passengers wishing to learn more about the mysteries of the ship; he was to preside over dinners with prominent passengers; he was to walk the ship and engage passengers in conversation about the weather, their reasons for crossing the Atlantic, the books they were reading.

Turner would sooner bathe in bilge. According to Mabel Every, he described passengers as "a load of bloody monkeys who are constantly chattering." He preferred dining in his quarters to holding court at the captain's table in the first-class dining room. He spoke little and did so with a parsimony that could be maddening; he also tended to be blunt. On one voyage, while in command of the *Carpathia*, he ran afoul of two priests, who felt moved to write to Cunard "complaining of certain remarks" that Turner had made when they asked permission to hold a Roman Catholic service for third-class passengers. Exactly what Turner said cannot be known, but his remarks were sufficient to cause Cunard to demand a formal report and to make the incident a subject of deliberation at a meeting of the company's board of directors.

At the start of another voyage, while he was in charge of the *Mauretania*, a woman traveling in first class told Turner that she wanted to be on the bridge as the ship moved along the Mersey River out to sea. Turner explained that this would be impossible, for Cunard rules expressly prohibited anyone other than necessary officers and crew from being on the bridge in "narrow waters."

She asked, what would he do if a *lady* happened to insist?

Turner replied, "Madam, do you think that would be a lady?"

Turner's social burden was eased in 1913 when Cunard, acknowledging the complexity of running the *Lusitania* and the *Mauretania*, created a new officer's position for both, that of "staff captain," second in command of the ship. Not only did this allow Turner to concentrate on navigation; it largely eliminated his obligation to be charming. The *Lusitania*'s staff captain as of May 1915 was James "Jock" Anderson, whom Turner described as more "clubbable."

The crew respected Turner and for the most part liked him. "I think I speak for all the crew if I say we all had the utmost confidence in Captain Turner," said one of the ship's waiters. "He was a good, and conscientious skipper." But one officer, Albert Arthur Bestic, observed that Turner was popular only "up to a point." Bestic noted that Turner still seemed to have one foot on the deck of a sailing ship, as became evident at odd moments.

One evening, while Bestic and other crewmen were off duty and playing bridge, the ship's quartermaster appeared at the door carrying a knot called a Turk's head. Complex to begin with, this was a four-stranded variant, the most complicated of all.

"Captain's compliments," the quartermaster said, "and he says he wants another of these made."

The bridge game stopped, Bestic recalled, "and we spent the rest of the 2nd. dog"—the watch from 6:00 to 8:00 P.M.—"trying to remember how it was made." This was not easy. The knot was typically used for decoration, and none of the men had tied one in a long while. Wrote Bestic, "It was Turner's idea of humor."

UNDER TURNER, the *Lusitania* broke all records for speed, to the dismay of Germany. In a 1909 voyage from Liverpool to New York, the ship covered the distance from Daunt Rock off Ireland to New York's Ambrose Channel in four days, eleven hours, and forty-two minutes, at an average speed of 25.85 knots. Until then that kind of speed had seemed an impossibility. As the ship passed the Nantucket lightship, it was clocked at 26 knots.

Turner attributed the speed to new propellers installed the preceding July and to the prowess of his engineers and firemen. He told a reporter the ship would have made it even faster if not for foul weather and a head-on sea at the beginning of the voyage and a gale that arose at the end. The reporter noted that Turner looked "bronzed" from the sun.

By May 1915 Turner was the most seasoned captain at Cunard, the commodore of the line. He had confronted all manner of shipboard crises, including mechanical mishaps, fires, cracked furnaces, open-sea rescues, and extreme weather of all kinds. He was said to be fearless. One seaman aboard the *Lusitania*, Thomas Mahoney, called him "one of the bravest Captains I sailed under."

It was Turner who experienced what may have been the most frightening threat to the *Lusitania*, this during a voyage to New York in January 1910, when he encountered a phenomenon he had never previously met in his half century at sea.

Soon after leaving Liverpool, the ship entered a gale, with a powerful headwind and tall seas that required Turner to reduce speed to 14 knots. By itself the weather posed no particular challenge. He had seen worse, and the ship handled the heavy seas with grace. And so, on Monday evening, January 11, at 6:00, soon after leaving the coast of Ireland behind, Turner went down one deck to his quarters to have dinner. He left his chief officer in charge.

"The wave," Turner said, "came as a surprise."

It was not just any wave, but an "accumulative" wave, known in later times as a rogue, formed when waves pile one upon another to form a single palisade of water.

The *Lusitania* had just climbed a lesser wave and was descending into the trough beyond it when the sea ahead rose in a wall so high it blocked the helmsman's view of the horizon. The ship plunged through it. Water came to the top of the wheelhouse, 80 feet above the waterline.

The wave struck the front of the bridge like a giant hammer and bent steel plates inward. Wood shutters splintered. A large spear of broken teak pierced a hardwood cabinet to a depth of two inches. Water filled the bridge and wheelhouse and tore the wheel loose, along with the helmsman. The ship began to "fall off," so that its bow was no longer perpendicular to the oncoming waves, a dangerous condition in rough weather. The lights of the bridge and on the masthead above short-circuited and went out. The officers and helmsman struggled to their feet, initially in waist-high water. They reattached the wheel and corrected the ship's heading. The wave's impact had broken doors, bent internal bulkheads, and shattered two lifeboats. By sheerest luck, no one was seriously injured.

Turner rushed to the bridge and found water and chaos, but once he assured himself that the ship had endured the assault without catastrophic damage and that no passengers had been hurt, he simply added it to his long list of experiences at sea.

Fog was one of the few phenomena that worried him. There was no way to predict its occurrence, and, once in fog, one had no way to know whether another vessel was thirty miles ahead or thirty yards. The Cunard manual, "Rules to Be Observed in the Company's Service," required that when encountering fog a captain had to post extra lookouts, reduce speed, and turn on his ship's foghorn. The rest of it was luck and careful navigation. A captain had to know his position at all times as precisely as possible, because fog could arise quickly. One instant there'd be clear sky, the next obliteration. The dangers of fog had become grotesquely evident one year earlier, also in May, when the *Empress of Ireland*, of the Canadian Pacific line, was struck by a collier—a coal-carrying freighter—in a fog bank in the Saint Lawrence River. The *Empress* sank in fourteen minutes with the loss of 1,012 lives.

Turner knew the importance of precise navigation and was considered to be especially good at it, careful to the extreme, especially in the narrow waters close to a port.

COME SATURDAY morning, May 1, Turner would make a detailed inspection of the ship, accompanied by his purser and chief steward. All preparations for the voyage had to be completed by then, rooms cleaned, beds made, all stores—gin, Scotch, cigars, peas, mutton, beef, ham—loaded aboard, all cargo in place, and the ship's supply of drinking water tested for freshness and clarity. Special attention was always to be paid to lavatories and bilges, and to maintaining proper levels of ventilation, lest the liner start to stink. The goal, in official Cunard parlance, was "to keep the ship sweet."

Everything had to be done in such a manner that none of the passengers, whether in first class or third, would be aware of the nature and extent of the week's travail. The needs of passengers were paramount, as the Cunard manual made clear. "The utmost courtesy and attention are at all times to be shown to passengers whilst they are on board the Company's ships, and it is the special duty of the Captain to see that this regulation is observed by the officers and others serving under him." On one previous voyage, this duty included allowing two big-game hunters, Mr. and Mrs. D. Saunderson of County Cavan, Ireland, to bring two four-month-old lion cubs aboard, which they had captured in British East Africa and planned to give to the Bronx Zoo. The couple's two-year-old daughter, Lydia, played with the cubs on deck, "much to the amusement of the other passengers," according to the *New York Times*. Mrs. Saunderson attracted a good deal of attention herself. She had killed an elephant. "No, I was not afraid," she told the *Times*. "I think I never am."

Complaints had to be taken seriously, and there were always complaints. Passengers grumbled that food from the Kitchen Grill came to their tables cold. This issue was at least partly resolved by changing the route waiters had to walk. The typewriters in the typing room were too noisy and annoyed the occupants of adjacent staterooms. The hours for typing were shortened. Ventilation in some rooms was less than ideal, a stubborn flaw that drove passengers to open their portholes. There was a problem, too, with the upper-level dining room in first class. Its windows opened onto a promenade used by third-class passengers, who had an annoying habit of peering in through the windows at the posh diners within. And there were always those passengers who came aboard bearing moral grudges against the modern age. A second-class passenger on a 1910 voyage complained that the ship's decks "should not be made a market place for the sale of Irish Shawls, etc.," and also that "card playing for money goes on incessantly in the smoking rooms on board the Company's steamers."

Cunard's foremost priority, however, was to protect its passengers from harm. The company had a remarkable safety record: not a single passenger death from sinking, collision, ice, weather, fire, or any other circumstance where blame could be laid upon captain or company, though of course deaths from natural causes occurred with regularity, especially among elderly passengers. The ship carried the latest in safety equipment. Owing to the epidemic of "Boat Fever" that swept the shipping industry after the *Titanic* disaster, the *Lusitania* had more than enough lifeboats for passengers and crew. The ship also had been recently equipped with the latest in life jackets, these made by the Boddy Lifesaving Appliances Company. Unlike the older vests, made of cloth-covered panels of cork, these resembled actual jackets. Said one passenger, "When you have it on you look and feel like a padded football player, especially around the shoulders." The new Boddy jackets were placed in the first- and second-class staterooms; third-class passengers and crew were to use the older kind.

No safety issue escaped the notice of Cunard's board. On one crossing, as the *Lusitania* moved through heavy seas, crewmen discovered that a section of third class was "full of water." The culprit was a single open porthole. The incident underscored the dangers posed by portholes in rough weather. The board voted to reprimand the stewards responsible for that section of the ship.

For all the respect afforded Turner by Cunard and by the officers and crew who served under him, his own record was far from impeccable. In July 1905, four months after he took command of the *Ivernia*, the ship collided with another, the *Carlingford Lough*. An investigation by Cunard found Turner to be at fault, for going too fast in fog. The company's directors resolved, according to board minutes, that he was "to be severely reprimanded." Three years later, a ship under his command, the *Caronia*, "touched ground" in the Ambrose Channel in New York and earned him another reprimand: "The *Caronia* should not have left the dock at such a state of tide."

The winter of 1914–15 was particularly hard on Turner. One of his ships, the newly launched *Transylvania*, caught a gust of wind while undocking in Liverpool and bumped against a White Star liner, causing minor damage. In a second incident that winter, the ship collided with another large liner, the *Teutonic*, and in a third got bumped by a tugboat.

But these things happened to all captains. Cunard's confidence in Turner was made clear by the fact that the company consistently put him in charge of its newest and biggest liners and made him master of the *Lusitania* for three different cycles.

The war had made the matter of passenger safety all the more pressing. For Turner's immediate predecessor, Capt. Daniel Dow, it had become too great a burden. On a March voyage to Liverpool, Dow had guided the *Lusitania* through waters in which two freighters had just been sunk. Afterward he told his superiors at Cunard that he could no longer accept the responsibility of commanding a passenger ship under such conditions, especially if the ship carried munitions intended for Britain's military. The practice of transporting such cargo had become common and made any ship that carried it a legitimate target for attack. Cowardice had nothing to do with Dow's decision. What troubled him was not the danger to himself but rather having to worry about the lives of two thousand civilian passengers and crew. His nerves could not take it. Cunard decided he was "tired and really ill" and relieved him of command.

THE LONELY PLACE

THE TRAIN CARRYING THE BODY OF ELLEN AXSON
Wilson pulled into the station at Rome, Georgia, at 2:30 in
the afternoon, Tuesday, August 11, 1914, under gunmetal
skies, amid the peal of bells. The casket was placed in a hearse,
and soon the cortege began making its way through town to the
church in which the funeral service would take place, the First
Presbyterian, where Mrs. Wilson's father had been a pastor. The
streets were thronged with men and women come to pay their last
respects to her and to show support for her husband, President
Woodrow Wilson. They'd been married twenty-nine years. Family
members carried the casket into the church as the organist played
Chopin's Funeral March, that dour, trudging staple of death scenes
everywhere. The service was brief; the chorus sang two hymns that
had been her favorites. Next the procession made its way up to the
cemetery on Myrtle Hill, and the rain began. The hearse rolled
past girls in white holding boughs of myrtle. Behind the girls stood
townspeople and visitors, their hats off despite the rain.

An awning had been erected over the gravesite to shelter Wilson
and the friends and family who made up the funeral party. The
rain became heavy and thudded against the cloth. Onlookers saw
the president tremble as he wept; those near at hand saw tears on
his cheeks.

Afterward, the mourners moved back to their cars, and the

spectators—a thousand of them—dispersed. Wilson stood alone beside the grave, neither speaking nor moving, until the coffin was fully covered.

With the death of his wife, Wilson entered a new province of solitude, and the burden of leadership bore on him as never before. His wife had died on Thursday, August 6, of a kidney illness then known as Bright's disease, two days after Britain entered the new war in Europe and just a year and a half into his first term. In losing her he lost not merely his main source of companionship but also his primary adviser, whose observations he had found so useful in helping shape his own thinking. The White House became for him a lonely place, haunted not by the ghost of Lincoln, as some White House servants believed, but by memories of Ellen. For a time his grief seemed incapacitating. His physician and frequent golf companion, Dr. Cary Grayson, grew concerned. "For several days he has not been well," Grayson wrote, on August 25, 1914, in a letter to a friend, Edith Bolling Galt. "I persuaded him yesterday to remain in bed during the forenoon. When I went to see him, tears were streaming down his face. It was a heart-breaking scene, a sadder picture no one could imagine. A great man with his heart torn out."

Later that August, Wilson managed to get away to a country home in Cornish, New Hampshire, called Harlakenden House, a large Georgian residence overlooking the Connecticut River on which he held a two-summer lease. Wilson's friend Col. Edward House came to join him and was struck by the depth of his sorrow. At one point as they talked about Ellen, the president, his eyes welling, told House that he "felt like a machine that had run down, and there was nothing in him worth while." The president, House wrote in his diary, "looked forward to the next two and a half years with dread. He did not see how he could go through with it."

There were crises on all fronts. The United States was still in the grip of a recession now in its second year. The South in particular suffered. Cotton, its main product, had been transported mainly on foreign vessels, but the war had brought an acute shortage of ships, whose owners, fearing submarine attack, kept them in port; the belligerents, meanwhile, commandeered their own merchant ships for military use. Now millions of bales of cotton piled up on southern wharves. There was labor trouble as well. The United Mine Workers of America were on strike in Colorado. The preceding April, the state had sent a force of National Guard troops to break the strike, resulting in a massacre at Ludlow, Colorado, that left two dozen men, women, and children dead. Meanwhile, south of the border, violence and unrest continued to plague Mexico.

Wilson's great fear, however, was that America might somehow find itself drawn into the war in Europe. That the war had begun at all was a dark amazement, for it had seemed to come from nowhere. At the start of that beautiful summer of 1914, one of the sunniest Europe would ever see, there had been no sign of war and no obvious wish for it. On June 27, the day before Europe began its slide into chaos, newspaper readers in America found only the blandest of news. The lead story on the front page of the *New York Times* was about Columbia University at last winning the intercollegiate rowing regatta, after nineteen years of failure. A Grape-Nuts ad dealt with warfare, but of the schoolyard variety, extolling the cereal's value in helping children prevail in fistfights: "Husky bodies and stout nerves depend—more often than we think—on the food eaten." And the *Times*' society page named dozens of New York socialites, including a Guggenheim and a Wanamaker, who were scheduled to sail for Europe that day, on the *Minneapolis*, the *Caledonia*, the *Zeeland*, and two German-owned ships, the *Prinz Friedrich Wilhelm* and the gigantic *Imperator*, 24 feet longer than the *Titanic*.

In Europe, kings and high officials set off for their country homes. Kaiser Wilhelm would soon board his yacht, the *Hohenzollern*, to begin a cruise of the fjords of Norway. The president of France, Raymond Poincaré, and his foreign minister departed by ship for a state visit to Tsar Nicholas II of Russia, who had moved to his summer palace. Winston Churchill, forty years old and already Britain's top naval official, First Lord of the Admiralty, went to the beach, a home in Cromer on the North Sea, 100 miles north of London, where he joined his wife, Clementine, and his children.

In England, the lay public was transfixed, not by any prospect of war, but by Sir Ernest Shackleton's planned expedition to the Antarctic in the square-rigger *Endurance*, set to depart August 8 from Plymouth, on Britain's southeast coast. In Paris, the big fascination was the trial of Henriette Caillaux, wife of former prime minister Joseph Caillaux, arrested for killing the editor of the Paris newspaper *Le Figaro* after the newspaper had published an intimate letter that the prime minister had written to her before their marriage, when they were having an adulterous affair. Enraged, Mrs. Caillaux bought a gun, practiced with it at the gunsmith's shop, then went to the editor's office and fired six times. In her testimony, offering an unintended metaphor for what was soon to befall Europe, she said, "These pistols are terrible things. They go off by themselves." She was acquitted, after persuading the court that the murder was a crime of passion.

Far from a clamor for war, there existed a widespread, if naive, belief that war of the kind that had convulsed Europe in past centuries had become obsolete—that the economies of nations were so closely connected with one another that even if a war were to begin, it would end quickly. Capital flowed across borders. Belgium had the sixth-largest economy in the world, not because of manufactures, but because of the money coursing through its banks. Enhanced communications—telephone, telegraph, cable, and most recently wireless—further entwined nations, as did the increasing capacity and speed of steamships and the expansion of railroads. Tourism grew as well. No longer just for the rich, it became a passion of the middle class. Populations increased, markets expanded. In the United States, despite recession, the Ford Motor Company announced plans to double the size of its manufacturing plant.

But old tensions and enmities persisted. Britain's King George V loathed his cousin Kaiser Wilhelm II, Germany's supreme ruler; and Wilhelm, in turn, envied Britain's expansive collection of colonies and its command of the seas, so much so that in 1900

Germany began a campaign to build warships in enough quantity and of large enough scale to take on the British navy. This in turn drove Britain to begin an extensive modernization of its own navy, for which it created a new class of warship, the *Dreadnought*, which carried guns of a size and power never before deployed at sea. Armies swelled in size as well. To keep pace with each other, France and Germany introduced conscription. Nationalist fervor was on the rise. Austria-Hungary and Serbia shared a simmering mutual resentment. The Serbs nurtured pan-Slavic ambitions that threatened the skein of territories and ethnicities that made up the Austro-Hungarian empire (typically referred to simply as Austria). These included such restive lands as Herzegovina, Bosnia, and Croatia. As one historian put it, "Europe had too many frontiers, too many—and too well-remembered—histories, too many soldiers for safety."

And secretly, nations began planning for how to use these soldiers should the need arise. As early as 1912, Britain's Committee of Imperial Defence had planned that in the event of war with Germany, the first act would be to cut Germany's transoceanic telegraph cables. In Germany, meanwhile, generals tinkered with a detailed plan crafted by Field Marshal Alfred von Schlieffen, the centerpiece of which was a vast maneuver that would bring German forces through neutral Belgium and down into France, thus skirting defenses arrayed along the French frontier. That Britain might object—indeed, would be compelled to intervene, as a co-guarantor of Belgian neutrality—seemed not to weigh heavily on anyone's mind. Schlieffen calculated that the war in France would be over in forty-two days, after which German forces would reverse course and march toward Russia. What he failed to take into account was what would happen if German forces did not prevail in the time allotted and if Britain did join the fray.

The war began with the geopolitical equivalent of a brush fire. In late June, Archduke Franz Ferdinand, inspector general of the Austro-Hungarian army, traveled to Bosnia, which Austria had annexed in 1908. While driving through Sarajevo, he was shot dead by an assassin sponsored by the Black Hand, a group devoted to unifying Serbia and Bosnia. On July 28, Austria stunned the world by declaring war on Serbia.

"It's incredible—incredible," Wilson said, during lunch with his daughter, Nell, and her husband, William McAdoo, secretary of the Treasury. Wilson could give the incident only scant attention, however. At the time, his wife lay gravely ill, and this alone consumed his heart and mind. He cautioned his daughter, "Don't tell your mother anything about it."

The dispute between Austria and Serbia could have ended there: a small war against a disruptive Balkan country. But within a week, the brush fire gusted into a firestorm, spiking fears, resurrecting animosities, triggering alliances and understandings, and setting long-laid plans in motion. On Tuesday, August 4, following the Schlieffen plan, German forces entered Belgium, dragging behind them giant fortress-busting guns capable of launching shells weighing 2,000 pounds apiece. Britain declared war, siding with Russia and France, the "Allies"; Germany and Austria-Hungary linked arms as the "Central Powers." That same day, Wilson declared America to be neutral in an executive proclamation that barred the warships of Germany and Britain and all other belligerents from entering U.S. ports. Later, a week after his wife's funeral, struggling against his personal grief to address the larger trauma of the world, Wilson told the nation, "We must be impartial in thought as well as in action, must put a curb upon our sentiments as well as upon every transaction that might be construed as a preference of one party to the struggle before another."

He had the full support of the American public. A British journalist, Sydney Brooks, writing in the *North American Review*, gauged America to be just as isolationist as ever. And why not, he asked? "The United States is remote, unconquerable, huge, without hostile neighbors or any neighbors at all of anything like her own strength, and lives exempt in an almost unvexed tranquility from the contentions and animosities and the ceaseless pressure and counter-pressure that distract the close-packed older world."

While easy in concept, neutrality in practice was a fragile thing. As the fire grew, other alliances were forged. Turkey joined the

Central Powers; Japan the Allies. Soon fighting was under way in far-flung corners of the world, on land, in the air, and on the sea, and even under the sea, with German submarines ranging as far as the waters off Britain's western shores. An isolated dispute over a murder in the Balkans had become a world conflagration.

The main arena, however, was Europe, and there Germany made clear that this would be a war like no other, in which no party would be spared. As Wilson mourned his wife, German forces in Belgium entered quiet towns and villages, took civilian hostages, and executed them to discourage resistance. In the town of Dinant, German soldiers shot 612 men, women, and children. The American press called such atrocities acts of "frightfulness," the word then used to describe what later generations would call terrorism. On August 25, German forces began an assault on the Belgian city of Louvain, the "Oxford of Belgium," a university town that was home to an important library. Three days of shelling and murder left 209 civilians dead, 1,100 buildings incinerated, and the library destroyed, along with its 230,000 books, priceless manuscripts, and artifacts. The assault was deemed an affront not just to Belgium but to the world. Wilson, a past president of Princeton University, "felt deeply the destruction of Louvain," according to his friend Colonel House; the president feared "the war would throw the world back three or four centuries."

Each side had been confident of a victory within months, but by the end of 1914 the war had turned into a macabre stalemate marked by battles in which tens of thousands of men died and neither side gained ground. The first of the great named battles were fought that autumn and winter—the Frontiers, Mons, Marne, and the First Battle of Ypres. By the end of November, after four months of fighting, the French army had suffered 306,000 fatalities, roughly equivalent to the 1910 population of Washington, D.C. The German toll was 241,000. By year's end a line of parallel trenches, constituting the western front, ran nearly five hundred miles from the North Sea to Switzerland, separated in places by a no-man's-land of as little as 25 yards.

For Wilson, already suffering depression, it was all deeply troubling. He wrote to Colonel House, "I feel the burden of the thing almost intolerably from day to day." He expressed a similar sentiment in a letter to his ambassador to Britain, Walter Hines Page. "The whole thing is very vivid in my mind, painfully vivid, and has been almost ever since the struggle began," he wrote. "I think my thought and imagination contain the picture and perceive its significance from every point of view. I have to force myself not to dwell upon it to avoid the sort of numbness that comes from deep apprehension and dwelling upon elements too vast to be yet comprehended or in any way controlled by counsel."

There was at least one moment, however, when his grief seemed to lessen. In November 1914, he traveled to Manhattan to visit Colonel House. That evening, at about nine o'clock, the two men set out for a walk from House's apartment, not in disguise, but also not advertising the fact that the president of the United States was now strolling the streets of Manhattan. They walked along Fifty-third Street, to Seventh Avenue, to Broadway, somehow managing not to draw the attention of passersby. They stopped to listen to a couple of sidewalk orators, but here Wilson was recognized, and a crowd gathered. Wilson and Colonel House moved on, now followed by a trailing sea of New Yorkers. The two men entered the lobby of the Waldorf Astoria, stepped up to the elevator, and directed the startled operator to stop at a high floor. They got off, walked to the opposite end of the hotel, found another bank of elevators, and returned to the lobby, then exited through a side door.

After a brief walk along Fifth Avenue, they caught a city bus and rode it uptown to House's building. As exhilarating as this escape may have been, it was no cure for Wilson's malaise. On their return, Wilson confessed to House that as they were out walking he had found himself wishing that someone would kill him.

In the midst of this darkness, Wilson still managed to see America as the world's last great hope. "We are at peace with all the world," he said in December 1914 in his annual address to Congress. In January, he dispatched Colonel House on an unofficial mission to Europe to attempt to discover the conditions under which the Allies and the Central Powers might be willing to begin peace negotiations.

House booked passage on the largest, fastest passenger ship then in service, the *Lusitania*, and traveled under a false name. On entering waters off Ireland, the ship's then-captain, Daniel Dow, following a tradition accepted in times of war, raised an American flag as a *ruse de guerre* to protect the ship from attack by German submarines. The act startled House and caused a sensation aboard, but as a means of disguise it had questionable value: America did not operate any liners of that size, with that distinctive four-funnel silhouette.

The incident highlighted the press of forces threatening to undermine American neutrality. The battles in Europe posed no great worry, with the United States so distant and secure within its oceanic moat. It was Germany's new and aggressive submarine war that posed the greatest danger.

AT THE beginning of the war, neither Germany nor Britain understood the true nature of the submarine or realized that it might produce what Churchill called "this strange form of warfare hitherto unknown to human experience."

Only a few prescient souls seemed to grasp that the design of the submarine would force a transformation in naval strategy. One of these was Sir Arthur Conan Doyle, who, a year and a half before the war, wrote a short story (not published until July 1914) in which he envisioned a conflict between England and a fictional country, Norland, "one of the smallest Powers in Europe." In the story, entitled "Danger!," Norland at first seems hopelessly overmatched, but the little country has a secret weapon—a fleet of eight submarines, which it deploys off the coast of England to attack incoming merchant ships, both cargo and passenger. At the time Doyle conceived his plot, submarines did exist, but British and German naval commanders saw them as having little value.

Norland's submarines, however, bring England to the verge of starvation. At one point, without warning, the commander of the submarine fleet, Capt. John Sirius, uses a single torpedo to sink a White Star passenger liner, the *Olympic*. England eventually surrenders. Readers found that last attack particularly shocking because the *Olympic* was a real ship. Its twin had been the *Titanic*, lost well before Doyle wrote his story.

Intended to sound the alarm and raise England's level of naval preparedness, the story was entertaining, and frightening, but was widely deemed too far-fetched to be believable, for Captain Sirius's behavior would have breached a fundamental maritime code, the cruiser rules, or prize law, established in the nineteenth century to govern warfare against civilian shipping. Obeyed ever since by all seagoing powers, the rules held that a warship could stop a merchant vessel and search it but had to keep its crew safe and bring the ship to a nearby port, where a "prize court" would determine its fate. The rules forbade attacks against passenger vessels.

In the story, Doyle's narrator dismisses as a delusion England's belief that no nation would stoop to such levels. "Common sense," Captain Sirius says, "should have told her that her enemy will play the game that suits them best—that they will not inquire what they may do, but they will do it first and talk about it afterwards." Doyle's forecast was dismissed as too fantastic to contemplate.

But Britain's own Adm. Jacky Fisher, credited with reforming and modernizing the British navy—it was he who had conceived the first *Dreadnought*—had also become concerned about how submarines might transfigure naval warfare. In a memorandum composed seven months before the war, Fisher forecast that Germany would deploy submarines to sink unarmed merchant ships and would make no effort to save the ships' crews. The strengths and limitations of the submarine made this outcome inescapable, he argued. A submarine had no room to bring aboard the crew of a merchant ship and did not have enough men of its own to put a prize crew aboard.

What's more, Fisher wrote, the logic of war required that if such a strategy were adopted it would have to be pursued to the fullest extent possible. "The essence of war is violence," he wrote, "and moderation in war is imbecility."

Churchill rejected Fisher's vision. The use of submarines to attack unarmed merchant ships without warning, he wrote, would be "abhorrent to the immemorial law and practice of the sea."

Even he acknowledged, however, that such tactics when deployed against *naval* targets constituted "fair war," but early on neither he nor his German counterparts expected the submarine to play much of a role in deep-ocean battle. The strategic thinking of both sides centered on their main fleets, the British "Grand Fleet" and the German "High Seas Fleet," and both anticipated an all-or-nothing, Trafalgar-esque naval duel using their big battleships. But neither side was willing to be the first to come out in direct challenge of the other. Britain had more firepower—twenty-seven *Dreadnought*-class battleships to Germany's sixteen—but Churchill recognized that chance events could nullify that advantage "if some ghastly novelty or blunder supervened." For added safety, the Admiralty based the fleet in Scapa Flow, a kind of island fortress formed by the Orkney Islands, north of Scotland. Churchill expected Germany to make the first move, early and in full strength, for the German fleet would never be stronger than at the war's beginning.

German strategists, on the other hand, recognized Britain's superiority and crafted a plan whereby German ships would make limited raids against the British fleet to gradually erode its power, a campaign that Germany's Adm. Reinhard Scheer called "guerrilla warfare," borrowing a Spanish term for small-scale warfare in use since the early nineteenth century. Once the British fleet was pared down, Scheer wrote, the German fleet would seek a "favorable" opportunity for the climactic battle.

"So we waited," wrote Churchill; "and nothing happened. No great event immediately occurred. No battle was fought."

At the start of the war, the submarine barely figured in the strategic planning of either side. "In those early days," wrote Hereward Hook, a young British sailor, "I do not think that anyone realized that a submarine could do any damage." He was soon to learn otherwise, in an incident that demonstrated in vivid fashion the true destructive power of submarines and revealed a grave flaw in the design of Britain's big warships.

At dawn, on the morning of Tuesday, September 22, 1914, three large British cruisers, HMS *Aboukir*, *Hogue*, and *Cressy*, were patrolling a swath of the North Sea off Holland known as the "Broad Fourteens," moving at eight knots, a leisurely and, as it happened, foolhardy pace. The ships were full of cadets. Hook, one of them, was fifteen years old and assigned to the *Hogue*. The ships were old and slow, and so clearly at risk that within Britain's Grand Fleet they bore the nickname "the live-bait squadron." Hook—who in later life would indeed be promoted to *Captain* Hook—was in his bunk, asleep, when at 6:20 A.M. he was awakened by "a violent shaking" of his hammock. A midshipman was trying to wake him and other cadets, to alert them to the fact that one of the big cruisers, the *Aboukir*, had been torpedoed and was sinking.

Hook sprinted to the deck, and watched the *Aboukir* begin to list. Within minutes the ship heeled and disappeared. It was, he wrote, "my first sight of men struggling for their lives."

His ship and the other intact cruiser, the *Cressy*, maneuvered to rescue the sailors in the water, each coming to a dead stop a few hundred yards away to launch boats. Hook and his fellow crewmen were ordered to throw overboard anything that could float to help the men in the water. Moments later, two torpedoes struck his own ship, the *Hogue*, and in six or seven minutes "she was quite out of sight," he wrote. He was pulled into one of the *Hogue*'s previously launched lifeboats. After picking up more survivors, the lifeboat began making its way toward the third cruiser, the *Cressy*. But another torpedo was now tearing through the water. The torpedo struck the *Cressy* on its starboard side. Like the two other cruisers, the *Cressy* immediately began to list. Unlike the others, however, the list halted, and the ship seemed as if it might stay afloat. But then a second torpedo struck and hit the magazine that stored ammunition for the ship's heavy guns. The *Cressy* exploded and sank. Where just an hour earlier there had been three large cruisers, there were now only men, a few small boats, and wreckage. A single German submarine, Unterseeboot-9—U-9, for short—commanded by Kptlt. Otto Weddigen, had sunk all three ships, killing 1,459 British sailors, many of them young men in their teens.

Weddigen and his U-boat were of course to blame, but the design of the ships—their longitudinal coal bunkers—contributed greatly to the speed with which they sank and thus the number of lives lost. Once ruptured, the bunkers caused one side of each ship's hull to fill quickly, creating a catastrophic imbalance.

The disaster had an important secondary effect: because two of the cruisers had stopped to help survivors of the initial attack and thus made themselves easy targets, the Admiralty issued orders forbidding large British warships from going to the aid of U-boat victims.

THROUGH THE fall and winter of 1914, Germany's submarines came to occupy more and more of Wilson's attention, owing to a new shift in German naval strategy that brought with it the steadily worsening threat of entanglement. The *Aboukir* incident, and other successful attacks against British ships, caused German strategists to view submarines in a new light. The boats had proved to be hardier and deadlier than expected, well suited to Germany's guerrilla effort to abrade the strength of Britain's Grand Fleet. But their performance also suggested another use. By year's end, Germany had made the interception of merchant shipping an increasingly important role for the navy, to stanch the flow of munitions and supplies to Allied forces. This task originally had fallen to the navy's big auxiliary cruisers—former ocean liners converted to warships—but these cruisers had been largely swept from the seas by Britain's powerful navy. Submarines by their nature offered an effective means of continuing the campaign.

They also raised the risk that an American ship might be sunk by accident, or that U.S. citizens traveling on Allied vessels might be harmed. Early in 1915, this risk seemed to increase sharply. On February 4, Germany issued a proclamation designating the waters around the British Isles an "area of war" in which all enemy ships would be subject to attack without warning. This posed a particularly acute threat to Britain, which, as an island nation that imported two-thirds of its food, was utterly dependent on seaborne trade. Neutral ships were at risk also, Germany cautioned, because Britain's willingness to fly false flags had made it impossible for U-boat commanders to rely on a ship's markings to determine whether it truly was neutral. Germany justified the new campaign as a response to a blockade begun previously by Britain, in which the British navy sought to intercept all cargoes headed to Germany. (Britain had more than twice as many submarines as Germany but used them mainly for coastal defense, not to stop merchant ships.) German officials complained that Britain made no attempt to distinguish whether the cargoes were meant for hostile or peaceful use and charged that Britain's true goal was to starve civilians and thereby "doom the entire population of Germany to destruction."

What Germany never acknowledged was that Britain merely confiscated cargoes, whereas U-boats sank ships and killed men. German commanders seemed blind to the distinction. Germany's Admiral Scheer wrote, "Does it really make any difference, purely from the humane point of view, whether those thousands of men who drown wear naval uniforms or belong to a merchant ship bringing food and munitions to the enemy, thus prolonging the war and augmenting the number of women and children who suffer during the war?"

Germany's proclamation outraged President Wilson; on February 10, 1915, he cabled his formal response, in which he expressed incredulity that Germany would even think to use submarines against neutral merchant ships and warned that he would hold Germany "to a strict accountability" for any incident in which an American ship was sunk or Americans were injured or killed. He stated, further, that America would "take any steps it might be necessary to take to safeguard American lives and property and to secure to American citizens the full enjoyment of their acknowledged rights on the high seas."

The force of his prose took German leaders by surprise. Outwardly, Germany seemed a fierce monolith, united in carrying out its war against merchant ships. But in fact, the new submarine campaign had caused a rift at the highest levels of Germany's military and civilian leadership. Its most ardent supporters were senior naval officials; its opponents included the commander of Germany's military forces in Europe, Gen. Erich von Falkenhayn, and the nation's top political leader, Chancellor Theobald von Bethmann Hollweg. Moral scruple had nothing to do with their opposition. Both men feared that Germany's undersea war could only lead to disaster by driving America to shed its neutrality and side with Britain.

Wilson's protest, however, did not impress Germany's submarine zealots. They argued that if anything Germany should intensify its campaign and destroy *all* shipping in the war zone. They promised to bring Britain to heel well before America could mobilize an army and transport it to the battlefield.

Both camps maneuvered to win the endorsement of Kaiser Wilhelm, who, as the nation's supreme military leader, had the final say. He authorized U-boat commanders to sink any ship, regardless of flag or markings, if they had reason to believe it was British or French. More importantly, he gave the captains permission to do so while submerged, without warning.

The most important effect of all this was to leave the determination as to which ships were to be spared, which to be sunk, to the discretion of individual U-boat commanders. Thus a lone submarine captain, typically a young man in his twenties or thirties, ambitious, driven to accumulate as much sunk tonnage as possible, far from his base and unable to make wireless contact with superiors, his vision limited to the small and distant view afforded by a periscope, now held the power to make a mistake that could change the outcome of the entire war. As Chancellor Bethmann would later put it, "Unhappily, it depends upon the attitude of a single submarine commander whether America will or will not declare war."

No one had any illusions. Mistakes would happen. One of Kaiser Wilhelm's orders included an acknowledgment of the risk: "If in spite of the exercise of great care mistakes should be made, the commander will not be made responsible."

WILSON'S GRIEF and loneliness persisted into the new year, but in March 1915 a chance encounter caused that curtain of gray to part.

His cousin, Helen Woodrow Bones, lived in the White House, where she served as a proxy First Lady. Often, she went walking with a good friend, Edith Bolling Galt, forty-three years old, who happened also to be a friend of Wilson's physician, Dr. Grayson. At five feet nine inches tall, with a full and shapely figure and a taste for fine clothes, including those designed in the Paris fashion house of Charles Frederick Worth, she was a striking woman, with a complexion and manner said to gleam, and eyes of a violet blue. One day while riding in a limousine with Wilson, Dr. Grayson spotted Galt and bowed toward her, at which point the president exclaimed, "Who is that beautiful lady?"

Born in October 1872 as the seventh of eleven siblings, Edith claimed family roots that dated back to Pocahontas and Capt. John Rolfe. She grew up in a small Virginia town, Wytheville, in a landscape still warm with residual passions of the Civil War. While a teenager, she began making periodic visits to Washington, D.C., to visit her eldest sister, who had married into a family that owned one of Washington's finest jewelry stores, Galt & Bro. Jewelers, situated near the White House. (The store was repairing Abraham Lincoln's watch at the time the Civil War began.) On one visit, when Edith was in her twenties, she met Norman Galt—a cousin of her sister's husband—who shared management of the store with other members of the family. They married in 1896.

Eventually Norman bought out his relatives to become sole owner of the business. Edith bore a son in 1903, but the baby died within days. Five years later, Norman died as well, suddenly, leaving substantial debts from his acquisition of the store. It was a difficult time, Edith wrote. "I had no experience in business affairs and hardly knew an asset from a liability." She placed the store's day-to-day operations in the care of a seasoned employee, and with his help the business began again to prosper so that Edith, while retaining ownership, was able to withdraw from daily management. She became a skilled golfer and was the first woman in Washington to acquire a driver's license. She tooled around the city in an electric car.

Her walks with Helen Bones usually began with Edith driving herself and Helen to Rock Creek Park in her car. Afterward, they invariably returned to Edith's house in Dupont Circle for tea. But one afternoon in March 1915, Helen arrived at Edith's home in a White House car, which took them to the park. At the end of the walk, Helen suggested that this time they have tea at her place, the White House.

Edith resisted. The walk had been a messy one. Her shoes were muddy, and she did not want to be seen by the president of the United States in this condition. As she told Helen, she feared being "taken for a tramp." In fact, shoes aside, she looked pretty good, as she herself later noted, with "a smart black tailored suit which Worth had made for me in Paris, and a tricot hat which I thought completed a very-good-looking ensemble."

Helen insisted. "There is not a soul there," she told Edith. "Cousin Woodrow is playing golf with Dr. Grayson and we will go right upstairs in the elevator and you shall see no one."

They rode to the second floor. As they emerged, they ran headlong into the president and Grayson, both of whom were in their golf clothes. Grayson and Wilson joined the women for tea.

Edith wrote later, "This was the accidental meeting which carried out the old adage of 'turn a corner and meet your fate.'" She noted, however, that the golf clothes Wilson had been wearing "were not smart."

Soon afterward Helen invited Edith to a dinner at the White House, set for March 23. Wilson sent his Pierce-Arrow to pick her up and to collect Dr. Grayson as well. Edith wore a purple orchid and sat at Wilson's right. "He is perfectly charming," she wrote later, "and one of the easiest and most delightful hosts I have ever known."

After dinner, the group went upstairs to the second-floor Oval Room for coffee and a fire, "and all sorts of interesting conversation." Wilson read three poems by English authors, prompting Edith to observe that "as a reader he is unequalled."

The evening had a profound effect on Wilson. He was entranced. Edith, sixteen years his junior, was an attractive and compelling woman. White House usher Irwin "Ike" Hoover called her an "impressive widow." That evening, Wilson's spirits soared.

He had little time to dwell in this new hopeful state, however. Five days later, on March 28, 1915, a British merchant ship, the *Falaba*, encountered a U-boat commanded by Georg-Günther Freiherr von Forstner, one of Germany's submarine aces. The ship was small, less than five thousand tons, and carried cargo and passengers bound for Africa. A sharp-eyed lookout first saw the submarine when it was three miles off and alerted the *Falaba*'s captain, Frederick Davies, who turned his ship full away and ordered maximum speed, just over thirteen knots.

Forstner gave chase. He ordered his gun crew to fire a warning shot.

The *Falaba* kept running. Now Forstner, using flags, signaled, "Stop or I fire."

The *Falaba* stopped. The U-boat approached, and Forstner, shouting through a megaphone, notified Captain Davies that he planned to sink the vessel. He ordered Davies and all aboard—242 souls—to abandon ship. He gave them five minutes.

Forstner maneuvered to within one hundred yards. The last lifeboat was still being lowered when he fired a torpedo. The *Falaba* sank in eight minutes, killing 104 people including Captain Davies. A passenger by the name of Leon C. Thrasher was believed among the lost, though his body was not recovered. Thrasher was a citizen of the United States.

The incident, condemned as the latest example of German

frightfulness, was exactly the kind of thing Wilson had feared, for it held the potential to raise a cry for war. "I do not like this case," he told his secretary of state, William Jennings Bryan. "It is full of disturbing possibilities."

Wilson's first instinct was to issue an immediate denunciation of the attack, in sharp language, but subsequent discussion with his cabinet and with Secretary Bryan caused him to hold off. Bryan, a staunch pacifist, proposed that the death of an American who knowingly traveled aboard a British ship through a declared war zone might not even merit protest. To him it seemed the equivalent of an American taking a stroll across the battlefield in France.

In a note to Bryan on Wednesday, April 28, the day after a cabinet meeting at which the *Falaba* incident was discussed, Wilson wrote, "Perhaps it is not necessary to make formal representations in the matter at all."

LEON THRASHER, the American passenger, was still missing, his body presumably adrift in the Irish Sea. It was one more beat in a cadence that seemed to be growing faster and louder.

SUCKING TUBES AND THACKERAY

THROUGHOUT THE WEEK BEFORE DEPARTURE, PASSEN-
gers who lived in New York started packing in earnest, while
the many who came from elsewhere began arriving in the city
by train, ferry, and automobile. They found a city steaming with
heat—91 degrees on Tuesday, April 27, with four days yet to go
until "Straw Hat Day," Saturday, May 1, when a man could at
last break out his summer hats. Men followed this rule. A *Times*
reporter did an impromptu visual survey of Broadway and spotted only two straw hats. "Thousands of sweltering, uncomfortable men plodded along with their winter headgear at all angles on
their uncomfortable heads or carried in their hot, moist hands."

The city seemed untroubled by the war. Broadway—"the Great
White Way," so dubbed for its bright electric lighting—came bril-
liantly alight and alive each night, as always, although now with
unexpected competition. A number of restaurants had begun providing lavish entertainment along with meals, even though they
lacked theater licenses. The city was threatening a crackdown on
these maverick "cabarets." One operator, the manager of Reisen-
weber's at Eighth Avenue and Columbus Circle, said he would
welcome a ban. The competition was wearing him out. His es-
tablishment was running a musical revue called "Too Much
Mustard," featuring "a Host of BEAUTIFUL GIRLS," and a separate "Whirlwind Cabaret" with a quintet of minstrels and a full

lunch—table d'hôte—for a buck, with dancing between courses. "The public," he complained, "is making such ridiculous demands for elaborate entertainment with meals that it is really dangerous for everybody in the restaurant business."

In case any of the newly arrived passengers needed some last-minute clothing for the voyage, there was New York's perennial attraction: shopping. Spring sales were under way or about to begin. Lord and Taylor on Fifth Avenue was advertising men's raincoats for $6.75, less than half their usual price. B. Altman, a few blocks south, didn't deign to list actual prices but assured female shoppers they would find "decided reductions" in the cost of gowns and suits from Paris, these to be found on its third floor in the department of "Special Costumes." And, strangely, a tailor of German heritage, House of Kuppenheimer, was advertising a special suit, "the British." The company's ads proclaimed, "All men are young in these stirring days."

The city's economy, like that of the nation as a whole, had by now improved dramatically, owing to the wartime boost in demand for American wares, especially munitions. The lull in shipping had ended; by year's end, the United States would report a record trade surplus of $1.5 billion, or $35.9 billion today. Real estate, ever an obsession in New York, was booming, with large buildings under construction on the East and West Sides. Work was about to begin on a new twelve-story apartment building at the corner of Eighty-eighth and Broadway. Expected cost: $500,000. There were extravagant displays of spending. It's possible that some of the *Lusitania*'s first-class passengers attended a big party at Delmonico's the Friday night before departure, thrown by Lady Grace Mackenzie, "the huntress," as the *Times* described her. The party had a jungle theme, with fifty guests, among them explorers, hunters, zoologists, two cheetahs, and "a black ape." Delmonico's had filled the banquet room with palm trees and layered the walls with palm fronds to create the effect of dining in an African glade. Black men in tights and white tunics kept watch on the animals, though in fact the black pigment proved to be the effect of burned cork and low lighting. The list of appetizers included stuffed eagles' eggs.

Although the city's newspapers carried a lot of war news, politics and crime tended to dominate the front page. Murder was a fascination, as always. On Thursday, April 29, in the midst of the heat wave, a city produce merchant who had recently lost his job sent his wife to the movies, then shot his five-year-old son to death and killed himself. A Bridgeport, Connecticut, man presented his girlfriend with an engagement ring and handed her one end of a ribbon; the other end disappeared into his pocket. "A surprise," he said, and urged her to pull it. She obliged. The ribbon was attached to the trigger of a revolver. The man died instantly. And on Friday, April 30, four criminals escaped from the drug ward at Bellevue Hospital, wearing pink pajamas. Three of the men were found, "after a thorough search of the neighborhood by policemen, hospital attendants, and small boys," the *Times* said. The fourth man was at large, presumably still dressed in pink.

And there was this: a report that plans had been completed for a ceremony to dedicate a memorial fountain to Jack Phillips, wireless operator aboard the *Titanic*, and to eight other Marconi operators likewise killed in maritime disasters. The article noted, "Space is left for the addition of other names in the future."

THE *LUSITANIA*'S roster of passengers included 949 British citizens (including residents of Canada), 71 Russians, 15 Persians, 8 French, 6 Greeks, 5 Swedes, 3 Belgians, 3 Dutch, 2 Italians, 2 Mexicans, 2 Finns, and 1 traveler each from Denmark, Spain, Argentina, Switzerland, Norway, and India.

The American complement, by Cunard's official tally, totaled 189. They came from locales throughout the country. Two men from Virginia were officials of a shipbuilding company on their way to Europe to explore the acquisition of submarines. At least five passengers hailed from Philadelphia, others from Tuckahoe, New York; Braceville, Ohio; Seymour, Indiana; Pawtucket, Rhode Island; Hancock, Maryland; and Lake Forest, Illinois. A number came from Los Angeles: the Blickes, husband and wife, traveling in first, and three members of the Bretherton family, in third. Christ traveled among them as well: Christ Garry, of Cleveland, Ohio, in second class.

They stayed in hotels and boardinghouses or with family and friends, at addresses in all parts of the city. At least six stayed at the Hotel Astor, another six at the Biltmore. They arrived at intervals during the week, bearing mountains of luggage. Cunard allowed each passenger 20 cubic feet. They brought trunks, some brightly colored—red, yellow, blue, green—and others with surfaces of leather embossed with checkerboard and herringbone patterns, braced with wood. They brought "extension suitcases" for transporting dresses, gowns, tuxedos, and business suits. The largest of these could hold forty men's suits. They brought large boxes built especially for footwear, and these smelled pleasantly of polish and leather. They carried smaller luggage as well, mindful of what they would need while aboard and of what could be left in the ship's baggage hold. Passengers arriving by train could check the most cumbersome bags straight through from their cities of origin to their staterooms or to the baggage hold of the ship, with confidence that their belongings would be there when they boarded.

They brought their best clothes, and in some cases, their only clothes. The dominant palette was black and gray, but there were cheerier items as well. A heliotrope-and-white-checked frock. A boy's red knitted jacket, with white buttons. A green velveteen belt. Babies complicated things. Their clothing was intricate. A single outfit for one infant boy consisted of a white wool wrapper; a white cotton bodice edged with red and blue piping; overalls of blue cotton embroidered with dotted squares, plaited down the front, fastened in back with white buttons; a gray wool jacket with four ivory buttons; black stockings; and shoes with straps. He topped this off with a "sucking tube," or pacifier, tied around his neck with cord.

The wealthiest passengers carried rings, brooches, pendants, necklaces, and necklets, embedded with diamonds, sapphires, rubies, and onyx (and sardonyx, its red sister). They brought bonds and notes and letters of introduction, but also cash. A thirty-five-year-old woman brought five one-hundred-dollar bills; another, eleven fifties. Everyone seemed to carry a watch, invariably in a gold case. One woman brought her Geneva-made "Remontoir Cylindre 10 Rubis Medaille D'Or, No. 220063," gold but with a face the color of blood. Later, the serial numbers of these watches would prove invaluable.

Passengers brought diaries, books, pens, ink, and other devices with which to kill time. Ian Holbourn, the famed writer and lecturer now returning from a speaking tour of America, brought along the manuscript of a book he had been working on for two decades, about his theory of beauty, whose pages now numbered in the thousands. It was his only copy. Dwight Harris, a thirty-one-year-old New Yorker from a wealthy family, brought with him an engagement ring. He had plans. He also had concerns. On Friday, April 30, he went to the John Wanamaker department store in New York and bought a custom life belt.

Another man packed a gold seal for stamping wax on the back of an envelope, with the Latin motto *Tuta Tenebo*, "I will keep you safe."

FIRST-CLASS PASSENGER Charles Emelius Lauriat Jr., a Boston bookseller, carried several items of particular value. Lauriat, forty, was a good-looking man, with an attentive gaze and well-trimmed brown hair. Since 1894 he had been president of one of the country's best-known bookstores, Charles E. Lauriat Company, at 385 Washington Street in Boston, several blocks from Boston Common, this at a time when a book dealer could achieve national recognition. It was "the golden age of American book collecting," according to one historian, when some of the nation's great private collections were amassed, later to become treasured libraries, such as the Morgan in New York and the Folger in Washington. Lauriat was an accomplished swimmer and yachtsman who played water polo and regularly raced his 18-foot sailboat and served as a judge in regattas that took place off the New England coast each summer. The *Boston Globe* called him a "born boat sailor." Something of a celebrity himself, at least in literary circles, he dined regularly at the city's Player's Club, often with one of the foremost critics and poets of the age, William Stanley Braithwaite.

The store, originally situated directly opposite Boston's Old South Church, had been founded by Lauriat's father and a partner, Dana Estes, in 1872, under the name Estes & Lauriat, which also published books. Three years later, the two partners divided the business into two companies, with Lauriat taking over the retail side. By the time of the split the store had already become a Boston institution, "as much a debating society as it was a bookshop," according to one account. It served as a meeting place for writers, readers, intellectuals, and artists and included among its regular customers Ralph Waldo Emerson and Oliver Wendell Holmes. The elder Lauriat was said to see himself as a "guide, counselor and friend" to his customers and produced in the store an atmosphere that one newspaper writer called "homeness."

The store was long and narrow and jutted far inward from the street, more mineshaft than showroom, with books shoring the walls all the way to the high ceilings and stacked on counters down the center. A flight of stairs led to a balcony full of collectors' books and "association books," those made valuable because their owners had been famous or otherwise noteworthy. One attraction for book aficionados was the store's Old Book Room, in the basement, filled with "great gems" that, according to a privately published history of the store, had come into the marketplace mainly "through the breaking up of old English country house libraries." The display windows on Washington Street drew crowds of onlookers at lunch hour. Rare books were displayed in the windows on one side of the front door, new books on the other, including those with the most garish covers known even then as "bestsellers." (One popular American author who turned out a bestseller every year was named, oddly enough, Winston Churchill.) The store was one of the first to sell "Remainders," stocks of once-popular books that remained unsold after the initial surge of sales and that publishers were willing to sell to Lauriat at a deep discount. He in turn sold them to customers for a fraction of their original price, a side of the business that grew so popular the store began printing a "Remainder Catalog," released each fall.

But the thing that set Lauriat apart from other booksellers, from the beginning, was the elder Lauriat's decision to make an annual trip to London to buy up old books and sell them in America for far higher prices, leveraging the differential in demand that existed on opposite sides of the Atlantic, while also taking advantage of the falling prices and faster speeds of shipping brought by the advent of transatlantic steamships. Lauriat made his first trip in 1873 on one of Cunard's earliest steamers, the *Atlas*. His purchases routinely made news. One acquisition, of a Bible dating to 1599, a Geneva, or "Breeches," Bible—so named because it used the word *breeches* to describe what Adam and Eve wore—drew nearly a full column in the *New York Times*. By century's end, the store had become one of the country's leading sellers and importers of rare books, manuscripts, and illustrations, its bookplates destined to be treasured by future bibliophiles.

Charles Lauriat Jr. continued his father's transatlantic harvest and in that last week of April 1915 was preparing to set out on his next buying trip. As always, Lauriat planned to stay in London for several months while he hunted for books and writerly artifacts to acquire, these to be crated and shipped back by sea to Boston. He transported his most valuable finds in his personal baggage and never thought to insure them against loss, "for the risk," as he put it, "is practically nil." Nor did the war prompt him to change his practice. "We considered the passenger steamers immune from submarine attack," he wrote.

He bought his ticket, No. 1297, from a Cunard agent in Boston, and while doing so asked whether the liner would be "convoyed through the war zone." The clerk replied, "Oh yes! every precaution will be taken."

Lauriat chose the *Lusitania* specifically because of its speed. Ordinarily he preferred small, slow boats, "but this year," he wrote, "I wanted to make my business trip as short as possible." At the *Lusitania*'s top speed of 25 knots, he expected to arrive in

Liverpool on Friday, May 7, and reach London in time to start work on Saturday morning, May 8. He planned to travel with a friend, Lothrop Withington, an authority on genealogy who had a particular expertise in the old records of Salem, Massachusetts, and Canterbury, England. Both men were married, but for this trip were leaving their wives behind. Lauriat had four children, one a baby, whose picture he planned to bring along.

He packed five pieces of luggage: a leather briefcase, a small valise, an extension suitcase, a large shoe case, and his steamer trunk. Dinner required formal wear and all that went with it. His various day suits required shoes of differing styles. There were braces and socks, ties and cufflinks. He also packed his favorite Knickerbocker suit, with its characteristic knickers, which he planned to wear while strolling the deck.

He and Withington were set to take the midnight train to New York, on Thursday, April 29, but first Lauriat stopped at his bookstore. There a colleague opened the store's safe and handed him two volumes, each with a cover that measured 12 by 14 inches. These were scrapbooks, but of a high order. One contained fifty-four line drawings, the other sixty-four drawings, all done by the Victorian author William Makepeace Thackeray to illustrate his own works. At one time, Thackeray, who died in 1863 and whose best-known work was *Vanity Fair*, had been nearly as popular as Charles Dickens, and his satirical stories, essays, and serialized novels were widely and avidly read in such magazines as *Fraser's* and *Punch*. His drawings and books and just about any other artifact from his life—all known as "Thackerayana"—were coveted by collectors on both sides of the Atlantic, but especially in America.

Lauriat took the scrapbooks back to his home in Cambridge, where he inspected them in the company of his wife, Marian. He then packed them, carefully, in his extension suitcase, and locked it. At the station later that night, he checked his trunk and shoe box for transport direct to the *Lusitania* but held back his other three pieces. He kept these with him in the railcar.

He and Withington reached New York early the next morning, Friday, April 30, the day before the *Lusitania* was scheduled to sail, and here they temporarily parted company. Lauriat took a taxi to the home of his sister, Blanche, and her husband, George W. Chandler, at 235 West Seventy-first Street in Manhattan. Lauriat had one more task to complete before departure.

AT THE Waldorf Astoria, at Fifth Avenue and Thirty-third Street, first-class passenger Margaret Mackworth, thirty-one, packed her things in a fog of gloom and depression. She dreaded her return to England. It meant going back to a dead marriage of seven years and a life oppressed by war.

She had arrived in New York the previous month, alone, after a tedious ten-day crossing, to join her father, D. A. Thomas, a prominent businessman, who was already in the city for discussions on ventures ranging from mines to Mississippi barges. She was delighted and relieved to find him waiting for her on the dock. "In 1915, to come out into sunlit April New York, care-free and happy, after being under the heavy cloud of war at home, was an unspeakable relief," she recalled.

The city charmed her. "In the evenings—almost every evening—we went out, either to the theatre or to dinner parties," she wrote. She bought dresses, paid for by her father, including a long black velvet gown that she loved. She saw her customary shyness—an "annihilating" shyness—begin to subside, and she began for the first time in her life to feel like a social asset to her father, rather than a liability. (Her shyness, however, had not kept her from fighting for women's suffrage back in England, in the course of which she jumped on the running board of a prime minister's car and blew up a mailbox with a bomb.) "Those weeks of open-hearted American hospitality and forth-comingness, of frankly expressed pleasure in meeting one, did something for me that made a difference to the whole of the rest of my life," she wrote.

She dropped her shyness "overboard" on that holiday. "I have always been grateful to New York for that," she wrote. "And, finally, it was one of the last times when I consciously felt quite young."

Although she and her father would be traveling in first class on one of the most luxurious vessels the world had known, all she felt now was sorrow and regret.

THAT FRIDAY morning, Captain Turner left the ship and made his way south to Wall Street, to the City Investing Building at 165 Broadway, an immense, ungainly structure that happened to stand beside one of the city's most beloved landmarks, the Singer Tower, built by the Singer Sewing Machine Company. Here Turner made his way up to the law offices of Hunt, Hill & Betts, where, at 11:00 A.M., he sat before eight lawyers for a deposition in one of the most compelling cases of the day, the attempt in U.S. Federal Court by the White Star Line, owners of the *Titanic*, to limit their financial liability in the face of claims by families of dead American passengers, who charged that the disaster had resulted from the company's "fault and negligence."

Turner, testifying on behalf of the families, had been summoned as an expert witness, an acknowledgment of his many years as captain of large passenger ships and of the respect afforded him by other mariners, but it became quickly evident to those present that being questioned by lawyers was not something he enjoyed. He offered only abrupt, clipped answers—seldom more than a single sentence or phrase—but nonetheless proved to be a damning witness.

The lawyers managed to pry from him his account of being at sea when he first learned of the *Titanic* disaster. He'd been captain of the *Mauretania* at the time. The *Titanic* had departed on April 11, 1912, and the *Mauretania* on April 13, a fact Turner remembered because the date posed a problem for superstitious passengers, even though in seafaring lore the number 13 presents no particular hazard. It is sailing on a Friday that causes sailors dread. Upon receiving reports by wireless of ice along his course, Turner decided to veer well south. His wireless man brought him first word of the *Titanic*'s collision with an iceberg.

Asked now whether he thought it had been prudent for the *Ti-*

tanic to travel at 20 knots or more with ice likely to be in the vicinity, Turner offered one of his most energetic replies: "Certainly not; 20 knots through ice! My conscience!"

The best way to proceed, Turner explained, was very slowly, or simply to stop. He allowed that wireless had become an effective tool for alerting captains to the presence of ice but dismissed sea studies that suggested that captains might derive warning by carefully monitoring the temperature of air and water as they sailed. This was useless, Turner explained: "No more effect than a blister on a wooden leg."

Turner also expressed ambivalence about the value of lookouts. The Cunard manual required two in the crow's nest at all times. "I call them Board of Trade ornaments," Turner said; "all they think about is home and counting their money."

Asked whether he gave lookouts binoculars, Turner replied: "Certainly not; might as well give them soda water bottles."

Still, he said, when traveling through waters where ice might appear, he always doubled the lookout, adding two men at the bow.

Turner warned that no matter what precautions were taken, what studies were made, ice would always be a hazard. Startled by this, one of the attorneys asked Turner, "Have you learned nothing by that accident?"

"Not the slightest," Turner said. "It will happen again."

At various points during the deposition, the lawyers focused on Turner's own ship, with emphasis on the *Lusitania*'s watertight decks and doors, and in particular its longitudinal bunkers.

"Which is very unusual with merchant vessels, but common enough with naval vessels, isn't it?"

"Yes," Turner said, "a protection."

Further questioning taught the lawyers that the captain had little interest in the structural design of ships, including his own.

"You are not a mechanical man," one asked, but "a navigator."

"Yes."

"You don't pay much attention to the construction of ships?"

"No, as long as they float; if they sink, I get out."

Asked if there was anything "peculiarly extraordinary" about the watertight doors on the *Lusitania* and her sister ship, the *Mauretania*, Turner answered: "Don't know."

A few moments later, the lawyer asked, "Before the 'Titanic,' it was supposed these great ships were non-sinkable?"

"Who told you that?" Turner snapped. "Nobody I ever went to sea with proved it."

The deposition concluded with a question as to whether a ship with *five* flooded compartments could continue to float.

Turner replied, "My dear sir, I don't know anything at all about it; it all depends on the size of the compartments, the amount of buoyancy; if she has buoyancy, she will float; if she has not, she will go down."

Turner returned to his ship.

THE HAPPIEST U-BOAT

THAT SAME DAY, FRIDAY, APRIL 30, A VESSEL OF A DIF-
ferent sort began making its way toward the British Isles, the
German submarine Unterseeboot-20, traveling under orders
that gave its new patrol a heightened urgency. The boat slipped
from its harbor at Emden, on the northwest coast of Germany, at
6:00 A.M., with no fanfare. The crews of U-boats nicknamed the
North Sea "Bright Hans," but today the sea and sky were gray, as
was the flat terrain that surrounded the harbor. Submarines stood
side by side at their moorage, roped to one another, their conning
towers like distant castles. The wind came onshore at 4 knots.

U-20 moved seaward along the Ems River, in silence, and left
almost no wake. Atop its conning tower stood Kptlt. Walther
Schwieger, the boat's captain, in his peaked cap and waterproof
leathers. The tower was a squat chamber jutting up from the boat's
midsection that housed an array of controls and two periscopes,
one his primary battle periscope, the other an auxiliary. During
underwater attacks, Schwieger would station himself here within
the tower's thick carbon-steel walls and use the main periscope to
direct his crew in launching torpedoes. When surfaced, the small
deck on top of the tower gave him a promontory from which to
scan the seascape around him but provided little shelter from the
weather. The morning was cold; the scent of coffee rose through
the hatch below.

Schwieger guided the submarine along the river and on into the shallows outside the harbor. The boat moved due west and by about 9:30 A.M. passed the lighthouse and wireless station on Borkum, a small barrier island that served as an important landmark for departing and returning submarines.

Schwieger had just turned thirty-two years old but already was considered one of the German navy's most knowledgeable commanders, so much so that he was consulted on submarine matters by his superiors, and his boat was used to try out new submarine tactics. He was one of the few captains who had been in the submarine service before the war began. He was tall and slender, with broad shoulders. "A particularly fine-looking fellow," one of his crew members said. His eyes were pale blue and conveyed coolness and good humor.

Around noon, Schwieger's boat entered the deep waters beyond Borkum, in a portion of the North Sea known variously as the German Bight or Heligoland Bight. Here the sea bottom fell away and on bright days the water turned a deep cobalt. In his War Log, kept for every patrol, Schwieger noted that the sea was running a three-foot swell from the west and that visibility was good.

Although he was free to submerge the vessel if he wished, he kept it on the surface, where he could travel farther and faster. His twin diesel engines could generate up to 15 knots, enough to overtake most conventional merchant ships. At routine cruising speeds, say 8 knots, he could travel up to 5,200 nautical miles. Once submerged, however, Schwieger had to switch to two battery-powered engines, lest the diesels consume all the oxygen in the boat. These engines could deliver 9 knots at best, and only for a brief period. Even at half that pace, a submerged U-boat could travel only about 80 nautical miles. These speeds were so slow that sometimes U-boats trying to make their way against the fast currents of the Strait of Dover, between England and France, were unable to advance. U-boats in fact traveled underwater as little as possible, typically only in extreme weather or when attacking ships or dodging destroyers.

For much of his first day at sea, Schwieger was able to maintain wireless contact with the station on Borkum Island and with a naval vessel in Emden Harbor, the *Ancona*, which was equipped with wireless apparatus that could communicate over long distances. Schwieger noted in his log that his ability to trade messages with the Borkum transmitter ceased when his U-boat was 45 sea miles out but that he maintained a good connection with the *Ancona*. Along the way his wireless operator repeatedly sent test signals, something U-boat wireless operators often did, as if to postpone the inevitable moment when the boat would be out of range of all friendly sources and utterly on its own.

This isolation made the U-boat distinct among Germany's naval forces. Surface ships usually traveled in groups and, given the height of their masts, could stay in contact with their bases; U-boats traveled solo and lost contact sooner, typically after sailing only a couple of hundred miles. Once at sea, a U-boat captain was free to conduct his patrol in whatever manner suited him, without supervision from above. He alone determined when and whether to attack, when to ascend or dive, and when to return to base. He had absolute control over the boat's periscope. "I want to stress that the submarine is only a one-eyed vessel," said a U-boat commander, Baron Edgar von Spiegel von und zu Peckelsheim, who knew Schwieger well. "That means, only the one who is at the periscope with one eye has the whole responsibility for attacking or the safety of his ship and crew."

The view it provided was a crabbed one at best. A captain got only a brief, platelike glimpse at the world around him, during which he had to make decisions about a ship's nature, its nationality, whether it was armed or not, and whether the markings it bore were legitimate or fake. And if he decided to attack, it was he alone who bore the responsibility, like pulling the trigger on a gun, but without having to see or listen to the result. All he heard was the sound of the exploding torpedo as transmitted through the sea. If he chose to watch the tragedy unfold, he saw only a silent world of fire and terror. Once, Spiegel attacked a transport carrying horses and watched one of the animals—"a splendid, dapple-gray horse with a long tail"—leap from the ship into an overloaded lifeboat.

After that, he wrote, "I could not endure the spectacle any longer." He pulled down his periscope and ordered his boat into a deep dive.

"It was a very hard task and entirely different from the fighting in the army," said Spiegel. "If you were bombarded by artillery and you had orders to leave your trenches and attack you were in full excitement personally. In the submarine perhaps you were sitting in your small cabin drinking your morning coffee and [eating] ham and eggs when the whistle or the phone rang and told you, 'ship in sight.'" The captain gave the order to fire. "And the results of these damn torpedoes were certainly very often heartbreaking." One ship, struck in the bow, sank "like an airplane," he said. "In two minutes the 10,000 ton ship disappeared from the surface."

Such authority could be thrilling but carried with it a certain loneliness, amplified by the fact that Germany had very few submarines at sea at any one time. As of May 1915, Schwieger's U-boat was one of only twenty-five in Germany's fleet that were capable of traveling long distances. Only seven were in service at a time, owing to the fact that after each cruise the boats often needed several weeks for repair and overhaul. When on patrol, Schwieger's U-boat occupied a pinpoint in a vast sea.

On this cruise, Schwieger carried with him a set of orders that had been delivered to him by hand. These were the result of a newly risen fear that Britain was about to launch an invasion of Germany itself, from the North Sea at Schleswig-Holstein, and that the ships carrying the invading troops would depart from ports different from those customarily used to resupply British forces in France. Intelligence reports had long suggested such an invasion might be in the works, but German naval officials were at first skeptical. Now, however, they had come to believe the reports might be true. Schwieger's orders directed him to hunt and attack these transports in a designated square of sea off Liverpool, between England and Ireland, and to sail there "on the fastest possible route around Scotland." Once there, the orders said, he was to hold that position "as long as supplies permit."

The mission must have been urgent indeed to cause the navy to override the maritime superstition about Friday departures.

THE SUBMARINE as a weapon had come a long way by this time, certainly to the point where it killed its own crews only rarely. The first submarine ever credited with sinking an enemy ship was the Confederate navy's *H. L. Hunley*, which, during the American Civil War, sank the Union navy's frigate, the *Housatonic*. The *Hunley*, propelled by a crew of eight using hand cranks to turn its propeller, approached the *Housatonic* after dark, carrying a large cache of explosives at the end of a thirty-foot spar jutting from its bow. The explosion destroyed the frigate; it also sank the *Hunley*, which disappeared with all hands. This fate was more or less foretold, however. During trials before its launch, the *Hunley* had foundered three times, killing three crews, twenty-three men in all. Although inventors in many different countries contributed to the development of the submarine, the man most often lauded for turning it into something other than a suicidal novelty—an "iron coffin," as members of the German navy were fond of saying—was an Irishman named John Philip Holland, who emigrated to America and began designing undersea vessels with the goal of helping Ireland defeat the British navy. A famous 1898 cartoon, based on a photograph taken in Perth Amboy, New Jersey, shows Holland emerging in top hat from the hatch of one of his submarines, with the caption, "What? Me worry?" Holland was first to incorporate electric engines for undersea cruising and gasoline for surface running, though gasoline, with its fumes and volatility and propensity for suffocating crews, was eventually replaced by diesel fuel. A Spaniard named Raimondo Lorenzo D'Equevilley-Montjustin, employed by the German arms maker Krupp, was responsible for designing Germany's first submarines, though he did so by incorporating the ideas of Holland and others. His boats prompted the German navy to establish, in 1904, a division devoted to their construction, the Unterseebootkonstruktionsbüro, though the navy remained skeptical about their value. By the start of the war, submarine disasters still occurred, but not at so high a frequency as to deter young men like Schwieger from joining Germany's U-boat service.

Schwieger's boat was 210 feet long, 20 feet wide, and 27 feet tall. Viewed head-on, it might have seemed to offer its crew a comfortable amount of living space, but in fact the portion occupied by the men was only a cylinder down the center. Much of the boat's apparent bulk consisted of giant tanks on both sides of the hull, to be filled with seawater when diving and to be emptied when surfacing. The space in between was crammed with berths for three dozen men, a kitchen, a mess room, a cubicle for the wireless operator, a central control room, two 850-horsepower diesel engines, tanks for 76 tons of diesel fuel, two 600-horsepower electric engines and the massive array of batteries that powered them, plus storage for 250 shells for the U-boat's sole deck gun and space for storing and handling seven torpedoes, known formally as "automobile torpedoes." The boat had two torpedo tubes in the bow, two in the stern. Linking all this apparatus was an array of pipes and cables as densely packed as the tendons in a human leg. "More dials and gauges than one might ordinarily see in a lifetime," one crew member said. Schwieger had his own tiny cabin, with an electric light over his bed.

Unlike large surface craft, a U-boat came to reflect the character and personality of its commander, as though the boat were a suit of steel tailored just for him. This arose from the fact that while on distant patrol the captain received no orders from superiors and had more direct control over his own men than would, say, an admiral aboard a flagship, with a fleet of ships and thousands of men under his command. There were cruel boats and chivalrous boats, lazy boats and energetic boats. Some captains made no attempt to save the lives of merchant seamen; others went so far as to tow lifeboats toward land. One U-boat commander sent the captain of a torpedoed ship three bottles of wine to ease the long row ashore.

Under U-20's previous commander, Otto Droescher, the boat

attained a reputation for daring. On one cruise, in September 1914, Droescher and another commander took their submarines into the Firth of Forth, the estuary off Edinburgh, Scotland, and sailed as far inland as the Forth Bridge, hoping to attack British warships anchored at the navy base at Rosyth, just beyond the bridge. The boats were spotted, however, and fled back to the North Sea.

On another patrol, the next month, Droescher became the first U-boat captain to circle all of Britain. He had sailed first into the English Channel, via the Strait of Dover, where he had encountered vigorous antisubmarine patrols. Gauging the strait as too dangerous for his return voyage, he traveled north instead, along the west coasts of England and Ireland and around the northern tip of Scotland, thus further demonstrating the range and endurance of U-boats. Germany kept the feat a secret.

Schwieger became captain of U-20 in December 1914, and within a short time the boat gained further notoriety, now for ruthlessness. On January 30, 1915, while patrolling off the coast of France, Schwieger sank three merchant steamers without warning. During that same cruise, he took his boat into the estuary of the Seine itself, though bad weather and fog forced him to remain submerged for 111 of 137 hours. On February 1, he fired a torpedo at a large ship painted white and marked with large red crosses, the hospital ship *Asturias*. He missed. But the attempt was considered a new low in German callousness. Even his superiors seemed surprised.

Yet among his peers and crew Schwieger was known for his kindness and good humor and for maintaining a cheerful atmosphere aboard his submarine. "She was a jolly boat, the U-20, and a kindly boat," said Rudolph Zentner, one of U-20's junior officers, in an interview with Lowell Thomas, for his 1928 book, *Raiders of the Deep*. Zentner attributed this wholly to Schwieger. "If you want a good and pleasant boat, you must have a good and pleasant skipper." Schwieger was the son of a long-established Berlin family, well educated, poised, urbane. "He was the soul of kindness toward the officers and men under him," Zentner said. "His temperament was joyous and his talk full of gaiety and pointed wit."

Baron von Spiegel, Schwieger's friend, said of him, "He was a wonderful man. He couldn't kill a fly."

Schwieger set the tone for life aboard U-20 early in his tenure. The boat was ordered to leave on patrol on Christmas Eve, 1914, a depressing time to be going to sea and to war. It was Zentner's first cruise. The boat was assigned to patrol the Heligoland Bight. The next day, Christmas—the first Christmas of the war—the crew awoke to a brilliant December morning, with bright sun, "frosty air," and a calm sea in its winter hue of blue-black. U-20 remained on the surface throughout the day, the better to watch for targets. In clear weather like this, the smoke from a steamer's funnels could be spotted twenty miles off. The lookouts saw nothing all day. "Apparently the enemy was at home spending Christmas as a Christian should," said Zentner.

That night, Schwieger ordered a dive to the sea bottom, 60 feet below the surface. He chose a spot where his charts indicated sand, not rock. For a time everyone was silent, listening as always for sounds of dripping or flowing water. The crew monitored gauges that measured interior pressure, keeping watch for the kind of sudden increase that might indicate a high volume of water penetrating the crew compartment. The refrain "All is tight" was relayed from bow to stern.

Spending the night on the ocean floor was common practice for U-boats in the North Sea, where depths rarely exceeded the maximum allowable for submarines. On the bottom, Schwieger and his crew could sleep without fear of being run over in the dark by a steamer or stumbling across a British destroyer. It was the one time a U-boat captain dared undress for bed. But on this particular night, Schwieger had something in mind other than sleep. "And now," Schwieger said, "we can celebrate Christmas."

A wreath was hung at one end of the mess room. The men piled food on the table. "It all came out of cans, but we didn't mind that," Zentner said. Schwieger and U-20's three other officers usually dined by themselves in a small officer's dining area, but now they joined the crew, thirty-six men in all. They spiked their tea with rum. "I lost count of the number of toasts that were drunk," Zentner said.

Schwieger stood and gave a little speech, "and a jolly ovation it was," said Zentner. Then came music. "Yes," Zentner said, "we had an orchestra." One man played a violin, another a mandolin. A third—a squat fisherman with a giant flaring red beard— brought out his accordion. He looked like a gnome and could neither read nor write but apparently had a certain appeal to the opposite sex, for twice Schwieger received letters from women demanding that he allow the sailor to go on leave to marry them. No effective means yet existed that allowed surface ships to track a submarine underwater, so no one aboard took much care about noise. The trio "played with soul," Zentner said, especially the accordionist. "His little eyes were half closed with ecstasy, and his bearded mouth was curved with a grin that was like the crescent of the moon."

The music and drinking went on into the night; the sea outside was cold, black, and impenetrable.

UNDER SCHWIEGER, U-20 had at least one dog aboard. At one time, it had six, four of them puppies, all dachshunds, the unexpected product of an attack off the coast of Ireland.

On that occasion, following cruiser rules, Schwieger chased and stopped a Portuguese ship, the *Maria de Molenos*. After waiting until its crew got away, he ordered his gun crew to sink the vessel. This was his favored mode of attack. He saved his few torpedoes for the best and biggest targets.

His gun crew was fast and accurate, and fired a series of shells into the freighter's waterline. Soon the ship disappeared from view, or, as Zentner put it, "settled down for her bit of vertical navigation."

Amid the usual debris left adrift on the surface, the men spotted a cow, swimming, and something else. The bearded accordion player saw it first and shouted, "*Ach Himmel, der kleine Hund!*"

He pointed to a box. A tiny head and two paws protruded over its edge. A black dachshund.

U-20 approached; the crew lifted the dog aboard. They named it Maria, after the sunken freighter. They could do nothing for the cow, however.

U-20 already had a dog aboard, a male, and in short order Maria became pregnant. She bore four puppies. The accordion player became the dogs' caretaker. Deeming six dogs too many for a U-boat, the crew gave three puppies away to other boats but kept one. Zentner slept with one in his bunk, next to a torpedo. "So every night," he said, "I slept with a torpedo and a puppy."

That Schwieger was able to conjure so humane an environment was a testament to his skill at managing men, because conditions in a U-boat were harsh. The boats were cramped, especially when first setting out on patrol, with food stored in every possible location, including the latrine. Vegetables and meats were kept in the coolest places, among the boat's munitions. Water was rationed. If you wanted to shave, you did so using the remains of the morning's tea. No one bathed. Fresh food quickly spoiled. Whenever possible crews scavenged. One U-boat dispatched a hunting party to a Scottish island and killed a goat. Crews routinely pillaged ships for jam, eggs, bacon, and fruit. An attack by a British aircraft gave one U-boat's crew an unexpected treat when the bomb it dropped missed and exploded in the sea. The concussion brought to the surface a school of stunned fish.

The crew of U-20 once scavenged an entire barrel of butter, but by that point in the patrol the boat's cook had nothing suitable on hand to fry. Schwieger went shopping. Through his periscope he spotted a fleet of fishing boats and surfaced U-20 right in their midst. The fishermen, surprised and terrified, were certain their boats would now be sunk. But all Schwieger wanted was fish. The fishermen, relieved, gave his crew all the fish they could carry.

Schwieger ordered the submarine to the bottom so his crew could dine in peace. "And now," said Zentner, "there was fresh fish, fried in butter, grilled in butter, sautéed in butter, all that we could eat."

These fish and their residual odors, however, could only have worsened the single most unpleasant aspect of U-boat life: the air within the boat. First there was the basal reek of three dozen men who never bathed, wore leather clothes that did not breathe, and shared one small lavatory. The toilet from time to time imparted to the boat the scent of a cholera hospital and could be flushed only when the U-boat was on the surface or at shallow depths, lest the undersea pressure blow material back into the vessel. This tended to happen to novice officers and crew, and was called a "U-boat baptism." The odor of diesel fuel infiltrated all corners of the boat, ensuring that every cup of cocoa and piece of bread tasted of oil. Then came the fragrances that emanated from the kitchen long after meals were cooked, most notably that close cousin to male body odor, day-old fried onions.

All this was made worse by a phenomenon unique to submarines that occurred while they were submerged. U-boats carried only limited amounts of oxygen, in cylinders, which injected air into the boat in a ratio that varied depending on the number of men aboard. Expended air was circulated over a potassium compound to cleanse it of carbonic acid, then reinjected into the boat's atmosphere. Off-duty crew were encouraged to sleep because sleeping men consumed less oxygen. When deep underwater, the boat developed an interior atmosphere akin to that of a tropical swamp. The air became humid and dense to an unpleasant degree, this caused by the fact that heat generated by the men and by the still-hot diesel engines and the boat's electrical apparatus warmed the hull. As the boat descended through ever colder waters, the contrast between the warm interior and cold exterior caused condensation, which soaked clothing and bred colonies of mold. Submarine crews called it "U-boat sweat." It drew oil from the atmosphere and deposited it in coffee and soup, leaving a miniature oil slick. The longer the boat stayed submerged, the worse conditions became. Temperatures within could rise to over 100 degrees Fahrenheit. "You can have no conception of the atmosphere that is evolved by degrees under these circumstances," wrote one commander, Paul Koenig, "nor of the hellish temperature which brews within the shell of steel."

The men lived for the moment the boat ascended to the surface and the hatch in the conning tower was opened. "The first breath of fresh air, the open conning-tower hatch and the springing into life of the Diesels, after fifteen hours on the bottom, is an experience to be lived through," said another commander, Martin Niemöller. "Everything comes to life and not a soul thinks of sleep. All hands seek a breath of air and a cigarette under shelter of the bridge screen."

All these discomforts were borne, moreover, against a backdrop of always present danger, with everyone aware they faced the worst kind of death imaginable: slow suffocation in a darkened steel tube at the bottom of the sea.

On one of U-20's patrols, this prospect came to seem all too real.

IT WAS EARLY in the war, when U-boat commanders and British defenders alike were developing new tactics to deploy against each other. Schwieger was scanning the sea through his periscope when he spotted two buoys ahead, spaced far apart. They had no obvious purpose, and their presence in that area of sea was unexpected.

Schwieger saw no danger. He called out, "Two buoys sighted. Keep exact depth." The boat continued forward at "periscope depth," 11 meters below the surface, about 36 feet, deep enough that only the top of the periscope showed above the water.

Something banged against the exterior, and then came a grating sound, like steel moving along the hull. "It sounded as if huge chains were banging against the boat and were being dragged over it," said Rudolph Zentner, then on duty in the boat's control room.

The men operating the ship's horizontal rudders, the dive planes, called out in alarm. The rudders weren't responding. Zentner checked the gauges that monitored depth and speed. The boat was slowing and sinking. It heaved and lurched from side to side.

Zentner watched the depth gauge and called each change to Schwieger. The boat sank deeper and deeper. At a depth of 100 feet, U-20 struck bottom. At this depth the pressure posed no threat, but the boat now seemed fused to the ocean floor.

Zentner climbed the ladder into the conning tower, and there looked out through one of the small windows of thick glass, the only means of observing the surrounding ocean while submerged. What he saw stunned him: a crosshatch of chain and cable. "Now we knew the meaning of those buoys," he said. A giant steel net had been suspended between them, a submarine trap, and U-20 had run right into it. The boat lay on the bottom, not just ensnared but pinned down by the weight of the net.

And now, something else: through the walls of the hull the crew heard the thrum of propellers overhead. They knew from experience that this particular pattern of sound was generated by destroyers—"a shrill, angry buzz." Depth charges did not yet exist, but the presence of destroyers waiting above was anything but reassuring. These were the ships that U-boat commanders most feared. A destroyer—a *Donnerwetter*—could move at 35 knots, or 40 miles an hour, and fire a lethal shot from a mile away. It could also kill a submarine by ramming. With a bow edged like a carving knife, a fast-moving destroyer could slice a U-boat in half.

The interior grew warm and close. Fear settled over the men like silt in a tide. "You can bet there was no laughing and singing on board now," Zentner said. "Each man thought of his home in Germany and how he would never see it again."

These were the hard moments of command. Schwieger was not permitted to show fear, though he undoubtedly felt it. In such close quarters, to act with anything other than confidence and reassurance would have amplified the fear already at play.

Schwieger ordered, "Reverse engines."

The engines responded. The boat strained. Steel rasped against the hull. Meanwhile, the propeller sounds above grew more distinct.

Zentner watched the dials and indicators in the control room. "The gauges were the whole world to us now," he said. "I had never gazed at anything so eagerly before."

The boat began slowly backing, amid the shriek of steel outside. And then, it was free.

Schwieger ordered ascent to cruising depth, 22 meters, or 72 feet, and full speed ahead. There was relief, until the men realized the propeller sounds above were not fading. The destroyers seemed to know the boat's exact location. Schwieger ordered a zigzag course, wide to right and left, but the destroyers always followed.

Schwieger traveled blind. He could not attempt to use his periscope because the destroyers would spot it immediately and begin shooting or attempt to ram the boat, or both. Schwieger ordered the helmsmen at the dive planes to maintain as deep a depth as the charts for these seas allowed. The pursuit continued "hour after hour," Zentner said, with U-20 following "a wild, weird course, going as fast as we could."

The best hope now was night. As darkness fell on the seas above, the propeller sounds began to fall away until they faded to nothing. Schwieger brought the boat back to periscope depth and took a fast look around, 360 degrees, to make sure no threat was near. This was a strenuous maneuver. The fittings on the periscope, where it jutted through the exterior of the conning tower above, had to be tight to keep water out and to withstand the pressures of a deep dive. Turning the apparatus required strength. The snugness of the fit was never perfect, however: a certain amount of oil-laced water inevitably dripped onto Schwieger's cap and face.

Once confident that the destroyers were gone, Schwieger ordered U-20 to the surface.

And there the final mystery was solved. In backing from the net, the boat had snagged a cable attached to one of the buoys. The buoy had followed on the sea above like a fisherman's bobber, revealing to the destroyers' lookouts every change of course, until darkness at last made the buoy invisible.

Schwieger was lucky. In coming months, the British would begin hanging pods of explosives off their submarine nets.

—⁓—

THROUGHOUT FRIDAY, April 30, as U-20 passed from the Heligoland Bight, Schwieger's wireless man continued to send messages reporting the submarine's position, apparently in an effort to determine the maximum range for sending and receiving signals. The last successful exchange was with the *Ancona* at a distance of 235 sea miles.

By seven that evening the U-boat was well into the North Sea, traversing the Dogger Bank, a seven-thousand-square-mile fishing ground off England. The winds picked up, as did the seas. Visibility diminished.

The submarine passed several fishing boats that flew Dutch flags. Schwieger left them alone. He signed his log, thereby marking the official end of the first day of the cruise.

LUSITANIA

MENAGERIE

THAT FRIDAY, CHARLES LAURIAT LEFT HIS SISTER'S apartment and traveled crosstown to 645 Fifth Avenue to pick up the final component of the collection of items he was bringing to London. He went to the home of a client named William Field, who, despite his address, described himself as a "gentleman farmer."

A few months earlier, Lauriat had sold Field a rare volume of Charles Dickens's *A Christmas Carol*, first published in December 1843. This copy had belonged to Dickens himself and was the one he entered into evidence in a series of legal actions he brought in early 1844 against "literary pirates" who had republished the story without his permission. On the inside of the book's front and back covers, and elsewhere within, were notes about the lawsuits that had been jotted by Dickens himself. It was an irreplaceable work.

Lauriat wanted to borrow it. Earlier in the year he had corresponded with a London solicitor who had written an account of Dickens's piracy litigation. The solicitor had asked Lauriat to bring the book with him on his next visit to London so that he could copy the various notations within. Its new owner, Field, "agreed rather unwillingly to do this," Lauriat wrote, and only after Lauriat promised to guarantee its safety.

Lauriat met Field at his apartment, and there Field handed over the book, a handsome volume bound in cloth and packaged in a "full Levant box," meaning a container covered in the textured goatskin used in morocco bindings. Lauriat placed this in his briefcase and returned to his sister's apartment.

AT PIER 54, on Friday morning, Turner ordered a lifeboat drill. The ship carried forty-eight boats in all, of two varieties. Twenty-two were Class A boats of conventional design—open boats hung over the deck from cranelike arms, or davits, strung with block and tackle. The smallest of these boats could seat fifty-one people; the largest, sixty-nine. In an emergency, the boats were to be swung out over the sea and lowered to the deck rails so that passengers could climb in. Once the boats were filled, two crewmen would manage the ropes—the "falls"—at the bow and stern of each boat and through careful coordination lower the boat in such a way that it would enter the water on a level keel. This was like being lowered down the face of a six-story building. Given that a fully loaded lifeboat weighed close to ten tons, the process took skill and coordination, especially in rough weather. But even in the best conditions it was a hair-raising operation.

The other twenty-six boats were "collapsibles," which looked like flattened versions of the regular boats. Capable of holding forty-three to fifty-four people each, these had canvas sides that had to be raised and snapped into place to make the boats seaworthy. The design was the product of a compromise. After the *Titanic* disaster, ocean liners were required to have enough lifeboats for everyone aboard. But in the case of a ship as large as the *Lusitania*, there simply was not enough room for all the Class A boats that would be necessary. The collapsibles, however, could be tucked underneath and lowered from the same davits after the regular boats were launched; in theory, they could also float free when a ship sank. The designers, however, seemed not to have taken into consideration the possibility that the boats might end up in the water before being properly rigged, with scores of panicked passengers hanging on and blocking all efforts to raise the sides. Taken together, the *Lusitania*'s lifeboats could seat as many as 2,605 people, more than enough capacity for all the ship's passengers and crew.

For the Friday drill, the ship's men were mustered on the boat deck, and the conventional boats were swung out from the hull. The boats on the starboard side were swung out over the wharf, but ten on the port side were lowered to the water, and several were rowed a distance from the ship. All were then raised back to the deck and returned to their positions.

It was Turner's belief, as he told his questioners during that morning's *Titanic* deposition, that an experienced and competent crew, operating in calm weather, could launch a boat in three minutes. But as he well knew, mustering such a crew was by now a near impossibility. The war had created shortages of labor in every industry, but especially shipping, with the Royal Navy drawing off thousands of able-bodied seamen. What made raising a crew even harder for Turner was the fact that Cunard's original deal with the Admiralty required that all the ship's officers and at least three-quarters of its crew had to be British subjects.

The unskilled character of Britain's wartime merchant crews was sufficiently pronounced that it drew the attention of U-boat commander Forstner, the man who had sunk the *Falaba*. He noted "the awkward way the men usually handled the lifeboats." Passengers also took notice. James Baker, a trader of oriental carpets, came to New York aboard the *Lusitania* earlier in the year, the first crossing with Captain Turner back in command. Baker idled away a portion of the first day of the voyage just watching the crew at work. His conclusion: "Some of them, I do not think could have been to sea before." He was struck by the haphazard way most of the men dressed. "The crew, with the exception of 4 or 5 . . . were in all sorts of costumes, confirming my first impression that outside of a few permanent men the balance of the crew were the type one sees on a tramp, a disgrace to such a ship."

Turner acknowledged the problem. His wartime crews bore no semblance to the sturdy and capable "sailormen" he had encountered earlier in his career. "The old-fashioned able seaman who could knot, reef, splice or steer disappeared with the sailing ships," Turner said. As to the crew's ability to handle lifeboats: "They are competent enough—they want practice. They do not get practice enough, and they do not get the experience."

For this upcoming voyage, however, Turner did manage to hire a number of hands who not only were experienced mariners but had gone to sea as he had done, aboard large square-rigged sailing vessels. One such was Leslie "Gertie" Morton, eighteen years old, close to achieving his second-mate's certificate, or "ticket." According to his official seaman's record, he was five feet, ten and a half inches tall, with fair hair and blue eyes. He also had two tattoos: crossed flags and a face on his left arm, a butterfly on his right. These were important details, should he be lost at sea and his body later recovered. He and his brother, Cliff, had signed aboard a square-rigger, the *Naiad*, as apprentice seamen, each under a formal agreement that bound them to the ship's owner for four years. Cliff's "indenture" was still pending; Leslie had completed his on March 28, 1915.

Sailing ships were still in wide use in commercial trade, even though voyages aboard them were inevitably slow and tedious. The brothers had arrived in New York after what Leslie Morton termed a "particularly vicious passage" from Liverpool that took sixty-three days with the ship all the while in ballast, meaning empty of cargo. They faced worse to come. In New York they were to pick up a load of kerosene in 5-gallon containers and haul it to Australia, then collect a load of grain in Sydney and bring it back to Liverpool. The whole journey promised to take a full year.

The brothers decided to jump ship, despite Cliff's obligation to serve out his indenture. Both wanted to get home to take part in the war, which they, like most people, expected would end soon. "We were still looking upon war in the light of Victorian and previous wars," Morton wrote later, adding that he and his brother had failed to appreciate that the "nature and method of war had changed for all time in August 1914 and that no war in the future would exclude anybody, civilians, men, women or children."

They planned to travel to England as paying passengers and wired home to ask for money to buy second-class tickets. Their father arranged a transfer of funds by return cable.

The Mortons learned that the next ship home was the *Lusitania* and bought tickets. They had heard so much about the liner that they felt they had to go to the wharf to see it. "What a sight she presented to our eyes," Leslie Morton wrote. "She seemed as large as a mountain. She had four funnels and tremendous length and, knowing that she could really move along, we were quite thrilled at the thought of traveling on her."

As they were standing on the wharf, staring at the ship, they realized that one of the ship's officers was staring at them. This proved to be Chief Officer John Preston Piper, who had just come down the gangplank to the wharf. "What are you boys looking at?" he asked.

They told him they had booked passage for the ship's upcoming voyage and just wanted to see it.

He watched them a moment, and asked, "What ship are you off?"

Morton, hedging the truth, told him they had just fulfilled their indentures and were heading back to Liverpool to take their certification exams.

"I thought you looked like seamen," Piper said. He asked the two why they wanted to pay for their voyage when they could work their way across. The *Lusitania* had just lost ten deckhands who had quit the ship, apparently to avoid having to serve in the British army. "I could use two boys like you," Piper said.

"I think there could be more, Sir," Morton said. "Some of our other shipmates have paid off."

Chief Piper told the brothers to be at the wharf Friday morning, "with as many as you can get."

The boys congratulated themselves. Now they could refund their tickets and devote their father's money to other pursuits. "We blew every penny" and spent Thursday night "in luxurious if doubtful surroundings," Morton wrote.

In all, eight members of the *Naiad*'s crew planned to jump to the *Lusitania*. History is silent on how the *Naiad*'s captain felt about this. Captain Turner, however, had no reservations about taking the men on and probably did not ask many questions. He needed all the crew he could find.

THE WAR RAISED other challenges as well. Turner readied the ship in a milieu suffused with fear and suspicion. Every merchant ship that left New York Harbor had to be inspected before departure to make sure, to the extent possible, that all cargo in its holds was identified on its shipping manifest, and that it wasn't armed, in violation of American neutrality laws. Turner received a visit from the port's "Neutrality Squad," under the supervision of Collector of Customs Dudley Field Malone, whose office was empowered to search all ships. Malone was said to be a dead ringer for Winston Churchill, so much so that years later he would be cast as Churchill in a film, *Mission to Moscow*. The squad conducted its inspection quickly, and Malone issued to Captain Turner a "Certificate of Loading," which allowed him to take the ship to sea, though Malone later conceded it was a "physical impossibility" to check every parcel of cargo.

Malone's office released the *Lusitania*'s preliminary manifest, a single sheet of paper that listed thirty-five innocuous shipments. As it happened, these shipments were just a fraction of the consignments that were already aboard the *Lusitania*. A more complete list would be released later, well after the ship had departed, the idea being to keep the information out of German hands as long as possible. For German spies and saboteurs, under the guidance of the German Embassy, were known to be at work along New York's wharves.

These spies seemed to have a particular interest in the *Lusitania* and had long monitored the ship. A report from the German naval attaché in New York, dated April 27, 1915, four days before the *Lusitania*'s departure, stated, "The crew of the *Lusitania* is in a

very depressed mood and hopes this will be the last Atlantic crossing during the war." The report noted as well that the crew was
incomplete. "It is difficult to service the machines adequately. Fear
of the U-boats is too strong."

A real possibility existed that German saboteurs might attempt
to harm the *Lusitania*. Cunard took the danger seriously enough
that it placed a Liverpool police detective, William John Pierpoint,
on board to keep watch during voyages. He occupied stateroom
A-1, on the boat deck, and kept to himself. Captain Turner took to
calling him "Inspector."

THROUGHOUT the day and night, the *Lusitania*'s crew came
aboard, in varying states of sobriety. Leslie Morton and his brother
and the other refugees from the *Naiad* climbed the gangway, still
suffering the effects of their previous night on the town. If Morton expected luxurious accommodations aboard the *Lusitania*, he
didn't get them. He was directed to a bunk three decks down, in
a chamber he likened to a "workhouse dormitory." He was heartened to find, however, that his bunk was right beside a porthole.

A junior crew member—a bellboy, or "steward's boy," named
Francis Burrows, age fifteen and a half—was met at the terminal
gate by a guard, who told him, "You're not going to get back this
time, sonny. They're going to get you this time."

Burrows laughed and continued on to his berth.

That evening a group of steward's boys, under orders not to
leave the ship for any reason, decided on a diversion to ease their
boredom. The boys, including one Robert James Clark, made their
way to a small cargo compartment, known in nautical parlance
as a lazaret, and there "began doing something we shouldn't have
been doing," according to Clark.

Clark and his accomplices found some electrical wires, then
stripped off the insulation and spread the wires on the floor. The
boys lay down and waited.

The ship had many rats. In fact, exactly one year earlier rats
had caused a small fire in one of the ship's public rooms by chew-

ing away the insulation on electric wires running through a wall, thereby allowing two bare wires to touch.

The boys waited with delight. The rats soon emerged and began following their usual routes through the chamber, unaware of the wires in their paths. "They got electrocuted of course," Clark said, "that was our pastime. That was Friday night." In later life, Clark would become Reverend Clark.

Whether out of professional pique or some instinct of fear, the ship's mascot—a cat named Dowie, after Captain Turner's predecessor—fled the ship that night, for points unknown.

CAPTAIN TURNER also left the ship that evening. He made his way to Broadway, to the Harris Theater on Forty-second Street, and there caught a play, *The Lie*, in which his niece, a rising actress named Mercedes Desmore, had a starring role.

Turner also indulged his passion for German food. He went to Lüchow's at 110 East Fourteenth Street, an easy walk from the Cunard docks, and dined in its Nibelungen Room, where an eight-piece orchestra played a brisk accompaniment of Viennese waltzes.

THAT EVENING, back at his sister's apartment, Charles Lauriat showed her and her husband the Dickens book and the Thackeray drawings and explained why he was bringing the drawings to England.

When he bought them in 1914, from Thackeray's daughter and granddaughter, Lady Ritchie and Hester Ritchie, of London, he paid a bargain price of $4,500, fully aware that he could sell them in America for five or six times as much. To get the best price, however, he had come to realize that he would need to present the drawings in a more appealing manner. At the moment they were pasted into the two scrapbooks, one drawing per page. He planned to have most of the drawings mounted individually and framed, but some he wanted to bind in combinations of three or four, in books with full Levant bindings. His main reason for bringing them back to England was so that Lady Ritchie could see them one more time and write a small note about each, thereby providing authentication and an extra element of interest.

He felt no guilt about paying Lady Ritchie so little for the drawings. That was the way the art business worked, especially if a seller wanted discretion, as the Ritchies did. They insisted that he keep the sale of the drawings as quiet as possible and barred him from attempting to sell them in Britain. He could offer them only in America, and even then he had to do so quietly, without advertising. Lady Ritchie was still smarting from the unexpected sequelae of a previous sale of drawings through a London dealer who had marketed them in a manner that the family found offensive and that had drawn unpleasant publicity and comment.

Lauriat's sister and her husband inspected the drawings "with a great deal of interest and admiration," Lauriat recalled. The husband, George, confessed to liking in particular a drawing entitled *The Caricature of Thackeray Himself Stretched Out on a Sofa in the Old Garrick Club*, and a series of six sketches "of negroes and their children" on the porch of a small house, which Thackeray had drawn while visiting the American South in the 1850s.

Afterward, Lauriat packed the book and drawings back into his extension suitcase and locked it.

ELSEWHERE in the city, a scheduled passenger named Alta Piper struggled through a restless night in her hotel room. She was the daughter of Leonora Piper, the famed spirit medium known universally as "Mrs. Piper," the only medium that William James, the pioneering Harvard psychologist and sometime psychic investigator, believed to be authentic.

Alta seemed to share her mother's gift, for throughout that Friday night, as she claimed later, she heard a voice telling her, "If you get into your berth, you'll never get out."

"THE MYSTERY"

THE DEPARTURE OF WALTHER SCHWIEGER'S U-20 WAS watched closely—from afar.

In London, two blocks from the Thames and adjacent to the parade ground of the Horse Guards, stood a five-story building with a facade of pale stone and whiskey-colored brick. Familiar to everyone in the Admiralty, the structure was known, for short, as the Old Building, or, for shorter, O.B. Far less familiar was a secret operation located along one of its corridors in a group of offices centered on Room 40. Here resided "the Mystery" or "the Holy of Holies," its function manifest only to its staff and to a coven of nine senior officials, including First Lord Churchill and Adm. Jacky Fisher, who by April 1915 had reentered the Admiralty as First *Sea* Lord, Churchill's number two. Fisher was seventy-four years old, three decades older than his chief.

Every day, the watchkeepers in Room 40 received hundreds of coded and enciphered German messages that had been intercepted by an array of wireless stations erected on the British coast, and then sent to the Old Building by land telegraph. Germany had been forced to rely almost exclusively on wireless communication after Britain, in the first days of the war, had followed through on its 1912 plan to cut Germany's undersea cables. The intercepted messages arrived in the basement of the Admiralty building and were then relayed to Room 40.

It was the task of Room 40 to translate these messages into the King's English, a process made possible by a series of nearly miraculous events that occurred in the closing months of 1914 and put the Admiralty in possession of three codebooks governing German naval and diplomatic communications. By far the most important, and secret, was the German navy's SKM code, short for *Signalbuch der Kaiserlichen Marine*. In August 1914, a German destroyer, the *Magdeburg*, ran aground and was cornered by Russian ships. Exactly what happened next remains unclear, but one story holds that the Russians found a copy of the codebook still clutched in the arms of a dead German signalman whose body had washed ashore after the attack. If so, it was probably the codebook that killed him: it was large and heavy, 15 inches by 12 inches by 6 inches, and contained 34,304 three-letter groups used to encode messages. The letters MUD, for example, stood for Nantucket; Liverpool was FCJ. The Russians in fact recovered *three* copies of the codebook, presumably not from the same body, and in October 1914 gave one to the Admiralty.

The codebooks were invaluable but did not by themselves reveal the contents of the intercepted messages. Their German authors used the volumes to obscure the original plain-text messages but then subjected the encoded versions to a further scrambling through the use of a cipher. Only holders of a cipher "key" could divine the underlying text, but possessing the codebooks made the whole process of solving the messages far simpler.

To exploit these treasures the Admiralty established Room 40. In a handwritten directive, Churchill set out its primary mission, "to penetrate the German mind," or, as one of the group's key officers put it, "to extract the juice." From the start, Churchill and Fisher resolved to keep the operation so secret that only they and a few other Admiralty officials would ever know it existed.

Equally mysterious—though unintentionally so—was the matter of who actually managed the group. On paper, at least, it reported to Adm. Henry Francis Oliver, the Admiralty's chief of staff, a man so tight-lipped and reticent he could seem almost mute, and this—given the British navy's predilection for nicknames—ensured that he would be known forever after as "Dummy" Oliver.

Within Room 40 itself, however, management of day-to-day operations fell largely, if informally, to Cdr. Herbert Hope, recruited in November 1914 to bring naval expertise to the interpretation of intercepted messages. His savvy was badly needed, for the group's staff were not navy officers but civilians recruited for their skill at mathematics and German and whatever else it was that made a man good at breaking codes and ciphers. The roster came to include a pianist, a furniture expert, a parson from northern Ireland, a wealthy London financier, a past member of the Scottish Olympic hockey team, and a dapper operative named C. Somers Cocks, who, according to one early member, William F. Clarke, was "chiefly remarkable for his spats." The unit's women—known as "the fair ladies in forty"—served in clerical roles and included one Lady Hambro, wife of a prominent financier, who according to Clarke startled everyone at one of the group's annual dinners by smoking a large cigar. Wrote Clarke, "It was the best of jobs and we were a happy band in those days with the best possible of chiefs in the person of Hope." Hope was modest and retiring, and a skilled manager, Clarke recalled, and "all of us became deeply attached to him."

Hope's authority was recognized outside Room 40 as well, much to the displeasure of Dummy Oliver, who was said to be obsessed with controlling who saw the deciphered intercepts and what was done with the information they revealed. When First Sea Lord Fisher made his initial visit to Room 40 and saw firsthand what the group was doing, he ordered Hope to bring him the latest intercepts in person, twice a day.

Hope also provided intercepts directly to another official who, of all those privy to "the Mystery," had perhaps the greatest appreciation for the value of its secrets: Capt. William Reginald Hall, director of naval intelligence. It was Hall who had recommended that Commander Hope, then a member of his intelligence division, should be transferred to Room 40. Despite being chief of naval intelligence, Captain Hall had no direct control over Room 40—as of early 1915 his intelligence division and Room 40 were separate entities—but his name more than any other would come to be associated with its achievements.

Hall was forty-four years old, and a former warship captain. He became director of naval intelligence in November 1914, filling a post once held by his father. He was short and brisk, with a face full of points and angles and a prominent bill-like nose, all of which gave him the look of a woodpecker in a captain's cap. This was reinforced by a neurological quirk that caused him to blink rapidly all day long and that earned him his own naval nickname, "Blinker." One of his most ardent admirers was America's Ambassador Page, in London, who in a letter to President Wilson heaped praise like a man in love. "I shall never meet another man like him," Page wrote; "that were too much to expect. For Hall can look through you and see the very muscular movements of your immortal soul while he is talking to you. Such eyes the man has! My Lord!"

Hall delighted in the gamesmanship of war and was said to be utterly ruthless, albeit in an engaging way. His secretary, Ruth Skrine—later to marry and bear the wedded name Mrs. Hotblack—recalled how one acquaintance had described Hall as being part Machiavelli, part schoolboy. The Machiavelli side "could be cruel," she said, "but the schoolboy was always round the corner, and his love of the dangerous game he, and all of us, were playing would bubble out, and the fun and hazard of it all would fill him with infectious delight." He was, she said, "uncannily quick at sizing up a man." When contemplating some new escapade, she recalled, Hall would rub his hands together, "grinning like a crafty little French Abbé."

IT WAS A vital game, in which Room 40 gave Britain an edge of inestimable value at a time when the war, far from concluding quickly, was expanding everywhere, with Germany ascendant. Battles raged in Russia, Austria, Serbia, Turkey, and Asia. In the

South China Sea a German torpedo boat sank a Japanese cruiser, killing 271 men. In the Pacific, off Chile, German warships sank two British cruisers, drowning 1,600 men and delivering a blow to Britain's pride and morale, the empire's first defeat in a naval battle since the War of 1812, when a British naval force on Lake Champlain had been defeated by the fledgling U.S. Navy. On New Year's Day, 1915, a German submarine sank the British battleship HMS *Formidable*, for a loss of 547 men. British warships nearby were forbidden to rescue survivors, in accord with the policy set up after the *Aboukir* disaster.

The war had grown darker and had sired new tactics for killing. German warships shelled the English coastal towns of Scarborough, Whitby, and Hartlepool, injuring over five hundred people and killing more than one hundred, most of them civilians. The dead in Scarborough included two nine-year-old boys and a fourteen-month-old baby.

On January 19, 1915, Germany launched its first-ever air raid against Britain, sending two giant zeppelins across the Channel—"zeps," in newly coined British slang, progeny of Count Ferdinand von Zeppelin. The raid caused minimal damage but killed four civilians. Another raid followed on January 31, during which nine airships flew as far as Liverpool, along the way sending terrifying shadows scudding across the landscape of Jane Austen's *Pride and Prejudice*.

And then came April 22, 1915. Late afternoon, near Ypres; bright sunshine; a light breeze blowing from east to west. The Allied trenches in this sector, or "salient," were occupied by Canadian and French forces, including a division of Algerian soldiers. The opposing Germans launched an offensive, which as usual began with shelling by distant artillery. This was terrifying enough, and the French and Canadians knew by experience it was a prelude to a head-on infantry attack across no-man's-land, but at about 5:00 P.M. the look of the battlefield abruptly changed. A gray-green cloud rose from the German side and began drifting across the blasted terrain as German soldiers opened the valves on six thousand tanks filled with over 160 tons of chlorine gas arrayed along a four-mile stretch of the front—the first ever use of *lethal* gas on a battlefield. As the gas reached the Allied side, its effects were immediate and terrible. Hundreds died at once; thousands ran from their trenches in a panic, many having experienced exposure that would kill them later. Their flight opened an eight-thousand-yard hole in the Allied line, but the effect of the gas attack seemed to surprise even its architects. German soldiers wearing respirators followed the gas cloud, but, instead of surging through the newly opened gap for a decisive victory, dug a new trench line and stayed put. Their commanders, intending mainly to test the gas, had not assembled the necessary reserve forces to take advantage of the opening in the line. Two thousand Canadian soldiers were killed, suffocated as fluid filled their lungs. Wrote one general, "I saw some hundred poor fellows laid out in the open, in the forecourt of a church, to give them all the air they could get, slowly *drowning* with water in their lungs—a most horrible sight, and the doctors quite powerless."

But these cataclysms played out on land. Where Room 40 promised to give Britain the clearest advantage was in the battle for control of the seas, and there Britain's strategy had undergone a change. Its centerpiece remained the destruction of Germany's fleet in battle, but the Admiralty gave new weight to interrupting the flow of war matériel to Germany and to combating the growing U-boat threat to British commerce. The Admiralty also harbored the persistent fear that Germany might attempt a full-scale invasion of Britain. Clearly any advance warning of German naval actions would be of critical importance.

Room 40 began providing such intelligence almost at once. From November 1914 until the end of the war, according to the group's William Clarke, "no major movement of the German Fleet could take place without the Admiralty knowing about it some time in advance." The information was detailed, right down to the movements of individual ships and submarines. But such detail raised a quandary. If the British navy acted in response to every foretold movement of the German fleet, it risked revealing to Germany that its codes had been broken. In a secret internal memorandum, Admiral Oliver wrote that "the risk of compromising the codes ought only to be taken when the result would be worth it."

But what did "worth it" mean? Some of the men within Room 40 contended that much useful information was stockpiled and never used because the Admiralty staff—meaning Dummy Oliver—had an obsessive fear of revealing the Mystery. For the first two years of the war, even the commander in chief of the British fleet, Sir John Jellicoe, was denied direct access to Room 40's decrypted intercepts, although he would seem to have been the one officer in the fleet most likely to benefit from the intelligence they conveyed. In fact, Jellicoe would not be formally introduced to the secret of Room 40, let alone given regular access to its intelligence, until November 1916, when the Admiralty, sensing bruised feelings, agreed to let him see a daily summary, which he was to burn after reading.

The tight control over intercepts exercised by Chief of Staff Oliver was also a source of irritation for Room 40's Commander Hope.

"Had we been called upon by the Staff to do so," Hope wrote, referring to Oliver, "we could have furnished valuable information as to movements of submarines, minefields, minesweeping etc. But the Staff was obsessed with the idea of secrecy; they realized that they held a trump card and they worked on the principle that every effort must be made to keep our knowledge to ourselves, so as to be able to keep it up our sleeves for a really great occasion such as the German Fleet coming out in all their strength to throw down the gage in battle. In other words the Staff determined to make use of our information <u>defensively</u> and not <u>offensively</u>." Commander Hope applied the underlines.

IT WAS tedious work. Hundreds of intercepted messages came chattering into the building's basement every day, where they were placed in dumbbell-shaped canisters, which in turn were shoved into vacuum tubes and, with a satisfying *fwump*, launched up through the building. Upon reaching Room 40, the containers tumbled into a metal tray with a clatter that "shook the nerve of any unwitting visitor," according to one of the group's code breakers. The noise of these arriving messages was especially hard on the men assigned to the night watch, who took turns sleeping in a bedroom that connected two larger offices. They endured an additional hardship: mice. The rodents infested the bedroom and late at night trotted over the faces of the sleeping men.

"Tubists" took the messages from the vacuum canisters and passed them on to the code breakers. The tubists were officers who had been injured badly enough in the war that they could no longer fight. This cadre included a one-legged man named Haggard and a one-eyed British officer named Edward Molyneux, who would go on to become an acclaimed designer of clothing in Paris.

The most tedious part of the job was writing the complete text of each message into a daily log. Churchill insisted that every intercept be recorded, no matter how routine. As the number of intercepts multiplied, this task became "soul destroying," according to one Room 40 member; the log "became an object of hatred." But Churchill paid close attention. In March 1915, for example, he scrawled on one of Hope's decrypts, "Watch this carefully."

The group learned over time that even a seemingly innocuous change in the character of routine messages could signal an important new action by the German navy. Wrote Commander Hope, "Any messages which were not according to routine, were to be looked on with great suspicion, and in this way we were able to build up a large number of signs and portents." The British wireless operators who listened in on German communications came to know just by the sound of a transmission whether it came from a submarine. They found that U-boats first took a few moments to tune their systems and then began each transmission with a kind of electrical throat-clearing, five Morse signals: dash dash dot dash dash. "The final note," Commander Hope said, "is high-pitched . . . and has a wailing or whining character when sending."

Thanks to captured charts, Room 40 also knew that the German navy had divided the seas around England into a grid to better direct the travels of surface ships and submarines. The North Sea had been broken into squares six miles on a side, with each square assigned a number, according to Hope. "Whenever any of their vessels was at sea, she was continually signaling her position by saying what square she was in." By plotting these on a chart, Hope wrote, Room 40 learned which routes German ships and U-boats followed. Some squares were consistently empty: "It was only reasonable to suppose that these blank spaces were mined areas."

Over time, thanks to Room 40's intercepts and information gleaned from interrogations of captured submariners, both Room 40 and Capt. Blinker Hall's intelligence division developed a sense of the flesh-and-blood men who commanded Germany's U-boats. A few, like Kapitänleutnant Weddigen, the man who sank the cruisers *Aboukir*, *Cressy*, and *Hogue*, were daring and pushed their crews to the limit. A captain of this kind was called a *Draufganger*, or dashing commander. Another commander, Claus Rücker, was said to be "a bully and a coward." In contrast, Walther Schwieger was described in several intelligence reports as a good-natured soul who was well liked by his crew and peers, "a very popular and pleasant officer," as one report put it.

Some U-boat captains were cold-blooded killers, like Schwieger's friend Max Valentiner. "He is said to be the most powerfully built officer in the German Navy," a British interrogator reported, and "one of the most ruthless submarine commanders." But another captain, Robert Moraht, saved lives "whenever possible." After his boat was sunk and he and four members of his crew were captured, interrogators learned through him and the others that the life of a U-boat commander was not all discomfort. Moraht woke each day at 10:00 A.M., and climbed to the deck "for a short stroll." He ate lunch by himself and afterward read in his cabin, "always keeping a stock of good books on board." At 4:00 he had tea, and at 7:00, supper, "after which he remained in the wardroom, talking, playing games, or listening to the gramophone." He went to bed at 11:00 P.M. "He made a habit of drinking a glass of wine just before turning in."

Room 40 and Hall's division also gained insight into the finer points of U-boat culture. They learned, for example, that U-boat commanders did not care about the *number* of ships they sank but rather their tonnage, because tonnage was what their superiors looked to when deciding to award honors. They learned, too, that the German navy had its own tradition of assigning nicknames. One very tall commander was nicknamed Seestiefel, or sea boot. Another had a reputation for smelling bad and thus was nicknamed Hein Schniefelig, or stinky person. A third was said to be "very childish and good-natured" and was commonly called Das Kind, the child.

The U-boat commanders had one thing in common, however. When it came to wireless, all were talkative, as Room 40 and Blinker Hall were delighted to learn. They used their wireless systems incessantly. In the course of the war, Room 40 would receive twenty thousand intercepted messages that had been sent by U-boats. This "extreme garrulity," as Room 40's Clarke put it, allowed the group to keep close watch over U-boat travels, all duly recorded in a ledger kept by Commander Hope.

In January 1915, Room 40 was able to pinpoint the first time a U-boat traveled as far as the Irish Sea, the body of water that separates England and Ireland. The group even identified the particular zone to which the U-boat's captain had been ordered—a square of sea near Liverpool. On that occasion, the value of the intelligence was immediately apparent, and the Admiralty acted at once. It sent a warning to the home fleet, identifying the source of its information only as a "reliable authority." Destroyers converged on the U-boat's patrol zone from north and south. Two large Cunard liners, the *Ausonia* and *Transylvania*, were en route to Liverpool at the time, carrying naval gun barrels made by Bethlehem Steel. The *Transylvania*, then under the command of Captain Turner, also carried passengers, among them forty-nine Americans. The Admiralty ordered both ships to change course immediately and speed as fast as possible to Queenstown, on the south coast of Ireland, and wait there until destroyers could arrive to escort them to Liverpool. Upon arriving safely, Turner expressed his relief at having evaded attack. "I fooled 'em that time," he said.

Room 40 had long followed Kptlt. Walther Schwieger's U-20

and kept a running record of his patrols: when he left, which route he took, where he was headed, and what he was supposed to do once he got there. In early March 1915, Commander Hope monitored a voyage Schwieger made to the Irish Sea that coincided with a disturbing message broadcast from a German naval transmitter located at Norddeich, on Germany's North Sea coast just below Holland. Addressed to all German warships and submarines, the message made specific reference to the *Lusitania*, announcing that the ship was en route to Liverpool and would arrive on March 4 or 5. The meaning was obvious: the German navy considered the *Lusitania* fair game.

The Admiralty found the message disconcerting enough that it dispatched two destroyers to rendezvous with the ship and escort it to port. One destroyer sent an uncoded message asking the ship's then captain, Daniel Dow, to report his position in order to arrange the meeting. Dow refused to give it, fearing that a U-boat had sent the message. The rendezvous never came off, but Dow succeeded in reaching Liverpool on his own. It was soon after this that he asked to be relieved, and Captain Turner took his place.

As that spring of 1915 advanced, the code solvers in Room 40 honed their skills, delighted and a bit astonished by the fact that the German navy still did not revise its codebooks. The Mystery remained secure and continued to yield revelations about the travels of German U-boats.

TOWARD THE end of April, as Captain Turner readied the *Lusitania* for its May 1 departure, Room 40 learned of a new surge of U-boat activity. Intercepts showed that on Friday, April 30, four U-boats left their bases. In response, war-staff chief Dummy Oliver sent an urgent, ultrasecret message to Jellicoe at Scapa Flow. "Four submarines sailed yesterday from Heligoland," the message read. It identified their expected destinations. "They appear to be making good 12½ knots. Do not divulge exact source of information in any steps you take." Within hours, Room 40 got word that two more U-boats also had departed, these from a base at

Emden, on Germany's North Sea coast. One of these was Schwieger's U-20. Considering that the German navy typically had only an average of two U-boats in the North Sea or the Atlantic at any one time, this was an extraordinary development.

Room 40's code breakers found it a simple matter to follow U-20 through the first day or so of its voyage: Schwieger's wireless man repeated the boat's position fourteen times in twenty-four hours.

Room 40 did not have to look far to find the reason for this new and dangerous assault by Germany's U-boats. As it happened, it was the German navy's response to a ruse concocted by intelligence chief Blinker Hall himself, in the application of what he described as one of the first principles of the profession, "that of mystifying and misleading the enemy."

A CAVALCADE OF PASSENGERS

B Y SATURDAY, MAY 1, THE HEAT WAVE HAD DISSIPATED. The morning was cold, the sky pewter. The temperature made it easier for passengers arriving at Cunard's Pier 54 to transport their belongings, for now they could simply wear their heavy coats, rather than bearing them draped over their arms along with all the other things they carried, their canes, umbrellas, valises, parcels, books, and babies, all in evidence on the sidewalk outside the terminal, as a long black line of taximeter cabs emerged from Eleventh Avenue and pulled close to the curb. Large bags traveled on the floor beside the drivers and were hauled from the cabs by squat, strong-looking men in open jackets and bully caps.

All these things were captured on film by a motion-picture camera stationed just outside the entrance to the terminal. Passengers crossed its plane of view: men in topcoats, fedoras, and snap-brim caps; women with large hats mounded with sewn-on flowers; toddlers bundled as if for the Arctic, one with a knit cap pulled low over the ears. Now and then a face appeared in startling closeup, with that look travelers have always had over time, stern, concentrating, trying to pay the cabbie, hold the cane and gloves—the empty glove fingers flexing like a cow's udder—and still keep track of the suitcase and trunk receding into the Cunard terminal.

At the far side of the building, the *Lusitania*'s hull rose high above the wharf in a black wall of steel and rivets. The ship seemed as indestructible as anything that could be imagined, even for an age that imagined well and placed so much trust in immensity and invention.

The furnaces in its boiler rooms flared as firemen raised steam for departure; its funnels exhausted braids of gray smoke into the mist above.

As always there were passengers who had achieved fame, and their arrival created a stir among the thousands of well-wishers, kin, and spectators now gathered along the wharf to see the ship off. Cunard had built grandstands to honor the custom, and these were full as always; they afforded a view not just of the ship but of a portion of Lower Manhattan and the wharves and vessels jutting from the shore on both sides of the Hudson. Just north stood the piers of the White Star Line, which three years earlier, almost to the month, were to have received the *Titanic*. Among the spectators the attention given to the *Lusitania* and its passengers was more acute than usual, given the German warning published in the city's papers that morning.

Here came Charles Frohman, the theater impresario, who had made Ethel Barrymore a star and had brought the play *Peter Pan* to America, for which he dressed Maude Adams in a woodsy tunic with a broad collar, and in so doing forever engraved a particular image of the boy in the world's imagination. Frohman also produced the stage show *Sherlock Holmes*, with William Gillette as its namesake hero, with deerstalker cap and meerschaum pipe. Frohman, wearing a blue double-breasted suit, walked with a marked limp and used a cane. A friend of his also came aboard, Marguerite Lucile Jolivet, twenty-five years old, known universally by her stage and film name, Rita Jolivet. Though she had already performed in Shakespearean plays in London, including a turn as Juliet, and had appeared in several silent films made in Italy, she was still only a fledgling star, but Frohman liked her, and his interest virtually assured her a vibrant career. She was traveling now to Europe to act in several more Italian films.

Another arrival was George Kessler, a wealthy wine importer known the world over as the "Champagne King." Bearded and spectacled, evoking a certain Viennese psychoanalyst, he was known for throwing elaborate parties, known as "freak dinners"—perhaps most notably the "Gondola Party" he hosted in 1905 at the Savoy Hotel in London, where he filled the hotel's courtyard with water, dressed everyone in Venetian garb, and served dinner to guests aboard a giant gondola. Lest this be deemed insufficient, he arranged to have a birthday cake—five feet tall—brought in on the back of a baby elephant.

By far the most glamorous passenger was Alfred Gwynne Vanderbilt I, son and primary heir of the late Cornelius, whose death in 1899 had left Alfred a rich man. Something of a rake, Alfred was tall and lean, with dark eyes and hair, and a taste for expensive suits. He was a welcome presence on board, especially among the women, despite the fact that he was married and carried with him a history of scandal. His first wife, Ellen French, had divorced him in 1908, charging him, as the *New York Times* put it, with "misconducting himself with an unknown woman" in his private railcar. The woman turned out to be Mary Ruiz, wife of a Cuban diplomat. The scandal drove Ruiz to commit suicide. Vanderbilt remarried, this time wedding Margaret Emerson, heiress to a trove of money that owed its existence to America's awful diet and its gastric consequences, the Bromo-Seltzer fortune. She was not on board. Vanderbilt was also a member of what a Minnesota newspaper called the "Just Missed It" club, a fortunate group whose roster included Theodore Dreiser, Guglielmo Marconi, and J. P. Morgan, all of whom had planned to sail on the *Titanic* but for one reason or another had changed their minds. Needless to say, Vanderbilt traveled in style, booking one of the *Lusitania*'s "Parlor Suites." He lodged his valet two doors down the corridor, in an interior room with neither porthole nor bath. Vanderbilt paid for both tickets in cash, $1,001.50, equivalent to over $22,000 in today's dollars.

Reporters came aboard, as usual, looking to interview famous or notorious passengers, only today their interest was more focused than usual. It was a mark of the importance of shipping and the frequency with which transatlantic liners called at New York that every newspaper had a "ship news" reporter. Each paper devoted a page to the arrivals and departures of the great liners and to advertisements and schedules for the many shipping lines with piers in the city. It was on these pages that the German warning had appeared in a number of Saturday morning editions.

The ship-news reporters worked out of a shedlike structure near Battery Park, in Lower Manhattan, adjacent to the terminal for the Staten Island Ferry, where a battered green door gave way to a room full of worn desks and telephones used by reporters for a dozen newspapers and one wire service. The reporters tended to favor certain ships, often for intangible reasons. "Ships do have personalities," wrote Jack Lawrence, the shipping writer for the *New York Evening Mail*. Some ships "have character and a warm, friendly atmosphere while others are only steel plates riveted around throbbing turbines." One of the favorites was always the *Lusitania*. The ship invariably provided news, because as the fastest and most luxurious ocean liner still in service it tended to draw the richest, most prominent passengers. Part of the ship's appeal was also due to the fact that its longtime chief purser, James McCubbin, sixty-two, welcomed the reporters' attention and directed them to passengers likely to be of interest. As purser, McCubbin had the responsibility to make sure all passengers were tucked into their cabins and berths as quickly as possible, to store their valuables, and—no small thing—to compile their bar bills at the end of the voyage. In the words of the Cunard officers' manual, he was "to give satisfaction to all classes of passengers."

The reporters met the *Lusitania* just before its departures, but also upon arrival, when they would sail out to the quarantine station in New York Harbor. A ritual followed. They gathered in McCubbin's cabin. He would order a cabin boy to bring some ice, club soda, and a couple of bottles of Cunard Line Scotch. He shut the door and handed out passenger lists. The last such session had taken place the previous week, when the *Lusitania* arrived from

Liverpool, and had brought the reporters some unwelcome news. McCubbin announced that his next voyage, the return to Liverpool departing Saturday, May 1, would be his last crossing. Company rules required that he retire. "I'm about to become the most useless mortal on earth," he told the reporters—"the sailor home from the sea." He called it a joke. "Sailors don't have homes," he said, and added, "When a sailor gets so old he can't work any more they ought to sew him up in a staysail rag and heave him over the side."

On Saturday morning, reporter Jack Lawrence went aboard as usual, but now with a particular story in mind. He carried with him a copy of the German Embassy's warning.

Lawrence stopped by the cabin of Alfred Vanderbilt and knocked on the door. Vanderbilt himself opened it, wearing an elegant suit with a pink carnation in one lapel. In the room beyond, his valet was hard at work unpacking a small mountain of baggage. Lawrence had tried to interview Vanderbilt in the past and had typically found it a pointless exercise because the man rarely had much to say. "Alfred Vanderbilt may have been a riot among the ladies," Lawrence wrote, "but in the presence of newspapermen he was a shy and shrinking violet."

Vanderbilt commented that there seemed to be an unusual amount of excitement aboard. "Lots of talk about submarines, torpedoes and sudden death," Vanderbilt said. "I don't take much stock in it myself. What would they gain by sinking the *Lusitania*?"

He showed Lawrence a telegram he had received after boarding. "The *Lusitania* is doomed," it read. "Do not sail on her." It was signed "Mort." Vanderbilt said he didn't know anyone named Mort but wondered if it might have been an allusion to death. "Probably somebody trying to have a little fun at my expense."

Out on deck, Lawrence came across Elbert Hubbard, at this point one of the most famous men in America—the soap salesman turned author who had founded a collective in East Aurora, New York, called the Roycrofters, where men and women built furniture, bound books, made prints, and produced finely crafted goods of leather and metal. As an author, he was best known for his inspirational book, *A Message to Garcia*, about the value of personal initiative, and for an account of the *Titanic* disaster that centered on one woman's refusal to enter a lifeboat without her husband; he was headed now to Europe with the goal of interviewing Kaiser Wilhelm. Hubbard was famous as well for coining crisp aphorisms, including "A friend is someone who knows all about you and still loves you." He wore a Stetson hat and a flamboyant black cravat—more like a large gift ribbon—and had long flowing hair. When Lawrence approached him, Hubbard was standing beside his wife and eating a large red apple.

Hubbard hadn't seen the warning. "When I showed it to him he merely glanced at it and went right on chewing his apple," Lawrence wrote. Hubbard took another apple out of his pocket and gave it to Lawrence. "Here, have an apple and don't bother your head about those Potsdam maniacs. They're all crazy."

Lawrence pressed him. What if the German navy really was planning an attack?

"What'll I do?" Hubbard said. "Why, I'll stay on the ship. I'm too old to go chasing after lifeboats and I never was much of a hand at swimming. No, we'll stay by the ship." He turned to his wife. "Won't we Ma?" It was Lawrence's impression that Mrs. Hubbard did not share his view.

Lawrence discovered that very few passengers had read the German warning. He did not find this surprising. "When you are getting ready to sail on a transatlantic liner at noon," he wrote, "you seldom have time to sit down and peruse the morning papers."

Even those who had seen the warning paid little attention. The idea that Germany would dare attempt to sink a fully loaded civilian passenger ship seemed beyond rational consideration. And even if a U-boat did try, common wisdom held that it would inevitably fail. The *Lusitania* was simply too big and too fast, and once in British waters would doubtless be too well protected by the British navy.

Only two passengers canceled because of the warning itself, a wealthy shoe dealer from Boston, named Edward B. Bowen, and his wife. They did so at the last minute. "A feeling grew upon me that something was going to happen to the *Lusitania*," Edward said, later. "I talked it over with Mrs. Bowen and we decided to cancel our passage—although I had an important business engage-, ment in London."

A few others canceled for reasons of illness and altered plans, or because they had resolved, warning aside, that sailing on a British ship in wartime wasn't prudent. The famed Shakespearean actress Ellen Terry planned initially to travel with producer Frohman on the *Lusitania*, but well before the warning appeared she canceled her booking and switched to an American ship, the *New York*. She encouraged Rita Jolivet to do likewise, but Jolivet kept her original booking. One of those who canceled citing illness was Lady Cosmo Duff-Gordon, a fashion designer who had survived the sinking of the *Titanic*. Another designer, Philip Mangone, canceled for unspecified reasons. Years later he would find himself aboard the airship *Hindenburg*, on its fatal last flight; he survived, albeit badly burned. Otherwise, the *Lusitania* was heavily booked, especially in the lesser classes. Second class was so full that a number of passengers learned to their delight that they had been given first-class rooms.

For those passengers who did feel unsettled by the German warning, Cunard offered comforting words. Wrote passenger Ambrose B. Cross, "From the very first the ship's people asseverated that we ran no danger, that we should run right away from any submarine, or ram her, and so on, so that the idea came to be regarded as a mild joke for lunch and dinner tables."

Moreover, a conviction existed among passengers that upon entering the waters off Britain's west coast, the so-called Western Approaches, the ship would be met by the Royal Navy and escorted to Liverpool. Cunard encouraged this belief, and may have believed it as well, on the basis of the Royal Navy's past efforts to direct and escort the company's ships. Long before the sailing, Oscar Grab, twenty-eight, a newly married clothing importer from New York, made an appointment to talk with a Cunard representative about submarines and the overall safety of transatlantic crossings. Grab's wife of thirty-nine days had begged him to take an American ship. Grab and the Cunard official had a long talk, during which Grab was told that steps would be taken to protect the ship during the crossing. He felt reassured enough to buy a first-class ticket, although he waited to do so until the day before departure.

Any passenger who read that morning's edition of the *New York Times* would have found explicit reassurance. In an article about the warning, the paper quoted Cunard's New York manager, Charles Sumner, as saying that in the danger zone "there is a general system of convoying British ships. The British Navy is responsible for all British ships, and especially for Cunarders."

The *Times* reporter said, "Your speed, too, is a safeguard, is it not?"

"Yes," Sumner replied; "as for submarines, I have no fear of them whatever."

Passenger Ogden Hammond, a real-estate developer and a member of the State Assembly of New Jersey, asked a Cunard official if it was safe to cross on the ship and got the reply, "Perfectly safe; safer than the trolley cars in New York City"—a possibly ill-advised answer, given the high frequency of fatal trolley accidents in the city.

Aboard the *Lusitania*, there was a good deal of gallows humor, but it was spoken from a position of comfort and confidence. "Of course we heard rumors in New York that they *were* going to torpedo us, but we didn't believe it for one moment," said May Walker, one of the ship's stewardesses. "We just laughed it off, and said they would never get us, we were too quick, too speedy. It was just the same kind of trip as it was any other trip."

One of her tasks was to help manage passengers' children. "There was all sorts of deck games. Quoits. And they had fancy dress parades for them," Walker said. Children whose birthdays happened to fall during a voyage were given a party—"a little private party," Walker said—and a birthday cake, with their names on it. "They had the time of their lives, and the run of the ship."

On this voyage, she would have her hands full. Many British

families were now returning home to do their part in supporting the nation in time of war, and the ship's size and speed provided a degree of reassurance. The passenger manifest listed ninety-five children and thirty-nine infants.

Whole families came aboard. Cunard set aside a group of first-class staterooms for Paul Crompton of Philadelphia and his wife and their six children—one "infant" included—and their nanny, twenty-nine-year-old Dorothy Allen. (Cunard tickets did not identify babies by name, possibly out of quiet resentment that they traveled free.) Crompton was a cousin of Cunard's chairman, Alfred Allen Booth, whose Booth Group owned the steamship line. Crompton headed the group's leather-goods subsidiary. Cunard's New York manager, Sumner, greeted the family just before boarding and "looked personally after their comfort for the voyage." On the opposite side of the ship, one deck down, the Pearl family of New York took three first-class staterooms, E-51, E-59, and E-67. Frederic Pearl was headed to London for a posting at the American Embassy, and brought his wife and four children: a five-year-old son, two daughters under the age of three, and one infant. The Pearls brought along *two* nannies. The children, including the baby, stayed with their nannies in E-59 and E-67; the parents lounged in comparative bliss by themselves in E-51. Mrs. Pearl was pregnant.

William S. Hodges, en route to Europe to take over management of the Paris office of the Baldwin Locomotive Works, was traveling with his wife and two young sons. When a *Times* reporter on the wharf asked Mrs. Hodges if she was afraid of making the trip, she merely laughed and said, "If we go down, we'll all go down together."

There were parents sailing to rejoin their children, and children to rejoin their parents, and wives and fathers hoping to get back to their own families, as was the case with Mrs. Arthur Luck of Worcester, Massachusetts, traveling with her two sons, Kenneth Luck and Elbridge Luck, ages eight and nine, to rejoin her husband, a mining engineer who awaited them in England. Why in the midst of great events there always seems to be a family so misnamed is one of the imponderables of history.

—◆—

AMONG THE less well-known, but still prominent, passengers who came aboard Saturday morning was a forty-eight-year-old woman from Farmington, Connecticut, by the name of Theodate Pope, Theo to her friends. She was accompanied by her mother, who came to see her off, and by a man twenty years her junior, Edwin Friend, with whom she was traveling to London. Prone to wearing a velvet turban, Theodate was an imposing figure, though she stood only a little over five feet tall. She had blond hair, a blunt chin, and vivid blue eyes. Her gaze was frank and direct, reflecting the independence that she had shown throughout her life and that had caused her to reject the path expected of women raised in high society. Her mother once scolded, "You never act as other girls do"; her contemporaries referred to her by that newly coined descriptive label *feminist*.

Theodate counted among her friends the painter Mary Cassatt, William James, and his brother, author Henry James, with whom she developed a particularly close friendship, to the point where she named a new puppy after him, Jim-Jam. She was one of America's few female architects of stature, designer of a revered house in Farmington, which she named Hill-Stead. When Henry James first saw the house, even before he came to know Theodate, he crafted one of the more novel analogies of architectural criticism, likening the joy he felt to "the momentary effect of a large slippery sweet inserted, without a warning, between the compressed lips of half-conscious inanition." Theodate had a competing passion, however. She was a spiritualist and served from time to time as an investigator of paranormal phenomena. Belief in such things was widespread in America and Britain at the start of the twentieth century, when an Ouija board was a regular fixture in drawing rooms, to be brought out after dinner for impromptu séances. With the advent of war, belief in an afterlife was poised for a resurgence, as Britons sought comfort in the idea that their dead sons might still be present, in some way, somewhere in the ether. It was

Theodate's interest in "psychical" research that explained why she and Edwin Friend were sailing to London.

As the sole child of a wealthy Cleveland couple, she had spent her early life mostly alone. Her father, Alfred, was an iron tycoon; her mother, Ada, a socialite. They lived on the city's Euclid Avenue, better known as Millionaire's Row. "I have no memory at all of ever sitting in my mother's lap," Theodate wrote. "My father was so occupied with [business] affairs that I was fifteen years old before he realized he was losing his child." She described her youth "as the extreme of what the lives of only children usually are" but credited this solitary time—punctuated by bouts of crushing boredom and depression—as instilling in her a strong sense of independence. From the age of ten on, she drew plans for houses and sketched their facades, and dreamed of one day building and living in a farmhouse of her own design.

To her parents, tuned to the high-society mores of the day, Theodate was doubtless a chore. At nineteen she changed her birth name, Effie, to Theodate, her grandmother's name, out of respect for the woman's devout belief in the Quaker principle of emphasizing the spiritual over the material. She had little interest in "coming out" as a debutante, and none in marriage, which she perceived to be a wall that foreclosed any future ambitions she might have. She called it the "gold collar." Her parents sent her to a private school in Farmington, Miss Porter's School for Young Ladies, expecting that once her education was completed she would return to take her place among Cleveland's upper crust. Theodate liked Farmington so much, however, that she decided to stay. She became a suffragist; at one point she also joined the Socialist Party, and she loved riling her father with her talk of socialism.

On a lengthy journey through Europe in 1888, when she was twenty-one, she grew closer to her father. He was devoted to travel and to collecting art and was among the first collectors to fully embrace the impressionists, at a time when their work was widely deemed eccentric, even radical. It was he who suggested she consider architecture as a profession. They spent time together scouring art galleries and artists' studios for works to bring back to Cleveland; they bought two paintings by Claude Monet. Theodate sketched elements of structures she found appealing, a pilaster here, a chimney there. She had little interest in Paris, which she described as "the greatest blot on the face of the earth," but she adored England, in particular its cozy country homes with sagging roofs, half-timbered walls, and welcoming doorways. She drew sketches of her vision of the ideal farmhouse.

Architecture being a field then largely barred to women, Theodate created an architectural education for herself, first through private studies with members of Princeton University's art department. With her father's support she bought a house in Farmington with 42 acres. Her parents, at her urging, resolved to retire to Farmington and build a house that would showcase Alfred's art collection, which, in addition to the two Monets, included works by Whistler and Degas. Her father suggested she design the house, under the supervision of a practicing architect. She chose the firm of McKim, Mead & White, which, no doubt because of Alfred's wealth, agreed to the plan. Theodate's subsequent letter to founding partner William Rutherford Mead revealed her to be a woman of strong if not imperious character. She wrote, "As it is my plan, I expect to decide in all the details as well as all more important questions of plan that may arise. . . . In other words, it will be a Pope house instead of a McKim, Mead and White."

The design and construction of the house became for Theodate an architectural apprenticeship. But the project, completed in 1900, exhausted her. That fall she wrote in her diary, "I have wrung my soul dry . . . over father's house."

By 1910 she was a full-fledged architect, soon to become the first female architect licensed in Connecticut. Three years later, in August 1913, her father died of a cerebral hemorrhage. It was a shattering blow, and in her grief she resolved to build a preparatory school for boys in his memory—a school, however, that would be very different from any then in existence. She envisioned a campus structured to mimic a small New England town, with shops, town hall, post office, and a working farm. Her plan was to emphasize the building of character by requiring that students devote a significant portion of their days to "community service," helping out on the farm and in the shops, where they would learn such arts as carpentry and printmaking. In this she was very much in step with the Arts and Crafts movement, then in full sway, which held that craftsmanship provided both satisfaction and rescue from the perceived dehumanization of the industrial revolution. By 1910 the movement had swept America, yielding collectives, like fellow passenger Elbert Hubbard's Roycrofters, and a new and simple approach to design, evident in the furniture of Gustav Stickley and in the simple, well-made homes of the so-called Craftsman style. It inspired as well the founding of magazines like *House Beautiful* and *Ladies' Home Journal*.

By Saturday morning, May 1, 1915, Theodate was again in the grip of a profound weariness. The past winter had been difficult, professionally and emotionally. One incident in particular underscored the challenge of being a woman in a male profession: a publisher, thinking the name Theodate was a man's, asked to include her photograph in a book on leading architects in New York. Upon learning in a phone call that she was female, he withdrew the offer. She also suffered one of her periodic descents into depression, this one sufficiently severe that she needed the assistance of a home nurse. In February 1915, she wrote, "I am having such persistent insomnia that my nights are waking nightmares."

She believed, however, in the regenerative power of setting off on a journey. "There is nothing like the diversion of travel for one who is mentally fagged."

Once aboard the *Lusitania*, Theodate was led by a steward to her cabin, a stateroom on D Deck on the starboard side. She deposited her hand luggage and made sure her cabin bags had arrived. If she hoped to sleep well that night, she was soon to be disappointed.

—m—

CHARLES LAURIAT, the Boston bookseller, now climbed the gangway, accompanied by his sister, Blanche, and her husband, George Chandler. "I was surprised that access to the steamer was allowed so freely," Lauriat wrote. He found it odd that his sister and brother-in-law "were allowed to pass aboard without question." Other passengers likewise noted the ease of access for friends and family who came aboard to see them off.

Chandler carried Lauriat's briefcase and valise; Lauriat carried the extension suitcase containing the drawings and Dickens's *Carol*. Chandler joked that the contents of that one were so valuable he "preferred not to touch it."

The three walked to Lauriat's room, B-5, the cabin closest to the bow on the starboard side of B Deck. Though seemingly a prime location, it was an interior stateroom, with no portholes. Lauriat was accustomed to traveling like this. One of the first things he did was place a matchbox in his room within easy reach, in case the ship's electric dynamo failed. He had crossed the Atlantic twenty-three times so far, mostly on Cunard ships, but this would be his first voyage on one of the celebrated "greyhounds."

Lauriat saw that the trunk and shoe case that he had checked at the station in Boston were already in his room. He tested the locks on his various bags, and then he, Blanche, and Chandler went back out on deck, where they remained until all visitors were asked to leave the ship. When Lauriat returned to his room, he took the drawings from the extension case and put them in the top tray of his shoe box, which was easier to lock; he put Dickens's *Carol* in his briefcase.

Before boarding, Lauriat had read about the German Embassy's warning but had paid little attention; the idea of canceling never entered his mind. He wore his Knickerbocker suit, and that new innovation, a stem-winding wristwatch, which he kept set to Boston time, always, no matter where he was; it was his way of grounding himself in the world. He told no one about the drawings.

—⁓—

DWIGHT HARRIS, the New Yorker with the engagement ring and custom life belt, took his valuables to the purser's office for safekeeping. These included a diamond-and-pearl pendant, a diamond-and-emerald ring, a large diamond brooch, $500 in gold, and of course the engagement ring. He took a few moments before sailing to write a thank-you note to his grandparents, who had given him a bon voyage present. He used *Lusitania* stationery. The German warning seemed not to have given him pause. His mood was full of exclamation points.

"A thousand thanks for the delicious Jelly Cake and Peppermint Paste!" he wrote. "I can hardly wait for tea time to come!" He noted that the weather had begun to improve. "I am glad it has cleared!—my cabin is most comfortable—and I shall proceed to unpack after lunch!" He added that his Cousin Sallie had sent a basket of fruit and that another family member, Dick, had sent a large supply of grapefruit. "So I am well supplied!"

His note was among those that made it into the last bag of mail to leave the ship before departure. The envelope was postmarked "Hudson Terminal Station."

THE STEWARDS announced that all visitors had to disembark. Ship reporter Jack Lawrence left without even trying to talk to Captain Turner. The captain, he wrote, "was of that brand of deep sea skipper who believes that a newspaperman's place is at his desk on Park Row or in Fleet Street and that there ought to be a law to prevent him from prowling around the decks of ships." On every prior encounter, Turner had been cold and unfriendly. "He seemed to me to be an austere, aloof sort of a man who knew his business and didn't wish to discuss it with anybody."

Lawrence admired Turner, however. He saw him on the ship's main stairway, talking to another officer, and noticed "what a splendid figure he made." His uniform was dark blue, double-breasted, with three-inch lapels and five buttons on each breast, only four to be actually buttoned, as specified in the Cunard officers' manual.

The jacket cuffs—the real show—were each edged with "four rows of gold wire navy lace ½-inch wide," according to the manual. Turner's cap, also dark blue, was trimmed in leather and black mohair braid, fronted with the Cunard badge: the Cunard lion, mocked gently by crew as the Cunard "monkey," surrounded by a wreath of gold stitching. "When a British skipper knows how to dress, and he usually does, he is the very last word in what the well-dressed merchant captain should wear," Lawrence wrote. "He knows not only what to wear but how to wear it. He achieves a jauntiness that is incomparable. Turner, that day, was master of one of the great greyhounds of the North Atlantic—and looked the part."

BLINKER'S RUSE

N LONDON, CAPTAIN HALL SAW THAT HIS NEW SCHEME for "mystifying and misleading the enemy" was beginning to have an effect.

It was a prime example of the kind of gamesmanship at which he excelled. His goal was to convince German military commanders that a British invasion of Schleswig-Holstein, on the North Sea, was imminent, and thereby cause the Germans to divert forces from the main battlefield in France. Teaming with an officer of Britain's domestic counterintelligence service, MI-5, Hall had supplied German espionage channels with detailed, but false, information, including a report that over one hundred warships and transports were being massed in harbors on Britain's west and south coasts, rather than the east-coast ports that were typically used to resupply Britain's continental forces. As a final touch, Hall persuaded the Admiralty to order a halt to all ship traffic between England and Holland starting on April 21, the kind of order that might precede the launch of an invasion.

German military leaders were at first skeptical, but this new announcement proved persuasive. Room 40 listened in on wireless messages sent on April 24, from a German station at Antwerp. "An untried agent reports from England: Large transport of troops from south and west coast of England to Continent. Large numbers of troops at Liverpool, Grimsby, Hull."

Then came the orders to Schwieger and commanders of the other five U-boats instructing them to depart and to destroy anything that resembled a troop transport.

Room 40 kept close watch on U-20. The boat's frequent use of wireless provided rich detail about its course and speed. At 2:00 P.M. on Friday, April 30, the submarine reported its location. Two hours later, it did so again, and it continued making reports every hour until midnight, and every two hours thereafter until eight o'clock the next morning, Saturday, May 1.

THE DISCOVERY of the new U-boat foray came against a backdrop of mounting threat.

The Admiralty received dozens of messages reporting submarine sightings, most false, but still unsettling. An Irish policeman claimed to have spotted three U-boats traveling together up the River Shannon, an unlikely scenario. Off England's east coast a steamer picked up an unexploded torpedo floating in the sea, with markings that identified it as belonging to U-22, a sister to Schwieger's submarine. Off the southeast tip of Italy a young Austrian U-boat commander named Georg von Trapp, later to gain eternal renown when played by Christopher Plummer in the film *The Sound of Music*, fired two torpedoes into a large French cruiser, the *Leon Gambetta*. The ship sank in nine minutes, killing 684 sailors. "So that's what war looks like!" von Trapp wrote in a later memoir. He told his chief officer, "We are like highway men, sneaking up on an unsuspecting ship in such a cowardly fashion." Fighting in a trench or aboard a torpedo boat would have been better, he said. "There you hear shooting, hear your comrades fall, you hear the wounded groaning—you become filled with rage and can shoot men in self defense or fear; at an assault you can even yell! But we! Simply cold-blooded to drown a mass of men in an ambush!"

ON SATURDAY, May 1, citing the new sortie by U-20 and the other U-boats, the Admiralty postponed the departures of two warships that were scheduled to hold gunnery practice in the open sea.

At some point that day, through Captain Hall, the Admiralty learned of the German Embassy's advertisement published in New York that morning that seemed to warn passengers against traveling on the *Lusitania*. By day's end the news was known to every Briton or American who happened to read a newspaper. The ship's date of departure and its expected arrival in Liverpool a week later were now in the foreground of public awareness.

But Room 40 and those officials privy to the Mystery knew much more: that the German wireless station at Norddeich was broadcasting the *Lusitania*'s schedule and that the six newly dispatched U-boats were now en route. Room 40 also knew that one of those boats was U-20, a prolific killer of ships and men, and that it was making its way toward a patrol zone in waters visited by every Cunard freighter and liner bound for Liverpool, and soon to be traversed by the *Lusitania* itself.

Although this accumulation of facts—a fresh swarm of submarines, a grand liner under way in the face of a public warning—would seem a stimulus for sleepless nights among the top men of the Admiralty, neither the new surge in U-boat activity nor the imminent arrival of U-20 was communicated to Captain Turner. Nor was any effort made to escort the *Lusitania* or divert it from its course, as the Admiralty had done for the ship the preceding March and for the *Transylvania* and *Ausonia* in January.

Like everyone else at Cunard, Captain Turner had no idea Room 40 even existed.

THE ADMIRALTY'S focus was elsewhere, on a different ship that it deemed far more valuable.

LOST

N WASHINGTON, EDITH GALT CAME INCREASINGLY TO OC-
cupy President Wilson's thoughts and imagination. Throughout
April she was a regular dinner guest at the White House, although for the sake of propriety she and Wilson always dined with
others present. At one point they discussed a book that Wilson
particularly liked, called *Round My House: Notes of Rural Life
in France in Peace and War*, by Philip Gilbert Hamerton. Wilson
ordered her a copy from a bookseller, but in the meantime he sent
over a copy from the Library of Congress. "I hope it will give you
a little pleasure," he wrote, on Wednesday, April 28. "I covet nothing more than to give you pleasure,—you have given me so much!"

He added, "If it rains this evening, would it be any fun for you
to come around [and] have a little reading—and, if it does not rain,
are you game for another ride?" By "ride," he meant one of the
drives that he so liked to take in the White House Pierce-Arrow.

She declined the invitation, gently, having promised to spend
the evening with her mother, but thanked him for his personal
note and told him how it helped "fill my goblet of happiness."
Her handwriting made a sharp contrast to Wilson's. Where his
leaned forward and proceeded in perfectly horizontal phalanxes
on the page, hers leaned backward and veered and bunched, in a
cross between block printing and cursive, with random curls here
and there, as if she wrote all her letters in a carriage rolling over

cobblestones. She thanked him for the way he had closed his note, "Your sincere and grateful friend, Woodrow Wilson." It had been particularly welcome on that Wednesday evening, after a day of gloom caused by depression, to which she appeared prone. "Such a pledge of friendship," she wrote, "blots out the shadows that have chased me today, and makes April Twenty Eighth a red letter day on my calendar."

The newly ordered book arrived at the White House soon afterward, and on Friday, April 30, Wilson sent it along to Edith's house near Dupont Circle, with a brief note. "It's a great privilege to be permitted to share any part of your thought and confidence. It puts me in spirits again and makes me feel as if my private life had been recreated. But, better than that, it makes me hope that I may be of some use to you, to lighten the days with whole-hearted sympathy and complete understanding. That will be a happiness indeed." He also sent flowers.

In seeking to brighten her days, he brightened his own. Here in Edith, in the midst of world chaos, he found a purpose to which he could devote himself that took him, if only temporarily, out of his apprehension about the widening war and the fate of the larger world. She was, to him, "a heaven—haven—sanctuary." More than this, her presence helped him clarify his thoughts about the nation's trials. On their evening rides in the White House Pierce-Arrow, he spoke to her of the war and his concerns as he probably would have spoken to his late wife, Ellen, thereby helping him order his own thoughts. "From the first," Edith wrote, "he knew he could rely on my prudence, and what he said went no further."

Edith, meanwhile, had begun to look at her own life through a new lens. Wilson's interest, and the dash and charm of the world into which he had brought her, had caused her own days to seem emptier and less worthy. Though her own education had been haphazard, she longed for life on a higher plane, for good talk about art, books, and the tectonic upheavals of world events. A friend of hers, Nathaniel Wilson, no relation to the president, once told her that he sensed she might one day influence great events—"perhaps the weal or woe of a country." But she had to be open to it, he warned. "In order to fit yourself for this thing that I feel will come to you, you must work, read, study, think!"

Edith saw her drives with President Wilson as "life giving." She felt an immediate bond. They traded recollections of the old South, the hard days that followed the Civil War. She had never met a man like Wilson—intensely bright, but also warm and solicitous of her feelings. It was all very unexpected.

What Edith did not yet appreciate was that Wilson was now a man in love, and as White House usher Ike Hoover observed, Wilson was "no mean man in love-making when once the germ has found its resting place."

The president's valet, Arthur Brooks, put it succinctly: "He's a goner."

As DISTRACTED as he was by the charms of Mrs. Galt, Wilson also grew increasingly concerned about the drift of world events. The western front had become a reciprocating engine of blood and gore, each side advancing then retreating across a no-man's-land laced with barbed wire, gouged with shell holes, and mounded with dead men. On Saturday, May 1, the Germans began a series of assaults in the Ypres Salient, in what would become known as the *Second* Battle of Ypres, and once again used poison gas. Neither side had gained any ground since the "first" battle the previous fall, despite combined casualty counts in the tens of thousands. On this day, however, the German offensive succeeded in pushing the British back almost to the town of Ypres. A Canadian physician caring for the wounded at a nearby aid station in Boezinge, in West Flanders, Belgium, would later write the most famous poem to arise from the war: "In Flanders fields the poppies blow / Between the crosses, row on row. . . ." By the end of the month, the British would regain their lost ground and advance another thousand yards, at a cost of sixteen thousand dead and wounded, or sixteen men per yard gained. The Germans lost five thousand.

One soldier in the Ypres Salient, at Messines, Belgium, wrote of the frustration of the trench stalemate. "We are still in our old positions, and keep annoying the English and French. The weather is miserable and we often spend days on end knee-deep in water and, what is more, under heavy fire. We are greatly looking forward to a brief respite. Let's hope that soon afterwards the whole front will start moving forward. Things can't go on like this for ever." The author was a German infantryman of Austrian descent named Adolf Hitler.

Elsewhere, a wholly new front was about to open. Hoping to break the impasse in Europe, Churchill orchestrated a massive naval bombardment and amphibious landing against Turkey in the Dardanelles. The idea was to force the strait and break through to the Sea of Marmara, and from there to link arms with the Russian navy in the Black Sea, and through a massive show of naval force off Constantinople compel Turkey to surrender. An offensive up the Danube River to Austria-Hungary was to follow. It looked easy. The planners even imagined they might be able to complete the drive to the Black Sea with ships alone. An old saying applied: Man plans, God laughs. The result was disaster—lost ships, thousands of men dead, and another immobile front, this one on the Gallipoli Peninsula.

Meanwhile, in the Caucasus, a Russian advance against Turkish forces steadily gained ground. The Turks blamed their losses on local populations of Armenians, whom they suspected of assisting the Russians, and began a systematic slaughter of Armenian civilians. By May 1, the Turks had killed over fifty thousand Armenian men, women, and children in Van Province, in eastern Turkey. The head of the Armenian church sent a plea for help directly to Wilson; he demurred.

America, secure in its fortress of neutrality, watched the war at a remove and found it all unfathomable. Undersecretary of State Robert Lansing, number two man in the State Department, tried to put this phenomenon into words in a private memorandum. "It is difficult, if not impossible, for us here in the United States to appreciate in all its fullness the great European War," he wrote. "We have come to read almost with indifference of vast military operations, of battle lines extending for hundreds of miles, of the thousands of dying men, of the millions suffering all manner of privation, of the wide-spread waste and destruction." The nation had become inured to it all, he wrote. "The slaughter of a thousand men between the trenches in northern France or of another thousand on a foundering cruiser has become commonplace. We read the headlines in the newspapers and let it go at that. The details have lost their interest."

But the tendrils of conflict seemed to reach more and more insistently toward America's shores. On April 30, five weeks after the sinking of the *Falaba* and the loss of American passenger Leon Thrasher, first details arrived in Washington about another attack, in which a German aircraft had bombed a U.S. merchant ship, the *Cushing*, as it traversed the North Sea. Three bombs fell, but only one struck. No one was hurt and the damage was minor. Just the day before, in another private memorandum, Lansing had written, "A neutral in time of international war must always show forbearance, but never in the course of history have the patience and forbearance of neutrals been put to so severe a test as today."

He saw grave meaning in the attack on the *Cushing*. "German naval policy is one of wanton and indiscriminate destruction of vessels regardless of nationality," he wrote to Secretary Bryan, on Saturday, May 1. But Wilson and Bryan, though troubled by the incident, resolved to treat it with more circumspection, as indicated in a report by the *New York Times*: "It was not thought in official quarters that any serious issue would be raised, because it is accepted that the bombs were not dropped deliberately, but under the impression that a hostile vessel was being attacked." This was a generous appraisal: at the time, the *Cushing* was flying an American flag, and its owners had painted the ship's name on its hull in six-foot letters.

Another piece of news, more troubling in nature, had not yet reached the *Times* or the White House. That Saturday—the day of the *Lusitania*'s departure—a German U-boat torpedoed an American oil tanker, the *Gulflight*, near the Isles of Scilly off England's Cornish coast, killing two men and causing the death by heart attack of its captain. The ship remained afloat, if barely, and was being towed to St. Mary's Island, the largest of the Scillies, 45 miles west of Cornwall.

In Washington the dawn brought only a lovely spring Saturday, with temperatures destined to rise into the seventies and send men to their haberdashers for their first straw "lids" of the season. The crowns of hats were expected to be shorter this year, the brims broader; gentlemen of course were expected to wear summer gloves made of silk, to keep their hands, as one ad put it, "cool and clean." The day promised to be one in which Wilson could indulge his dream, his hope, of love and an end to loneliness.

UNDER WAY

THE SHIP WAS SCHEDULED TO DEPART AT 10:00 A.M., but now came a delay. In wartime, Britain's Admiralty held the power to requisition for military service any ship under British flag. At very much the last minute, the Admiralty commandeered a passenger ship docked at New York, the *Cameronia*, which provided service to Liverpool and Glasgow. The *Cameronia*'s captain received his orders just as his ship was about to depart. Now some forty passengers and their belongings, and five female crew, were to be transferred to the *Lusitania*. Exactly how these passengers all felt about it, given the morning's news about the German warning, cannot be known, though at least one account holds that the passengers were pleased, for the *Lusitania* represented the pinnacle of seaborne luxury and would, they believed, get them to Liverpool much faster than the smaller and slower *Cameronia*.

Aboard the *Lusitania*, one passenger, Richard Preston Prichard, took advantage of this delay to unpack one of his two cameras and bring it up on deck so that he could take photographs of the city and harbor. This camera was a Kodak No. 1, which collapsed into a form compact enough to fit into a coat pocket.

Prichard was twenty-nine years old, and stood five feet ten inches tall. His mother and brother called him Preston, possibly to avoid the unfortunate rhythm inherent in saying Richard Prichard.

They offered this description of him: "Dark brown hair, with high forehead, blue eyes, and prominent features. <u>Very Deep dimple in chin.</u>" The underlining was theirs, and indeed the cleft in Prichard's chin was a salient landmark. In another man it might have been disfiguring, but for him it was one feature in an indisputably handsome face, otherwise graced by full lips, dark eyebrows, pale skin, and rich dark hair combed up in a wave from his forehead, all anchored by those blue eyes, so striking in a man with dark hair and brows—"a most interesting face," one passenger said, "with marked features which any one once seeing could scarcely forget."

Prichard was a medical student at McGill University in Montreal, Canada, where he had enrolled after trying his hand at various jobs, including lumberjack and farmer. He had moved to Canada after the death of his father, to earn money to send back to his mother in England. He was traveling in second class, room D-90, an interior cabin opposite the *Lusitania*'s barbershop, and shared the room with three other men, all strangers to one another. He had an upper berth and carried with him three "grips," or suitcases. He often wore a tie clip with a gold ring inlaid with tiny red and white "lava heads," decorative faces carved from the kind of lava rock often used for cameos and brooches. He had packed two suits for the crossing, one dark blue, the other a more casual suit in green.

On deck, he encountered another young man, Thomas Sumner, of Atherton, England, who also had a camera. (Sumner bore no relation to Cunard's New York manager, Charles Sumner.) Both hoped to take photographs of the harbor. The day was cool and gray—"rather dull," as Sumner put it—and this caused the two to wonder what exposures to use. They fell to talking about photography.

Sumner liked Prichard immediately. He saw him as "such another fellow as myself." Both were traveling solo, and they were destined to encounter each other often during the voyage. Sumner liked Prichard's ability to take great delight in life but without intruding on others. He "seemed very pleasant and enjoyed himself in a very quiet manner," Sumner wrote, "—you will understand what I mean, [he] didn't go about in a rowdy fashion like lots of fellows do having a time." A fellow second-class passenger, Henry Needham, said of Prichard, "He was a great favorite on board, he arranged the whist drives & seemed to do most of the work." A whist drive was a social event during which passengers grouped themselves in pairs and played game after game of whist until one team won.

Now Prichard was on his way back to England for a visit, and according to one of his cabin mates, Arthur Gadsden, he was very excited to be doing so—"counting the time" until his arrival, Gadsden said.

THE TRANSFER of the *Cameronia*'s passengers took two hours. Although later this delay would prove significant to a degree far greater than its brevity might suggest, for now it was merely maddening. Captain Turner prided himself on his skill at deftly managing the *Lusitania*'s arrivals and departures, which meant casting off precisely on schedule.

Turner had no concern about the German warning. Shortly before departure, he was standing on the ship's promenade deck, talking with Alfred Vanderbilt and Charles Frohman, when one of the ship-news men—apparently not Jack Lawrence—approached and asked Vanderbilt if he thought he'd be as lucky this time as he had been in deciding not to sail on the *Titanic*. Vanderbilt smiled but said nothing.

Turner put his hand on Vanderbilt's shoulder and said to the reporter, "Do you think all these people would be booking passage on board the *Lusitania* if they thought she could be caught by a German submarine? Why it's the best joke I've heard in many days, this talk of torpedoing the *Lusitania*."

Both Vanderbilt and Turner laughed.

ANOTHER DELAY occurred, but for this one Captain Turner was at least partly responsible. His niece, the actress Mercedes Desmore, had come aboard for a quick tour and was nearly stranded when the crew, having boarded all the extra *Cameronia* passengers, removed the gangway. Turner angrily ordered it replaced so that his niece could get off. The process further postponed the ship's departure.

One passenger, set designer Oliver Bernard, took note. "Captain Turner," he wrote, later, "neglected his duty at the wharf in New York at a time when the vessel should have been sailing—by having a relative on board." By the time Bernard made this charge, he had come to understand what few others seemed to grasp, which was that on this particular voyage, given the convergence of disparate forces, timing was everything. Even the briefest delay could shape history.

THE MEN operating the motion-picture camera outside the Cunard terminal moved it to a higher prospect, apparently the building's roof, until the camera was at about the height of the ship's bridge, with its lens aimed downward to capture scenes on the decks below. In the film, passengers crowd the starboard side, many waving white handkerchiefs the size of cloth diapers. One man flourishes an American flag, while nearby a woman props her baby on a deck rail.

A few moments later, a young sailor climbs a stairway to the docking bridge, an elevated, narrow platform spanning the deck near the ship's stern. He raises a white flag on a pole on the port side, then sprints across to raise a duplicate flag on the starboard side, a visual signal that departure is imminent. Soon afterward, just past noon, the *Lusitania* begins to ease backward. The camera remains stationary, but the slow, smooth motion of the ship produces the illusion that it is the camera that is moving, panning across the ship's full length.

A crewman standing atop a lifeboat works on its ropes. A first-cabin steward steps smartly out of a doorway and walks directly to a male passenger, as if delivering a message. At the top of a stairway, staring directly at the camera, is a man the filmmakers instantly recognize, Elbert Hubbard, in his Stetson, though his cravat is barely visible under the buttoned front of his overcoat.

The ship's bridge now passes by, at camera level, and there is Turner, in frame 289. He stands at the starboard end of the bridge wing. As the ship slides past the camera, the captain, smiling, turns toward the lens and removes his hat, once, in a brief wave, then leans comfortably against the rail.

Once the ship has backed fully into the Hudson, two tugboats gingerly nudge its bow toward the south, downstream, and the ship begins to move under its own power. As the *Lusitania* at last exits the frame, the wharves of Hoboken become visible in the distance, heavily hazed with smoke and mist.

The film ends.

WHILE MOVING downriver Turner kept his speed slow, as freighters, lighters, tugs, and ferries of all sizes adjusted their own courses to make way. The Hudson here was busy. A 1909 sea chart shows the shore of Manhattan so closely packed with piers as to evoke a piano keyboard. The river was also surprisingly shallow, just deep enough to accept the *Lusitania*'s nearly 36-foot draft. Turner's crew had balanced the vessel so well that at the time of departure the draft at the bow, as indicated by markings on the hull, was just 4 inches deeper than at the stern.

The river was lined on both sides with piers and terminals; on the New Jersey flank—the right side as the ship moved down the river—lay the vast track-covered wharves of various railroads, among them the Erie, the Pennsylvania, and the New Jersey Central. On the left was a succession of piers, bearing, in order of descent down the Hudson, names that spoke to the ubiquity of sea travel:

South Pacific Co.
Colonial Line
Albany Line
Clyde Line

Savannah Line
People's Line
Old Dominion Line
Ben Franklin Line
Fall River Line
Providence Line

Here too were the many ferries that carried goods and people between New Jersey and the city, with terminals at Desbrosses, Chambers, Barclay, Cortland, and Liberty Streets. The ferry to the Statue of Liberty operated from the southernmost tip of Manhattan.

As the *Lusitania* made its way through the harbor, signs of the war became evident. The ship passed one of Germany's crack liners, the giant *Vaterland*, tied to a Hoboken wharf. Over 60 percent larger in gross tonnage than the *Lusitania*, the *Vaterland* had once held the Blue Riband, but on the first day of the war the ship had ducked for safety into New York Harbor, to avoid being captured and put to use by the British navy, a very real possibility, as the passengers of the *Lusitania* soon would discover. The *Vaterland* and its crew had been effectively interned in New York ever since. At least seventeen other German liners were likewise stranded.

Below the Battery, where the Hudson and East Rivers met to form New York Bay, the waters grew deeper and more spacious. Here Turner encountered familiar landmarks. To the right, Ellis Island and next, of course, Miss Liberty on Bedloe's Island; on his left, Governors Island with its circular fortress-prison, Castle Williams, followed by Red Hook in Brooklyn and the breakwater of the Erie Basin. In the distance sprawled the Black Tom wharves, a vast munitions depot, which before the war's end would be destroyed in an apparent act of sabotage. Ever mindful of traffic, Turner maintained a slow speed, especially in the Narrows, which were always clogged with ocean liners and freighters, and perilous in fog. Bells peeled in the haze as random wakes tipped buoys, evoking the sounds of churches on Sunday morning.

Meanwhile, the *Lusitania*'s purser and stewards conducted

their usual inspection to detect stowaways. This being wartime, they did so with extra care and soon had three men in custody. The men appeared to speak only German; one carried a camera.

The discovery was reported to Staff Captain Anderson. He in turn requested the assistance of Pierpoint, the Liverpool detective, and called as well for the ship's interpreter. They learned little, other than that the three men were indeed German. What the stowaways intended to accomplish was unclear, but later speculation held that they hoped to find and photograph evidence that the ship was armed or carried contraband munitions.

The three were locked below decks in a makeshift brig, pending arrival in Liverpool, at which point they were to be turned over to British authorities. News of the arrests was kept from the passengers.

ALTA PIPER, the daughter of the famous medium, never made it aboard; neither did she refund her ticket. Unable to ignore the night's voices, but also apparently unable to step forth and just cancel, she chose the path taken by indecisive people throughout history and spent the morning of departure packing and repacking her bags, over and over, letting the clock run out, until at last she heard the distant horn marking the ship's departure.

TOWARD FAIR ISLE

AT DAWN, SATURDAY, ABOARD U-20, THERE WAS COFfee, bread, marmalade, cocoa. The boat's ventilators issued a monotonous buzz. Schwieger, atop the conning tower, noted that the sea was calm, "here and there rain and fog." A steamship appeared up ahead but was so obscured by mist and gray that he chose not to attack. Members of the crew took turns smoking on deck, a pastime forbidden within the boat itself.

The fog grew dense, so much so that at 7:15 A.M. Schwieger ordered a dive to U-20's customary cruising depth, 72 feet. The depth was great enough to ensure that U-20 would pass underneath vessels of even the deepest draft. This was prudent practice, for U-boats, despite their fearsome reputation, were fragile vessels, complex and primitive at the same time.

Men served as ballast. In order to quickly level or "dress" his boat, or speed a dive, Schwieger would order crewmen to run to the bow or the stern. The chaos might at first seem funny, like something from one of the new Keystone Cops films, except for the fact that these maneuvers were executed typically at moments of peril. U-boats were so sensitive to changes in load that the mere launch of a torpedo required men to shift location to compensate for the sudden loss of weight.

The boats were prone to accident. They were packed with complicated mechanical systems for steering, diving, ascending, and regulating pressure. Amid all this were wedged torpedoes, grenades, and artillery shells. Along the bottom of the hull lay the boat's array of batteries, filled with sulfuric acid, which upon contact with seawater produced deadly chlorine gas. In this environment, simple errors could, and did, lead to catastrophe.

One boat, U-3, sank on its maiden voyage. When it was about two miles from the naval yard, its captain ordered a trial dive. Everything seemed fine, until the deck of the U-boat passed below the surface and water began pouring into the boat through a pipe used for ventilation.

The boat sank by the stern. The captain ordered all the crew, twenty-nine men, into the bow; he and two other men stayed in the conning tower. As the crew squeezed forward, water filled the boat behind them, causing air pressure to build to painful levels. All this occurred in absolute darkness.

The batteries began generating chlorine gas, which rose in a greenish mist. Some gas entered the bow compartment, but the boat's air purification system kept it from reaching deadly concentrations. The air supply dwindled.

On shore, naval officials did not learn of the crisis for two hours and then dispatched two floating cranes and a salvage ship, the *Vulcan*. The rescuers devised a plan to raise the bow to the surface so that the men within could climb out through the two forward torpedo tubes.

It took eleven hours for divers to place the necessary cables around the bow. The cranes began lifting the boat. The bow became visible.

The cables broke.

The boat fell backward into the sea. The divers tried again. This attempt took fourteen more hours. By then the twenty-nine crewmen had been sitting crammed into the bow in nearly airless darkness for more than twenty-seven hours. But this attempt worked. The men emerged through the tubes, tired and gasping for air, but alive.

The conning tower containing the captain and the two other men remained underwater. Five more hours passed before the

Vulcan at last managed to bring the entire boat to the surface. When the rescuers opened the conning-tower hatch, they found its interior to be nearly dry, but the three men within were dead. Chlorine gas had seeped upward into the tower through speaking tubes designed to allow officers to communicate with the control room below.

A subsequent investigation found that the indicator governing the ventilation valve through which the water entered the boat had been installed incorrectly. It showed the valve was closed when in fact it was open.

This outcome, though, was still better than what befell a training U-boat that sank with all aboard and could not be raised for four months. Divers who participated in an early, failed attempt at rescue heard tapping from within. When the boat was finally raised, the cause of the disaster was obvious. It had struck a mine. As to what had occurred within, a seaman present when the hatch was forced open found vivid evidence of the kind of death submariners most feared. He wrote, "The scratches on the steel walls, the corpses' torn finger-nails, the blood-stains on their clothes and on the walls, bore all too dreadful witness."

THE FOG remained dense until about eleven o'clock Saturday morning, when Schwieger gauged visibility to be good enough to allow him to surface and continue under diesel power. It was always important to recharge the batteries, in case of a chance encounter with a destroyer or the sudden appearance of a choice target.

Soon after surfacing, Schwieger's wireless man attempted to communicate with the *Ancona*, back at U-20's base in Germany. There was no response. The wireless man reported, however, that he had picked up "strong enemy wireless activity" nearby, at 500 meters. Schwieger told him to stop signaling, to avoid revealing the boat's presence.

U-20 continued north, well off the eastern coast of England, following a course that would take it over the top of Scotland, then south along Scotland's west coast. From there Schwieger would make his way farther south to Ireland and sail down Ireland's west coast, then turn left to enter the Celtic and Irish Seas between Ireland and England and proceed to his destination, Liverpool Bay. This route was far longer, certainly, than traveling through the English Channel but also much safer.

The boat moved through 4-foot swells, against winds that now came from the northeast. Schwieger's lookouts watched for other ships, but in such gray and dreary conditions it was hard to spot the plumes of smoke exhausted by steamers.

Visibility remained poor throughout the day, and in late afternoon again worsened, until Schwieger once more found himself enclosed in fog. By this time, U-20 was crossing the sea-lanes off Edinburgh, Scotland, that funneled into the Firth of Forth. On a sunny day, with so many ships coming and going, the possibility of finding a target in these waters would have been high; but now, in the fog, attack was impossible and the risk of collision great. At four o'clock he ordered the boat to submerge and descend again to cruising depth.

That night the skies cleared, and stars arced from horizon to horizon. U-20 surfaced and Schwieger set a course toward Fair Isle, in the Shetland Islands, astride the imaginary line that divided the North Sea and the North Atlantic.

Two days out, and no longer able to communicate with his superiors, Schwieger was now wholly on his own.

RENDEZVOUS

Once outside New York Harbor, the *Lusitania* accelerated, but Captain Turner did not yet order its cruising speed. He first had a rendezvous to make, after the ship exited American territorial waters, and it was pointless to waste the coal necessary to reach top speed when he soon would have to bring the ship to a complete stop.

The ship's decks grew markedly cooler, subject now to the winds of the open Atlantic and the breeze generated by the ship's own forward motion. Some passengers still lingered at the rails to watch the coastline recede, but most went inside to settle into their accommodations and unpack their belongings. Older children roamed the decks, making friends and testing out various means of recreation, including, yes, shuffleboard on the top deck. Younger children—at least those in first and second class—met the stewardesses who would tend to them during the voyage and occupy them while their parents dined in their respective dining rooms.

Theodate Pope, the architect-spiritualist, and her companion, Edwin Friend, went to the ship's first-class reading and writing room, part of which was reserved for women, but which also served as the ship's library, to which men also had access. It was a large but comfortable place that spanned the width of A Deck, the ship's topmost level, and was fitted with writing desks and chairs. Its walls were covered with pale silk in soft gray and cream. Silk curtains in a pinkish hue called Rose du Barry hung at its windows. The carpet was a soft rose. Men had exclusive use of a separate similarly sized chamber farther back on A Deck, called the Smoking Room, paneled in walnut.

Theodate found a copy of that morning's *Sun*, a New York newspaper, and began to read.

The paper devoted a good deal of attention to a visit that Secretary of State William Jennings Bryan had made to New York the previous day. He had taken time off from foreign concerns to speak at a rally at Carnegie Hall, in support of a campaign by evangelist Billy Sunday to persuade people to renounce alcohol, and to sign a pledge of "total abstinence." For a previous talk on the subject, in Philadelphia, Secretary Bryan had drawn an overflow crowd of 16,000 people. The organizers in New York expected a similar crush at the hall. It didn't happen. Only about 2,500 people showed up, leaving about a third of the house empty. Bryan wore a black suit, a black alpaca coat, and his black string tie. At the end of his talk, toasting the audience, he raised a glass—of ice water. Booker T. Washington, newly turned fifty-nine, got up to speak as well and signed one of Billy Sunday's pledge cards.

Another item, this out of Washington, reported President Wilson's unhappiness at the fact that critics continued to take him to task for allowing the film *The Clansman*, by D. W. Griffith, to be screened at the White House. It was May now; the screening had taken place on February 18, with Wilson, his daughters, and members of the cabinet in attendance. Based on the novel *The Clansman*, by Thomas Dixon, which was subtitled *An Historical Romance of the Ku Klux Klan*, the film described the purported evils of the Reconstruction era and painted the Klan as the heroic savior of newly oppressed white southerners. The film, or "photoplay," as it was called, had become a huge hit nationwide, though its critics, in particular the six-year-old National Association for the Advancement of Colored People, decried its content and held protests outside movie theaters, prompting Griffith to give the film a more palatable name, *The Birth of a Nation*. On Friday, April 30, the president's personal secretary, Joseph Tumulty, had issued a statement saying, "The President was entirely unaware of the character of the play before it was presented and has at no time expressed his approbation of it." Wilson had agreed to the showing, Tumulty said, as a "courtesy extended to an old acquaintance."

And of course, there was the latest news of the war. A German drive against the Russians along the Baltic Sea had gained ground; back-and-forth fighting in Champagne and along the Meuse had gained nothing. German troops reinforced their position in the Ypres Salient. In Van Province, the Turks renewed their attacks against Armenian civilians; far to the west, Allied forces on the Gallipoli Peninsula were said to have routed the Turks, though this account would shortly be proven inaccurate. There was also a brief report about the bombing of the American ship *Cushing*.

THEODATE LOATHED the war. She saw Germany as wholly at fault and rejected German attempts to shift blame to Britain. "Whatever else could they expect when they have insulted England for years, and she is now simply and honorably keeping her agreement with the Triple Alliance?" Theodate wrote, referring to England's intervention in defense of Belgian neutrality. She longed for a crushing Allied victory that would leave Germany blasted "beyond recognition." She did not want the United States to get involved, however. The preceding October she had heard from a spirit medium, an acquaintance, who claimed to have received a message from the beyond: "Under no circumstances, whatever, should the United States participate belligerently in the European conflict." Theodate had forwarded the message to President Wilson.

What most caught Theodate's attention in Saturday's *Sun* was an item at the top of page 1, about the German Embassy's warning. This was the first she had heard of it. The only warning of any kind that she had seen thus far was in the "Information for Passengers" brochure she had received from Cunard after buying her ticket, which named her fellow first-class travelers and included this notice: "Passengers are informed that Professional Gamblers are reported as frequently crossing on Atlantic Steamers, and are warned to take precautions accordingly."

The *Sun* cast the German announcement in benign terms, under the headline "Germany Moves to Stop Tours Abroad." The item included the text of the warning, calling it the first step in a campaign by Germany "to head off American travel to Europe during the coming summer."

Theodate told Friend about it and said, "That means of course that they intend to get us." She was certain, however, that when the *Lusitania* reached British waters it would receive an escort. The prospect gave her comfort.

NELLIE HUSTON, thirty-one years old and on her way back to England after nearly a year staying with her aunt and uncle in Chicago, began a long letter to a woman named Ruth, which she planned to continue writing throughout the voyage. It was full of chatty details. She was traveling in second class and noted how crowded it was because of the additional passengers from the *Cameronia*—so crowded that the breakfast service had been divided into two sittings. She complained that she had been assigned to the first, at 7:30 A.M., which meant she would have to get up each morning at 7:00. She noted as well that the day was surprisingly cold and that she was glad she had brought her heavy coat.

A lot of her friends and family knew she was sailing that day on the *Lusitania*. "My!" she wrote. "The mail I got today. The steward who was giving it out was amused. He said it might be my birthday." Friends and relatives had sent her letters and gifts. "I had a pair of silk stockings from Prue and a piece of silk from Aunt Ruth and a rose. I had cards from Nellie Casson, Will Hobson, Tom, Edith Klaas and a nice letter from Lu which I'm going to answer."

Some were concerned about her voyage. "I'm so surprised to hear that Will and Bee cried, I didn't think it would worry them." She herself hated to cry, but, she wrote, "I've felt like doing it quite a lot since I've left."

—⁓—

UPON ENTERING international waters, Turner slowed the ship. In the distance, three large vessels materialized from the haze. These were British warships, stationed there to keep the *Vaterland* and the other German liners locked in New York Harbor. Turner ordered "full astern" to bring the *Lusitania* to a complete stop.

Two of the three ships were cruisers, HMS *Bristol* and *Essex*; the third was the *Caronia*, a Cunard liner converted to military use and now heavily armed. Turner had once been its captain. The two cruisers lay off the *Lusitania*'s starboard side, the *Caronia* off the port, each at a distance of about a "cable's length," equivalent to a tenth of a nautical mile, or roughly 600 feet. All three warships lowered a small boat, and the sailors in each began rowing toward the *Lusitania*, through "swirling mist-veils," as Capt. James Bisset, the *Caronia*'s master, recalled. The boats carried mail bound for England. "There was scarcely a breeze to ruffle the surface of the ocean," Bisset wrote. "A light mist clung around the ships, like a shroud."

Bisset spotted Captain Turner on the bridge, and Staff Captain Anderson. He knew the two men well. Some years earlier Bisset had served under both as junior third officer on the *Umbria*, an older passenger liner.

Turner and Anderson stepped out onto the port-side wing of the bridge and waved to the officers on the *Caronia*'s bridge. Everyone seemed to know one another, having served under, beside, or over one another through the years. After Turner and Anderson went back inside the bridge, the *Lusitania*'s second officer, Percy Hefford, appeared on the port wing. "He was a special friend of mine," Bisset recalled. Before both joined Cunard, they had served together on an ancient tramp steamer. The thing Hefford had wanted most was to serve aboard the *Lusitania*. "Now, there he was," Bisset wrote.

The two men used their arms to semaphore greetings and good-byes.

"Cheerio!"

"Good luck!"

"Good voyage!"

After the boats pulled away to return to their respective ships, Captain Turner gave the order for maximum speed. Full ahead. The *Lusitania*'s giant propellers raised a Niagara of water at the stern, and the ship began to move. Turner sounded his foghorn three times, the "Sailor's Farewell."

Ordinarily, all the *Lusitania*'s furnaces and boilers would be fully engaged during a crossing, with all four funnels belching smoke, but the war had caused a decline in travel so dramatic that Cunard had been compelled to seek cost reductions wherever it could find them. Turner was under orders issued the preceding November to run the ship using only three of its four boiler rooms, for a savings of 1,600 tons of coal per trip. But this also reduced the ship's maximum speed by 16 percent, from 25 knots to 21, ironic considering the ship's original mandate. Though seemingly a modest reduction, it nonetheless cut the distance the *Lusitania* could travel each day by 100 nautical miles, adding one full day to a transatlantic crossing.

A man aboard one of the warships took a photograph, believed to be the last ever taken of the *Lusitania*, which showed the ship steaming off into the mist-shrouded Atlantic, smoke pouring from just three funnels. Cunard did not publicize the change, and few, if any, passengers knew it had been made.

CADENCE

INTERCEPTED POSITION REPORTS: U-20
SATURDAY, MAY 1, 1915

2:00 A.M.: "IN 25D AREA 7 (55.21 N [LATITUDE] 3.15 E [LONGITUDE])"

4:00 A.M.: "IN 157A AREA 5 (55.39 N 2.45 E)"

6:00 A.M.: "IN 124A AREA 5 (55.51 N 2.15 E)"

8:00 A.M.: "IN 59A AREA 5 (56.15 N 1.18 E)"

REPORTS CEASE.

PART II

JUMP ROPE AND CAVIAR

"THE BLIND MOMENT"

B Y 8:25 A.M., SUNDAY, FAIR ISLE WAS VISIBLE 3 SEA MILES
ahead, to starboard, but Schwieger could not yet make out the
"Mainland" of the Orkneys archipelago, off the northernmost
tip of Scotland, which by now he expected to see off his port side.
The Mainland was the largest island in the Orkneys and had the
highest elevation.

On this third day of the cruise, there was new tension in the
boat. U-20 was about to leave "Bright Hans" behind and enter the
closely watched waters of the North Atlantic, north of Scotland, in
the vicinity of the big British base at Scapa Flow. Schwieger could
not have been surprised, therefore, when just after logging his location, he spotted two destroyers in the distance, moving with a
deliberation that suggested they were on patrol.

He ordered a fast dive, climbed down into the conning tower,
and closed the hatch behind him.

SIMPLE ENOUGH in concept, diving was in fact a complex and
perilous process that took time and left a U-boat exposed to attack. With a well-trained crew, a submarine of U-20's class could
descend from a fully surfaced condition to a level deep enough to
clear the hulls of the largest ships in as little as seventy-five seconds. In a crisis, however, each of those seconds could seem very

long. Certain older boats needed from two and a half minutes to as many as five. Their crews nicknamed them "suicide boats." While diving, a U-boat was at its most vulnerable, subject to ramming by warships, and to gunfire from long distances away. Penetration by a single shell would prevent a U-boat from submerging, thus eliminating its one advantage and its sole means of escape.

The men controlling U-20's bow and stern hydroplanes—horizontal rudders—now adjusted them for maximum dive, bow planes down, stern planes up. To submerge, a submarine did not simply fill its dive tanks with water and sink. As the boat moved forward under power, water flowed over the planes in the same way that air passes over the wings and flaps of an aircraft, driving the boat below the surface. Seawater would be pumped into the tanks only to the degree necessary to achieve a particular depth. Finding this point took skill, for it varied from day to day, even moment to moment, as sea conditions changed and the weight of the boat steadily declined. The firing of a torpedo made a U-boat suddenly 3,000 pounds lighter. Even the consumption of food diminished the boat's weight by a perceptible amount. The boxes and crates in which food was stored went overboard; the supply of fresh water, a significant source of weight, fell daily.

The buoyancy of seawater changed in accord with shifts in temperature and salinity. In the Baltic, boats descended much more readily than in the more heavily salted waters of the North Sea. A submarine passing the mouth of a river might suddenly find itself dropping because of the outrush of fresh water, like an airplane passing through an air pocket. Changes in water temperature due to current and depth also affected buoyancy. A miscalculation could cause catastrophe. A submarine might bob unexpectedly to the surface within view of a destroyer.

Bad weather further complicated things. High waves could prevent the hydroplanes from digging fully into the sea. Commander Paul Koenig recalled one terrifying morning when, after surfacing into a storm, he spotted the smoke plume of a nearby destroyer and ordered an emergency dive. The men in the control room below opened vents to admit water into the tanks at both sides of the bow to reduce buoyancy. The boat stayed on the surface. Koenig watched through one of the tiny windows in the conning tower with increasing anxiety as each new wave lifted the bow into the air.

Koenig ordered the hydroplanes tilted to their maximum angles and called for full speed ahead, hoping the acceleration would increase the downward drive of the planes. Still the boat stayed on the surface, rising and falling in the waves.

At last the planes dug in, and the boat began to descend. But now a new problem presented itself. The boat plummeted downward at an angle so steep that Koenig had to grasp the periscope eyepiece to keep from falling. The "manometer," which registered depth, showed a startling rate of descent. Then came an impact. Men were propelled forward, along with everything else in the boat that wasn't bolted in place.

There was silence. The face of the manometer cast a reddish light through the control room. One officer broke the tension. "Well, we seem to have arrived," he said.

The boat stood at a steep angle, about 36 degrees. The stern oscillated up and down. The engines continued running, "raving at intervals in a way that made the whole boat roar from stem to stern," Koenig wrote. The chief engineer was first to grasp what was happening. He ordered full stop.

Koenig understood. The submarine's bow was lodged in the seabed, which here, according to his charts, was 31 meters below the surface, about 100 feet. His boat was twice that in length. With the action of the waves, the stern at intervals protruded from the surface, and the propellers spun in open air, stirring a geyser of foam visible a long way off. Koenig feared—expected—that at any moment a shell from the destroyer would come crashing through the hull.

Now, with the problem defined, Koenig directed the crew to fill the stern diving tanks and blow water from the bow. Gradually the submarine rose and righted but stayed safely submerged. Koenig ordered full speed and away.

—⚓—

IN DIVING, timing was crucial. As U-20 began its descent, its engineers shut down the diesel engines and engaged the electric. All vents and exhaust ports leading to the exterior of the hull had to be closed and hatches sealed. Once this was done, Schwieger gave the order to begin admitting water to the dive tanks. Air was forced out through valves at the top, and seawater entered through valves below. Suction engines helped draw the water in. To speed the process, Schwieger sent a contingent of men into the bow.

Just as U-20 neared its cruising depth, Schwieger ordered air pumped back into the tanks to halt the boat's descent. The crew always knew when this point was reached because the pumps would engage with an angry growl.

In the control room, the helmsmen maintained depth by adjusting the hydroplanes. To ascend to periscope depth, they maneuvered only with the planes, not by filling the dive tanks with air. This allowed more precision and reduced the possibility that the boat might unexpectedly surface. While submerged, a U-boat had to keep moving at all times, held trim and steady by the hydroplanes. The only exception was when a boat was in shallow waters, where it could sit on the bottom. In deep seas like the North Atlantic, this was impossible, for the pressures at the seabed would crush a boat's hull. The constant forward motion caused a problem. When the periscope was up, it produced a wake on the surface, a white feather of water visible for miles.

As U-20 descended, all activity ceased for a few moments, save for those tasks that made no noise. As always, the crew listened for leaks and monitored internal air pressure.

Then came the moment crews found so thrilling, when the boat was fully submerged and moving forward through the sea in a way unlike that of any other vessel, not grinding through waves like surface ships, but gliding, like a bird in air.

A sightless bird, however. The windows in the conning tower afforded a view only of things near at hand and in any case were usually covered by steel shutters. Traveling like this required a great deal of confidence, because Schwieger now had no way of knowing what lay ahead. In this day before sonar, a submarine traveled utterly blind, trusting entirely in the accuracy of sea charts. One great fear of all U-boat men was that a half-sunk derelict or an uncharted rock might lie in their path.

SHORTLY AFTER NOON on Sunday, Schwieger gave orders to ascend. Now came "the blind moment," as commanders called it, that dismayingly long interval just before the periscope broke the surface. Everyone listened carefully for the sounds of ships transmitted through the hull—the rush of water past a prow, the thrum of propellers. There was no other way to tell what lay above. As Schwieger stared through the eyepiece, the water became brighter and more clear. These seconds were, according to one commander, "some of the most nerve-racking that a man can endure."

The biggest fear for Schwieger and fellow commanders was that the periscope would emerge within close range of a destroyer, or worse, in the destroyer's path. One U-boat surfaced so close to a ship that the vessel's black hull filled the lens. The commander at first thought he was looking at a particularly dark storm cloud.

The instant Schwieger's periscope cleared the surface, he made a fast 360-degree sweep of the surrounding seascape. He saw nothing of concern. Here a U-boat had a significant advantage over surface ships. Schwieger could see the smoke coming from the funnels of steamships at a great distance, but the lookouts aboard those ships had to be much closer to spot him.

Schwieger gave the order to bring the submarine fully to the surface. Now, in addition to using the hydroplanes, the crew adjusted the air-water mix in the dive tanks to increase buoyancy. Within U-20, the crew heard a roar as compressed air was blasted into the tanks to force seawater out. Sometimes a commander chose to come all the way up, exposing the boat's deck; at other times he ran "awash," with just the conning tower above the surface, imparting a sensation akin to walking on water.

U-20 EMERGED, but now Schwieger found a situation very different than his initial view through the periscope had led him to expect. The sea ahead was swarming with British patrol vessels—six of them—strung in a line between Fair Isle and the northernmost island of the Orkneys, North Ronaldsay, whose lighthouse was familiar to any mariner traversing these waters.

And behind him, Schwieger spotted two more destroyers. He had seen these earlier in the day but believed he had outdistanced them. In his log he wrote, "they heave in sight again, course towards 'U20'; one of the patrol boats turns towards us."

A SUNDAY AT SEA

AFTER HIS RENDEZVOUS WITH THE THREE BRITISH warships, Captain Turner brought the *Lusitania* to the speed he hoped to maintain throughout the voyage, 21 knots. He set a northeasterly bearing to begin a "circle course" that would take him across the Atlantic. This being May, when icebergs calved in northern seas, Turner chose the "long course," which veered farther south than the route followed in late summer and fall. Assuming all went well, Turner would arrive at the Mersey Bar outside Liverpool Harbor shortly before dawn on Saturday, May 8. Timing was crucial. Large ships could cross the bar only at high tide. Before the war, this had posed no particular problem. If a captain arrived too early or too late he could just stop and loiter awhile in the Irish Sea. But now that any such pause could prove fatal, captains timed their arrivals to cross the bar without stopping.

Throughout Sunday, May 2, the ship encountered rain and fog, and seas just turbulent enough to cause seasickness. Many passengers retreated to their rooms, but hardier souls walked the decks, played cards, engaged the ship's typists for their correspondence, and sipped tea in the Verandah Cafe, a calming gardenlike place with five hanging baskets, six shrubs in containers, and forty other plants in boxes around the room. Some passengers read books on C Deck—also called the Shelter Deck—protected from rain by the underside of the deck above. Passengers could rent deck chairs for a dollar per voyage; another dollar got them a blanket, known in the ship's vernacular as a "rug."

At 10:30 Sunday morning, church services began for two denominations: Church of England, in the first-class saloon; Roman Catholic in second. Many passengers slept late, planning to wake at about eleven, in time for lunch.

THEODATE POPE awoke after a difficult night. Her cabin had been noisy, owing to its proximity to the three staterooms booked by the Crompton family, who proved to be a boisterous group, as families of six, including an infant, tend to be. Always prone to insomnia, she found the noise intolerable and asked the purser, McCubbin, to find her a more suitable stateroom. Changing accommodations while under way could be a tricky business, but McCubbin obliged and placed her in a new stateroom three decks up.

SECOND-CLASS PASSENGER William Uno Meriheina, a twenty-six-year-old race-car driver from New York traveling to South Africa as a "special agent" for the General Motors Export Company, got up early and took "a dandy salt water bath." The tubs on board were supplied with heated seawater. Afterward, he dressed and went to breakfast. "Plenty of seasickness on board," he noted, in a long day-by-day letter he was writing to his wife, Esther, "but I feel splendid."

Meriheina—who, except when traveling, went by the name William Merry Heina—had been born in Russia, in the Duchy of Finland (which would become independent in 1917), and emigrated to New York in 1893. He had a fascination with speed and by 1909 was racing cars in Brighton Beach, Brooklyn, including one race that lasted twenty-four hours. He was also one of the first drivers to race at the Indianapolis Motor Speedway after it opened in 1909. He survived two crashes, one in which his car, a Lozier, rolled over twice, but left him unhurt. He also tried his hand at flying and survived a collision at an airfield in Garden City, Long Island, in which another aircraft settled on top of his in midair. Once again he emerged unscathed. Said his wife, "A braver man never lived."

He had chosen the *Lusitania* because he believed it to be the "safest" ship. In the rush to board and say good-bye to his wife and their daughter, Charlotte, he had not had a chance to open the newspaper he had bought before boarding. It was only when the ship was about fifty miles from New York that he read about the German warning.

He wasn't worried. Now and then the ship encountered French and British warships. One French dreadnought turned around and followed, but the *Lusitania* left it behind.

Like other passengers, he was unaware that the liner was traveling at reduced speed with one boiler room closed, despite the obvious visible clue provided by the lack of smoke coming from the fourth funnel. He believed the ship was moving at its top speed of 25 knots and took pride in the pace. "We have passed quite a few vessels bound both ways," he wrote. "Owing to our great speed we don't stay in sight of any one ship very long."

He was also under the impression the ship was being watched over by British naval forces. "Evidently," he wrote, "we are being carefully convoyed all the way across."

THAT MORNING Charles Lauriat got up at 8:00 A.M., called back to consciousness by his steward. He also took a sea bath. Once dressed, he strolled the first-class promenade, stopping to chat with the Hubbards and other acquaintances. He dined with his traveling companion, Lothrop Withington. They took their meals together in the opulent first-class dining room at the center of D Deck, where some 470 passengers at a time dined at tables arrayed on two levels under a dome frescoed with cherubs, amid palm trees, potted plants, white plaster walls, and fluted Corinthian columns with gilded capitals. Gold leaf seemed to coat every raised surface, from plaster wreaths and vines to balustrade rails.

Lauriat was sufficiently well known to Cunard officers and crew that on some past voyages he had been allowed to climb up into the crow's nest on the ship's forward wireless mast and stay there throughout the day. This was not, however, something Captain Turner was likely to let him do. Dealing with bloody monkeys on deck was one thing; having them climbing the wireless mast was another.

Lauriat knew well the routines of shipboard life, including the daily pools where passengers placed bets on how many miles the ship would travel in a given day. Places in the pool denoted a particular distance and were auctioned by a ship's officer. Passengers based their bets on their sense of how the ship would fare given the weather and sea conditions likely to prevail over the next twenty-four hours. The most unpredictable factor was fog, which if it persisted would sharply limit a ship's progress, for the only safe way of coping with fog was to cut speed and start blowing the ship's foghorn. The mileage pool and its associated strategizing and arguing and the cigars and whiskey consumed by those present invariably helped spark friendships and break down barriers of formal courtesy and convention.

On Sunday, the ship's first full day at sea, it traveled 501 miles, according to Lauriat's recollection. He found this surprising. He too assumed the ship was moving at 25 knots. At that rate, equivalent to about 29 miles an hour, it should have covered 700 miles. The periodic fog accounted for part of this sluggishness, he gauged, but certainly not all. At noon the next day, Lauriat and Withington would discover the ship was traveling even more slowly. "At this rate," Lauriat told Withington, "we're not going to make Liverpool on time."

Lauriat retired to his stateroom to examine the Thackeray drawings. He looked them over, mulling what he would ask Lady Ritchie to write and planning how each drawing would be mounted.

—⚓—

FOR CAPTAIN TURNER, the voyage thus far was routine, and it was likely to remain so for at least the next four days. The weather was peaceful, for the most part, and there was little likelihood of encountering a German submarine in mid-ocean. When the ship neared Ireland, however, the danger of attack would grow. While Turner himself expressed little anxiety about submarines, within Cunard there was a growing sense that the threat they posed was becoming more acute.

Before each crossing, the company gave Turner confidential advisories and notices about conditions that might affect the voyage. Lately these had included Admiralty memoranda that delineated the growing submarine threat and offered advice on what to do if confronted by a U-boat. Cunard's managers still shared the widely held belief that no U-boat commander would dare sink a passenger liner; at the same time, they had watched as Germany began conducting attacks against other merchant ships without scruple. U-boats now ventured as far as Liverpool. One merchant victim, the *Princess Victoria*, was torpedoed just off the Mersey Bar.

These attacks prompted the Admiralty to issue new advisories to address the danger. Cunard relayed to Turner orders to halt all wireless transmissions from the ship's Marconi room except when "absolutely necessary." Its wireless operators were expressly prohibited from "gossiping." Passengers could receive messages but could not send them. Another Admiralty advisory warned, in italics, *"Ships should give prominent headlands a wide berth."*

The Admiralty issued its most comprehensive set of instructions in February 1915, in a secret memorandum that captains were to store "in a place where it can be destroyed at a moment's notice." The document revealed a mixture of naïveté and sophistication about the nature of the submarine threat. It called the deck gun of a submarine "an inferior weapon" and stated, "Gun-fire from most submarines is not dangerous." The instructions also advised that if a vessel got hit with a torpedo, there was no need to worry: "There will generally be ample time for the crew to escape in the boats, if the latter are kept ready for service." The memorandum evaded entirely the matter of *passengers* and how they might fare under the same circumstances.

But it also embodied a realistic appraisal of the vulnerabilities of U-boats and urged captains to exploit these at every opportunity. "If a submarine comes up suddenly close ahead of you with obvious hostile intention, steer straight for her at your utmost speed, altering course as necessary to keep her ahead." In short, the Admiralty was asking merchant captains to transform their ships into offensive weapons and ram their attackers. This was an effective maneuver given the inherent fragility of submarines, as would be proved a month later when the HMS *Dreadnought* rammed and sank Kapitänleutnant Weddigen's U-29, thereby avenging the dead crews of the *Aboukir*, the *Cressy*, and the *Hogue*. The memorandum recommended that British ships disguise themselves as neutrals whenever possible and fly false colors. "It is not in any way dishonorable. Owners and masters will therefore be within their rights if they use every device to mislead the enemy and induce him to confuse British vessels with neutrals."

The memorandum also included a strict order, the codified effect of the *Aboukir* disaster: "No ocean-going British merchant vessel is permitted to go to the assistance of a ship which has been torpedoed by a submarine."

THE ADMIRALTY later claimed that Turner possessed still another advisory, dated April 16, which reported, "War experience has shown that fast steamers can considerably reduce the chance of successful surprise submarine attack by zigzagging that is to say altering the course at short and regular intervals say in ten minutes to half an hour." The memo noted that this tactic was used by warships in waters likely to be patrolled by submarines.

The Admiralty may have erred, however, in presuming Turner really did have this particular memo among his papers at the time the ship sailed from New York. (Cunard's lawyers later would hedge the point with a heroic bit of legal prose in which they stated that while Cunard believed such a notice had been given to the captain, the company had no knowledge of what the delivered memo actually said.) Whether such a communiqué had in fact been delivered to Turner became a matter of debate. The Admiralty's Board of Trade had indeed crafted a statement on zigzagging, but one prominent naval historian asserted that the advisory was not approved by First Lord Churchill until April 25 and was not actually distributed to captains and shipping companies until May 13, long after the *Lusitania*'s May 1 departure.

Even had this memo been in Turner's possession, it probably would have made little impression. For one thing, the memo did not order captains to zigzag; it merely described the practice. For another, zigzagging at the time was a proposition that merchant captains considered worthy of ridicule, and that none was likely to endorse, especially not the master of a grand ocean liner. The idea of subjecting passengers, many of them prominent souls in first class, to the hard and irregular turns of a zigzag course was beyond contemplation.

Now, in open seas, the *Lusitania* maintained an average speed of 21 knots, 6 knots faster than the maximum speed a U-boat could attain while surfaced and more than twice what it could achieve while fully submerged.

This was also faster than any other civilian ship still in service. On Sunday afternoon the *Lusitania* quickly overtook and passed the American liner *New York*, with the Shakespearean actress Ellen Terry aboard.

That Sunday, Dwight Harris, the New Yorker traveling to England to get married, planned what he would do if in fact the *Lusitania* were torpedoed. He wrote, "I took a look around and decided that if anything did happen in the 'War Zone' I would go to the bow if possible." First, however, he planned to grab the custom life belt he had bought at Wanamaker's in New York.

PROTECTING ORION

THE GERMAN WIRELESS MESSAGES INTERCEPTED BY ROOM 40 caused deep anxiety within the Admiralty. But it was not the *Lusitania* the Admiralty was concerned about. It was the HMS *Orion*, one of Britain's largest and most powerful battleships, a "superdreadnought." The ship had undergone a refitting in Devonport, on England's southwest coast, and was now ready to sail north to rejoin the Grand Fleet at Scapa Flow.

On Sunday, May 2, Admiralty Chief of Staff "Dummy" Oliver sent a note to First Sea Lord Jacky Fisher, in which he recommended that the *Orion*'s departure be postponed. "There will be less moon & less risk every night now that we wait," he wrote.

Fisher agreed, and at 1:20 P.M. Oliver sent a telegram to the commander in chief of the fleet, Admiral Jellicoe, ordering him to hold the *Orion* in Devonport a while longer. That same afternoon the Admiralty also urged Jellicoe, "in view of the submarine menace West of the West Coast of Ireland," to take precautions to protect lesser ships, such as colliers and tenders.

Over the next several days, Oliver would send explicit warnings to two other warships, HMS *Gloucester* and HMS *Duke of Edinburgh*, and would direct a third, HMS *Jupiter*, to take a newly opened route, the so-called North Channel, deemed far safer than alternative paths. The Admiralty had closed the route previously because of German mines but had declared it clear on April 15 and promptly made it available to navy ships but not merchant vessels. The route passed between Scotland and Ireland, through waters bracketed by friendly shores and heavily patrolled by the Royal Navy.

Despite the North Channel's safety, Admiral Oliver issued orders to have the *Jupiter* escorted by destroyers.

THAT SUNDAY there was more news of the North Channel. Adm. Richard Webb, head of the Admiralty's Trade Division, which in wartime held dominion over all British merchant shipping, received notice that the new route would now in fact be open to *all* vessels, merchant and military alike. This meant that civilian freighters and liners sailing to Liverpool could henceforth avoid the Western Approaches altogether and sail instead over the top of Ireland, then turn right and go *south* to Liverpool.

Admiral Webb did not transmit this new information to Cunard or to the *Lusitania*.

Through much of Sunday, the Admiralty also tracked the progress of the wounded American tanker *Gulflight*, under tow and escorted by the navy. At 4:05 that afternoon the ship was reported making "good progress." Two hours later it arrived at St. Mary's Island in the Scillies, with its foredeck nearly submerged, its propeller visible at the stern.

IN QUEENSTOWN, IRELAND, America's local consul opened a newspaper and read for the first time about the warning the German Embassy had published in American newspapers the previous day.

The consul was Wesley Frost, now just beginning his second year of service in Queenstown. The town was still a major port, although Cunard's largest liners no longer stopped there, having "touched bottom" in its harbor once too often. Although Frost knew the *Lusitania* was at this moment on its way to Liverpool, he felt no particular concern. "The reference to the *Lusitania* was obvious enough," he recalled later, "but personally it never entered my mind for a moment that the Germans would actually perpetrate an attack upon her. The culpability of such an act seemed too blatant and raw for an intelligent people to take upon themselves."

THAT SAME SUNDAY, well to the south in London, U.S. ambassador Walter Page, Frost's chief, took a few moments to write a letter to his son, Arthur, an editor at the New York publishing company that the ambassador and his partner, Frank Doubleday, had founded in 1899.

Page was an Anglophile through and through. His dispatches consistently favored Britain and time and again struck President Wilson as being decidedly un-neutral. In fact, Wilson had by now lost confidence in Page, though the ambassador did not yet seem to know it. The president had left enough hints, however, often failing to respond to Page's communiqués. The presence of Colonel House in London as Wilson's personal emissary should, by itself, have been evidence enough of Page's diminished influence, but the ambassador still seemed not to grasp just how little Wilson cared for him and the information he supplied.

Page wrote often to his son and now, in his Sunday letter, told him of his concern that America might be drawn into the war. Later this letter would seem prescient to an uncanny degree.

"The blowing up of a liner with American passengers may be the prelude," the ambassador wrote. "I almost expect such a thing."

He added, "If a British liner full of Americans be blown up, what will Uncle Sam do? What's going to happen?"

A PERILOUS LINE

AT 12:30 P.M. SUNDAY, FINDING HIMSELF BRACKETED by patrol boats and destroyers, Schwieger ordered another fast dive. The line of vessels ahead seemed to be an antisubmarine cordon, with Fair Isle at the top and North Ronaldsay in the Orkneys at the bottom. Schwieger suspected the cordon might be a permanent presence in these waters. If so, he wrote in his log, by way of warning other captains, "it would not seem advisable to pass this line during the day, especially when visibility is very good."

U-20 traveled submerged for the next four hours. At 4:30 P.M., Schwieger ascended to periscope depth and immediately spotted a patrol boat off to starboard. He dove back to cruising depth.

So much underwater travel was taxing for his crew. The atmosphere grew close and warm. But it was especially taxing for the submarine's batteries. Even moving at a mere 5 knots, a boat of U-20's class could cover a maximum of only 80 nautical miles before the batteries failed.

Schwieger kept the boat submerged for another two and a half hours. He noted in his log that his batteries were making a crackling noise. By this point U-20 had traveled 50 nautical miles on electric power.

At 7:00 P.M. Schwieger again tried his periscope and to his relief saw no imminent threat. "Emerged," he wrote, "and steered towards the open sea in order to get away from the patrol boats whose smoke is still visible astern."

In an addendum to his log, he noted that if still more destroyers had been posted beyond this Fair Isle–Ronaldsay line, thus forcing his boat to stay submerged even longer, "our situation could have been critical as our battery was pretty nearly gone." These were deep waters—too deep for U-20 to hide on the bottom. Had the batteries failed here, Schwieger would have had no choice but to come to the surface and run until his diesel engines succeeded in recharging the system. But destroyers, capable of moving at speeds more than twice U-20's maximum, would have had no difficulty overtaking him and would have begun firing long before.

Once safely out to sea and past the northern lip of Scotland, Schwieger set a course that would take him down the west flank of the Outer Hebrides, a bulwark of islands situated off Scotland's northwest coast. His patrol zone off Liverpool was still a three-day voyage away.

The heave of the sea had lessened, producing swells of only 3 feet. Schwieger kept the boat on the surface. At 9:30 P.M. he signed his log to close the third day of his patrol.

Three days out, and he had sunk nothing—had not even fired his deck gun.

LATER THAT NIGHT, Schwieger was summoned into the shelter atop the conning tower. A lookout had spotted a potential target. In his log Schwieger described it as a "huge neutral steamer, its name lighted." He judged it to be a Danish passenger liner out of Copenhagen, bound for Montreal. To determine this, Schwieger may have relied on his "War Pilot," a merchant officer named Lanz, who served aboard U-20 to help identify ships. Between Lanz's expertise and an immense book carried aboard every submarine that provided silhouettes and descriptions of nearly all ships afloat, Schwieger could be reasonably certain of the identities of any large vessel that came into view.

Though it's clear Schwieger considered the Danish ship a potential target, he made no attempt to attack. The ship was too far ahead and moving too fast; he estimated its speed to be at least 12 knots. "An attack on this ship impossible," he wrote in his log.

This entry revealed much about Schwieger. It showed that he would have been more than willing to attack if circumstances had been better, even though he recognized the ship was neutral—and not just neutral but heading *away* from Britain and thus unlikely to be carrying any contraband for Germany's enemies. The entry revealed as well that he had no misgivings about torpedoing a liner full of civilians.

HALIBUT

THE WEATHER REMAINED GLOOMY THROUGHOUT SUN-day and into Monday. Rain and wind made the decks cold, and for the second day in a row passengers inclined to sea-sickness withdrew to their cabins.

Each day Captain Turner ordered lifeboat and fire drills and tests of the bulkhead doors between the ship's waterproof compartments. During lifeboat drills at sea the crew did not actually launch any boats, as they had at the wharf in New York, because to do so while the ship was moving would likely have fatal consequences for anyone in the lifeboat. A ship had to be fully stopped before the crew could lower a boat safely.

These daily drills involved only the ship's two "emergency boats," which were kept swung out at all times in order to be ready should a passenger fall overboard or some other incident arise. These were boats 13 and 14, on opposite sides of the ship. Every morning a squad of crewmen would gather at whichever boat was on the lee side of the deck, meaning away from the wind. John Lewis, senior third mate, directed the drills. The men stood at attention. At Lewis's command—"Man the boats!"—they climbed in, put on their life jackets, and sat in their assigned places. Lewis then dismissed the crew.

Lewis also participated in Staff Captain Jock Anderson's daily inspections of the entire ship, which began every morning at 10:30.

Four other men typically went along as well: the ship's senior surgeon, the assistant surgeon, the purser, and the chief steward. They gathered outside the purser's office, or "Purser's Bureau," at the center of B Deck, opposite the ship's two electric elevators, then set off to tour the ship. They checked a sample of cabins and the ship's dining rooms, lounges, lavatories, boilers, and passages, from A Deck to steerage, to "see that everything was clean and in order," Lewis said. They paid particular attention to whether any portholes—"air ports," Lewis called them—had been left open, especially in the lower decks.

The inspections, drills, and other activities of the crew provided an element of diversion for passengers. Seaman Leslie Morton became something of an attraction aboard ship because of his skill at tying complex knots. "I remember putting an eye splice in an eight stranded wire hawser on the fore deck, with a crowd of admiring passengers watching me, which called forth all my latent histrionic abilities," Morton wrote. The performance, at least according to his own recollection, drew " 'Oos' and 'Ahs' and gasps."

No one aboard knew, as yet, about the May 1 torpedoing of the American oil tanker *Gulflight* or that in Washington the incident had sparked concern as to the safety of the *Lusitania* itself. The attack, coming as it did on the same day as publication of Germany's advisory against travel through the war zone, suggested that the warning was more than mere bluff. The *Washington Times*, without identifying sources, stated, "The liner *Lusitania*, with several hundred prominent Americans on board, is steaming toward England despite anonymous warnings to individual passengers and a formally signed warning published in the advertising columns of American newspapers—warnings, which, in view of late developments in the sea war zone, it is beginning to be feared, may prove far from empty." The article noted further that "hundreds of Americans are holding their breaths lest relatives on board such vessels go down."

It reported that federal officials were perplexed about Germany's intentions. One question seemed to be on everyone's mind: "What is the German government driving at? Is it bent on incurring war with the United States?"

No one had any doubts that the *Gulflight* incident would be resolved through diplomacy, the article said. "But what is worrying everybody is the accumulation of evidence that Germany is either looking for trouble with the United States or that her authorities are reckless of the possibilities of incurring trouble."

As THE *LUSITANIA* steamed on, the usual shipboard tedium began to set in, and meals became increasingly important. In these first days of the voyage, passengers adapted themselves to their assigned table mates. For Charles Lauriat, this was simple: his friend Withington was his dining companion. For Liverpool police detective Pierpoint, it was even simpler: he dined alone. Unaccompanied travelers, however, faced the potential of being seated among tiresome souls with whom they had nothing in common. Invariably one encountered charmers and boors, sheep and braggarts; one young woman found herself seated beside "a very dyspeptic sort of fellow." Sparks flew, or got damped. Romances got kindled.

But the food was always good and plentiful, even in third class, where blue marrowfat peas were a staple, as were Wiltshire cheeses and tinned pears, peaches, apricots, and pineapples. In first class, the food was beyond good. Lavish. First-class passengers were offered soups, hors d'oeuvres, and a multitude of entrées at each meal. On one voyage the menu for a single dinner included halibut in a sauce Orleans, mignons de sole souchet, and broiled sea bass Choron (a sauce of white wine, shallots, tarragon, tomato paste, and eggs); veal cutlets, tournedos of beef Bordelaise, baked Virginia ham, saddle of mutton, roast teal duck, celery-fed duckling, roast guinea chicken, sirloin and ribs of beef; and five desserts—a Tyrollean soufflé, chocolate cake, apple tart, Bavaroise au citron, and ice cream, two kinds: strawberry and Neapolitan. There were so many items on the menu that Cunard felt obliged to print a separate sheet with suggested combinations, lest one starve from befuddlement.

Passengers drank and smoked. Both; a lot. This was a significant source of profit for Cunard. The company laid in a supply of 150 cases of Black & White Whiskey, 50 cases of Canadian Club Whiskey, and 50 of Plymouth Gin; also, 15 cases each of an eleven-year-old French red wine, a Chambertin, and an eleven-year-old French white, a Chablis, and twelve barrels of stout and ten of ale. Cunard stockpiled thirty thousand "Three Castles" cigarettes and ten thousand Manila cigars. The ship also sold cigars from Havana and American cigarettes made by Phillip Morris. For the many passengers who brought pipes, Cunard acquired 560 pounds of loose Capstan tobacco—"navy cut"—and 200 pounds of Lord Nelson Flake, both in 4-ounce tins. Passengers also brought their own. Michael Byrne, a retired New York merchant and former deputy sheriff traveling in first class, apparently planned to spend a good deal of the voyage smoking. He packed 11 pounds of Old Rover Tobacco and three hundred cigars. During the voyage, the scent of combusted tobacco was ever present, especially after dinner.

The dominant topic of conversation, according to passenger Harold Smethurst, was "war, and submarines."

FOR THEODATE POPE, there was tedium, but also depression. Ever since childhood she had struggled with it. Theodate described herself once as being afflicted with "over consciousness." During her time at Miss Porter's School in Farmington she had often become depressed and was hobbled by fatigue. In 1887, when she was twenty, she wrote in her diary, "Tears come without any provocation. Headache all day." The school's headmistress and founder, Sarah Porter, offered therapeutic counsel. "Cheer up," she told Theodate. "Always be happy." It did not work. The next year, in March 1888, her parents sent her to Philadelphia, to be examined and cared for by Dr. Silas Weir Mitchell, a physician famous for treating patients, mainly women, suffering from neurasthenia, or nervous exhaustion.

Mitchell's solution for Theodate was his then-famous "Rest Cure," a period of forced inactivity lasting up to two months. "At first, and in some cases for four or five weeks, I do not permit the patient to sit up or to sew or write or read," Mitchell wrote, in his book *Fat and Blood*. "The only action allowed is that needed to clean the teeth." He forbade some patients from rolling over on their own, insisting they do so only with the help of a nurse. "In such cases I arrange to have the bowels and water passed while lying down, and the patient is lifted on to a lounge at bedtime and sponged, and then lifted back again into the newly-made bed." For stubborn cases, he reserved mild electrical shock, delivered while the patient was in a filled bathtub. His method reflected his own dim view of women. In his book *Wear and Tear; or, Hints for the Overworked*, he wrote that women "would do far better if the brain were very lightly tasked."

Theodate complied with the rules of Mitchell's rest cure, even though she believed rest to be the last thing she needed. She wrote, "I am always happy when I keep so busy that I cannot stop to think of the sadness of life." The cure didn't help. And in fact, Dr. Mitchell's approach was soon to undergo a nationwide reevaluation. In 1892 a writer named Charlotte Perkins Gilman published a popular short story, "The Yellow Wall-Paper," in which she attacked Mitchell's rest cure. Gilman had become a patient of his in 1887, a year before Theodate's treatment, suffering from what a later generation would describe as postpartum depression. Gilman spent a month at Dr. Mitchell's clinic. Afterward, he wrote out a prescription for how she was to proceed after treatment: "Live as domestic a life as possible. Have your child with you all the time. Lie down an hour after each meal. Have but two hours intellectual life a day."

And this: "Never touch pen, brush, or pencil again as long as you live."

Gilman claimed that Mitchell's cure drove her "to the edge of insanity." She wrote the story, she said, to warn would-be patients of the dangers of this doctor "who so nearly drove me mad."

Theodate continued fighting depression throughout her thirties. By the autumn of 1900, when she was thirty-three, it threatened even to deaden her love of art and architecture. "I find that my material world is losing its power to please or harm me—it is not vital to me anymore," she wrote in her diary. "I am turning in on myself and am finding my pleasure in the inner world which was my constant retreat when I was a child." Even her interest in paintings began to wane. She wrote, "Pictures have been dead long ago to me—the ones that please me, please me only at first sight—after that they are paint and nothing more; to use a vulgar expression, 'sucked lemons.' " Architecture continued to engage her, but with less ferocity. "My interest in architecture has always been more intense than my interest in any other art manifestation. And on my word I think it is not dead yet—not quite." She was, she wrote, "tired of seeing these fluted flimsy highly colored hen houses going up—and am gnashing my teeth over them."

She and Edwin Friend dined together, and at least for a time shared their table with a young doctor from Saratoga Springs, New York, named James Houghton, and with one of the ship's more famous personages, Marie Depage, a nurse who, along with her physician-husband, Antoine, had gained fame for tending Belgians wounded in the war. Depage had spent the previous two months raising money to support their work, but was now on her way back to Europe to see her son, Lucien, before he was sent to the front. Dr. Houghton, en route to Belgium to help Depage's husband, at one point revealed that on the night before the *Lusitania*'s departure he had signed a new will.

Such talk did not move Theodate. She wrote, "I truly believe there was no one on the ship who valued life as little as I do."

MARGARET MACKWORTH and her father, D. A. Thomas, were seated at a table in the first-class dining room with an American doctor and his sister-in-law, Dorothy Conner, twenty-five, from Medford, Oregon. Conner was a woman of energy and candor. She was also bored and given to impetuous remarks. At one point, Conner said, "I can't help hoping that we get some sort of thrill going up the Channel."

Margaret took note of the curiously high number of children on the passenger list. "We noticed this with much surprise," she wrote. She attributed this to families moving from Canada to England to be near husbands and fathers fighting in the war.

She took the German Embassy's warning seriously and told herself that in case of trouble she would have to override her instinct to run immediately to the boat deck and instead go first to her cabin and get her life jacket.

PRESTON PRICHARD, the young medical student heading home from Canada, found himself seated at a long table in the second-class dining hall directly opposite a young woman named Grace French, of Renton, England, who was among those passengers transferred to the ship from the *Cameronia*. She seemed to take an interest in Prichard or at least found him worth examining in some detail. She saw that he had a narrow tie with a red stripe, and she paid close enough attention to realize that he had only two suits, "one very smart navy blue serge and a green suit; more for knock-about wear." She also noted his lava-head tie clasp. "About the heads I remember them distinctly because my father once had ones similar and they took my eye, and so far as I can remember he wore it all the time."

Prichard was kind and funny and full of stories. And very good looking. "He kept us in good spirits relating different experiences he had during his travels and was very nice to everybody," she wrote. "I appreciated his efforts as I was very sick"—seasick—"during the whole journey, and [he] was especially nice to me."

She also took note of the lucky young woman, also English, who'd been assigned the seat right next to Prichard. With a whiff of a meow, Miss French described this potential rival as "very short," with "light brown hair, blue eyes, lots of color in her face, and I think she was visiting in California, at least she talked a great deal about its beauties and advantage." She added: "They were great friends at the dining table."

In addition to playing whist, Prichard took part in the mileage betting pools and in various deck sports, including tug-of-war and an improvised obstacle course. "A party of us used to have a game of skipping every day," one young woman recalled. At a certain point another participant, a young man, tried to use the jump rope to lasso her but failed. Prichard stepped forward and showed the group how to do it. He seemed to be an expert at lassoing and roped many of the players. "I never saw him again after this," the woman said.

She touched on a peculiar aspect of life aboard such a large ship: you might meet someone who interested you in one way or another, but unless that person happened to be assigned to your table or your room, or occupied the deck chair next to yours, you had little opportunity to build a closer association. The ship was too big. Gertrude Adams, a passenger in second class traveling with her two-and-a-half-year-old daughter, wrote later, "There were so many on the ship that it really was like living in a town, one saw fresh people every day & never knew who they were."

It was a mark of Prichard's popularity that so many casual acquaintances remembered him at all.

IN THE EVENING, select guests would be invited to sit at a table presided over by Staff Captain Anderson, or at Captain Turner's table, on those occasions when Turner was willing to suppress his antipathy toward social engagement. As a rule, he preferred to take his meals in his cabin or on the bridge. He was particularly fond of chicken and during one meal drove his first officer nearly mad with his effort to gnaw every last morsel off a chicken leg.

THE TROUBLE WITH TORPEDOES

ARLY ON MONDAY MORNING U-20 WAS SAILING THROUGH a world of cobalt and cantaloupe. "Very beautiful weather," Schwieger noted, in a 4:00 A.M. entry in his log. The boat was abreast of Sule Skerry, a small island west of the Orkneys with an 88-foot lighthouse, said to be the most remote and isolated light in the British Isles.

Schwieger sailed a southwesterly course. He saw no targets but also no threats and was able to stay on the surface the entire day. Toward nightfall, at 6:50 P.M., he at last spotted a potential target, a steamer of about two thousand tons. It flew a Danish flag off its stern, but Schwieger's war pilot, Lanz, believed the flag was a ruse, that the ship was in fact a British vessel out of Edinburgh. It was heading toward U-20. Schwieger ordered a fast dive, to periscope depth.

Now began the complex choreography that would determine whether he could add this ship to his personal tally of sunk tonnage. Men ran back and forth under the direction of the ship's chief engineer, to help keep the boat level, as the helmsmen adjusted the horizontal and vertical planes. Schwieger raised and lowered the periscope at brief intervals to keep the steamer in sight but minimize the amount of time the periscope and its wake were visible on the surface.

With his rangefinder, Schwieger gauged the ship's distance and speed. Another indicator of velocity was the height to which water rose on the target's bow. The higher and whiter, the faster. If this had been a French battleship, Schwieger would have had to watch especially closely, for the French navy painted false wakes on the bows of its warships, in an effort to confuse the calculations of U-boat commanders.

Schwieger had two kinds of torpedoes aboard—an old bronze model and the newest G6 torpedoes. The G6, or "gyro," torpedo was bigger and more reliable, but Schwieger selected one of the bronze models, presumably in order to conserve the better torpedoes for more important targets, like the troop transports he would be hunting in Liverpool Bay. The crew armed it and flooded its launching tube, one of the two tubes in U-20's bow. The boat had two others in its stern.

The men at the hydroplanes worked to keep the boat as steady and level as possible, lest the conning tower rise too high and betray the submarine's presence, or the periscope sink below the surface and make aiming impossible.

The freighter approached, clearly unaware that U-20 was ahead. Schwieger positioned his boat at a right angle to the ship's course and advanced slowly to maintain "steerage," just enough forward motion to keep the hydroplanes and rudder engaged. The submarine was, in effect, a gun barrel and had to be pointed in the right direction at the time the torpedo was launched.

From the bow a crewman called, "Torpedo ready."

TORPEDOES WERE weapons of great power—when they worked. Schwieger distrusted them, and with good reason. According to a German tally 60 percent of attempted torpedo firings resulted in failure. Torpedoes veered off course. They traveled too deep and passed under their targets. Their triggers broke; their warheads failed to explode.

Aiming them was an art. Through the restricted view afforded by the periscope, a captain had to estimate the forward speed of the target, its course, and its distance away. He aimed not at the target itself but at a point well ahead, as if shooting skeet.

Stories of torpedo mishaps were rife among crews. One U-boat experienced three torpedo failures in twenty-four hours. In the third of these, the torpedo turned unexpectedly and traveled in a circle back toward the boat, and nearly hit it. Another submarine, UB-109, of a class used primarily for coastal patrols, tried launching an attack while surfaced. The first torpedo, fired from its stern, left the tube and immediately sank. The captain maneuvered the boat so that he could take another shot, this time from the bow. But, according to a British intelligence report, "This torpedo broke surface 5 or 6 times, described a complete circle, and also missed the target."

Torpedoes were expensive, and heavy. Each cost up to $5,000— over $100,000 today—and weighed over three thousand pounds, twice the weight of a Ford Model T. Schwieger's boat had room only for seven, two of which were to be held in reserve for the homeward voyage.

If the performance measured by the German navy were to hold true for Schwieger on this patrol, it would mean that if he fired all seven of his torpedoes, only three would succeed in striking a ship and exploding.

SCHWIEGER'S TARGET—the presumed British ship, flying Danish colors—continued its approach. It was 300 meters away, the U-boat equivalent of point-blank range, when Schwieger gave the order to fire. The command was repeated throughout the boat.

What should have come next was a whoosh and a tremor as the torpedo left its tube, followed by a sudden, perceptible rise of the bow due to the lost weight, this immediately suppressed by the men at the hydroplanes.

But Schwieger heard nothing and felt nothing. There was only silence.

The torpedo never left the tube. A misfire—a locking mechanism had failed to release.

The target continued on its way into the safe, deep waters of the North Atlantic, its crew apparently unaware of how close they had come to disaster.

LUSITANIA

SUNSHINE AND HAPPINESS

William Meriheina, of General Motors: "Tuesday—Resumption of games on deck today. Dandy sunshine weather."

Nellie Huston, thirty-one, second class, heading home to England: "Tuesday: I didn't write a letter each day you will notice. On Saturday night after I'd written to you I went to bed and had a fine night. I've got the top bunk and really I don't know if I was supposed to be able to spring right into it but I tried and couldn't so had to ring for the steward to bring me some steps. They seem to be short of everything so I had to wait quite a while. He tried to persuade me to jump in but I'm too heavy behind."

Jane MacFarquhar, of Stratford, Connecticut, traveling with her daughter, Grace, sixteen; second class: "I think a happier company of passengers would be impossible to find. They were of all ages: a large number of babies in their mothers' arms, children of various ages and men and women up to the age of seventy.

"Games were heartily enjoyed on the decks during the daytime and concerts were enjoyed in the evenings—sunshine and happiness making thoughts of danger almost impossible."

CHARLES LAURIAT: "As the days passed the passengers seemed to enjoy them more and more, and formed those acquaintances such as one does on an ocean crossing."

DOROTHY CONNER, twenty-five, of Medford, Oregon, in first class: "I'd never seen a more uneventful or stupid voyage."

THE ORION SAILS

O N TUESDAY, MAY 4, THE ADMIRALTY DECIDED IT could no longer hold the HMS *Orion* at Devonport but took precautions to make sure the superdreadnought made it safely to the fleet's base at Scapa Flow.

Admiral Oliver ordered the ship to depart that night, under cover of darkness, and gave strict instructions that it sail 50 miles west past the Scilly Islands before turning north and then keep at least 100 miles out to sea for the remainder of the voyage up the Irish coast. He also assigned four destroyers—HMS *Laertes*, *Moorsom*, *Myngs*, and *Boyne*—to provide an escort until the *Orion* reached deep ocean.

A succession of reports to the Admiralty provided a step-by-step account of the *Orion*'s progress, including changes in speed. It was the most closely watched ship on the high seas.

The Admiralty's telegraphic records show no reference made at all to the *Lusitania*, by now four days into its voyage and halfway across the Atlantic.

IN LONDON, at the Admiralty's War Room, messages arrived reporting fresh submarine sightings and new attacks. On the morning of Sunday, May 2, a French ship, the *Europe*, was torpedoed and sunk off the Scillies. A lighthouse keeper elsewhere reported spotting a "steamer chased by submarine." An Admiralty collier, the *Fulgent*, was torpedoed off the Skelling Rocks west of Ireland; nine members of its crew were rescued and landed at Galway on Monday evening. Early on the morning of Tuesday, May 4, an observer reported spotting a submarine on the surface northwest of Frenchman's Rock in the Scillies. He watched it move east, then dive. That same morning, at 3:15 A.M., a coast watcher reported a "large sheet of flame" rising from the sea off County Mayo.

But in Room 40, Commander Hope and his code breakers heard nothing new from Kptlt. Walther Schwieger. The submarine was too far from Germany to attempt wireless communication. Room 40 could only presume that Schwieger was still on his way to his patrol zone in the Irish Sea.

It was a curious moment in the history of naval warfare. Room 40 knew a U-boat was heading south to Liverpool—knew the boat's history; knew that it was now somewhere in the North Atlantic under orders to sink troop transports and any other British vessel it encountered; and knew as well that the submarine was armed with enough shells and torpedoes to sink a dozen ships. It was like knowing that a particular killer was loose on the streets of London, armed with a particular weapon, and certain to strike in a particular neighborhood within the next few days, the only unknown being exactly when.

The quiet meant nothing. At some point U-20 would make its presence known.

FRUSTRATION

AT 7:40 P.M., TUESDAY, SCHWIEGER AT LAST SIGHTED the coast of Ireland. A lighthouse lay on the horizon, barely visible in the rising mist.

The day had been a disappointment. Strong swells had made the going uncomfortable for the crew below, and Schwieger had found no targets worthy of attack. An armed trawler briefly had come into view, but he realized its draft was so shallow that a torpedo would likely run underneath its keel. Visibility had been poor for most of the day, though by evening it improved to the point where he could see distant objects. The gathering haze, however, foretold a night of fog.

Fifteen minutes later, a steamship appeared, heading in U-20's direction. It was still far off but looked to be a vessel of significant tonnage. Schwieger ordered a dive to periscope depth and prepared his attack. He placed U-20 at a 90-degree angle to the ship's course, to set up what he called a "clean bow shot," and once again selected a bronze torpedo.

As the ship approached, however, it seemed to shrink in size. Something about the fading light and mist had produced an optical illusion that made the vessel at first look large, but the closer it got, the smaller it got. Schwieger estimated its tonnage at a mere 1,500 tons. Still, it was something. He maneuvered so that when the ship's course intersected his, he would be just 300 meters away. The target was still a mile off.

And then, as he watched through the periscope, the ship sheered from its course. At that distance, there was no chance for him to catch up.

Even in the spare prose of his log, Schwieger's frustration was evident. "It was impossible that the steamer could have seen us," he wrote. He identified the ship as a Swedish vessel, the *Hibernia*, "with neutral signs, without flag."

Schwieger brought U-20 back to the surface, and continued south, through a night he described as being exceptionally dark.

COMFORT DENIED

O N THAT WEDNESDAY, MAY 5, BRITAIN'S TOP NAVAL official, Winston Churchill, First Lord of the Admiralty, left London for Paris. He could do so with relative safety because a combination of protective measures—sea mines and submarine nets at the eastern end of the English Channel and heavy patrols along its length—had made the channel too dangerous for submarines to traverse on a routine basis. Although Churchill traveled incognito and checked into his hotel under a false name, there was little mystery about his visit. He was to meet with Italian and French officials to determine how the Italian navy should be used in the Mediterranean Sea, now that Italy—on April 26—had joined the war on the side of Britain, France, and Russia. Afterward, as he had done on previous occasions, Churchill planned to travel to the front to spend time with Field Marshal Sir John French—Sir John Denton Pinkstone French—commander of the British Expeditionary Force in France.

With Churchill absent, the Admiralty became a much quieter place. Ordinarily, he kept a very close hand on naval matters, including details of day-to-day operations that, at least in theory, were supposed to be left to the number two Admiralty official, the First Sea Lord. This put the forty-year-old Churchill in direct conflict with the seventy-four-year-old occupant of that post, Adm. Jacky Fisher.

If Churchill resembled a bulldog, Fisher was a large bulb-eyed toad, dead ringer for a future actor named László Löwenstein, better known by the stage name Peter Lorre. Like Churchill, Fisher was strong-willed and tended to consume himself with the minute details of naval operations. When both men were present, tension was the order of the day. One naval official wrote to his wife, "The situation is curious—two very strong and clever men, one old, wily and of vast experience, one young, self-assertive, with a great self-satisfaction but unstable. They cannot work together, they cannot both run the show." Churchill seemed bent on usurping Fisher's role. Churchill's "energy and capacity for work were almost frightening," wrote intelligence chief Blinker Hall. "Notes and memoranda on every conceivable subject would stream forth from his room at all hours of the day and night. What was worse, he would demand information which would ordinarily and properly have gone only to the First Sea Lord or Chief of Staff, a fact which more than once led to some confusion and an unmerited word of rebuke."

What made their relationship still more turbulent was the fact that Fisher seemed to be tottering on the verge of madness. Wrote Hall, "Gradually we in the Admiralty could not help becoming aware that the Fisher we had known was no longer with us. In his place was a sorely harassed and disillusioned man who was overtaxing his strength in the attempt to carry on. He might still on occasion show the old flashes of brilliance, but, beneath the surface, all was far from being well. . . . At any moment, we felt, the breaking-point would come." Admiral Jellicoe, commander of the Grand Fleet, likewise grew concerned. "The state of affairs at Head Quarters," he wrote, in an April 26 letter to a fellow officer, "is as bad or worse than I feared. It is lamentable that things should be as they are, and there is no doubt whatever that the Fleet is rapidly losing confidence in the administration."

Churchill acknowledged Fisher's energy and prior genius. "But he was seventy-four years old," Churchill wrote, in an oblique evisceration. "As in a great castle which has long contended with time, the mighty central mass of the donjon towered up intact and seemingly everlasting. But the outworks and the battlements had fallen away, and its imperious ruler dwelt only in the special apartments and corridors with which he had a lifelong familiarity." This, however, was exactly what Churchill had hoped for in bringing Fisher back as First Sea Lord. "I took him because I knew he was <u>old</u> and <u>weak</u>, and that I should be able to keep things in my own hands."

By May 1915, Churchill wrote, Fisher was suffering from "great nervous exhaustion." With Churchill gone to Paris, Fisher was in charge and seemed barely up to the task. "He had evinced unconcealed distress and anxiety at being left alone in sole charge of the admiralty," Churchill wrote. "There is no doubt that the old Admiral was worried almost out of his wits by the immense pressure of the times and by the course events had taken."

In Churchill's absence, an incident took place that seemed to reinforce his concerns about Fisher's sanity. Before leaving for France, Churchill had told his wife, Clementine, "Just look after 'the old boy' for me," and so Clementine invited Fisher to come to lunch. She neither liked nor trusted Fisher and doubted he could withstand the stress of having to run the Admiralty in her husband's absence. The lunch went well, however, and Fisher departed. Or so Clementine thought.

Soon afterward, she too left the sitting room, and found that Fisher was still in the house, "lurking in the passage," according to an account by the Churchills' daughter Mary. Clementine was startled, Mary recalled. "She asked him what he wanted, whereupon, in a brusque and somewhat incoherent manner he told her that, while she no doubt was under the impression that Winston was conferring with Sir John French, he was in fact frolicking with a mistress in Paris!"

To Clementine, this was a ludicrous charge. She snapped, "Be quiet, you silly old man, and get out."

With Churchill in Paris, the torrent of notes and telegrams he generated daily—"the constant bombardment of memoranda and minutes on every conceivable subject, technical or otherwise," as Fisher's assistant described it—abruptly subsided. Relative to the turmoil that ordinarily existed in its halls, the Admiralty now became quiescent, if not to say inattentive.

AT THE U.S. EMBASSY in Berlin, Ambassador James W. Gerard received a curt, two-paragraph note from the German Foreign Office. The message, dated Wednesday, May 5, cited the fact that in preceding weeks "it has repeatedly occurred" that neutral ships had been sunk by German submarines in the designated war zone. In one case, the note said, a U-boat sank a neutral ship "on account of the inadequate illumination of its neutral markings in the darkness."

The note urged Gerard to convey these facts to Washington and to recommend that the United States "again warn American shipping circles against traversing the war zone without taking due precautions." Ships, the note said, should be sure to make their neutral markings "as plain as possible and especially to have them illuminated promptly at nightfall and throughout the night."

Gerard relayed this to the State Department the next day.

IN WASHINGTON, President Wilson found himself in emotional turmoil, for reasons unrelated to ships and war.

By now he had fallen ever more deeply in love with Edith Galt, and with the prospect of no longer being alone. On the evening of Tuesday, May 4, Wilson sent his Pierce-Arrow to pick up Edith and bring her to the White House for dinner. She wore a white satin gown with "creamy lace, and just a touch of emerald-green velvet at the edge of the deep square neck, and green slippers to match," she recalled. Afterward, Wilson led her out onto the South Portico, where they sat by themselves, without chaperone. The evening was warm, the air fragrant with the rich perfume of a Washington spring. He told her he loved her.

She was stunned. "Oh, you can't love me," she said, "for you don't really know me; and it is less than a year since your wife died."

Wilson, unfazed, said, "I was afraid, knowing you, that I would shock you," he said, "but I would be less than a gentleman if I continued to make opportunities to see you without telling you what I have told my daughters and Helen: that I want you to be my wife."

So not just love, itself a striking declaration—but marriage.

Edith turned him down. She leavened her rejection with a note she composed later that night, after Wilson dropped her at her apartment. "It is long past midnight," she wrote, early Wednesday morning, May 5. "I have been sitting in the big chair by the window, looking out into the night, ever since you went away, my whole being is awake and vibrant!"

She told him that his expression of love and confession of loneliness had left her anguished. "How I want to help! What an unspeakable pleasure and privilege I deem it to be allowed to share these tense, terrible days of responsibility, how I thrill to my very finger tips when I remember the tremendous thing you said to me tonight, and how pitifully poor I am, to have nothing to offer you in return. Nothing—I mean—in proportion to your own great gift!"

Here she joined the universal struggle shared by men and women throughout time, to temper rejection so as not to lose a friend forever.

"I am a woman—and the thought that you have <u>need</u> of me—is sweet!" she wrote. "But, dear kindred spirit, can you not trust me and let me lead you from the thought that you have forfeited anything by your fearless honesty to the conviction that, with such frankness between us, there is nothing to fear—we will help and hearten each other."

She added, "You have been honest with me, and, perhaps, I was too frank with you—but if so forgive me!"

Later that morning, with the sun up and the day under way, Edith and Helen Bones went for another walk in Rock Creek Park. They sat on some rocks to rest. Helen glared at Edith and said, "Cousin Woodrow looks really ill this morning." Helen loved her cousin and was protective of him. She nicknamed him "Tiger," not because of some lascivious bent, but because, as Edith later told the story, "he was so pathetic caged there in the White House, longing to come and go, as she did, that he reminded her of a splendid Bengal tiger she had once seen—never still, moving, restless, resentful of his bars that shut out the larger life God had made for him." Now, in the park, Helen burst into tears. "Just as I thought some happiness was coming into his life!" she said. "And now you are breaking his heart."

In a strangely cinematic intervention, Dr. Grayson suddenly appeared from a nearby stand of trees, riding a horse—a large white horse no less. He asked Helen what had happened, and she quickly answered that she had tripped and fallen. "I don't think he believed her," Edith wrote, "but he pretended to and rode on."

His arrival was a timely thing, she added, "for I was starting to feel like a criminal, and guilty of base ingratitude." She tried to explain to Helen that she wasn't being an "ogre"; rather, she simply could not "consent to something I did not feel." She told Helen that she understood she was "playing with fire where [Wilson] was concerned, for his whole nature was intense and did not willingly wait; but that I must have time really to know my own heart."

Edith's rejection caused Wilson great sorrow and left him feeling almost disoriented as world events clamored for his attention. Even Britain had become a growing source of irritation. In its drive to halt the flow of war matériel to Germany, British warships had stopped American ships and seized American cargoes. Early in the war Wilson had grown concerned that Britain's actions might so outrage the American public as to cause serious conflict between the two nations. Diplomacy eased tensions, for a time. But then on March 11, 1915, in response to Germany's "war zone" declaration of the preceding month, the British government issued a new, and startling, "Order in Council" proclaiming its formal intent to stop every ship sailing to or from Germany, whether neutral or not, and to stop ships bound even for neutral ports, to determine whether their cargoes might ultimately end up in German hands. Britain also sharply increased the list of products it would henceforth view as contraband. The order outraged Wilson, who sent a formal protest in which he described Britain's plan as "an almost unqualified denial of the sovereign rights of the nations now at peace."

The note achieved nothing. Complaints poured in from American shippers whose cargoes had been detained or confiscated, although the State Department did succeed in securing the prompt release of an automobile shipped by an American socialite. For the British the stakes were simply too high to allow compromise. As Britain's ambassador to America, Cecil Spring Rice, had written the previous fall, "In the life and death struggle in which we are now engaged it is essential to prevent war supplies reaching the German armies and factories."

America's neutrality seemed harder and harder to maintain. In a letter to a female friend, Mary Hulbert, Wilson wrote, "Together England and Germany are likely to drive us crazy, because it looks oftentimes as if they were crazy themselves, the unnecessary provocations they invent."

Still, Wilson recognized the fundamental difference that existed between how the two sides executed their campaigns against merchant traffic. The Royal Navy behaved in civil fashion and often paid for the contraband it seized; Germany, on the other hand, seemed increasingly willing to sink merchant ships without warning, even those bearing neutral markings. The torpedo attack on the *Gulflight* was a case in point. Within the State Department, Undersecretary Robert Lansing warned that in light of the *Gulflight* attack the United States was duty bound to adhere to Wilson's February declaration vowing to hold Germany "to a strict accountability" for its actions. Wilson made no public comment, but he and Secretary of State Bryan, in background conversations with reporters, signaled that the administration would treat the incident in judicious fashion. "No formal diplomatic action will be taken by the United States Government . . . until all the facts have been ascertained and a determination reached," the *New York Times* reported in a front-page story on Wednesday, May 5.

In fact, Wilson found the *Gulflight* incident disquieting. This was an American ship; the attack had killed three men. What's more, it had occurred without warning. While the incident didn't strike Wilson as having the magnitude to draw the nation into war, it did demand some kind of protest. That Wednesday, he cabled his friend Colonel House, still in London, to ask his advice on what kind of response to send to Germany.

House recommended "a sharp note" but added, "I am afraid a more serious breach may at any time occur, for they seem to have no regard for consequences."

THE MANIFEST

A BOARD THE *LUSITANIA*, THE *CUNARD DAILY BULLETIN* kept passengers abreast of war news but, like its counterparts on land, reported only broad movements of forces, as if war were a game played with tiles and dice, not flesh-and-blood men. These reports did not begin to capture the reality of the fighting then unfolding on the ground, particularly in the Dardanelles, where the Allied naval and ground offensive had stalled and British and French forces had dug trenches that mimicked those on the western front.

The most terrifying part of battle was the exit from a trench—standing up and climbing out, knowing that the opposing force would at that moment unleash a fusillade that would continue until the offensive concluded, either with victory, meaning a few yards gained, or defeat, a few yards lost, but invariably with half one's battalion dead, wounded, or missing. "I shall never forget the moment when we had to leave the shelter of the trenches," wrote British private Ridley Sheldon, of combat at Helles, at the southwest tip of the Gallipoli Peninsula. "It is indeed terrible, the first step you take—right into the face of the most deadly fire, and to realize that any moment you may be shot down; but if you are not hit, then you seem to gather courage. And when you see on either side of you men like yourself, it inspires you with a determination to press forward. Away we went over the parapet with fixed bayonets—one line of us like the wind. But it was absolute murder, for men fell like corn before the sickle."

The wounded lay in the open or in shell holes awaiting stretcher bearers who might not come for hours, or even days. Injuries ranged from minor penetrations by shrapnel to grotesque disfigurements. "I got back into the trench, and saw what I had not seen before, for the smoke had cleared now," wrote Capt. Albert Mure, also on Helles. A shell had just landed in his trench, in the spot where moments earlier he had been writing messages to be delivered by two orderlies. One orderly survived, the other did not. "His body and his head lay 4 or 5 feet apart. Two of my signalers were killed also, and mutilated so horribly that to describe their condition would be inexcusable."

Elsewhere at Helles, Sgt. Denis Moriarty and his First Royal Munster Fusiliers fought off a Turkish assault that began at ten o'clock at night. "They crept right up to our trenches, they were in thousands, and they made the night hideous with yells and shouting, 'Allah, Allah!' We could not help mowing them down." Some managed to reach Moriarty's trench. "When the Turks got to close quarters the devils used hand grenades and you could only recognize our dead by their identity discs. My God, what a sight met us when day broke this morning." By the time the Allied invading force would finally be evacuated, in January 1916, some 265,000 Allied troops and 300,000 Turks would be dead, wounded, or missing.

Men in the ships massed offshore fared little better. The armada was an impressive one—hundreds of vessels, ranging from minesweepers to giant dreadnoughts. But many were in easy range of Turkish artillery embedded in high ground, which dropped thousands of tons of high explosives onto their decks. The French battleship *Suffren* was struck by a shell that destroyed a gun turret and ignited a fire deep within its hull; another shell destroyed its forward funnel. Rear Adm. Émile Guépratte descended from the bridge to survey the damage and bolster the morale of his sailors. "The scene," he wrote, "was tragically macabre: the image of desolation, the flames spared nothing. As for our young men, a few minutes ago, so alert, so self-confident, all now [lay] dead on the bare deck, blackened burnt skeletons, twisted in all directions, no trace of any clothing, the fire having devoured all."

Aboard the *Lusitania*, there was quiet. There were books, and cigars, and fine foods, afternoon tea, and the easy cadence of shipboard life: strolling the deck, chatting at the rails, doing crochet, and just sitting still in a deck chair in the sea breeze. Now and then a ship appeared in the distance; closer at hand, whales.

BACK IN New York, on Wednesday, May 5, Cunard at last provided the customs office with the *Lusitania*'s full cargo manifest. Unlike the initial one-page version filed by Captain Turner before departure, this "Supplemental Manifest" was twenty-four pages long and listed over three hundred consignments.

Here were muskrat skins, nuts, beeswax, bacon, salt brick, dental goods, cases of lard, and barrels of beef tongues; machinery from the Otis Elevator Company; and enough candy—157 barrels of it—to populate the fantasies of all the schoolchildren in Liverpool. The manifest also listed one case of "Oil Paintings," these accompanying first-class passenger Sir Hugh Lane, a Dublin art collector. To identify this consignment merely as oil paintings was an understatement. The paintings were insured for $4 million (about $92 million today) and were rumored to have included works by Rubens, Monet, Titian, and Rembrandt.

More problematic, but entirely legal under U.S. neutrality laws, were the 50 barrels and 94 cases of aluminum powder and 50 cases of bronze powder, both highly flammable under certain conditions, as well as 1,250 cases of shrapnel-laden artillery shells made by the Bethlehem Steel Company, bound for the British army, and badly needed on the western front, where British forces were hampered by a severe shortage of artillery ammunition. (Wrote Churchill, "The army in France was firing away shells at a rate which no military administration had ever been asked to sustain.") The shrapnel shells were essentially inert. They contained only a minimum bursting charge; their associated fuses were packed separately and stored elsewhere. The cartridges that held the powerful explosives needed to propel the shells from a gun were *not* among the ship's cargo; these would be attached later, at an arsenal in Britain.

Also aboard, according to the manifest, were 4,200 cases of Remington rifle ammunition, amounting to 170 tons.

AT LAST

Throughout the morning of Wednesday, May 5, heavy fog lingered over the sea off Ireland. From 4:00 A.M. on, every time Schwieger checked on the weather through his periscope all he saw was a dark opacity. He held U-20 on a southerly course and kept its speed slow, probably about 5 knots, to conserve battery power. At 8:25 A.M. Schwieger gauged visibility as good enough to bring the boat to the surface, though banks of fog persisted all around him.

His crew now decoupled the two electric engines and engaged the diesels to bring U-20 to cruising speed and recharge the batteries. Somewhere off to his left, in the murk, was the southwest coast of Ireland, here a phalanx of stone cliffs jutting into the North Atlantic. He would soon pass Valentia Island, where the British had built a powerful wireless transmitter. Schwieger's own wireless man would by now be picking up strong signals from the Valentia tower, but could not read the codes in which they were sent.

U-20 moved through curtains of fog. By 12:50 P.M. Schwieger believed himself to be abreast of the Fastnet Rock, though he could not see it. The rock was one of Britain's most prominent maritime landmarks, a road sign to the Western Approaches. Irish immigrants in the nineteenth century knew it as "Ireland's Teardrop" because it was the last bit of Ireland they saw before their ships entered the North Atlantic en route to America. Here Schwieger ordered a left turn, to begin sailing along Ireland's south coast toward Liverpool. This was the upper edge of a great funnel of ocean called the Celtic Sea, where inbound ships converged from north, west, and south. It was the perfect hunting ground for a U-boat, but Schwieger saw nothing.

He wrote, "During the whole afternoon no steamer sighted in spite of the clearing weather, although we found ourselves within one of the main shipping lanes."

Visibility improved. Soon Schwieger was able to see the Irish coast, but only for a few moments. Over the next three hours, U-20 cruised on the surface and encountered no ships of any kind. The evening haze began to gather once again.

Just before five o'clock, while off the coast of County Cork, Schwieger spotted what at first seemed to be a large square-rigged sailing ship. In the haze, it cut a lovely figure, its three masts billowing with canvas. Unlike other U-boat commanders, who sank such ships with reluctance, Schwieger was unmoved. He saw a target. U-20 turned toward the ship, and Schwieger's men loaded and aimed its deck gun.

As Schwieger got closer, he saw that once again the light and haze had deceived him. The ship did have three masts, but it was only a small schooner. He signaled the vessel to stop. Although he had fired on ships many times without warning, here he returned, briefly, to cruiser rules. "As no danger existed for our boat in approaching," he wrote, "we made for the stern of the sailer."

He ordered the schooner's captain and four-man crew to abandon ship and bring its registry and cargo manifest over to U-20. The schooner proved to be the *Earl of Lathom*, out of Liverpool, carrying rocks from Limerick. It weighed all of 99 tons.

As the schooner's crew began rowing away, Schwieger ordered his men at the gun to begin firing at the schooner's waterline. Despite its small size and decidedly nonbuoyant cargo, the vessel proved a stubborn target. Shot after shot boomed across the sea and exploded against its hull. Schwieger's gun crew needed twelve shells to sink it.

—⁓—

SEVERAL HOURS later, as dusk and fog gathered, Schwieger found another target. A steamship emerged from the fog, very near—too close to allow Schwieger to prepare an attack. He turned U-20 away, to gain sea room, but kept the boat on the surface. The steamship stopped, apparently expecting an examination under cruiser rules.

Outwardly, the vessel weighed about 3,000 tons and seemed to be Norwegian, but Schwieger and his pilot, Lanz, sensed something amiss. The markings were unusually high on the hull, and Schwieger suspected they might have been painted onto tarpaulins.

Schwieger maneuvered for a torpedo attack. He ordered a bronze torpedo, set to run at a depth of 8 feet. When U-20 was about 330 yards away from the steamer, Schwieger gave the order to fire.

He missed.

The bubbles rising to the surface from the torpedo's compressed-air engine revealed its path. As the torpedo track moved toward the target, the ship began a sudden acceleration and veered away. As best Schwieger could tell, the torpedo went past or under the stern.

Now it was Schwieger's turn to flee. He feared the ship might be armed. "After the shot I turned around hard and ran away in order to avoid the danger of being fired upon," he wrote. "For this reason I did not consider a second attack. Steamer disappeared quickly in the fog."

In his log entry at 8:10 that night, he contemplated what had occurred. The torpedo had seemed to lose speed as it approached the target, he wrote. "I had considered a miss out of the question, even after the torpedo had been fired, considering our favorable position and the fact that [the] steamer could not make much headway." Remarkably the ship had then managed to accelerate from a dead stop to make its escape.

Over the next hour the dense fog returned and once again forced Schwieger to submerge. This was the end of his sixth day at sea, and all he had sunk was a 99-ton sailboat.

SIGHTING

From: Head of Kinsale
To: Admiralty

May 5, 1915

Sent 7:55 p.m.
Received 8:52 p.m.

Small boat containing five men South East one
mile hoisted oar with a garment attached. Steam
drifter D 145 took crew on board making Kinsale.
Coast Guard Kinsale informed.

SCHWIEGER REVEALED

IRST CAME A REPORT OF GUNFIRE IN THE FOG, SENT ON the evening of Wednesday, May 5, from a station perched on the Old Head of Kinsale, a promontory that jutted into the Celtic Sea near Queenstown, Ireland. The Old Head was well known to mariners, who often used it to fix their locations.

Kinsale followed this message with a report that a schooner, the *Earl of Lathom*, had been sunk off the Old Head. This was relayed to Blinker Hall and First Sea Lord Fisher, temporarily in charge of the Admiralty. Churchill was expected to arrive in Paris by midnight. The new message, received in London at 10:46 P.M. and noted in a record of U-20's travels compiled by Room 40, stated that the schooner's crew had been rescued and brought to Kinsale. The crew reported that when they had last seen the submarine it was heading southeast toward a large steamer.

At about the same time another telegram reached the Admiralty, this from the Naval Center at Queenstown. The captain of a British ship, the *Cayo Romano*, was reporting that a torpedo had been fired at his vessel off Fastnet Rock. He never saw the submarine that fired it. This too was noted in Room 40 and relayed to Hall and Fisher.

Now came a fourth message, also circulated, that a submarine had been sighted 12 miles south of the Daunt Rock Light, a lightship anchored outside the entrance to Queenstown Harbor. The time of the sighting was 9:30 P.M.

By comparing the locations of these attacks with previously intercepted wireless reports, it should have become obvious to someone—to Chief of Staff Oliver, Captain Hall, or Fisher—that the U-boat involved was Kptlt. Walther Schwieger's U-20 and that Schwieger was now operating in the heart of one of Britain's primary sea-lanes. A detailed record of U-20's travels kept by Room 40 included a precise location for that evening, "51.32 N, 8.22 W." These coordinates put the U-boat just south-southeast of the Old Head of Kinsale.

The Admiralty was well aware the *Lusitania* would soon traverse these same waters but made no effort to provide specifics of the night's events directly to Captain Turner. Meanwhile, the closely watched HMS *Orion* continued on its course to Scapa Flow, guarded all the while by the four destroyers assigned as escorts. They accompanied the dreadnought until it was safely in the Atlantic and heading north before beginning their own return voyages. At that point the four destroyers were within range of U-20's last position and the path the *Lusitania* soon would follow on its way to Liverpool. No attempt was made to divert the destroyers. One, the HMS *Boyne*, went directly back to Devonport; the other three returned via the Scilly Islands.

The *Orion* continued north on a zigzag course, at 18 knots, a speed deemed more than sufficient to outrun a U-boat.

NOW FIVE DAYS into its voyage, the *Lusitania* made its way toward Britain alone, with no escort offered or planned, and no instruction to take the newly opened and safer North Channel route—this despite the fact that the ship carried a valuable cache of rifle cartridges and desperately needed shrapnel shells.

The absence of any protective measures may simply have been the result of a lapse of attention, with Churchill off in France and Fisher consumed by other matters and seemingly drifting toward madness. It would take on a more sinister cast, however, in light of a letter that Churchill had sent earlier in the year to the head of England's Board of Trade, Walter Runciman, in which Churchill wrote that it was "most important to attract neutral shipping to our shores, in the hopes especially of embroiling the United States with Germany."

Though no one said it explicitly, Britain hoped the United States would at some point feel moved to join the Allies, and in so doing tip the balance irrevocably in their favor.

After noting that Germany's submarine campaign had sharply reduced traffic from America, Churchill told Runciman: "For our part, we want the traffic—the more the better; and if some of it gets into trouble, better still."

HELPFUL YOUNG LADIES

A T 5:30 A.M., THURSDAY, MAY 6, PASSENGERS IN FIRST-class staterooms arrayed along the port side of the *Lusitania*'s boat deck—A Deck—heard a commotion outside. Theodate Pope, in A-10, recalled being "wakened by shouts and the scuffling of feet." Metal clanked against metal; ropes moved through squealing tackle. All this was mingled with muffled curses and the sounds of men working at a task requiring strength, which the crew possessed, and coordination, which it did not.

With the ship about a day away from entering the Celtic Sea, Captain Turner had ordered the crew to uncover and swing out all the ship's conventional lifeboats, meaning those that hung from davits along both sides of the boat deck. The two emergency boats were already in position.

Turner was being prudent. If an emergency were to occur, the boats could be launched from this position more quickly, and with less hazard, than if they were still locked in their deep-sea positions. At this hour, few passengers would be out on deck and thus would be less likely to interfere with the effort or, worse, be injured, though Turner risked causing annoyance by awakening them so early—and these were some of the most expensive staterooms on the ship.

Third Officer John Lewis, who ran the daily lifeboat drills, also directed this operation. First, he said, "we mustered the cooks, the stewards, the watch of sailors on deck, and any other day men that we could raise." The crew began with the boats on the port side. Lewis climbed to the navigation deck and positioned himself at its midpoint, outside the Marconi room, so that he could monitor the entire operation at once. Six to eight men were assigned to each boat. To avoid tangled falls and guy lines, all the boats had to be swung out at once, according to Lewis. Next, the men—some eighty in all—shifted to the starboard side and repeated the process. Lewis then dismissed the cooks and stewards, but ordered the deck crew to secure the guy lines and pile the falls in tidy "Flemish" coils. Last, he had the men make sure that each boat contained its required complement of survival gear, including oars, mast, sails, matches, sea anchor, lamp, provisions, and drinking water.

The process did not go smoothly. First-class passenger Joseph Myers, up early, watched the crew work. "The men were not efficient," he said. "I saw them trying to throw out the boats, trying to break away the boats from the davits, and it seemed to me that they were not equal to it. They were clumsy handling the ropes. They were bossed by some petty officer; I don't know who it was but the men did not look to me as if they had been handling the boats before. They handled the ropes and falls like men building a house; they looked more like day laborers than seamen."

Passengers who awoke later that morning were greeted by the sight of all the boats swung out and uncovered, with no explanation posted. For most the change was of minor interest; some may not even have noticed. For others, it was disconcerting. "On Thursday morning I felt rather uneasy when I discovered that the lifeboats were hung over the side of the ship," wrote Jane MacFarquhar, of Stratford, Connecticut. "On inquiry, I was informed that it was essential that they should be so—according to law. I thought it rather strange that they had not been put ready after clearing New York instead of waiting until we were so near the other side. I noticed the other passengers did not seem to bother, so I also began to forget the lifeboats."

Nellie Huston, adding a few more paragraphs to her diary-like letter, wrote, "This morning we have all the lifeboats swung out ready for emergencies. It's awful to think about but I guess there is some danger." She noted that she and fellow passengers expected British naval vessels to rendezvous with the ship that day, to provide escort.

She switched to cheerier observations. "What a crowd there are in the boat and all English. I was so pleased to see the Union Jacks on this boat when we were in New York, there are quite a lot of distinguished people in the 1st class but of course you couldn't touch them with a soft pole! There is a Vanderbilt, one or two bankers. I have made lots of friends and if it wasn't for the worry I could say we've had a lovely trip."

THE DECK MEN did the usual "sailoring" to maintain the ship, a process that never ended. Every morning a group of sailors cleaned the brass and glass in the portholes that opened onto the decks. There was always a peek of rust that needed sanding and painting; the brine and dried mist that collected on the deck rails overnight had to be ragged off in the morning, so that the rails shone and did not spoil the dresses and suits of passengers. All the ship's plants had to be watered, including the twenty-one large palm trees that stood at the heads of stairwells. Deck chairs had to be straightened, to avoid the haphazard look of a wedding after all the guests had left.

Seaman Morton was assigned to touch up the paint on the hull of one of the lifeboats. The crew must have swung the boat back in for this, because Morton had to lie underneath to administer the paint. The paint was gray and was known as "crab fat." It was a messy task. "We were not issued with paint brushes, we had instead a swab of waste"—meaning a rag—"and the paint pot into which we dipped the waste and then applied it to the hull of the lifeboat."

Morton was hard at work when he heard the sound of small shoes charging toward him, and looked out from under the boat to see two girls intently watching. These were Anna and Gwendolyn Allan, ages fifteen and sixteen, the two daughters of Lady Hugh

Montagu Allan, of Montreal, one of the ship's most prominent passengers. The three occupied a Regal Suite on B Deck, which included two bedrooms, bathroom, dining room, and parlor. The Allans traveled with two maids, who stayed in a tiny room squeezed between one of the ship's funnels and the dome of the first-class dining salon.

The girls were a popular and vivid presence aboard. "I could not help thinking what lovely children they were and how beautifully dressed," Morton wrote. "I seem to remember the eldest one was wearing a white accordion pleated skirt and sailor blouse."

One girl asked, "What are you doing, sailor?"

Morton answered, "I am painting the lifeboat."

"May we help you?"

Morton noted again the girls' clothing and also the sound of heavier steps quickly approaching—these the footfalls of a woman who appeared to be a nanny. The woman did not look pleased.

Morton said, "I don't think this is a job for little girls."

The eldest girl, clearly accustomed to having her way, grabbed the improvised brush, which was soaked with paint, and started applying it to the boat and in the process applied it to her clothing as well.

"I was horrified," Morton wrote. He heard the still heavier footsteps of his approaching supervisor, the bosun, or senior deck man, "coming along at the double."

The girls fled, and so did Morton. He eased out from under the boat, toward the water, and climbed over the side to the deck below. "I did not feel there was any purpose in stopping to argue the point with either the irate bosun or the extremely angry looking Nannie."

A BOY NAMED Robert Kay missed all the morning's excitement. Kay, seven years old, was an American citizen from the Bronx, in New York City, traveling to England with his British mother, Marguerita Belsher Kay, who was in an advanced phase of pregnancy. She wanted badly to return to her parents' home in England to have the baby and was willing to brave the passage, despite the German warning and her own tendency to get seasick.

By midweek Robert himself had begun to feel poorly. The ship's surgeon examined him and diagnosed a full-blown case of measles. The boy, he said, would have to spend the rest of the voyage in quarantine, two decks down. The Kays were traveling in second class, but his mother chose to go below as well, to room with her son.

The monotony was crushing, but there was, at least, a porthole through which the boy could watch the sea.

CAPTAIN TURNER ordered the usual midmorning lifeboat drill. The team of "picked" crewmen climbed into one of the emergency boats as an audience of passengers looked on. One witness was George Kessler, the "Champagne King," who went up to the sailor in charge, and told him, "It's alright drilling your crew, but why don't you drill your passengers?"

The man replied, "Why not tell Captain Turner, sir?"

Kessler resolved to do so.

SPECTACLE

THURSDAY MORNING, MAY 6, FOUND U-20 ADVANCING slowly along the southwest coast of Ireland, into waters mariners knew as the St. George's Channel. Though the term *channel* connotes a narrow body of water, the St. George's at its broadest was about 90 miles wide, tapering to 45 miles between Carnsore Point on the Irish coast and St. David's Head in Wales. A lightship was anchored at the Irish side to steer ships away from a notorious hazard, the Coningbeg Rock, routinely misspelled by telegraph and wireless operators as Coningberg or Koninbeg. Beyond this point, the waters broadened again to form the Irish Sea, Muir Éireann, with Liverpool another 250 nautical miles to the north and east. Even at Schwieger's best speed of 15 knots, he would need another sixteen hours to reach his assigned patrol zone.

But the weather was not cooperating. Persistent fog had forced him to remain submerged throughout the night. Just before 8:00 A.M., he found signs of clearing and brought the boat to the surface, but did so using only its hydroplanes. He kept the diving tanks filled with seawater in case of emergency. The boat moved through striations of heavy fog.

A steamship appeared ahead, off to starboard. It flew no flag and showed no other indicator of registry. Schwieger ordered his gun crew on deck for a surface attack. Despite the poor visibility, some sharp-eyed soul aboard the steamer spotted the submarine. The ship turned hard and fled at full speed.

Schwieger raced after it, his gun crew firing round after round. Two shells hit the steamer, but it continued to run. The ship entered a fog bank and disappeared from view. Schwieger followed.

Clarity returned. Schwieger's men resumed fire. U-20 was making 15 knots; the steamer probably only 8 to 10. The attack went on for nearly two hours, with U-20 gradually gaining, until one shell struck the target's bridge. This proved persuasive. The steamship stopped and lowered its boats. One foundered, Schwieger saw, but three others pulled away, "full to capacity."

Schwieger brought the submarine closer. He fired a bronze torpedo into the hull, from a distance of 500 meters (550 yards). It exploded at a point opposite what Schwieger believed to be the ship's engine room. "Effect slight," he wrote. The ship sagged at the stern but did not sink.

Schwieger's gun crew began firing at the ship's waterline as he brought U-20 slowly around to its stern. The ship's name had been painted over, but up close Schwieger was able to read it: *Candidate*. His ship-identification book showed it to be a British freighter of about 5,000 tons, owned by the Harrison Line of Liverpool, a company prone to giving ships such romantic names as *Auditor*, *Administrator*, and *Electrician*.

Schwieger's men continued firing until the ship's bow rose high out of the water and the stern began to sink. He recorded the latitude and longitude of the wreck, which put it 20 miles south of the Coningbeg lightship, at about the middle of the narrowest portion of the Saint George's Channel. The time was 10:30 A.M.

Ten minutes later, he sighted another potential target coming over the horizon, this one the biggest yet, on a course that would converge with his. Fog obscured the ship. Schwieger ordered full speed and set a course that he anticipated would put U-20 ahead of the ship and in position to fire a torpedo.

The big steamer burst from the fog, moving fast. Schwieger saw now that it was a passenger liner of about 14,000 tons. A true prize. He ordered a fast dive and raced at the highest speed his battery-powered engines could muster, 9 knots, but this proved not nearly enough. The ship was still 2 miles off and moving at full speed. Schwieger realized that the best he could do would be to position U-20 so that a torpedo would strike the liner at a glancing 20-degree angle—too oblique to be successful. He called off the attack.

Although he didn't name the ship in his log, the liner was the *Arabic*, of the White Star Line, which had owned the *Titanic*.

AN HOUR LATER, shortly before one o'clock, Schwieger spotted yet another target, ahead and to port.

He set up his attack. This time he chose one of the newer G6 torpedoes and ordered its depth set at 3 meters, about 10 feet. He fired from a distance of 300 meters. The torpedo struck the ship at a point below its forward mast. The bow took on water, but the ship stayed afloat. Its crew fled in boats. Schwieger surfaced.

He determined that the vessel was an English freighter, the *Centurion*, about 6,000 tons, owned by the same line that owned the freighter he had sunk earlier in the day.

The fog again began to build. Schwieger did not want to take a chance that the *Centurion* would survive. He fired a second torpedo, "to make foundering sure." This too exploded on contact, and Schwieger heard the telltale hiss of air that fled the ship as water filled its hull. U-boat commanders always found this a satisfying moment. Kapitänleutnant Forstner, in his memoir, described how the air "escapes with a shrill whistle from every possible aperture, and the sound resembles the shriek of a steam siren. This is a wonderful spectacle to behold!" Often at this point stricken ships gave one last exhalation as water filled their boiler rooms, causing a final explosion and releasing a cloud of black smoke and soot, known to U-boat commanders as "the black soul."

Schwieger did not wait to see the ship disappear below the surface. The fog had grown too thick. At 2:15 p.m., he submerged and set a course that would take U-20 well out to sea so that he could recharge its batteries in safety and consider how next to proceed.

Schwieger faced a decision. His fuel was running low—surprisingly so—and he had yet to reach his assigned hunting zone off Liverpool, still nearly a day's voyage away.

LIFE AFTER DEATH

THAT THURSDAY AFTERNOON, THEODATE POPE AND Edwin Friend sat in their deck chairs enjoying the fine weather and blue vista. They were not lovers, but Theodate spent most of her time in Friend's company. While on deck, Friend read aloud to her from a book, Henri Bergson's *Matière et mémoire*, or *Matter and Memory*, published in 1896. Broadly, it dealt with the relationship between mind and body. Bergson, a past president of Britain's Society for Psychical Research, was sympathetic to the idea that some element of an individual persisted after death.

Theodate too was a member of the society, an organization founded in London in 1882, not by crackpots or would-be mediums, but by philosophers, writers, scientists, and journalists who sought to bring the principles of scientific rigor to the investigation of paranormal phenomena. Its membership included dozens of scientific and literary notables, among them H. G. Wells, Mark Twain, William James, and Oliver Lodge, a leading British physicist who would lose his own son to the war in September 1915 and spend the rest of his life trying to reach him beyond the veil. From time to time Theodate had assisted Lodge and James in an investigation of Mrs. Piper, the medium, for which James convened seventy-five séances. The medium's apparent talents so resisted his attempts to debunk her skills that James came to believe she might be legitimate. "If you wish to upset the law that all crows are black," he wrote, famously, "you must not seek to show that no crows are, it is enough if you prove the single crow to be white. My own white crow is Mrs. Piper."

Theodate also participated in séances independently of William James and in an unpublished memoir described a 1909 sitting with another famed medium, Eusapia Palladino, during which Theodate claimed her own turban levitated from her scalp and settled on the table in front of her. Palladino was subsequently proven to be a very talented fraud.

Theodate began serious study of the powers of the mind and the occult in her thirties. In 1900, at thirty-three, she read her first issues of *Proceedings of the Society for Psychical Research*, which included investigations of supposed hauntings and incidences of "survival," the society's preferred term for life after death; the *Proceedings* were also where Sigmund Freud in 1912 published his first detailed articulation of his theory of subconscious thought. Theodate joined the society in 1904 and soon afterward began helping William James with his investigation of Mrs. Piper. (James's brother Henry, though the author of ten ghost stories including *Turn of the Screw*, scorned spiritualism and paranormal dabbling.) In 1907, the year Theodate turned forty, she helped found a new institute for psychical research in New York and contributed $25,000, over $600,000 today. Her traveling companion, Edwin Friend, had been editor of the institute's journal until a decidedly non-astral conflict over what sorts of articles to publish led to his removal. Though only in his twenties, Friend had already received bachelor's and master's degrees from Harvard and had taught classics at Princeton, Harvard, and the University of Berlin. Theodate, angered by his removal, resigned from the institute's board. Her reason for traveling with him now on the *Lusitania* was to visit Oliver Lodge and others in London to seek support for the founding of a wholly new American society.

Bergson's book was in French, but Friend translated as he read. This was no mean feat. *Matter and Memory* was a stupefying read in any language. Yet there they sat, contentedly filling the warm afternoon air with murmured language and knowing smiles, grasping the ungraspable.

"There were passages that illustrated so wonderfully some of the common difficulties in communication," Theodate wrote—and by *communication* she meant contact with the dead. "They were most illuminating and I could see the vividness of the inspiration they were to Mr. Friend; and as we sat side by side in our deck chairs I marveled to myself that such a man as Mr. Friend had been found to carry on the investigations. I felt very deeply the quality of my respect and admiration for him. He was endowed so richly in heart and mind."

She saw Friend as an intellectual helpmate and believed that in coming years he would be an important, albeit platonic, presence in her life.

AMONG THE younger crowd, shipboard life gained a new intensity with the end of the voyage so near. New-made friends asked each other to sign memento books. Flirtations became more flirty; the ongoing sporting competitions more zesty, with prizes offered at the ship's barbershop. The boundaries between families began to blur. Children roamed the deck in packs, led by stewardesses. One stewardess had charge of twenty-two children, whom she watched while their parents dined. Ethel Moore Lamping Lines, thirty-four, traveling with her husband, Stanley, befriended a young couple from Toronto who were on their way home to Scotland with their three children: a toddler and a pair of one-and-a-half-year-old twins. "All around us were nice little growing families," Mrs. Lines wrote, "and all so happy."

She and a friend joked about what to do if the ship were attacked. "Our stewardess laughed," Mrs. Lines recalled, "and said we would not go down, but up, as we were well loaded with munitions."

THAT AFTERNOON, Captain Turner and Staff Captain Anderson toured the ship to make sure all the lifeboats were in fact swung out and ready for lowering. Turner also ordered Anderson to see that all the ship's portholes were closed, up to B Deck, and that all bulkhead doors likewise were closed.

As of noon Thursday, the ship was 465 miles west of Ireland's Fastnet Rock, and moving at 21 knots.

CHANGE OF PLAN

On Thursday afternoon, with U-20 submerged and headed out to sea, Schwieger made his decision: he resolved to abandon his effort to reach Liverpool, despite his orders. Within the culture of U-boat leadership, this was his prerogative. Out of touch with superiors and friendly vessels, only a commander could know how his patrol was unfolding and what threats or challenges he faced. Still, Schwieger devoted nearly a full page of his War Log to his rationale.

The weather was the biggest factor in his decision. The barometer, and the fog that had dogged his course all day and the previous night, and the strangely calm weather—here he used the lovely German word *Windstille*—suggested to him that the fog would linger for days. "The poor visibility," he wrote, "makes it impossible to sight the numerous enemy patrols, trawlers and destroyers, which may be expected in the St. George['s] Channel and the Irish Sea; therefore we will be in constant danger and compelled to travel submerged."

He assumed that any troop transports leaving Liverpool would do so at night, with destroyer escorts. The only way to spot these ships was to remain on the surface, he wrote, but doing so in fog and darkness was too dangerous, both because of the risk of being run over and because the destroyers—fast and heavily armed— could not be spotted in time for him to evade attack.

Also, he had only three torpedoes left, of which he wanted to hold two in reserve for his return journey, standard practice for U-boat commanders.

And then there was the fuel problem. If he continued forward to Liverpool, his supply would run so low that he would be unable to return by the same route that had brought him here. He would be forced to take the North Channel, between Scotland and Ireland. While the route had become much safer for British merchant ships, for U-boats it had become increasingly dangerous. The last time he had gone that way he had encountered heavy patrols and unceasing danger. He vowed not do it again "under any circumstances."

He planned to continue attacking ships, he wrote, but in waters well short of Liverpool, at the entrance to a different passage—the Bristol Channel—through which ships traveled to reach the English port cities of Swansea, Cardiff, and Bristol, "since chances for favorable attacks are better here and enemy defensive measures lesser than in the Irish Sea near Liverpool." Though he had only one torpedo available for immediate use, apart from his two in reserve, he had plenty of shells. He resolved to continue attacks until two-fifths of his remaining fuel was used up.

But once again he was stymied by the weather. At 6:10 that evening he looked through his periscope and again found only fog, with visibility limited to 30 yards in any direction. He continued out to sea, beyond the heaviest lanes of traffic, to spend the night. He planned to surface the next morning, Friday, to run his diesels and recharge his batteries, in preparation for the day's hunting.

MESSAGES

THERE WAS DINNER, OF COURSE, AS ELABORATE AND filling as usual, though now more appreciated, given that this was the second-to-last dinner of the voyage before arrival in Liverpool on Saturday morning.

As the passengers dined, one of the ship's Marconi men picked up a message chattering through the ether. The time was 7:50 P.M. The message, sent *en clair*, meaning in plain English, was from the Admiralty's office in Queenstown, Ireland. The first version must have been distorted, for the *Lusitania*'s operator asked Queenstown to send it again. The repeat was sent at 7:56. Moments later Captain Turner had the message in hand: "Submarines active off South Coast of Ireland."

At about the same time the ship received another message, this one directed to all British ships and sent in a special Admiralty code reserved for merchant vessels. Once decoded, it too was delivered to Turner. The message warned ships in the English Channel to stay within 2 miles of England's southern coast but ordered those ships en route to Liverpool to avoid headlands, stay in midchannel, pass the entrances to harbors at high speed, and finally take on a harbor pilot at the Mersey Bar to guide them to their wharves in Liverpool. The message ended: "Submarines off Fastnet."

Coming one after the other, the two messages were disconcerting—and confusing. The second seemed to contradict itself. On the one hand, it advised ships in the English Channel to stay close to shore. On the other, it recommended that ships on Turner's route stay in midchannel. It urged captains to race past harbors, but at the same time told them to stop and pick up a pilot at the entrance to the Mersey River. Nor did these messages offer any clue as to the actual number of submarines or their precise locations. The waters off the south coast of Ireland formed an immense expanse of ocean. The phrase "submarines off Fastnet" could mean half a mile or a hundred miles. Together, the two messages suggested waters teeming with U-boats.

For Captain Turner, one fact was certain: the *Lusitania* would be passing the Fastnet Rock the next morning and would be off the south coast of Ireland for the remainder of the voyage to Liverpool.

AFTER DINNER, Preston Prichard led the night's "whist drive" in the second-class lounge, while in first class the evening concert got under way. The night's program has vanished from history, but one passenger reportedly dressed up as Bonnie Prince Charlie, in full Highland regalia, and sang six Scottish songs. On past voyages, passengers recited poetry, displayed their skills at "legerdemain," read aloud from books, and gave "comic recitations"; they sang songs like "Down by the Old Mill Stream," "Genevieve," and "Tip Top Tipperary Mary"; and they showed off their instrumental talents, with solos on the euphonium and mandolin and cello—Godard's "Berceuse d'Jocelyn" and Schumann's "Traumerei." There was one regular feature: each concert ended with the audience standing to sing "God Save the King" and its American cousin, "My Country 'Tis of Thee." Same tune, very different lyrics.

It was here, during intermission, that Turner stepped forward to offer his sobering remarks about submarines and the war zone and assured the audience they would soon be securely in the embrace of the Royal Navy.

While the concert was under way, a team of officers conducted a night inspection of the ship, another measure prompted by the submarine threat. In addition to wanting all portholes closed, Captain Turner now ordered that they all be curtained to prevent the escape of light, and that all doors that led to outside decks be closed. Turner also turned off the ship's running lights.

The inspection team, led by Senior Third Mate John Lewis, checked all the portholes and windows in public rooms throughout the ship, and those that could be examined from the decks, but Cunard rules forbade the men from entering staterooms. The inspection team left a list of open portholes for the room stewards, tucked into a corridor light fixture. Passengers had been instructed to keep their portholes closed, but the weather was so mild that many opened them for ventilation.

Book dealer Charles Lauriat made it his business to observe the inspections and other shipboard operations. "I was keenly interested in all that was done aboard ship as we approached the Irish Coast," he wrote, "and in fact all through the voyage I kept my eyes unusually wide open." That Thursday night, as he walked to his room on B Deck—which, being an interior room, did not have a porthole—he saw the list of open portholes, "stuck right in the lantern as you walk along the passageway."

Captain Turner's concern about open portholes was shared by all captains, whether in peace or war. A porthole was just what its name indicated: a hole in the side of a ship. Under certain conditions, a single open porthole could admit water at a rate of 3.75 tons a minute.

THAT EVENING a group of passengers got together and formed a committee to teach one another how to put on the new "Boddy" life jackets, "these being of a different pattern from the usual cork waistcoat," said passenger Arthur J. Mitchell, a representative of the Raleigh Cycle Company. Mitchell had reason to be concerned. In his travels thus far he had survived two shipwrecks.

Captain Turner approved the idea, Mitchell said, provided "that no suggestion would be made to the passengers that the use of the preservers was in any way imminent."

There was enough unease as it was. A first-class passenger named Josephine Brandell, twenty-three years old, was so frightened she decided she could not sleep in her own cabin, and asked another passenger, Mabel Gardner Crichton, forty-two, if she could spend the night in hers.

Mrs. Crichton assented.

Wrote Brandell, "She was only too happy to be of any assistance to me and did all she could during that whole night to quiet my nerves."

THE SHIP'S Marconi room now received a new message, this of a different sort. It was for Alfred Vanderbilt, from a woman. It read, "Hope you have a safe crossing looking forward very much to seeing you soon."

TENSION

NEWS OF THE SINKING OF THE *CANDIDATE* TOOK TIME to reach the Admiralty. A trawler, the *Lord Allendale*, stumbled across the ship's three lifeboats at about three o'clock Thursday afternoon. The men had been adrift in the fog for five hours. The trawler was not equipped with wireless and so could not report the sinking or the rescue until it returned to its base at Milford Haven, on the English coast, far from where the *Candidate* had sunk. The commander of naval forces at Milford Haven notified the Admiralty of the attack in a telegram sent shortly after midnight.

A telegram from the Queenstown Naval Center came in that day as well, with another report of a submarine sighted off Daunt Rock, this one at 9:45 that morning. The U-boat had remained "in sight for five minutes" before submerging. This was relayed to Director of Intelligence Hall as well as to First Sea Lord Fisher. A copy also was circulated to Churchill's office, though he was still in France.

The HMS *Orion* continued on its way north, zigzagging in open sea 150 miles west of Ireland.

IN WASHINGTON, President Wilson struggled anew with depression. Edith Galt's rejection had cast him into a state akin to grief, to the extent that he found it difficult to concentrate on world events, though these continued to press. The *Gulflight* was still major news. An inquest by an English coroner had confirmed that the ship's captain, Alfred Gunter, had died of "heart failure, accelerated by shock, caused by the torpedoing of the ship." The *Gulflight*'s second officer testified that the submarine captain had to have realized the ship was American, for the day had been clear and the tanker was flying a large American flag. There was also news of fresh U-boat predations. The *Washington Times* reported on Wednesday evening that a German submarine, "running amok," had sunk eleven unarmed fishing trawlers in the North Sea, off England.

That night, however, Wilson's attention was focused solely on Edith. He resolved that despite his new grief he would not—*could not*—let her exit his life. He composed a long letter, really a prose poem of despair, in which he, the man so many Americans thought of as distant and professorial, wrote, "There are some things I must try to say before the still watches come again in which the things unsaid hurt so and cry out in the heart to be uttered."

He was willing to accept friendship, he told her—for now. "If you cannot give me all that I want—what my heart finds it hard now to breathe without—it is because I am not worthy. I know instinctively you could give it if I were—and if you understood,—understood the boy's heart that is in me and the simplicity of my need, which you could fill so that all my days would be radiant."

He made it clear that she *would* come to love him. "Do not misunderstand," he added, in one of three impassioned postscripts. "What I have now at your generous hands is infinitely precious to me. It would kill me to part with it,—I could not and I hope you could not. And I will be patient, patient without end, to see what, if anything, the future may have [in] store for me."

Not so patient, as it happened, for the next morning, Thursday, May 6, before sending off this letter, he added a codicil that was five pages long.

He had read her letter again, he told her, and now appraised it in a more hopeful light. "I can hardly see to write for the tears as I lift my eyes from it,—the tears of joy and sweet yearning."

For the time being, he chose to position himself as her knight. "I seem to have been put into the world to serve, not to take, and serve I will to the utmost, and demand nothing in return."

Edith's resistance, meanwhile, had begun to waver, but amid a crush of conflicting anxieties. The fact Wilson was president of the United States placed a barrier in her thoughts that she found hard to overcome. His power, his ever-present detail of Secret Service men, his visibility in the public eye, and corollary restraints on his private behavior all complicated matters, as did the simple fact that any woman inclined to marry Wilson was likely to have her motives questioned, given his high office. "There was the fear," she wrote, "that some might think I loved him for that; then the terrible thought of the publicity inevitably entailed; and the feeling that I had no training for the responsibilities such a life held." On the other hand, she felt deep affection for the man. "Oh, so many things swarmed in my thoughts," she wrote; "and yet each time I was with him I felt the charm of his presence." She was enthralled, too, by the trust he placed in her and his willingness to discuss with her "all the problems which confronted him and the fears, even then, that the fires of war raging in Europe might leap the Atlantic and involve our own country."

They could not see each other too often, lest they draw "unwelcome publicity," she wrote; and when they did see each other, it had to be at the White House, or during a drive with a chaperone always at hand, whether Helen Bones, or Dr. Grayson, or Wilson's daughter Margaret. A car full of Secret Service men invariably followed. The only wholly private means of communication was by mail, and so their letters continued, his ever passionate and filled with declamations of love, hers welcoming and warm but at the same time curiously distant.

IN BERLIN, Germany's Chancellor Bethmann was growing increasingly perturbed. The war in the trenches was not going well, and he feared that Germany's U-boats might make things much worse. A month earlier, Kaiser Wilhelm had issued an order that permitted U-boat commanders to keep their vessels submerged when attacking merchant ships in order to avoid the danger inherent in surfacing and approaching suspected enemy freighters to first confirm their identity. The effect was to give commanders still more freedom. Combined with improved spring weather at sea, this had led to a startling increase in attacks on neutrals, like that against the American tanker *Gulflight*.

On Thursday, May 6, Bethmann wrote a letter to Germany's top naval official, in which he complained that over the preceding week U-boats had sunk "more and more" neutral ships. "This fact is eminently bound not only to alter our good relations with the neutral states but also to create the gravest complications and, finally, to throw those states into the enemy's camp." The empire's situation was "tense" enough as it was, he wrote, and warned, "I cannot accept the responsibility of seeing our relations with the neutral states further worsened, to which the pursuit of the submarine war in its present form will certainly lead."

He demanded that the naval high command "take necessary measures to guarantee that our submarines will in all circumstances avoid attacking neutral ships."

THAT EVENING, the *Washington Times* reported that four more ships had been sunk, including two neutral steamers and an English schooner. Two of the ships had been attacked by submarines; the other two were destroyed by a sea mine and shellfire from a German warship.

THE *LUSITANIA* was now two days out from Liverpool. At midnight that Thursday, May 6, the powerful German transmitter at Norddeich broadcast a message to all U-boats that the *Lusitania* would begin its return trip to New York on May 15.

This message was intercepted and relayed to Room 40.

U-20

FOG

SCHWIEGER AND HIS CREW SPENT A PEACEFUL NIGHT FAR out at sea. At five o'clock Friday morning, May 7, he ordered the submarine back to the surface and climbed into the conning tower. He shifted to diesel power and began charging the batteries below.

At intervals U-20 passed through mist and clarity. "From time to time, it clears up a little," Schwieger wrote. These brief periods of clearing at first gave hope of better visibility to come, but soon all sunshine disappeared and the fog returned as dense as ever.

It was discouraging and affirmed Schwieger's earlier decision not to proceed to Liverpool. He later recounted the story of that morning to his friend and fellow U-boat commander Max Valentiner. The heavy fog allowed "small chance of sinking anything," Schwieger told him. "At the same time, a destroyer steaming through the fog might stumble over us before we knew anything about it."

Schwieger wrote in his War Log, "Since the fog didn't subside, decided already to begin the return trip now."

He set a new course for home. As far as he was concerned, this patrol was over.

PART III

DEAD WAKE

ENGINES ABOVE

ARLY FRIDAY MORNING A NUMBER OF PASSENGERS awoke and dressed and climbed to the topmost decks to watch the sun come up. Although sunrise would not officially occur until 5:30, already the eastern sky was beginning to brighten. Elbridge and Maude Thompson of Seymour, Indiana, both thirty-two years old and traveling in first class, were in position by 4:30 A.M., as were second-cabin passengers Belle, forty-nine, and Theodore Naish, fifty-nine, of Kansas City. At about five, the two couples spotted a warship off the port side, distant, traveling fast on a course parallel to the *Lusitania*. Mrs. Thompson called it a "battleship," though in fact it was the HMS *Partridge*, a high-speed destroyer with three funnels. Aboard the *Partridge*, the officers and crew of the early morning watch also saw the *Lusitania*.

For early risers like the Naishes and Thompsons the sight of this robust warship was a comfort. Its presence affirmed the reassuring remarks Captain Turner had made at the previous night's concert. Said Mrs. Naish, "We had been told that we were protected all the way by warships, wireless, and that submarine destroyers would escort us in the channel." By "channel" she was referring to the St. George's Channel.

The *Partridge* had no such orders. The destroyer, capable of making over 30 knots, continued past at a brisk pace.

—w—

AT ABOUT 6:00 A.M. the *Lusitania* encountered heavy fog. Captain Turner reduced speed to 15 knots and ordered the ship's foghorn activated. Like other passengers aboard, the Naishes had a penchant for timing things, a function perhaps of the fact that there was little else to do aboard ship. They clocked the blasts of the foghorn at one a minute. Theodore found the horn unsettling. "I do not like this," he told his wife; "it is too much like calling for trouble."

Throughout the ship, passengers awoke abruptly and upon looking out their portholes and windows saw only a milky blur. Charles Lauriat stayed in bed until his usual shipboard wake-up time of eight o'clock, then got up and took his usual sea bath. This morning he had little enthusiasm for the process. "As the horn was blowing and the weather was thick, I returned to my berth for a few hours' extra snooze. I instructed the steward that if he didn't hear from me by 12 o'clock he was to call me, as that would give me ample time to get ready for lunch at one." The foghorn seemed not to bother Lauriat, possibly because of his inside room and its lack of portholes.

Captain Turner placed extra lookouts to watch for other vessels. One of these was Leo Thompson, a crewman assigned "special lookout" duty for the two-hour watch that began at 10:00 A.M. He climbed the ladder to the crow's nest, about one-third the way up the forward mast. There he and another crewman, George Clinton, were to spend the next two hours staring into the fog, sometimes with marine glasses—Thompson owned a pair of his own—sometimes just with the naked eye. It was tedious but crucial work.

Fog was dangerous, especially in crowded waters like these. But it also afforded protection from submarines. In heavy fog, only chance could bring a submarine commander close enough to a ship to see it through his periscope or from his conning tower, and if he was that close, he was too close, at great risk of collision. As long as the fog persisted, Captain Turner had little cause to worry about U-boats.

At eleven o'clock, the fog began to dissipate.

—⁂—

IN THE crow's nest Thompson and Clinton now had the extraordinary experience of moving through the dispersing fog as if flying in an aircraft through clouds. At intervals sun warmed their perch and leavened the morning chill. Sometime between eleven and noon, Thompson caught his first sight of the Irish coast. He was able to see it over the top of the fog, but only with his binoculars, and even then the terrain was obscured by mist. What he saw, he said later, was "just the loom of the land through the haze."

He called out to the bridge below, "Land on the port beam."

The fog continued to fade, and soon the decks were bathed in a yellowing mist that foretold sunshine to come.

IN LONDON, a mosaic of information had by now accumulated in Blinker Hall's intelligence division and in Room 40 that showed that only one submarine was in the waters off County Cork, and that it had to be U-20, commanded by Capt. Walther Schwieger, a talented and aggressive commander.

As the morning progressed, more information arrived, in the form of two messages that provided additional details about the demise of the *Centurion*. The ship had been attacked at 1:00 P.M. Thursday; all forty-four of its crew were rescued after spending ten hours at sea in lifeboats. One message stated, "Number and directions of submarine unknown."

But by then, news about the attacks on the *Centurion*, the *Candidate*, and the schooner *Earl of Lathom* was already in Liverpool newspapers. Alfred Allen Booth, chairman of Cunard, learned of the attacks while reading his morning paper, over breakfast at his home. The meaning was clear, at least to him. He knew his company's flagship was due to travel the same waters that very day.

Booth quit breakfast and rushed to see the senior naval officer at Liverpool, Capt. Harry Stileman, and pleaded with him to take measures to protect the *Lusitania*. Booth urged that a message be sent to Turner, notifying him that the two Harrison Line ships had been torpedoed and sunk. Under war rules, Booth was not himself empowered to send a warning, or any other command, directly to Turner. At the start of the war, all ships of British registry came under the dominion of the Admiralty's trade division, to give the Admiralty maximum flexibility in commandeering ships for military use, as well as to prevent confusion that might arise if conflicting orders were sent to a ship from both its owners and the Admiralty, a circumstance that Cunard chairman Alfred Booth conceded could be "very dangerous."

Exactly what else occurred during Booth's meeting with Admiral Stileman is unclear, but Booth came away believing that a detailed message would be sent and that the Admiralty would order the *Lusitania* to divert to Queenstown, well short of Liverpool, until the immediate U-boat threat was past.

OFF IRELAND, the *Lusitania* moved through pockets of fog, but visibility improved by the minute, and the threat of collision rapidly receded. Turner ordered the foghorn deactivated. Now, however, the risk of detection by a submarine increased.

Anxiety on the bridge rose sharply with the arrival, at 11:30 A.M., of a wireless message from the Admiralty, which stated: "Submarines active in Southern part of Irish channel last heard of 20 miles South of Coningbeg Light Vessel."

The sender added, "Make certain 'Lusitania' gets this."

The Coningbeg Light Vessel was dead ahead on Turner's course, just before the narrowest expanse—45 miles across—of the St. George's Channel. The message also indicated there was more than one submarine.

If the submarines, *plural*, were in fact 20 miles south of the lightship, they were positioned about halfway across the channel. On a clear day—and by now the fog was nearly gone—the smoke from the *Lusitania*'s three operating funnels would be visible for 20 miles in any direction, meaning a lookout on a submarine at the center of the channel would have an excellent chance of spotting the ship. The warning described the submarines as being "active," but what exactly did "active" mean?

The message was apparently the product of Chairman Booth's plea, but it fell short of what he had asked for. Only eighteen words long, it conveyed no details about what had occurred over the previous twenty-four hours. Captain Turner, the one man at that moment who needed details the most, never learned of the loss of the two Harrison Line vessels and the *Earl of Lathom*.

With the fog now dissipated, Turner brought his speed up to 18 knots. He ordered maximum pressure maintained in his three available boiler rooms in the event a sudden burst of speed became necessary.

AT NOON, as per Charles Lauriat's request, the steward assigned to his cabin arrived to awaken him. The steward told Lauriat the ship had "picked up Cape Clear," a familiar landmark at the southwest tip of Ireland, and that the ship's time had been set ahead to Greenwich Mean Time. Lauriat got out of bed, put on his Knickerbocker suit, and was up on deck by 12:50. He knew the time because he checked his wristwatch, set as always to Boston time, and calculated the Greenwich equivalent.

Lunch for first-class passengers began at one o'clock; he wanted to take a ten-minute stroll first. He noted that the ship seemed to be "loafing along" and saw as well that the results of the mileage pool, posted at noon, showed the ship had traveled only 484 miles. Although Lauriat found this slow, in fact it worked out to an average of slightly more than 20 knots, and that included several hours through fog at 15. Still, this was well below the 25-knot pace he had expected the ship to maintain.

"It was a beautiful day then, light wind, a smooth sea, and bright sunshine," Lauriat wrote. Along the port side, he saw "the good old Irish Coast." The coast, though, was still a long way off, merely a green slash on the horizon. The fine weather made Lauriat uneasy. "I thought to myself that if a German submarine really meant business, she would have to wait weeks for a more ideal chance than the present weather conditions. With a flat, unbroken sea, such as that around us, the periscope of a submarine could certainly carry a long distance."

The smoothness of the sea was the remarkable thing. Lauriat likened it to a pancake; one of the ship's bellboys said it was "just flat as a billiard table."

CONNECTICUT PASSENGER Jane MacFarquhar climbed to one of the upper decks and looked out over the glittering seascape. She and her sixteen-year-old daughter had just finished setting out the clothes they would wear upon arrival in Liverpool the next morning. They planned to leave their current outfits behind, on the ship. "The view was grand," MacFarquhar said, "the sun shining, the water smooth and land visible on either side. As I gazed around the beautiful scene, I thought:—'Where is this spoken-of danger?' The end of our voyage is almost in view and we have had no sign of danger whatever."

ON FRIDAY MORNING, Schwieger kept U-20 on the surface to continue recharging its batteries. He stood atop the conning tower. The sea was quilted with fog, but here and there sunlight gleamed through. Visibility improved quickly. The sea was flat, under a 1-knot breeze.

"All of a sudden visibility has become very good," Schwieger wrote in his log. While this gave him a long view of the surrounding sea, it also provided that view to any British patrol boat or destroyer that happened to be in the vicinity. The flatness of the surface increased the danger that enemy lookouts would spot U-20, even when submerged to periscope depth, for the feathery white wake of Schwieger's periscope would be visible for miles.

And in fact, a trawler off in the distance now began moving in U-20's direction. Schwieger ordered a fast dive and raised his periscope. The vessel approached slowly, in a manner he found unsettling. "Therefore," he wrote, "we dive to a depth of 24 meters to get away from the trawler." The time was 10:30 A.M. "At 12 P.M.," he wrote, "I shall rise again to a depth of 11 meters and take a periscopic observation."

But shortly before that was to happen, at 11:50 A.M., a surge of excitement passed through the submarine. Even 80 feet below the surface, the men in U-20 could hear the sound of a ship overhead, transmitted through the hull. Schwieger wrote in his log, "A vessel with a very heavy engine passes over our boat."

From the sound, Schwieger knew it was neither a destroyer nor a trawler but something far larger, moving fast. It passed directly above, confirming the prudence of cruising at a depth that cleared even the largest ships' keels.

Schwieger waited a few minutes, then returned to periscope depth to try to identify the ship.

WITH THE foghorn off, and the sun high and bright, the *Lusitania*'s passengers took to the open decks to play shuffleboard, throw medicine balls, and take part in other deck games. Older children played jump rope, as always. The youngest paraded the decks with nannies and stewardesses, on foot or in prams, with their sucking tubes hung around their necks or affixed to their clothing. In the shaded portions of the deck and in those areas exposed to the 18-knot breeze generated by the ship's forward motion, it was still cool enough to require coats. One woman wore a large black fur.

This being the last full day of the voyage, with the sun so bright and the air so clear, passengers seemed to take a special effort to dress well and with a little flair. A seven-year-old girl wore a pink-and-white-striped cotton frock under a black velvet coat lined with red silk, then added a gold ring, a red coral necklet, and a mother-of-pearl brooch. The coat imparted to her the look of a red-winged blackbird. Pink seemed to be a popular color—for boys. One five-year-old boy tore around in a pink wool coat over a checked jacket and knickers. A man in his late twenties dressed with clear intent to dazzle. He wore:

Blue serge trousers
Striped cotton shirt ("Anderson Bros., Makers,
   27, Bridge Street, Glasgow")
White merino pants
Light lace-up boots (stamped inside with "Holober Bros.,
   501, West 14th Street, New York")
Gray socks, with light-blue soles
Light-colored suspenders
Leather belt and nickel buckle

And this:

A pink merino vest.

MANY PASSENGERS settled into deck chairs to read, just as they'd done over the preceding six days. Dwight Harris sat on deck for a time reading a book about the Medicis, then went to the purser's office to retrieve his engagement ring, his other jewels, and the $500 in gold that he had parked there at the start of the voyage. He went to his cabin and used a watch chain to hang several pieces around his neck, including the ring. "I pinned the big diamond brooch inside the pocket of my coat," he wrote, "and before leaving my cabin unlocked the camera bag that held my life belt." This was the belt he had bought at Wanamaker's in New York the day before sailing. Harris had not yet run out of exclamation points. "I put the gold in my trousers pocket, and then went down to lunch!"

Despite the calm weather, Kansas City passenger Theodore Naish was seasick, as he had been throughout the voyage. He urged his wife, Belle, to go up on deck without him to see the Irish coast and its islands in sunshine. He knew from past experience how lovely the view was. Belle at first demurred: "I replied that his word was enough, I would see them when we returned, and if fog prevented, pictures would satisfy me." But Theodore insisted, and she obliged; she was glad that she had. "A lovelier day cannot be imagined—the air was warm, no wind, bright sun, smooth sea."

Throughout the ship there was that mix of sorrow and expectation that always marked the end of a voyage, but now it was joined by the relief of having made it to England safe and sound.

ON THE BRIDGE, Turner received a new message from the Admiralty that confused things further: "Submarines 5 miles south of Cape Clear, proceeding west when sighted at 10 A.M."

The *Lusitania* had already passed Cape Clear. If correct, this message indicated the threat might also be past—the submarines, plural again, were behind and heading out to sea. Captain Turner congratulated himself on apparently missing these in the fog. He knew that even if their commanders now spotted the smoke from the ship's funnels and turned around, they would have no hope of catching up.

While this offered some comfort, there was still the matter of the earlier report of submarines active in the St. George's Channel, south of the Coningbeg Light Vessel, dead ahead.

AT HIS PERISCOPE, Schwieger made a fast 360-degree sweep of the sea, then rotated the apparatus until he found the ship that had just passed overhead. It was a prize indeed, and not just in terms of tonnage. Long and narrow, with a razor bow, it sliced easily through the flat sea. Its funnels blew thick black smoke that showed its engine crew were working hard to achieve maximum speed. Schwieger did not need his war pilot, Lanz, to help identify this ship. It was a large armored cruiser, British, of about 6,000 tons.

He let it go. He had no choice. At his top submerged speed of 9 knots, Schwieger had no chance of catching the cruiser. Even his surface maximum of 15 knots would not have helped, for the cruiser was speeding away at what he estimated to be 18 knots. And had Schwieger for some reason been foolhardy enough to try surfacing, the warship's guns would have sunk his boat within minutes.

Schwieger followed anyway, at periscope depth, in case the cruiser happened to change its course in a manner that would allow him to overtake it and launch an attack. But the ship ran at top speed, zigzagging, and soon was far in the distance. Schwieger later told his friend Valentiner how at this point, exasperated, he unleashed a torrent of profanity. "After the early days of the war," Valentiner explained, "you rarely had a chance to loose a torpedo at any warship as big as a cruiser, and many a U-boat never caught sight of one during the entire war." The British navy, like its German counterpart, kept its big warships locked safely away "and did not send them roaming around to act as good targets for U-boats."

The ship was in fact the HMS *Juno*, an old cruiser now serving as a coastal patrol vessel. It was based in Queenstown and was speeding back to port precisely because of the latest submarine alerts issued by the Admiralty. As it traveled, its crew took a routine measure of water temperature and found it to be 55 degrees Fahrenheit.

"After I was through swearing," Schwieger told Valentiner, "I noticed that the fog was lifting. Presently I could see blue sky."

Schwieger recorded the encounter at 12:15 P.M. Half an hour later, he surfaced and returned to his westward course, to continue his voyage home. Conservation of fuel was now a priority. He could not delay—the journey back to Emden would take another week.

By now the weather had cleared to a degree that was almost startling. "Unusually good visibility," Schwieger noted; "very beautiful weather."

On the horizon, something new caught his eye.

THE KING'S QUESTION

I n London, on Friday, Colonel House, still acting in his role as President Wilson's unofficial emissary, met with Sir Edward Grey, Britain's foreign secretary, and the two traveled to the Royal Botanic Gardens at Kew for a walk among the garden's beds of spring flowers, its alleys, or "vistas," of cedars, and its most celebrated structure, the Palm House, an immense conservatory built of glass and iron said to have influenced the design of London's Crystal Palace. The two men discussed the submarine war. "We spoke of the probability of an ocean liner being sunk," House wrote, "and I told him if this were done, a flame of indignation would sweep across America, which would in itself probably carry us into war."

Oddly enough, the subject came up again a couple of hours later, when Colonel House paid a call on King George V at Buckingham Palace.

The king turned to House at one point, and asked, "Suppose they should sink the *Lusitania* with American passengers aboard?"

EARLY THAT MORNING, Churchill, having concluded his naval negotiations with his French and Italian counterparts, left Paris on his journey to the headquarters of Britain's forces in France, at St. Omer, where Sir John French was planning an offensive against

German forces at Aubers despite a severe shortage of artillery shells.

Seeking to experience battle firsthand, Churchill hoped to get as close to the front as possible, while not, as he put it, "incurring unjustifiable risks." He saw shellfire and smoke but little else. "Without actually taking part in the assault it was impossible to measure the real conditions," he wrote. "To see them you had to feel them, and feeling them might well feel nothing more. To stand outside was to see nothing, to plunge in was to be dominated by personal experiences of an absorbing kind."

He received his most vivid sense of the war at a "casualty clearing station" in a convent at Merville, about 40 miles east of headquarters, where men "suffering from every form of horrible injury, seared, torn, pierced, choking, dying, were being sorted according to their miseries." Ambulance after ambulance pulled up at the door. The dead were carried out the back and buried. As Churchill passed the operating theater, he saw doctors at work trepanning a soldier, that is, cutting a hole in his skull. "Everywhere was blood and bloody rags," Churchill wrote.

AT THE White House, with a fresh spring Friday in the offing, Wilson wrote again to Edith. She had come to dinner the night before, and he was feeling far more optimistic about the possibility of one day marrying her.

"In this clear morning air," he wrote, "the world seems less in the way, seems less to stand between us."

FUNNELS ON THE HORIZON

U-20 MOVED THROUGH A BLUE-ON-BLUE MORNING. THE fog was gone, the sky was empty of clouds, the sea was still. Schwieger trained his binoculars—his Zeiss "godseyes"—on a smudge at the horizon and was startled to see "a forest of masts and stacks," as he later described it to Max Valentiner. "At first I thought they must belong to several ships," he said. "Then I saw it was a great steamer coming over the horizon. It was coming our way. I dived at once, hoping to get a shot at it."

In his log, at 1:20 P.M., Schwieger wrote, "Ahead and to starboard four funnels and two masts of a steamer with course triangular to us comes into sight (coming from SSW it steered towards Galley Head). Ship is made out to be a large passenger steamer."

Once at periscope depth, Schwieger ordered his maximum submerged speed—9 knots—and set a course "converging with that of the steamer." The ship was still miles off, however. When the liner was 2 miles away, it veered onto a new course that further widened the gap. Frustrated again, Schwieger wrote, "I had no hope now, even if we hurried at our best speed, of getting near enough to attack her."

Schwieger followed anyway, just as he had done earlier with the cruiser *Juno*, in case the liner happened to make another course change that would bring it back onto a converging trajectory.

He called for his pilot, Lanz, to come to the periscope to take a look. Why he felt the need to do so is unclear. The ship was one of the most distinctive on the high seas, and a prize of the first order. He was near despair: this one ship, by itself, would have given him his best monthly tonnage count of the war.

The day remained startlingly clear and still. This meant that Schwieger could not keep the periscope raised for long, lest it be detected by the target's lookouts or, worse, by a destroyer on patrol. In weather this clear and with seas this smooth there'd be little chance for escape. On two previous occasions, the wake cast by his periscope on a flat sea had forced him to abort attacks. One would-be target, a Royal Mail steamer, had turned toward him with obvious intent to ram, causing him to order a fast dive and full speed away.

Lanz entered the control room. At about the same moment, something happened that Schwieger deemed the equivalent of a miracle.

ON THE *Lusitania*'s bridge, Captain Turner faced a dilemma that nothing in his long experience at sea had prepared him to manage. If the morning's wireless messages were correct, there were U-boats directly ahead of him, and behind.

On top of this, he faced a timing problem. Liverpool at this point still lay about 250 nautical miles ahead. At the entrance to the city's harbor lay the notorious Mersey Bar, which he could pass only at high tide. If Turner accelerated and proceeded at the highest speed he could achieve with only three boiler rooms in operation, or 21 knots, he would arrive far too early. With stopping out of the question, he would be forced to circle in the Irish Sea, smoke billowing from the ship's three operating funnels in open invitation to any submarine within a radius of twenty miles.

There was another dimension to the problem. The time was now just past noon. No matter what speed Turner traveled, he would end up having to pass through the St. George's Channel at night, with fog an ever-present danger. As it was, the fog that had enclosed the ship all morning had left Turner with a less precise sense of his location than he would have liked. Compounding this imprecision was the fact that he was farther from the coast than usual—about 20 miles, when in fine weather he might come as close as 1 mile.

He called his two most senior officers to the bridge, Staff Captain Anderson and First Officer John Preston Piper, to ask their advice, and at length reached a decision. First, he would pinpoint his location. The Irish coast was by now visible, but the ship's distance from shore was difficult to reckon precisely. Being a sailor of the old school, Turner liked to use a procedure known as a four-point bearing. This would require him to run parallel to the coast at a steady speed for roughly thirty minutes while First Office Piper took four bearings off a single shore landmark, in this case the lighthouse atop the Old Head.

Once Turner knew his precise position, he planned to maintain a speed of 18 knots so that he would arrive at the Mersey Bar early the next morning, at just the right time to enter the harbor without pause. Though slower than the 21 knots his three operating boiler rooms would allow, it was still faster than any other merchant ship then in service and certainly faster than any submarine. Turner planned as well to alter his course later in the day to bring the *Lusitania* closer to shore, so that he would pass near the Coningbeg Light Vessel before entering the narrowest portion of the St. George's Channel. He understood that this contravened the Admiralty's advisory that captains pass lightships and other navigational markers at "mid-channel." But the Admiralty had reported submarines 20 miles south of the lightship, a location that any mariner traversing that 45-mile-wide stretch would have described as midchannel. To follow the Admiralty's advisory would have meant sailing directly toward the waiting submarines.

At about 1:30 P.M. Captain Turner ordered the officer at the helm to make a turn to starboard, to bring the ship in line with the coast, so that Piper could take the first of the four bearings. This turn and several previous course changes persuaded some passengers that Turner was directing the ship on a zigzag course to evade submarines, though in fact he was not. Paradoxically, owing to the shape of the coastline, the turn would have seemed to passengers like a turn toward open sea.

Measles-wracked Robert Kay peered through his porthole in quarantine. The Bronx boy, now spotted and enflamed, watched the world pass, his only diversion. The day outside was full of sunshine and sparkle, the Irish coast a vivid green. But as he watched, the ship began its turn to starboard, and to his great disappointment the land began to recede.

THAT MORNING "Champagne King" George Kessler followed through on his decision to talk to Captain Turner about including passengers in the ship's drills. The two men smoked as they talked.

Kessler wrote, "I suggested that the passengers should be given tickets with a number denoting the number of the boat they should make for in case anything untoward happened, and that it seemed to me this detail would minimize the difficulties in the event of trouble."

Turner told him that the idea had come up in the wake of the *Titanic* disaster but that Cunard had rejected it as "impractical." He added that he did not have the authority to institute the practice on his own without first getting approval from the Admiralty's Board of Trade.

The conversation shifted to "the torpedo scare which neither of us regarded as of any moment," Kessler recalled. Turner may have downplayed his own concerns to put Kessler at ease.

JUST AS Pilot Lanz arrived at U-20's periscope, Schwieger saw the giant steamer change course again, this time to starboard. "She was coming directly at us," Schwieger told Valentiner. "She could not have steered a more perfect course if she had deliberately tried to give us a dead shot."

The time was 1:35 P.M. The ship's new heading suggested it was bound for Queenstown. Schwieger set a course that would put U-20 in front of the ship, at a 90-degree angle. He ordered full ahead, and for the next twenty-five minutes sped forward on an intersecting course, as the ship grew steadily larger in his viewfinder. "A short fast run, and we waited," he told Valentiner.

Although this patrol had affirmed Schwieger's distrust of torpedoes, he had no choice but to use one. His deck gun would have been useless against such a large vessel, and dangerous, for after the first couple of shells the big ship likely would have turned and run, or even attempted to ram his boat. Schwieger selected a G6 torpedo.

Within the submarine the tension mounted. All the ship had to do was make another turn, away from U-20, and the chase would be over. Queenstown was near. There was also the possibility the ship's lookouts would spot Schwieger's periscope and that its captain would summon a pride of destroyers.

Strangely, the ship had no escorts whatsoever. Even stranger, in Schwieger's view, was that the vessel was in these waters at all, especially after his two successful attacks the day before. That the ship "was not sent through the North Channel is inexplicable," he wrote in his log.

Schwieger ordered the torpedo set to run at a depth of 3 meters, about 10 feet. He had not yet had time to let Lanz take a look at the target. The big ship continued its approach, its giant hull black against the otherwise gleaming seascape.

Schwieger's firing crew armed the torpedo and flooded its tube.

THE LUSITANIA was now about sixteen hours from Liverpool, or, put another way, three meals out—one lunch, one dinner, and, on Saturday, a last breakfast in Liverpool Harbor. Now came the lunch. First-class passengers had only one seating, in the dining saloon at the center of the ship under the great dome; second-class had two, at 12:30 and 1:30. Over lunch there was talk of the talent show the night before, and of the latest war news, published in the ship's daily Cunard Bulletin, and, of course, of the fact that the ship was now well into the "war zone."

Charles Lauriat went to lunch with Lothrop Withington, as always, and they sat at their usual table in the first-class saloon. Lauriat noted that portholes on either side of the room were open. He was certain of this, he said later, because the unusual warmth of the day had conjured an annoyance that had plagued the two men throughout the voyage. Owing to the warm weather, the stewards had opened portholes throughout the dining room and turned on a large electric fan positioned directly over Lauriat's table, thereby creating a draft that was strong enough to be irritating. The same thing had happened several times previously during the voyage, and each time, as now, Lauriat felt compelled to ask the steward to turn the fan off.

Otherwise, the lunch was a pleasant one. The two men looked forward to the ship's arrival. "We had a jolly time together," Lauriat wrote, "and made plans for seeing each other in London, as his rooms were near our London office."

It was clear now that the unexpectedly slow pace of the *Lusitania* would cost Lauriat a day's work in London, but soon enough he'd be handing off the Dickens *Christmas Carol* and meeting with Thackeray's daughter, Lady Ritchie, to plan the notes she would write for each of the 118 drawings still locked in the shoe case in his cabin. Next he would meet with the framers and binders who would transform those drawings into items worth far more than the paltry $4,500 he had paid for them.

ELSEWHERE IN the dining room, Theodate Pope and her companion, Edwin Friend, were finishing up their lunch. "A young Englishman at our table had been served with his ice cream and was waiting for the steward to bring him a spoon to eat it with," Theodate recalled. "He looked ruefully at it and said he would hate to have a torpedo get him before he ate it. We all laughed and then commented on how slowly we were running. We thought the engines had stopped."

The ship, however, was still moving at a brisk 18 knots. This perception of slowness was likely caused by the fact that the sea was so smooth, which reduced the level of vibration transmitted through the hull.

Dwight Harris, with his engagement ring hanging snug under his shirt, joined his usual luncheon companions but did not share the cheerful anticipation that colored the talk around him. He was ill at ease, uncannily so. He wrote, "While at table I had a most intense nervous feeling come over me, and I got up and left without finishing my lunch!"

He went to his stateroom, A-9, to get his coat and hat, and his Medici book, and went back out on deck to read.

MEDICAL STUDENT Preston Prichard and his roommate, Arthur Gadsden, were very much aware of the ship's entry into the danger zone. They had become friends during the voyage and talked often, owing to the fact that both had the upper berths in their room. On Friday, Prichard and Gadsden spent part of the morning "talking about Submarines & wondering if we should see one at all, never having the least fear but what we should get away from them," Gadsden wrote.

Shortly after noon, Prichard walked to the smoking lounge to join the other men who had gathered there to see the results of the mileage pool and then set off to the second-class dining saloon for lunch. As usual he sat opposite Grace French.

Today there seemed to be a certain charge between Prichard and Miss French. He wore his green suit—not his best blue—but handsome was handsome, and after six days in the sun and weather Prichard was very handsome indeed. He mentioned to Grace that he had seen a young woman aboard who could be her double, and that he had even gone up to this other woman to start a conversation before realizing his mistake. This was not merely a flirty line meant to ignite conversation. One or two of the other men at the table had encountered the same woman and had done likewise. Prichard "volunteered to point her out for me after lunch," Grace recalled. "I agreed and went down for my hat and coat."

One of the ship's stewards noted that Prichard left the dining room around 1:20 P.M.

As Miss French was making her way back up the stairs to meet Prichard, she ran into two shipboard friends, who asked where she was going. "I replied that Mr. Prichard was going to present me to my double and passed on. I then joined him and we walked around laughing at the idea. I said to him, I wonder if I could recognize this girl myself."

They joked as they hunted. The time passed happily, and then it was 2:09 P.M. The sun shone, the sea glittered.

SCHWIEGER ESTIMATED his target's speed at 22 knots—25 miles an hour—and gauged its range at 700 meters, just under half a mile. If his calculations were correct, the torpedo would strike the ship at an ideal angle of 90 degrees.

At 2:10 P.M. Schwieger gave the order to fire. The torpedo burst from the submarine in what Schwieger called a "clean bow shot" and soon reached a speed of about 44 miles an hour. At that rate, it would reach the target's hull in thirty-five seconds.

With the sea so smooth, the possibility of the torpedo's track being discovered was high. Each passing second reduced the likelihood that the ship would be able to turn hard enough and fast enough to evade it, but still, for Schwieger and his men, those thirty-five seconds constituted a long interval.

Schwieger watched through his periscope. He didn't realize it, yet, but he had erred in his calculation of the target's speed. In fact, it was moving more slowly than he had gauged—by 4 knots, or roughly 5 miles an hour.

BEAUTY

SHORTLY BEFORE TWO O'CLOCK, SCORES OF CREWMEN were gathered in the baggage room at the *Lusitania*'s bow, on F Deck, half coming on duty, half coming off. The task at hand was to get the thousands of pieces of passenger luggage ready for arrival.

Seaman Morton spent two hours helping load suitcases and trunks onto the electric elevator that provided the only access to the room. The shifts changed at two o'clock—"four bells"—when Morton was to begin a two-hour stint as a special lookout, to watch for submarines. He was assigned to the forecastle, or *fo'c'sle*, the portion of the main deck just behind the bow.

"At five minutes to four bells," he said, "I went on deck to put my sweater and gear ready for going on the lookout at two o'clock. My place was extra lookout right up in the eyes of the ship on deck; my responsibility being the starboard side of the bow from ahead to the beam."

BY NOW the ship had expended about six thousand tons of coal, and the bunkers that ran the length of the hull on both the port and the starboard sides were for the most part empty tunnels, grimed with coal dust and pierced here and there by portals through which men known as trimmers moved the coal to the furnaces.

On the bridge, Captain Turner ordered the helmsman to hold the ship on its course parallel to shore so that his first officer could continue the four-point bearing. The protective screen of fog had by now wholly dissipated.

"All lookouts had been warned to keep a sharp lookout and report anything that appeared suspicious," said Thomas Mahoney, a seaman who was sharing the noon to 2:00 P.M. watch. "At approximately 1:50 p.m. we spotted an object 2 points on the starboard bow, conical in shape." It looked to him like a buoy. "We reported it to the officer of the watch and it caused a little commotion on the bridge, over what it might be."

A seaman named Hugh Johnston, quartermaster, was at this point just taking over the helm, his "trick at the wheel." The bridge was crowded with officers, who also were changing watch.

Soon after Johnston took the wheel, he heard the cry that something had been spotted off the starboard bow. A number of officers raised binoculars and speculated that the object might indeed be a buoy, or a porpoise, or a fragment of drifting debris. No one expressed concern. "We carried on," said Johnston.

At two o'clock, Seaman Leslie Morton took his position in the forecastle. He stood on the starboard side. Another seaman scanned the waters off the port side. Four other lookouts were stationed elsewhere on the ship, including in the crow's nest.

Morton's brother lay below decks, sleeping, so as to be ready for his own shift later in the day. Half the ship's crew was still gathered in the luggage bay.

The ship sliced through the calm like a razor through gelatin.

Morton was so intent on doing his job well that he started "seeing a dozen things every few minutes."

BY TWO O'CLOCK the second-class passengers assigned to the second lunch seating were midway through their meals. First-class passengers rode between decks aboard the ship's two electric elevators, which were powered by the ship's dynamo. A group of children was jumping rope on an upper deck with the help of a member of the engineering crew, John Brennan, a trimmer.

The weather by now was perfect, the day vividly clear—so lovely that families from Queenstown and Kinsale had gathered on the Old Head to picnic in the balmy air and watch the passage of ships. They could just see the *Lusitania*, about 20 miles off, her funnels pouring smoke into the sky.

For Morton, in the ship's "eyes," the vista off to starboard toward open sea was clear and bright. "At ten minutes past two," he said, "I looked at my watch and putting it into my pocket, I glanced round the starboard side and, as roughly as I could judge, I saw a big burst of foam about 500 yards away, four points on the starboard bow." It looked to him like a giant bubble bursting onto the surface.

An instant later, he saw something moving across the flat plane of the sea, a track, as clear as if it had been made by "an invisible hand with a piece of chalk on a blackboard."

He reached for his megaphone.

CAPTAIN TURNER left the bridge and went below to his quarters. At about 1:30, Quartermaster Johnston, no longer at the wheel, was sent below to give Turner a message that the Old Head of Kinsale was now "10 points on the port bow and 20 miles away." The ship's course was taking it gradually closer to the coast.

Johnston returned to the bridge. Half an hour later, just after two o'clock, he heard the cry, "Here is a torpedo coming."

AFTER FINISHING lunch and parting from his friend Lothrop Withington, Charles Lauriat went down to his cabin to get a sweater. He put it on under the jacket of his Knickerbocker suit, then headed back up for "a *real walk*." He climbed the main companionway and walked out onto the port side of the ship, with the Irish coast visible in the distance. Here he ran into Elbert Hubbard, the writer, and his wife, Alice. Hubbard joked that he probably would not be welcome in Germany, given a pamphlet he had written, entitled *Who Lifted the Lid Off Hell?*, in which he laid blame for the war on Kaiser Wilhelm. He had given Lauriat a copy earlier in the voyage. Lauriat described it as "a piece of vitriolic English."

On B Deck, starboard side, Theodate Pope stood beside her companion, Edwin Friend, leaning on the rail and admiring the sea, "which was a marvelous blue and very dazzling in the sunlight." There was so much glare that Theodate wondered aloud, "How could the officers ever *see* a periscope?"

Oliver Bernard, the set designer, was standing in the Verandah Cafe leaning "lazily" against a window, looking out at the view. He saw what seemed to be the tail of a fish, well off the starboard side. Next "a streak of froth" began arcing across the surface, toward the ship.

An American woman came up beside him, and said, "That isn't a torpedo, is it?"

"I was too spellbound to answer," he said. "I felt absolutely sick."

Here it was, this thing everyone had feared. "We had all been thinking, dreaming, eating, sleeping 'submarine' from the hour we left New York, and yet with the dreaded danger upon us, I could hardly believe the evidence of my own eyes."

There was little fear, Bernard said. "I did not think that anybody, even women and children, were so much terrified as they were astounded and stunned by the consciousness that the fears, cherished half in ridicule for five days previous, had at last been realized. The German 'bluff' had actually come off."

The track continued its approach.

THAT FIRST TURMOIL, that first bubble of foam, was the expulsion of compressed air from the submarine's launching tube as the torpedo exited. The torpedo itself was 20 feet long and 20 inches in diameter; its nose, shaped like the top of a corn silo, contained 350 pounds of TNT and an explosive called Hexanite. Though

German commanders typically set the depth at 15 feet, this one traveled at 10 feet. It moved at about 35 knots, or 40 miles an hour, powered by compressed air stored in a tank toward its nose, just behind the compartment that contained the explosives. The air rushed against the pistons in its engine, geared to spin two propellers, one clockwise, the other counterclockwise, to keep the torpedo from rolling and veering. The air was then exhausted into the sea, where it bubbled to the surface. These bubbles needed a few seconds to rise, which meant the torpedo itself was always well ahead of the track that appeared above.

As the torpedo advanced, the water rushing past its nose turned a small propeller, which unscrewed a safety device that prevented detonation during storage. This propeller slipped from the nose and fell to the sea bottom, thereby exposing a triggering mechanism that upon impact with a ship's hull would fire a small charge into the larger body of explosives. A gyroscope kept the torpedo on course, adjusting for vertical and horizontal deflection.

The track lingered on the surface like a long pale scar. In maritime vernacular, this trail of fading disturbance, whether from ship or torpedo, was called a "dead wake."

THE SMOOTHNESS of the sea presented some passengers with a view of the torpedo that was startling in its clarity.

Dwight Harris, his Medici book in hand, was walking toward the stern, along the starboard side, when something caught his eye. He wrote, "I saw the torpedo coming!—a white and greenish streak in the water!—I stood transfixed!"

Passenger James Brooks, a chain salesman who came from Connecticut, was walking along the boat deck, when friends on the next deck up—the Marconi deck—called to him to join them for a round of shuffleboard. These friends were Mr. and Mrs. Montagu Grant, of Chicago. He climbed the stairs, and as he walked toward them across the upper deck he saw a foam trail moving fast across the water.

"Oh, yes, I saw the torpedo coming, and exclaimed, 'Torpedo!'

and rushed to the rail just aft of the staircase and stood on one foot and leaned forward, over, to watch the explosion which I expected to see occur on the outside of the ship."

Any other man would have found this scene terrifying. Brooks was entranced. He saw the body of the torpedo moving well ahead of the wake, through water he described as being "a beautiful green." The torpedo "was covered with a silvery phosphorescence, you might term it, which was caused by the air escaping from the motors."

He said, "It was a beautiful sight."

HAD THERE BEEN more time, had the idea of a torpedo attack against a civilian liner not seemed so incomprehensible, had submarine tactics and evasion stratagems been better understood, there would have been a chance—a tiny one—that Turner could have maneuvered the ship to lessen the damage or even avoid the torpedo altogether. He could have engaged the ship's reverse turbines, thereby slowing the ship and nullifying the calculations made by the submarine commander as to its range and speed, causing the torpedo to miss. He could also have taken advantage of the *Lusitania*'s proven agility and ordered a full turn to port or starboard, to dodge the oncoming torpedo or cause it to glance off the hull.

In just two months, another Cunard captain, Daniel Dow, back at work, would do exactly that, and win a citation from the company's board. On July 15, 1915, at dusk, a lookout aboard Dow's *Mauretania* spotted a periscope about half a mile out. An instant later two torpedoes began racing toward his ship, their tracks clearly visible. He ordered an immediate full turn to starboard, *toward* the submarine. Both torpedoes missed; the submarine submerged and fled.

"TREFF!"

S CHWIEGER'S LOG ENTRY FOR 2:10 P.M., MAY 7, BEGAN with the German word *Treff*, for impact. He wrote, "Torpedo hits starboard side close behind the bridge. An unusually great detonation follows with a very strong explosive cloud (cloud reaches far beyond the forward funnel). The explosion of the torpedo must have been accompanied by a second one (boiler or coal or powder?)."

By now his pilot, Lanz, was standing next to him at the periscope. Schwieger stepped aside and let Lanz peer through the eyepiece. Lanz could identify ships, even small ones, by their silhouettes and deck configurations. This one was easy. An instant after looking through the eyepiece, Lanz said, "My God, it's the *Lusitania*."

Schwieger's log indicates that he only now learned the ship's true identity, but this seems implausible. The ship's profile—its size, its lines, its four funnels—made it one of the most distinctive vessels afloat.

Schwieger again took the periscope. What he saw now shocked even him.

PART IV

THE
BLACK SOUL

IMPACT

A S THE TORPEDO PASSED FROM VIEW BELOW THE EDGE of the deck, there was an interval when nothing happened and one could indulge the notion that it had missed or malfunctioned. "I saw it disappear," one passenger said, "and for a bare second we all had a kind of hope that maybe it wouldn't explode."

In the next instant, 350 pounds of explosives detonated against the plates of the hull, at a point under the bridge about 10 feet below the waterline. Immediately the payload turned from solid to gas. This "phase change" released heat at a temperature exceeding 5,000 degrees Centigrade, 9,000 Fahrenheit, at immense pressure. As one early-twentieth-century submarine builder put it, "The side of the ship is nothing but tissue paper in the hands of these enormous forces."

A geyser of seawater, planking, rope, and shards of steel soared upward to twice the height of the ship. Lifeboat No. 5 "was blown to atoms," one lookout said. The ship continued forward through the geyser, which almost immediately collapsed back onto the decks. Seawater drenched passengers; debris thudded off the shuffleboard courts. The children jumping rope on A Deck stopped jumping.

A hole the size of a small house now existed below the waterline. Its shape was more horizontal than vertical, roughly 40 feet wide by 15 feet high. The effects of the blast spread well beyond this, however. Thousands of rivets and the steel plates they anchored came loose over an area about fifteen times greater than the hole itself; the glass in nearby portholes fractured. Bulkheads were damaged and watertight doors dislodged. The relatively small doors and chambers of passenger ships did not dispel explosive forces as readily as the open holds of cargo vessels and thus were prone to destruction. The *Lusitania*'s builders had installed these barriers with collisions and groundings in mind; none had imagined that a torpedo might one day be detonated against the hull from underwater.

Just inside the hull, at the point of impact, stood the starboard end of a major watertight bulkhead that spanned the width of the hull, one of a dozen such dividers in the ship. This particular bulkhead also formed a wall between the forward-most boiler room—Boiler Room No. 1—and a large coal storage chamber just beyond, toward the bow, called the "cross-bunker," the only coal bunker in the ship arrayed across the full width of the hull. The rest were the longitudinal bunkers that ran along the hull walls. At this point in the voyage all the bunkers were nearly empty.

The forward motion of the ship, initially 18 knots, caused "forced flooding," which drove seawater into the ship at a rate estimated at 100 tons a second. Water surged into the cross-bunker and into Boiler Room No. 1, a cavern that housed two one-ended boilers and two double boilers, and the beginning of a main steam line. Water also flowed into the longitudinal bunkers along the starboard side, nearest the impact zone. As these bunkers filled with water, the ship began to list to starboard. At the same time, the water filling Boiler Room No. 1 and the forward cross-bunker caused the bow to begin sinking. The stern began to rise and the hull to twist.

CAPTAIN TURNER was standing on A Deck, just outside the entry to his rooms, when he heard the lookout's cry that a torpedo was coming. He saw the track and watched it pass below the starboard rail. There was a brief silence, and then a column of water and wreckage erupted from the sea. The shock of the explosion and the sudden list to starboard threw Turner off balance.

With debris and seawater falling behind him, Turner ran up the stairway to the bridge.

HOW PASSENGERS experienced the blast depended on where they were situated when it happened. The ship was so long—nearly 800 feet—and so elastic that those standing or seated toward the stern, in the second-class smoking and dining rooms and the Verandah Cafe, or on the stern "counter," where the deck swept out over the rudder, felt it as a dull thud. Oliver Bernard recalled thinking, "Well, that wasn't so bad." Those closest to the bridge felt the impact in a manner more vivid and tactile. "Water, bits of coal, splinters of wood, etc., coming down on our heads!" recalled Dwight Harris. "I flattened up against the side of the ship, but got soaked!"

Preston Prichard and Grace French were happily searching for her "double" when they heard the explosion and felt the ship lurch to starboard. "The ship listed so much that we all scrambled down the deck and for a moment everything was in confusion," she recalled. "When I came to myself again, I glanced around but could find no trace of Mr. Prichard. He seemed to have disappeared."

Too frightened to go to her own cabin, Miss French set off to look for a life jacket on deck, apparently unaware that all jackets were stored in passengers' rooms.

Out came the watches. William McMillan Adams, nineteen years old and always handy with a timepiece, put the moment of impact at 2:05. "I timed everything," he said, later. When asked why, he replied, "I just did it; I don't know why." Charles Lauriat checked his stem-winding wristwatch and pegged the impact at 9:08 A.M., Boston time, or 2:08 P.M. Greenwich Mean Time. Others put the time at 2:10; this would later become the agreed-upon benchmark.

Within seconds Lauriat felt the ship roll to the right and tilt toward the bow. "You could feel the two separate motions very distinctly," Lauriat wrote. "It seemed as if she were going down at once, but then she stopped suddenly as if the sea had met the water-tight bulkheads and she seemed to right herself and even raise her bow a little. This gave me a feeling of security, and I at first thought she would stay afloat."

Moments later a second explosion occurred. (The ever-precise William McMillan Adams timed this at thirty seconds after the first.) Its character was different. Where the first had been a single, sharp detonation, this one, Lauriat said, was "very muffled." A shudder traveled the length of the ship and seemed to rise from deep within the hull, "more like an explosion of a boiler, I should think," said Lauriat. He was unable to identify the location with any precision. The sound was not "distinct enough," he said.

In the dining rooms, the plants set out on tables shifted; glassware fell to the floor.

MARGARET MACKWORTH and her father, D. A. Thomas, having finished lunch, were about to enter the elevator on D Deck when Thomas joked, "I think we might stay up on deck to-night to see if we get our thrill."

Before Mackworth could answer, she heard a dull explosion, not loud, more a heavy thud that rose from somewhere below. "I turned and came out of the lift; somehow, the stairs seemed safer."

Her father set off to try to learn more about what had happened. Mackworth, in accord with her earlier plan, went straight to her room on B Deck to get her life jacket. The degree of list made progress difficult. She moved along the lower side of the passage in the angle between wall and floor and collided with an oncoming stewardess. The two, Mackworth wrote, "wasted a minute or so making polite apologies to each other."

After retrieving her life jacket, Mackworth ran to her father's cabin and got one for him as well. She climbed to the open boat deck and moved to the higher side—the port side—judging it safer to be "as far away from the submarine as possible."

There she encountered her tablemate Dorothy Conner, and asked if she could stand with her while she waited for her father. She put on her life jacket.

A crowd of third-class passengers emerged from below, with great energy and noise.

Mackworth turned to Conner and said, "I always thought a shipwreck was a well-organized affair."

"So did I," Conner replied, "but I've learnt a devil of a lot in the last five minutes."

CHARLES LAURIAT was standing next to Elbert Hubbard and his wife. He urged them to go to their room and get their life jackets, but the couple seemed paralyzed. "Mr. Hubbard stayed by the rail affectionately holding his arm around his wife's waist, and both seemed unable to act."

Lauriat told Hubbard, "If you don't care to come, stay here and I will get them for you." Lauriat set off for his own quarters.

For the many parents aboard, the blast brought a unique sort of terror. The Cromptons of Philadelphia had six children scattered over the ship; the Pearl family of New York had four. The ship was immense, and older children had the run of its decks. Parents were compelled to hunt for their children among the ever-growing crowds of passengers swarming the boat deck, while at the same time holding babies and corralling toddlers.

Norah Bretherton, the thirty-two-year-old wife of a journalist in Los Angeles, had booked passage aboard the *Lusitania* so that she could bring her two children, Paul and Elizabeth, to meet her parents in England. Paul was three years old; Elizabeth—"Betty"— was one and a half. Bretherton, pregnant, was traveling alone with the children because her husband had to stay behind in California to work.

Her cabin was a second-class room toward the stern of C Deck, the shelter deck. Before lunch she had dropped her daughter off at a "play yard" on the deck above, then placed her son in the cabin for a nap and left him there.

When the torpedo struck, she was in a stairwell between the two decks. She froze. She had no idea where to go first—up one deck to retrieve her baby girl, or down a deck to get her napping son? All lamps went out. The sudden list of the ship threw her from one side of the stairwell to the other.

She ran for the baby.

ON ENTERING the bridge, Captain Turner began issuing commands. He ordered the engines "full astern." The reverse turbines were the ship's brakes, the only way to bring it to a stop, and the ship had to be stopped before any lifeboats could be launched with safety. The engines did not respond.

Turner told the helmsman, Quartermaster Hugh Johnston, to turn the ship hard toward the coast, still a dozen miles off. If worst came to worst, he would beach the ship and at least eliminate the danger of sinking.

Johnston stood inside the wheelhouse, a small enclosure within the bridge. He repeated Turner's command to confirm that he understood. He rotated the wheel to produce what should have been a 35-degree turn toward shore.

"All right, boy," Turner said.

The ship responded, according to Johnston.

Captain Turner now ordered him to "steady" the ship, that is, to adjust the wheel to counter the tendency to continue turning once the desired heading was achieved. Johnston gave the ship 35 degrees helm in the opposite direction.

"Keep her head on Kinsale," Turner said, directing Johnston to aim the bow toward the lighthouse on the Old Head. Johnston echoed the order and began its execution.

This time the helm failed to answer. The ship began to veer, "to pay off," toward open sea. Johnston attempted to counter the drift. "I was doing all I was supposed to do, steadying the ship,"

Johnston said, "but she was swinging off again." Turner repeated his order for a turn toward shore.

Johnston tried. "I put the wheel round, but she would not answer her helm but kept on swinging out toward the sea."

Turner told Second Officer Percy Hefford to check the ship's spirit indicator, a marine version of a carpenter's level, to gauge the severity of the list.

Hefford called out, "Fifteen degrees to starboard, sir."

Turner gave the order to close the ship's watertight doors, below the passenger decks, which were operated with a control along the front wall of the bridge. To make sure the doors really did close, Turner told Hefford to go down into the forecastle and check.

Hefford stopped at the wheelhouse and told Johnston to keep his eye on the spirit indicator and "sing out if she goes any further." Hefford left the bridge. He did not reappear.

Turner ordered the lifeboats lowered "to the rails," that is, to a level where they could be safely boarded by passengers. The boats still could not be launched, however, for sheer momentum continued to propel the *Lusitania* forward, initially at 18 knots. Had the reverse turbines responded, the ship could have been stopped in under three minutes, but now only the drag of the sea could bring it to a halt. The liner moved in a long arc away from shore. The forced flooding continued.

At the wheel, Johnston checked the spirit gauge. The list held steady at 15 degrees.

Turner stepped out onto the bridge wing. Below him, the boat deck was filling with passengers and deckhands. Firemen black with soot worked their way through the crowd like shadows. Some of them climbed out of the ship's vents.

DOWN IN QUARANTINE, Robert Kay and his mother felt the torpedo blast, which Robert described as a "violent explosion." This was followed by a second, more muted eruption that seemed to come from within the ship. The lights went out.

His mother was tense but oddly calm, Robert recalled, though she expressed concern that in her condition, so deeply pregnant, they might never reach the upper decks safely.

The door to quarantine was no longer plumb in its frame. They forced it open. The corridor outside was dark, tilted both to starboard and toward the bow.

They moved slowly. Robert tried to help, but "every step was an effort, and our progress was painfully slow," he wrote. The combined starboard and forward list made stairways dangerous. The Kays held tight to handrails, "but with each moment it seemed that the surroundings became more and more crazily distorted."

Everyone else seemed to have gone. There was quiet, though now and then Robert heard a shout from far above. With great effort, he and his mother worked their way upward.

Five minutes had elapsed since the initial explosion.

CHARLES LAURIAT returned to deck, carrying all the life jackets he could. He put his on first, then helped others. These were the new Boddy life jackets. If worn properly, they were effective in keeping even an oversized man afloat, comfortably on his back, but Lauriat saw that nearly everyone around him had put the jackets on incorrectly. Cunard had not yet established a policy of having passengers try on life jackets at the start of a voyage. The only guide was an illustrated instruction sheet posted in each room, in the apparent belief that passengers would have the time and presence of mind to read and follow it. The fault in this logic now became evident. "In their hurry, they put them on every way except the right way," Lauriat wrote. "One man had his arm through one armhole and his head through the other; others had them on around the waist and upside down; but very few had them on correctly."

Lauriat was standing within earshot of the bridge when he heard a woman call out to Captain Turner, her voice steady and calm, "Captain, what do you wish us to do?"

"Stay right where you are, Madam, she's all right."

"Where do you get your information?" she asked.

"From the engine room, Madam," he said. But the engine room clearly had told him no such thing. Apparently he was seeking to calm the crowd below and avoid setting off a panicked race for the boats.

This was the last Lauriat saw of Turner. Lauriat and the woman now headed back toward the stern, and as they walked they told other passengers what the captain had said.

Second-class passenger Henry Needham may have encountered the pair, for he recalled that a passenger approaching from the direction of the bridge had shouted, "The Captain says the boat will not sink."

"The remark," Needham wrote, "was greeted with cheers & I noticed many people who had been endeavoring to get a place in the boats, turn away in apparent contentment."

Turner's words merely confirmed what the passengers and many of the crew already believed, or wanted to believe: that no torpedo could cause the ship mortal damage. The ship's purser and surgeon spent the moments after the two explosions calmly strolling along the boat deck, smoking cigarettes, assuring passengers the ship was not in any danger. And this seemed entirely plausible. The *Lusitania* was simply too big and too well built to sink. What made the idea even more incongruous was the setting: a gleaming May afternoon, warm and still, the sea smooth and the headlands of Ireland visible in the distance, so green they seemed to luminesce in the sunshine.

Isaac Lehmann, the New York businessman, did not share this confidence in the ship's unsinkability. He went to his stateroom to get his life jacket and found that someone had entered his room and taken it. A nervous man, Lehmann feared chaos. "I don't know what possessed me," he said, "but I looked in my dress suit case and got hold of my revolver, as I figured this would come in handy in case there was anybody not doing the proper thing."

THERE WERE shipbuilders among the *Lusitania*'s passengers, and at first they too believed the ship would remain afloat. One of them, Frederic J. Gauntlett, an executive with the Newport News Ship Building and Dry Dock Company, was on his way to Europe to meet with builders of submarines with an eye to starting a venture in the United States. He was traveling with the company's president, Albert Hopkins.

Gauntlett was at lunch with Hopkins and another shipbuilder, a Philadelphian named Samuel Knox. (It was Knox's company that had built the *Gulflight*, the American oil tanker torpedoed a week earlier.) They sat at their usual table, the sixth one back, on the starboard side. They wore suits; the tablecloths were white, and each table had clear glass vases with cut flowers. Sunlight streamed through the windows.

The room tilted to the right. A vase fell from Gauntlett's table. "I left my coffee and nuts," he said, "and rose from the table and shouted to the stewards to close the ports." As a shipbuilder, he understood the danger posed by open portholes. He shouted half a dozen times. "The stewards evidently had business elsewhere," he said, "and when they left the dining saloon I followed suit and left the dining room also."

He and his lunch mates did not themselves attempt to close the ports, and these remained open. Gauntlett went to the coatrack, got his hat, and retrieved Knox's as well. They walked up three flights to the boat deck.

Gauntlett was reassured that the list seemed to stabilize at 15 degrees. He was convinced the angle would not worsen and "never for one moment supposed she was going to sink." He said as much to a woman standing nearby, surrounded by her children. She asked him what to do. "I told her there was no danger," he said; the ship "was not going to sink."

Gauntlett expected the bulkheads and watertight doors to keep the hull from flooding further, but then he sensed a change. The list became more pronounced, as did the tilt toward the bow, at which point, he said, "I made up my mind that it was up to me to take a look around and see what the trouble was."

He made his way to the railing at the forward end of the deck and looked over at the bow below. The forecastle was partially submerged.

He went to his room and put on his life jacket.

ALL THE ship's systems were now dead. The rudder no longer operated. The main electric dynamo had failed. All lights were out; anyone walking along an interior corridor now found himself in blackness. The operator in the Marconi room on the topmost deck switched to emergency power. The two first-class elevators at the center of the ship stalled. According to one account, passengers within began to scream.

The elevator that provided the only access to the ship's baggage room also stopped. The scores of men working to get passengers' luggage ready for arrival either were dead from the torpedo blast, or would be soon, as water filled the bow. A fireman who escaped Boiler Room No. 2, Eugene McDermott, described a "rush of water that knocked me off my feet." Many of the dead crewmen were precisely those who would have been assigned to help launch the ship's lifeboats.

Now the sea found a new path into the hull. Water began to flow through open portholes, many of which were barely above the water to begin with. Those of E Deck, for example, normally cleared the water by only 15 feet. By one estimate, at least 70 portholes had been left open in the starboard side. Multiplied by 3.75 tons of water per minute per porthole, that meant that 260 tons was entering the ship each minute through the starboard portholes alone.

It was now about 2:20 P.M., ten minutes since the torpedo struck. For the next few moments, as deckhands and passengers waited for the ship to slow enough to allow the safe launching of boats, there was quiet. "A strange silence prevailed," said Albert Bestic, junior third officer, "and small, insignificant sounds, such as the whimper of a child, the cry of a seagull or the bang of a door, assumed alarming proportions."

FIRST WORD

THE TELEGRAMS ARRIVED AT THE ADMIRALTY IN London and the Naval Center in Queenstown in rapid and jarring sequence, sent from various points:

2:15 FROM VALENTIA STATION TO QUEENSTOWN:
" 'LUSITANIA' IN DISTRESS OFF KINSALE. BELIEVED."

2:20 FROM GALLEY HEAD TO ADMIRALTY:
" 'LUSITANIA' S.E. 10 MILES SINKING BOW FIRST
APPARENTLY ATTACKED BY SUBMARINE."

2:25 FROM QUEENSTOWN TO ADMIRALTY:
" 'LUSITANIA' TORPEDOED REPORTED SINKING 10 MILES
S. OF KINSALE. ALL AVAILABLE TUGS AND SMALL CRAFT
BEING SENT TO HER ASSISTANCE. ABERDEEN, PEMBROKE,
BUNCRANA, DEVONPORT, LIVERPOOL INFORMED."

DECISIONS

THE FIRST ATTEMPTS TO LAUNCH THE *Lusitania*'S LIFE-boats revealed the true degree of danger now faced by the ship's passengers and shattered the illusion of safety projected by having so many boats aboard. The list was so severe that the boats on the starboard side now hung well away from the hull, leaving a gap between the boats and the deck of 5 to 8 feet, with the sea 60 feet below. Members of the crew tried using deck chairs to span the opening, but most passengers chose to jump. Parents handed small children across. One boy took a running leap and landed in a boat feet-first.

Meanwhile, the lifeboats on the opposite side, the port side, had swung inward over the deck. These were all but unusable. Only a great effort could move them into position for launch. Capt. Turner ordered them emptied, but as the ship's condition worsened, passengers and crew tried to launch them anyway.

Ogden Hammond, the New Jersey real-estate developer who'd been assured the ship was as safe as a New York trolley, walked along the port side of the boat deck with his wife, Mary, until they found themselves at Boat No. 20, which a group of crewmen and male passengers had somehow muscled to a point outside the rail. Women and children were climbing aboard.

Neither Mary nor Ogden wore a life jacket. He had wanted to go down to their stateroom and retrieve the jackets stored there, but Mary had pleaded with him not to leave her. They had hunted for jackets on deck but found none.

At the lifeboat, Ogden balked at climbing aboard, out of respect for the maritime custom that gave women and children priority. Mary refused to go unless Ogden came too, so the couple stood aside, watching the process and waiting. At last Ogden agreed to get in. He and Mary took a place near the bow. The boat was half full, with about thirty-five people, when the attempt to launch it began.

Men at the bow and stern manipulated the ropes—the falls— that ran through block and tackle at each end of the boat. A sailor at the bow lost control of his rope. Ogden tried to grab it, but the rope was running so fast it tore the skin from his hands. The bow plunged; the stern rope held. Everyone fell from the boat into the sea, 60 feet below.

Ogden came to the surface; his wife did not. He reached for an oar floating nearby.

AT THE NEXT port-side boat, No. 18, another launching attempt had stalled. This boat contained forty women and children, and was held in place by a restraining pin. The sailor in charge refused to lower it, in accord with Turner's orders, but held an ax, ready to knock the pin loose should the orders change. Several dozen passengers stood between the boat and the outer wall of the first-class smoking room.

Isaac Lehmann, the New York businessman, was shocked that no effort was being made to launch the boat. He had managed to find a life jacket; his revolver was in his pocket. He glanced toward the ship's bow and saw water advancing along the deck. He demanded to know why the sailor didn't act.

"It is the captain's orders not to launch any boats," the sailor replied.

"To hell with the captain," Lehmann said. "Don't you see the boat is sinking?" He drew his revolver. "And the first man that disobeys my orders to launch the boat I shoot to kill!"

The sailor complied. He swung his ax to knock out the restraining pin. The boat was heavy to begin with, but now loaded with three tons of humanity it swung inward, crushing everyone between the boat and the wall. At least two passengers, sisters in their fifties, died instantly, of injuries associated with severe crushing. Lehmann's right leg was damaged, but he managed to crawl from the mass of wounded bystanders. This was not easy. He was a large, round man and wore a long overcoat and a life jacket.

Passengers and crew again attempted to launch the lifeboat. They were making progress when something went awry and this boat too dumped its passengers into the water. At about the same time, Lehmann said, a "terrific explosion" rose from the deck in the direction of the bow. This new convulsion was likely caused by water infiltrating yet another boiler room and coming in contact with a superheated tank, one of a number of such secondary eruptions. Only about fourteen minutes had passed since the torpedo impact, but the sea was climbing fast.

MANY PASSENGERS decided to forgo the boats and take a more direct path. Dwight Harris headed toward the bow, as per his plan. He climbed over the port rail on A Deck and scuttled down the side of the ship, two decks, then went toward the bow, which had sunk to the point where all he would have to do was step into the water. He took off his shoes and discarded his overcoat, his hat, and his Medici book. He had no life jacket, not even his custom Wanamaker's belt. He too had been afraid to go to his cabin for fear of being trapped. But now, at the water's edge and facing the real prospect of drowning, he changed his mind.

"I took a look at things and decided I must have a life belt so I climbed up again to 'A' deck and rushed to my cabin," he wrote. He put the belt on and returned to the bow. An officer called to him to come up to the lifeboats, "but I realized that all available space in them was badly wanted, so I shook my head no!—I got up on the rail, swung my feet over, and when the water got right up to the deck I jumped overboard!"

As he swam away, he looked up, and saw the ship's giant funnels move past against the sky.

THEODATE POPE and Edwin Friend had planned that if an emergency arose they would rendezvous on the boat deck with Theodate's maid, Emily Robinson. "The deck suddenly looked very strange crowded with people," Theodate wrote, "and I remember two women were crying in a pitifully weak way." Theodate and Friend looked over the port side and watched a boat being lowered. One end fell too fast and everyone plummeted into the sea. This could have been Ogden Hammond's boat, or the one Lehmann tried to launch at gunpoint. "We looked at each other, sickened by the sight, and then made our way through the crowd for deck B on the starboard side."

As they stood at the rail, they saw that efforts to launch the lifeboats on this side were having more success. Boats came down past them, winched slowly from the deck above. The two feared the ship was sinking so quickly and with so pronounced a list that it might roll onto the boats after they reached the water.

They climbed back up to the boat deck but made no attempt to board any of the remaining lifeboats.

"We walked close together, side by side, each with an arm around the other's waist," Theodate recalled. The two met a passenger whom by now they knew well, Marie Depage, the Belgian nurse. Depage seemed stunned. "She had a man on either side of her, friends of hers, so I did not speak," Theodate wrote. "It was no time for words unless one could offer help."

Theodate and Friend headed toward the stern, now an uphill climb. Her maid came up beside them and Theodate noted the tense smile etched on her face. "I could only put my hand on her shoulder and say, 'Oh Robinson.'"

They searched for life jackets. They entered several cabins and found three. Friend helped the women put them on; they all walked to the rail. The ship's giant funnels towered above them at an exaggerated slant. The water was far below.

Theodate glanced at Friend. The two looked down at the water. The time had come. "I asked him to go first," she wrote.

Friend climbed down one deck, then jumped. He disappeared briefly, but soon bobbed to the surface, and looked up at the women. The ship continued to move forward; his form receded.

Theodate said, "Come Robinson," and stepped off the rail.

GRACE FRENCH ran back to where she and Preston Prichard had been standing at the moment of impact. He was nowhere in sight. She went to the rail, took off her coat, and jumped. She had no life jacket. Her plan was to swim until she found a piece of floating debris. The jump took her deep under the surface, where an eddy caused by the passing ship held her down.

BY NOW, Captain Turner knew the ship would sink. He put on a life jacket but remained on the bridge, as did fellow officers and his helmsman, Hugh Johnston. In the Marconi house behind the bridge, the ship's chief wireless man, Robert Leith, used auxiliary power to send message after message asking all ships in the vicinity to come at once.

Turner asked Johnston for another readout of the spirit gauge.

Johnston called, "Twenty-five degrees."

Turner said, "My God."

His view from the bridge was of water surging over the forecastle below. He told Johnston, "Save yourself." The time was about 2:25 P.M.—fifteen minutes since impact.

Johnston left the bridge and found one of the ship's thirty-five life buoys. Water had reached the starboard bridge wing. Johnston entered the sea and was washed across the deck. "I simply had to go wherever the tide took me," he said.

Turner remained on the bridge.

SCHWIEGER'S VIEW

"I TOOK MY POSITION AT THE PERISCOPE AGAIN," SCHWIEGER told his friend Max Valentiner. "The ship was sinking with unbelievable rapidity. There was a terrific panic on her deck. Overcrowded lifeboats, fairly torn from their positions, dropped into the water. Desperate people ran helplessly up and down the decks. Men and women jumped into the water and tried to swim to empty, overturned lifeboats. It was the most terrible sight I have ever seen. It was impossible for me to give any help. I could have saved only a handful. And then the cruiser that had passed us was not very far away and must have picked up the distress signals. She would shortly appear, I thought. The scene was too horrible to watch, and I gave orders to dive to twenty meters, and away."

In his final log entry on the attack, at 2:25 P.M., Schwieger wrote: "It would have been impossible for me, anyhow, to fire a second torpedo into this crushing crowd of humanity trying to save their lives."

Schwieger directed his U-boat out to sea. His crew was jubilant: they had destroyed the *Lusitania*, the ship that symbolized British maritime prowess.

THE LITTLE ARMY

Certain now that the ship would sink, Charles Lauriat went back to his cabin at the forward end of B Deck to rescue what he could of his belongings. As he moved along the corridor toward his room, he found vivid evidence of just how much the ship had listed. The floor was canted to a degree that made it impossible to walk without also stepping on the wall. The awkward bulk of his life jacket further impeded his progress. He passed open staterooms whose portholes had once provided views of sky and horizon but now looked down onto water made dark by the shadow of the leaning hull. The only light in the corridor was a shifting, silvery glow raised by sunlight glinting off the sea from beyond the ship's shadow. Lauriat was startled to see that many of the portholes were open.

His room was a black box. He found his matches and used these to locate his passport and other items he hoped to rescue. He grabbed his leather briefcase with the Dickens *Christmas Carol* inside but left the Thackeray drawings in his shoe case. He hurried back onto the deck, which now was close to the water.

A lifeboat containing women and children was floating just off his deck, on the starboard side, but had not yet been released from the ropes that tied it to the davits on the boat deck above. This was Boat No. 7. Someone needed to act, and soon, Lauriat realized, before the ship dragged the lifeboat under. He climbed into the

boat and placed his briefcase on the bottom, then set about trying to free the stern. The bow remained tethered. Another man,
a steward, was struggling to cut it loose with a pocketknife. "The
steamer was all the time rapidly settling," Lauriat recalled, "and
to look at the tremendous smokestack hanging out over us only
added to the terror of the people in the boat."

Being this close to the hull brought home just how big the *Lusitania* truly was. Arthur Mitchell, the Raleigh Bicycle agent who had
wanted to hold lifeboat drills for passengers, was in Boat No. 15,
four astern of Lauriat's. He said, "Never could one realize the size
of the ship so well as at this moment, her great deck towering above
us, and her enormous funnels clear against the sky belching forth
smoke which almost blinded the people in the boats around her."

The ship was still moving but sinking fast, the deck visibly descending. Lauriat stood on a seat in the lifeboat, intending to go
forward to help with the bow. The curved arm of a descending
davit struck him from behind and knocked him down. He got up,
this time mindful of the davit, and moved forward by stepping
from seat to seat, forcing his way through the mass of passengers.

The boat seemed to be full of oars—"an infinite number," he
wrote. He stepped on one. It rolled. He fell.

By the time Lauriat got to his feet, the now partially submerged
forward davit was pressing on the bow of the lifeboat and the
boat's stern was rising. It was as though the ship had reached out
with a clawed hand to drag the lifeboat down. There was nothing
to be done. Lauriat stepped from the boat into the water. He urged
the other occupants to do likewise, but few did. The davit gripped
the lifeboat and tipped it inward, toward the deck, then pulled it
under the water, with women and children and the Dickens *Carol*
still aboard.

SHIPBUILDER SAMUEL KNOX came across Paul Crompton, the
Philadelphian traveling to England with his wife and six children.
Crompton had corralled four of the children and was trying to
put a life jacket on the youngest, "a mere baby," Knox said. One

of Crompton's older girls could not get her own jacket adjusted properly. With no apparent concern, she asked Knox, "Please will you show me how to fix this?" Knox did so. The girl thanked him.

NORAH BRETHERTON, the Los Angeles woman who had run to rescue her infant daughter, Betty, while leaving her three-year-old son asleep in her cabin, carried the baby up a stairway crammed with passengers. She forced the girl into the arms of a passing stranger, a man, then turned and went back down to get her son.

The interior stairs were empty of people. She ran. Smoke came through the floors of the corridor and the cabin itself. She grabbed the boy, Paul, and carried him up to B Deck, to the starboard side, which by this point was canted so steeply that another woman, also holding a small boy, slid past along the deck, on her back.

Bretherton came to a lifeboat in process of being lowered. A male passenger told her she could not get in, that the boat was too full, but a friend of Bretherton's, already in the boat, persuaded the other passengers to allow her aboard.

Bretherton had no idea where her baby was. On the way to the lifeboat, she had seen the man to whom she had given the child, but the man's arms were empty.

THEODATE POPE struggled to come to the surface but found herself pressed against a barrier of some sort. Something made of wood. She swallowed salt water.

"I opened my eyes," she wrote, "and through the green water I could see what I was being dashed up against; it looked like the bottom and keel of one of the ship's boats." She was certain death was near, she wrote, and "committed myself to God's care in thought—a prayer without words." Then, something struck her, and she lost consciousness.

She awoke floating on the surface, held up by her life jacket. For a few moments, everything she saw was gray. The limbs of frantic people jostled her. There was screaming and shouting.

Color returned to her vision. A man, "insane with fright," grabbed her around the shoulders. He had no life jacket. His bulk pushed her downward.

"Oh please don't," she said. Then she and the man sank below the surface. She passed out again.

When she regained consciousness, the man was gone and she was afloat. There was sunshine and cerulean sky. The ship was well past, and still moving. The men and women drifting in the sea around her were spaced more widely than before, and they were quieter. Some were alive, some clearly dead. Blood flowed from a gash in one man's forehead.

An oar floated near. Her life jacket kept her buoyant, but even so she reached for the oar and draped her right foot over the blade. She raised her head to see if help was coming, but saw that none was. "Then I sank back, very relieved in my mind, for I decided it was too horrible to be true and that I was dreaming, and again lost consciousness."

ELSEWHERE IN THE SEA, a kindred soul also lay adrift—Mary Popham Lobb, a British citizen and spiritualist from the island of St. Vincent, in the Caribbean. For her this time in the water was mystical and moving. She found herself drifting farther and farther from the dense mass of bodies and wreckage left behind as the ship slid by. The cries of survivors became faint, as did the clatter of oars and the shouts of men in boats.

She gave up all hope of rescue and told herself the time to cross over had come, but another voice within told her, no, this was not her moment. "The gulls were flying overhead," she wrote, "and I remember noticing the beauty of the blue shadows which the sea throws up to their white feathers: they were happy and alive and made me feel rather lonely; my thoughts went to my people, looking forward to seeing me, and at that moment having tea in the garden. The idea of their grief was unbearable; I had to cry a little."

—⁓—

GRACE FRENCH, having jumped without a life jacket, sank deep into the sea. "It got blacker and blacker, until it became calm and peaceful and I thought I must be in heaven," she wrote. "The next thing I saw was the water getting lighter and lighter until I popped to the surface and grabbed hold of a plank of wood and it helped keep me afloat. With that I felt I was saved; I grabbed hold of a lifejacket which had a dead young man in it. We floated together for a while until a big wave washed him away."

DWIGHT HARRIS swam from the ship. "I had no feeling of fear when I went overboard." He felt as comfortable as if he had simply entered a swimming pool—so composed that when he came across a floating book, he picked it up and examined it.

The *Lusitania* moved past. "I was carried by the whole length of the ship and saw everything that happened!—The first life boat (starboard side) was in the water with only two sailors in it. They called to me to swim to it, but I kept on. The second boat was suspended and hanging straight down, the ropes at one end having jammed; the third and fourth boats were crowded with people."

He saw that the sea was now level with the bridge. As the ship passed him, its stern rose into the air.

FOR THE FAMILY of Joseph Frankum, of Birmingham, England, traveling with his wife, three-year-old daughter, and two sons, ages five and seven, these last moments were terrifying. Frankum gathered them all in a lifeboat on the port side, at the stern. The boat still hung from its davits, but Frankum hoped it would float free when the sea arrived.

The view downhill was of chaos and death, punctuated with eruptions of black smoke as boilers exploded in succession. The mounting air pressure in the hull caused portholes to burst and seams and apertures to howl.

But, strangely, there was also singing. First "Tipperary," then "Rule, Britannia!" Next came "Abide with Me," but it was so moving and so sad that women began to cry, and the singers switched to "Pull for the Shore," and then another round of "Rule, Britannia!"

Frankum said, "I clung to my wife and children and held them tight."

MARGARET MACKWORTH stayed with the ship, on the boat deck, next to Dorothy Conner. Conner's brother-in-law was somewhere below, looking for life jackets. A strange calm settled over the deck. People moved "gently and vaguely," Mackworth recalled. "They reminded one of a swarm of bees who do not know where the queen has gone."

For a moment, the ship seemed about to right itself. Word spread that the crew had at last been able to close its watertight bulkheads and that the danger of sinking was past. Mackworth and Conner shook hands. "Well, you've had your thrill all right," Mackworth said.

"I never want another," Conner said.

Conner's brother-in-law returned. He had been unable to reach his cabin because of water in the corridor but had managed to find jackets elsewhere. The three put them on. Mackworth released the hook on her skirt, to make it easier to take off later if the need arose.

The ship's list returned, steeper than before. Seventeen minutes had elapsed since impact. They resolved to jump. The idea terrified Mackworth. She chided herself on this, "telling myself how ridiculous I was to have physical fear of the jump when we stood in such grave danger as we did."

Conner and her brother-in-law moved to the rail. Mackworth held back.

Conner wrote, "One gets very close in three minutes at such a time, and just before we jumped I grabbed her hand and squeezed to try and encourage her."

But Mackworth stayed behind. Her last recollection was of water up to her knees, and the ship sliding away, pulling her down.

—⁓—

THEODORE AND Belle Naish, the Kansas City couple who just hours earlier had been admiring the sunrise from the ship's top deck, also stood at the rail. They wore life jackets and stood arm in arm, talking quietly. Having watched one lifeboat dump its occupants into the sea, they made no effort to get into another. A member of the crew told them, "She's all right, she will float for an hour." But Belle did not believe him. She'd been watching the rail and the horizon line. The changing differential told her the ship was sinking quickly. She said, "We'll be gone in a minute."

She took her arm from Theodore's, so as not to drag him under. "We watched the water, talked to each other; there seemed to be a great rush, a roar and a splintering sound, then the lifeboat or something swung over our heads." The boat struck her and cut her scalp. She held out an arm to protect Theodore. A sudden shift in the deck brought water to her armpits. "It seemed as if everything in the universe ripped and tore."

And then she was deep underwater—by her estimate, 20 or 30 feet. She looked up and saw the brilliant blue of the sky through the water. "I thought about how wondrously beautiful the sunlight and water were from below the surface," she wrote. She was not afraid. "I thought, 'Why, this is like being in my grandmother's feather bed.' I kicked, and rose faster."

Her head struck something, and continued to bump against it. "I put up my right hand, saw the blue sky and found myself clinging to the bumper of life boat 22." A man reached for her. She was so grateful she asked him to write his name on the inside of her shoe, "lest in the experience to follow I might forget."

The name was Hertz, for Douglas Hertz, a young man who was returning to England to join the South Lancashire Regiment, after living for a time in St. Louis. The sinking crowned a troubled period for Hertz. In 1913, he had lost his wife in a train wreck on their honeymoon; that same year, his mother had died in a house fire.

Belle saw no sign of her husband.

—⁂—

AFTER HELPING to launch a starboard boat, No. 13, Seaman Leslie Morton went to help with a second, also on the starboard side. He and another sailor, under the direction of a petty officer, struggled to help passengers get across the gap between the ship and the boat. The final angle of list, by Morton's estimate, was 30 degrees. Sixty passengers made it. Asked later how this feat had been achieved, Morton answered, "If you had to jump six or seven feet, or certainly drown, it is surprising what 'a hell of a long way' even older people can jump."

Morton worked the stern falls, as the petty officer directed the operation. The ship was still moving at 4 or 5 knots. The men lowered the lifeboat until its keel was just above the surface, and then, in accord with procedures for just this kind of circumstance, they let the lines play out so that when the boat touched water it would slip backward.

It drifted back one boat's length. The falls and the forward motion of the ship caused the boat to ride against the ship's hull. Morton was just about to climb down the stern ropes to clear the lifeboat when a group of less experienced men—Morton thought they might be stewards or waiters—began lowering the next boat back and lost control of its descent. The boat dropped 30 feet onto Morton's boat and the passengers within.

There was no time "to waste in either horror or sympathy," Morton wrote. He looked for his brother, amid mounting confusion, "many people losing their hold on the deck and slipping down and over the side, and a gradual crescendo of noise building up as the hundreds and hundreds of people began to realize that, not only was she going down very fast but in all probability too fast for them all to get away."

He found his brother at another lifeboat and helped him to lower it. The brothers then slid down and released the falls and used boat hooks to try shoving the lifeboat away from the hull. The passengers wouldn't let go of the ship. They held tight to various ropes and to the deck rails, "in some mistaken belief," Morton wrote, "that they would be safer hanging on to the big ship rather than entrusting their lives in the small lifeboat." The *Lusitania*'s deck came steadily downward.

Something snagged the gunnel of the lifeboat and began tipping it toward the ship's hull. "The time for heroics was obviously past," Morton wrote, "and my brother yelled at the top of his voice, 'I'm going over the side, Gertie.'"

The brothers waved at each other, then both dove into the sea. Neither wore a life jacket.

Morton wrote, "As I hit the water, and it is strange what one thinks about in times of stress, I suddenly remembered that my brother had never been able to swim."

Morton came to the surface and looked for his brother, "but seeing the turmoil of bodies, women and children, deck chairs, lifebelts, lifeboats, and every describable thing around me, coupled with no less than 35,000 tons of *Lusitania* breathing very heavily down my neck and altogether too close for my liking," he began to swim. Hard.

He glanced back. Two images became impressed in his memory. One was of a collapsible lifeboat slipping from the ship, still sheathed in its protective cover; the other, of Captain Turner in full dress uniform still on the bridge as the *Lusitania* began its final dive.

LAURIAT SWAM clear of the ship—or thought he had. He turned to watch its final moments. The bow was submerged, and slipping deeper into the sea; the stern was high in the air. The list to starboard had become so pronounced that passengers could stand upright only by propping themselves against the starboard rail, where they accumulated three or four deep in a long line that extended up toward the stern. Another witness called this assemblage "a little army." If anyone still harbored a hope that the *Lusitania* would not sink, that hope now failed.

Passengers back toward the stern, and therefore higher, watched as those ahead in line lost their grip on the rail. Those wearing life jackets floated, as if levitated from the deck; the many without jackets attempted to swim or sank from view.

Third Officer Bestic, still aboard, felt the ship make a "peculiar lurching movement" and looked down the deck. "An all-swallowing wave, not unlike a surf comber on a beach, was rushing up the boat deck, enveloping passengers, boats, and everything that lay in its path," he wrote. A mass wail rose from those it engulfed. "All the despair, terror and anguish of hundreds of souls passing into eternity composed that awful cry."

AS MEASLE-POXED Robert Kay and his pregnant mother struggled to ascend to the boat deck, the sounds of commotion above became more and more clear. They emerged to find themselves in a crush of people climbing toward the stern to escape the water ascending the deck. Robert watched people jump from the rails.

The ship continued to move; its stern rose higher. His mother held him close. And then the sea seemed to leap forward, and his mother was gone. They were separated; he was cast into a roiling turbulence. The ship disappeared.

Later, a passenger reported seeing a woman giving birth in the water. The idea that this might have been his mother would haunt the boy for the rest of his life.

AS CHARLES LAURIAT watched the ship pass and descend, something struck his head with shocking force. Whatever the thing was, it slipped back onto the shoulders of his life jacket, and caught there, and dragged him under. "I couldn't imagine what was landing on me out of the sky," he wrote. "I wouldn't have been as much surprised if the submarine had risen and I had found myself on her, but to get a bolt from the blue did surprise me."

He turned his head and saw that the thing that had snagged him was a wire stretched between the ship's two masts. This, he realized, was the *Lusitania*'s wireless antenna. He tried to shake it off but failed. It turned him upside down and pushed him ever deeper below the surface.

TELEGRAM

FRIDAY,
MAY 7, 1915
2:26 P.M.

"S.O.S. FROM 'LUSITANIA.' WE THINK WE ARE OFF
KINSALE. LATE POSITION 10 MILES OFF KINSALE COME AT
ONCE BIG LIST LATER PLEASE COME WITH ALL HASTE."

A QUEEN'S END

ONLY SIX OF THE *LUSITANIA*'S TWENTY-TWO CON-
ventional lifeboats got away before the ship made its final
plunge; a seventh, from the port side, reached the water,
but without a crucial plug. The boat filled, and foundered.

Those passengers who had already jumped from the ship swam
to get as far away as possible, for fear that the ship's descent would
generate suction that would drag them down as well. This did not
occur, although three passengers did experience a kindred effect.
One woman, Margaret Gwyer, a young newlywed from Saska-
toon, Canada, was sucked into one of the ship's 24-foot-wide funnels. Moments later an eruption of steam from below shot her back
out, alive but covered in black soot. Two other passengers accompanied her into the funnel—Harold Taylor, twenty-one, also newly
married, and Liverpool police inspector William Pierpoint. They
too emerged alive, with blackened faces and bodies.

As the ship's bow nosed down, its stern rose, exposing its four
giant propellers, which glinted gold in the sun. By now the *Lusitania* was 2 miles from the point where the torpedo had struck,
and about 12 miles from the Old Head of Kinsale. In these last
moments, the angle of starboard list decreased to only about 5 degrees, as water filled the rest of ship.

Seaman Morton turned onto his back and watched. He saw
passengers swept from the deck and hundreds of others struggling

to climb toward the stern. The *Lusitania* again heeled to starboard and slipped from view, in "a slow, almost stately, dive by the head, at an angle of some forty-five or fifty degrees."

Dwight Harris, floating a good distance astern in his Wanamaker's life belt, watched as the ship "plunged forward like a knife blade into the water—funnels, masts, boats, etc., all breaking to pieces and falling about everywhere! A <u>terrible</u> mass of iron, wood, steam, and water! And worst of all, human forms!—A great swirling greenish white bubble formed where the ship went down, which was a mass of struggling humanity and wreckage! The bubble got bigger and bigger, and fortunately only came to within twenty or thirty yards of me shoving wreckage with it."

THIS UPHEAVAL was a singular feature of the ship's demise, commented upon by many survivors. The sea rose as a plateau of water that spread in all directions. It carried bodies and masses of debris, and was accompanied by a strange sound.

Charles Lauriat emerged just as the *Lusitania* disappeared. By kicking hard he somehow managed to free himself of the antenna wire. "As she went under," Lauriat wrote, "I was not conscious of hearing cries; rather it was a long, lingering moan that rose, and which lasted for many moments after she disappeared." Lauriat was overtaken by the wave. "The mass of wreckage was tremendous," he wrote. "Aside from the people brought out with it, there were deck chairs, oars, boxes, and I can't remember what. I simply know that one moment one was jammed between large objects, and the next moment one was under the water."

Countless souls struggled in the sea around him. There was little he could do beyond shoving an oar or some other piece of floating debris in their direction. Many passengers wore heavy coats; women wore multiple layers of clothing—corsets, camisoles, petticoats, jumpers, furs—and all these quickly became sodden and heavy. Passengers without life jackets sank. The complicated clothing of children and infants bore them under as well.

One of the most disconcerting sights reported by survivors was of hundreds of hands waving above the water, beseeching help. But soon there was quiet. Survivors reported seeing a plume of smoke from a steamer to the south, but it came no closer. The time that had elapsed since the impact of the torpedo was eighteen minutes.

Seagulls came now and moved among the floating bodies.

CAPTAIN TURNER was still on the bridge as the navigation deck submerged. The sea in the distance was a shimmery blue, but up close, green and clear. The sun penetrating the upper strata of water caught the paint and brightwork of the deck as it fell away below him.

Helmsman Hugh Johnston saw Turner on the bridge wing, moving from port to starboard and back, wearing a life jacket but otherwise making no attempt to dodge the customary fate of a sea captain. Johnston said, later, that he'd "never met anyone as 'cool' " as Turner.

The ship at that point was still moving, but slowly, with a wake full of wreckage and corpses spreading behind it, fed by the hundreds of men, women, and children who through accident or fear had remained on the ship. They streamed off like the knots in a kite's tail.

AT 2:33 P.M., the wireless station at the Old Head of Kinsale sent the Admiralty a two-word message: " 'Lusitania' sunk."

Observers on the Old Head had seen it happen. A great ship, present one moment, gone the next, leaving what appeared at a distance to be an empty blue sea.

Captain Turner's pocket watch, which would eventually make its way into a Liverpool museum, stopped at 2:36:15.

ALL POINTS

RUMOR

T HE AMERICAN CONSULATE IN QUEENSTOWN, IRELAND, was located in a suite of rooms above a bar, overlooking the harbor. Behind the building stood the great spire of St. Colman's Cathedral, which dwarfed every other structure in town. That afternoon, Consul Wesley Frost was at work revising his annual report on commercial conditions in various Irish counties when, at 2:30, his vice-consul came pounding up the stairs to report a fast-spreading rumor that a submarine had attacked the *Lusitania*.

Frost walked to the windows and saw an unusual surge of activity in the harbor below. Every vessel, of every size, seemed to be leaving, including the big cruiser *Juno*, which had arrived only a short while earlier. Frost counted two dozen craft in all.

He went to his telephone and called the office of Adm. Charles Henry Coke, the senior naval officer for Queenstown, and spoke to the admiral's secretary. Frost chose his words with care, not wishing to appear to be a dupe of someone's practical joke. He said, "I hear there is some sort of street rumor that the *Lusitania* has been attacked."

The secretary replied, "It's true, Mr. Frost. We fear she is gone."

Frost listened in a daze as the secretary told him about the SOS messages and the report from eyewitnesses on Kinsale Head confirming the disappearance of the ship.

After hanging up, Frost paced his office, trying to absorb what had occurred and thinking about what to do next. He telegraphed the news to U.S. ambassador Page in London.

ADMIRAL COKE had dispatched all the rescue craft he could, including the *Juno*, and telegraphed the Admiralty that he had done so.

The *Juno* was the fastest ship available. Queenstown was two dozen miles from the reported site of the attack. Most of the smaller vessels would be lucky to cover that distance in three or four hours; given the calm air, sail-powered craft would take even longer. The *Juno*, capable of making 18 knots, or 20 miles an hour, could do it in just over one hour. Its crew moved with great haste, and soon the old cruiser was under way.

But the Admiralty fired back a reply: "Urgent: Recall *Juno*." The order was a direct offspring of the *Aboukir*, *Cressy*, and *Hogue* disaster: no large warship was to go to the aid of victims of a U-boat attack. The risk was too great that the submarine might still be present, waiting to sink ships coming to the rescue.

Coke apparently had second thoughts of his own, for even before the Admiralty's message arrived he ordered the *Juno* back into port. His rationale for deciding to recall the ship did not conform to the Admiralty's, however. After dispatching the *Juno*, he explained, "I then received a telegram stating that the *Lusitania* had sunk. The urgent necessity for the *Juno* no longer obtaining I recalled her."

This was curious logic, for the "urgent necessity" was if anything far greater, with hundreds of passengers and crew now adrift in 55-degree waters. It testified to the importance the Admiralty placed on protecting its big warships and heeding the hard lesson taught by the *Aboukir* disaster, to never go to the aid of submarine victims.

—⁓—

IN LONDON, at four o'clock that afternoon, U.S. ambassador Walter H. Page learned for the first time that the *Lusitania* had been attacked and sunk, but, in an eerie echo of the *Titanic* disaster, initial reports also indicated that all passengers and crew had been saved. Since no lives had been lost, there seemed little reason to call off a dinner party the ambassador and his wife had scheduled for that evening to honor President Wilson's personal emissary, Colonel House.

By the time Page got home at seven o'clock that night, the news from Queenstown had grown darker, but by then it was too late to cancel dinner. The guests arrived and spoke of nothing but the sinking. The telephone rang repeatedly. Each call brought fresh reports from Page's staff at the embassy, which were delivered to the ambassador on small slips of yellow paper. He read each aloud to his guests. The news grew steadily more dire, until it became clear that this was a disaster of historic proportions. The guests spoke in quiet tones and debated the potential consequences.

Colonel House told the group, "We shall be at war with Germany within a month."

THAT MORNING, in New York, where the time was far behind that in London, Jack Lawrence, the ship-news reporter for the *New York Evening Mail*, went to a bar on Whitehall Street in Lower Manhattan frequented by sailors, harbor pilots, and the like and ordered a gin daisy, which the bartender delivered to him in a stone mug. *Daisy* was a bastardization of "doozy." Lawrence saw a harbor pilot whom he knew. The pilot, just back from docking a small freighter in Hoboken, New Jersey, suggested they move to the quiet end of the bar, where he told Lawrence something he had overheard that morning.

The pilot explained that he had docked the freighter next to the *Vaterland*, the big German ocean liner interned for the war. After disembarking, he went to a nearby sidewalk café that was full of the *Vaterland*'s crewmen, all clearly in high spirits, slapping one another on the back and speaking animated German. A woman tending the bar, who spoke English and German, told the pilot that the *Vaterland* had just received a message, via wireless, that the *Lusitania* had been torpedoed off Ireland and had sunk rapidly.

Lawrence set his drink aside and left the bar. The Cunard offices were a short walk away, on State Street. As soon as he walked in, he concluded that the pilot's report had been false. The bureau operated just as it always had, with typewriters clacking and passengers buying tickets. A clerk who knew Lawrence commented on the weather. The reporter continued past and climbed a stairway to the next floor, where he walked unannounced into the office of Charles Sumner, Cunard's New York manager. The heavy carpet on Sumner's floor suppressed the sound of his entry.

Sumner was a tall man who dressed well and always wore a white carnation in his lapel. "My first glimpse of him told me that something was wrong," Lawrence recalled. "He was slumped over his desk. He looked all caved in." Lawrence moved closer and saw two telegrams on Sumner's desk, one in code, the other apparently a decoded copy. Lawrence read it over Sumner's shoulder.

Sumner looked up. "She's gone," he said. It was more gasp than declaration. "They've torpedoed the *Lusitania*." The message said the ship had gone down in fifteen minutes (though this would later be revised to eighteen). Sumner had no illusions. "I doubt if they saved anybody. What in God's name am I to do?"

Lawrence agreed to wait one hour before telephoning the news to his editor. Fifteen minutes later, he was on the phone. This news was too big to hold.

THE FIRST REPORT reached President Wilson in Washington at about one o'clock, as he was about to leave for his daily round of golf. The report bore no mention of casualties, but he canceled his game anyway. He waited in the White House, by himself, for more news to arrive. At one point he left to take a drive in the Pierce-Arrow, his tried-and-true way of easing inner tension.

The day had begun clear and warm, but by evening a light rain was falling. Wilson had dinner at home and had just finished when, at 7:55 P.M., he received a cable from Consul Frost in Queenstown warning, for the first time, that it was likely that many of the *Lusitania*'s passengers had lost their lives.

At this, Wilson left the White House, on his own, telling no one, and took a walk in the rain. "I was pacing the streets to get my mind in hand," he wrote later, to Edith Galt.

He walked across Lafayette Square past the cannon-surrounded statue of Andrew Jackson on a rearing horse, then continued up Sixteenth Street toward Dupont Circle, Edith's neighborhood. He passed newsboys hawking fresh "Extra" editions of the city's newspapers that already carried reports of the sinking. At Corcoran Street, Wilson made a right turn, then headed back down Fifteenth to return to the White House, where he went to his study.

At ten o'clock the worst news arrived: an estimate that the *Lusitania* attack had taken as many as one thousand lives. That some of the dead would prove to be Americans seemed certain. The thing Wilson had feared had come to pass.

As U-20 traveled west, Schwieger took a final look back through his periscope.

He wrote in his War Log: "Astern in the distance, a number of lifeboats active; nothing more seen of the *Lusitania*. The wreck must have sunk." He gave the location as 14 sea miles from the Old Head of Kinsale, 27 sea miles from Queenstown, in waters 90 meters deep, about 300 feet.

What he did not know was that among his many victims were the three German stowaways arrested on the first morning of the *Lusitania*'s voyage. The men were still locked away in the ship's improvised brig.

ADRIFT

A LIFE JACKET DID NOT GUARANTEE SURVIVAL. MANY who entered the sea had their jackets on incorrectly and found themselves struggling to keep their heads out of the water. The struggle did not last long, and soon survivors who did manage to outfit themselves properly found themselves swimming among bodies upended in poses their owners would have found humiliating. Able-bodied seaman E. S. Heighway wrote, with a degree of exaggeration, "I saw myself hundreds of men & women dead with life belts on in the water after the ship had gone."

For children—those who did not drown outright—the killer was hypothermia. Fifty-five degrees was not nearly as cold as the water confronted by passengers of the *Titanic*, but it was cold enough to lower the core temperatures of people large and small to dangerous levels. A drop in the body's internal temperature of just 3 or 4 degrees, from the norm of 98.6 degrees Fahrenheit to 95, was enough to kill over time. Passengers in the water found that their lower bodies went numb within minutes, despite the warm sun above. Those who wore coats under their life jackets were better off than those who had stripped down, for coats and other warm clothing, even though wet, provided insulation for the heart. Thin people, old people, women, and children, and especially infants, lost body heat the fastest, as did any passenger who had drunk wine or spirits with lunch. With the onset of hypothermia, those in the water began to shiver severely; as the danger rose, the shivering subsided. With a water temperature of 55 degrees, adults could be expected to experience exhaustion and loss of consciousness within one to two hours; after this the skin took on a blue-gray pallor, the body became rigid, and the heart rate slowed to almost imperceptible levels. Death soon followed.

DWIGHT HARRIS swam toward an overturned lifeboat. "The most frightful thing of all was the innumerable dead bodies floating about in the water!," he wrote. "Men, women and children. I had to push one or two aside to reach the lifeboat!"

On the way he came across a little boy, Percy Richards, calling for his father. "I swam to him and told him not to cry, and to take hold of my collar, which he did. The bravest little chap I ever saw."

Harris pulled the child with him to the overturned boat and pushed him onto its hull. Nearly exhausted by the effort, Harris climbed on after him. "I could hardly move, my limbs were so cold!—I must have been in the water about one-half to three quarters of an hour."

He spotted one of the ship's collapsible lifeboats, manned by two sailors and partially filled with passengers. He called to them. Soon the boat was near enough for Harris and the boy to climb aboard. The sailors picked up a dozen more survivors but had to leave others in the water because the collapsible was on the verge of being swamped. "The cries for help from those in the water were most <u>awful</u>!" Harris wrote.

No ships were in sight.

AS THE *LUSITANIA* descended, Margaret Mackworth was pulled along with it. The water around her seemed black, and a fear suffused her of being trapped by debris. She became frightened when something snagged her hand, but then she realized it was the life jacket she had been holding for her father. She swallowed seawater.

She surfaced and grabbed one end of a board. At first she

imagined it was this alone that kept her afloat, but then remembered that she was wearing a life jacket. "When I came to the surface I found that I formed part of a large, round, floating island composed of people and debris of all sorts, lying so close together that at first there was not very much water noticeable in between. People, boats, hencoops, chairs, rafts, boards and goodness knows what besides, all floating cheek by jowl."

People prayed and called out for rescue. She clung to her board, despite her life jacket. She saw one of the ship's lifeboats and tried swimming toward it, but did not want to let go of the board and thus made little progress. She stopped swimming. She grew calm and settled back in her life jacket. She felt "a little dazed and rather stupid and vague" but was not particularly afraid. "When Death is as close as he was then, the sharp agony of fear is not there; the thing is too overwhelming and stunning for that."

At one point, she thought she might already be dead: "I wondered, looking round on the sun and pale blue sky and calm sea, whether I had reached heaven without knowing it—and devoutly hoped I hadn't."

She was very cold. As she drifted, she thought up a way to improve life jackets. Each, she proposed, should include a small bottle of chloroform, "so that one could inhale it and lose consciousness when one wished to." Soon hypothermia resolved the issue for her.

CHARLES LAURIAT swam to one of the *Lusitania*'s collapsible rafts, floating nearby. This was the one that Seaman Morton had seen fall from the ship. Morton swam to it also, as did shipbuilder Fred Gauntlett. Morton called it "an oasis in the desert of bodies and people."

The three men stripped off its cover. Other survivors clambered aboard. The canvas sides and seats were meant to be raised and locked into position, but with so many terrified people now clinging to the raft, the men found the task difficult. "We were picking people out of the water and trying at the same time to raise these seats," said Gauntlett; "most everybody that came on board flopped on the seats and it was practically impossible to get the thing to work properly. We could not get it up far enough to bring the parts home so that they would stay so."

They tried to persuade people to let go just briefly so the seats could be raised, "but that was impossible," Lauriat said. "Never have I heard a more distressing cry of despair than when I tried to tell one of them that that was what we were doing."

They positioned the survivors on the floor of the raft. To Lauriat's later regret, he became annoyed with one man who seemed unwilling to move from his seat. Lauriat "rather roughly" told him to get off. The man looked up and said, "I would, old chap; but did you know I have a broken leg and can't move very fast?"

With a great heave, the men managed to raise the seats and the attached canvas sides, but only partway. They jammed pieces of wood into the mechanism to prop them in place.

The collapsible had no oars within, but the men found five floating nearby. Lauriat used one for steering while Gauntlett, Morton, and two other passengers rowed. Lauriat guided the raft through wreckage and corpses, looking for more survivors. Seagulls by the hundreds wheeled and dove. It was startling to see men and women in the water still wearing the suits and dresses they had worn at lunch. The men picked up Samuel Knox, the Philadelphia shipbuilder who had shared Gauntlett's table. They came across a woman who appeared to be African. Seaman Morton swam to get her and brought her back to the boat. This was Margaret Gwyer, the woman who had been sucked into a funnel and ejected. Lauriat wrote, "The clothes were almost blown off the poor woman, and there wasn't a white spot on her except her teeth and the whites of her eyes." He described her as a "temporary negress."

She revived quickly and brightened the spirits aboard with her optimism and cheer and "her bright talk," Lauriat wrote.

The boat was nearly full when Lauriat steered it past a dense jam of floating debris. "I heard a woman's voice say, in just as natural a tone of voice as you would ask for another slice of bread and butter, 'Won't you take me next? You know I can't swim.' " Lauriat looked over and saw a woman's head protruding from the wreckage, her long hair splayed over the surrounding debris. She was wedged so tightly that she could not raise her arms. Even so, she had a "half smile" on her face, Lauriat recalled, "and was placidly chewing gum."

The men pulled her in, and set off rowing toward the lighthouse on the Old Head of Kinsale, a dozen miles away.

EVEN THOUGH the sinking had occurred so near the Irish coast, there was still no sign that rescuers were approaching. Those passengers in the water came to terms with their situations in varying ways. Rev. Henry Wood Simpson, of Rossland, British Columbia, put himself in God's hands, and from time to time repeated one of his favorite phrases, "Come, Holy Ghost, our souls inspire." He said later he knew he would survive—"It is too long a story to tell how I knew"—and that this gave him a sense of calm even when at one point he was underwater, asking himself, "What if I don't come out?"

He did come out. His life jacket held him in a position of comfort, "and I was lying on my back smiling up at the blue sky and the white clouds, and I had not swallowed much sea water either." For him, these moments in the water were almost enjoyable—aside from the dead woman who for a time floated beside him. "I found it a most comfortable position," he said, "and lay there for a bit very happily."

He pulled the woman's body to an overturned collapsible and maneuvered her onto its hull, then swam toward another collapsible, this one right-side up and occupied by survivors. There were corpses on this raft as well. An engineer from the ship started singing a hymn, "Praise God, from Whom All Blessings Flow," Simpson recalled, and noted, "We put a good deal of heart into it." But upon its conclusion no one tried to sing another. "Then we just waited, hoping that they had been able to get out a wireless for help before she went down. It was beautifully calm, fortunately for us, because a very little would have washed us off. We were better off than the people floating on planks in the water or kept up by their lifebelts, or than the people in the water-logged boat [nearby], which kept capsizing."

A porpoise—Simpson called it "a monster porpoise"—surfaced "and played near us, coming up with its shiny black skin and triangular fin showing for a moment."

An hour passed, then two hours. The sea remained calm; the afternoon light shifted hue. "It was a beautiful sunset," Simpson recalled, "and all so calm and peaceful."

SURVIVORS DRIFTED—in the water, on boats, on pieces of wreckage—for three hours, in hopes that rescuers were on their way. Had the *Juno* come, the wait would have been far shorter, the chances of survival much higher. But the Admiralty had adopted a harsh calculus, and indeed no one knew whether the submarine was still in the vicinity or not. Some passengers claimed to have seen a periscope after the *Lusitania* sank, and feared the U-boat might even now be among them. As one survivor wrote, "I was fully expecting the submarine to come up and fire on the Lucy's boats or wait until the rescue ships came up and then sink them."

The first sign of rescue was smoke on the horizon, and then came a long, rag-tag armada of torpedo boats and trawlers and small fishing vessels, these more expendable than the large cruiser *Juno*. Here were the *Brock*, *Bradford*, *Bluebell*, *Sarba*, *Heron*, and *Indian Empire*; the *Julia*, *Flying Fish*, *Stormcock*, and *Warrior*.

In Queenstown, suspense mounted. None of these ships had wireless, wrote Consul Frost: "No news could be had until they returned."

ONCE A LIFEBOAT was emptied, the seamen aboard rowed back to look for more survivors, but as evening approached the retrieval of corpses began to outpace the rescue of living souls. The last vessel to arrive was a shore-based lifeboat, the *Kezia Gwilt*, with a crew of fifteen. Ordinarily the men would have raised sail to make the journey, but there was so little wind that they realized they could cover the distance more quickly if they rowed. And so they did—some 14 miles.

"We did everything we could to reach the place, but it took us at least three and a half hours of hard pulling to get there only in time to pick up dead bodies," wrote Rev. William Forde, in charge of the lifeboat. There, in that gorgeous dusk, they moved through the wreckage. "It was a harrowing sight to witness," Forde wrote, "the sea was strewn with bodies floating about, some with lifebelts on, some holding on to pieces of rafts, all dead."

LAURIAT AND COMPANY rowed their collapsible boat 2 miles until they came upon a small sail-rigged fishing boat, known in these waters as a fishing smack.

As they approached the vessel, Margaret Gwyer, still coated in soot, saw her husband standing at its rail and called to him. His expression, Lauriat wrote, was "perfectly blank." He had no idea who this blackened young woman could be.

He recognized her only when the collapsible came right under the smack's rail, and he was able to look directly into her face. He wept.

It was now 6:00 P.M. Lauriat counted the number of survivors that he and his companions had picked up along the way: thirty-two. Fifty other survivors were already on the smack. Before climbing aboard, Lauriat pocketed one of the collapsible's oarlocks as a souvenir.

An hour later, he and the rest were transferred to a steam side-wheeler, the *Flying Fish*, which then set out for Queenstown. The survivors crowded into its engine room, for the warmth. Here was Ogden Hammond, the New Jersey real-estate developer. No one had seen his wife. The heat was exquisite, and "and before very long," reported Arthur Mitchell, the Raleigh Bicycle man, "songs were being sung, indicating not only a spirit of thankfulness but even of gaiety."

A number of corpses were on board as well: a five-year-old boy named Dean Winston Hodges; two unidentified boys, about two and six years old; and the body of fifteen-year-old Gwendolyn Allan, one of the girls who had helped seaman Morton paint a lifeboat.

DWIGHT HARRIS helped row his collapsible boat toward a distant sailboat. The going was slow and difficult. Another lifeboat got there first and unloaded a cache of survivors and bodies, then came back for Harris and his companions and put them aboard the sailboat as well. Next all were transferred to a minesweeper called the *Indian Empire*, whose crew spent the next several hours searching for survivors and bodies. When the ship began its return to Queenstown after seven o'clock that evening it carried 170 survivors and numerous dead.

On board, the little boy whom Harris had rescued now found his father, mother, and brother—alive and well. His baby sister, Dora, was lost.

THEODATE POPE awoke to a vision of blazing fire. A small fire, in a stove. She had no recollection of the sinking. She saw a pair of legs in trousers and then heard a man say, "She's conscious." Despite the warmth from the stove, tremors rattled her body.

She was in the captain's cabin of a ship named *Julia*. Another survivor aboard, Belle Naish, later told Theodate how she came to be there. Crew members had pulled Theodate aboard using boat hooks. Presuming her to be dead, they had left her on deck among other recovered bodies. Naish and Theodate had become friends during the voyage, and when Naish saw Theodate lying there she touched her body and sensed a trace of life. Naish called for help. Two men began trying to revive Theodate. One used a carving knife from the ship's kitchen to cut off her sodden layers of clothing. The men worked on her for two hours until confident they had revived her—though she remained unconscious. A lurid bruise surrounded her right eye.

There was no sign of Theodate's companion, Edwin Friend, or of her maid, Emily Robinson.

PARTING SHOT

L ATER, A WOMAN WHO CLAIMED TO BE SCHWIEGER'S FI-
ancée told a newspaper reporter that the attack on the *Lusitania* had left Schwieger a shattered man. (The reporter did not
disclose her name.) When Schwieger visited her in Berlin after his
return to base, she had no idea, at first, that it was he who had
torpedoed the ship. "All we thought of was that one of the fastest
and biggest English ships had been sunk, and we were all very
glad," she said. But Schwieger seemed not to share the elation. "Of
course, his mother and I saw right away that something dreadful
had happened to him. He was so haggard and so silent, and so—
different."

Schwieger told her the story of the attack. "Of course he
couldn't hear anything, but he could see, and the silence of it all
in the U-boat was worse than if he could have heard the shrieks.
And, of course, he was the only one in the U-boat who could even
see. He didn't dare let any of the others in the U-boat know what
was happening." After the attack he took the boat straight back to
Germany, his fiancée said. "He wanted to get away from what he
had done. He wanted to get ashore. He couldn't torpedo another
ship."

The woman's account, while compelling, stands at odds with
Schwieger's own War Log. If Schwieger felt any sense of remorse,
he did not express it by his actions.

Just five minutes after taking his last look at the *Lusitania*, he spotted a large steamer ahead, coming toward him, and prepared to attack. He was supposed to keep two torpedoes in reserve for the voyage home—ideally one in the bow, one in the stern—but this was an irresistible target, a 9,000-ton tanker. Schwieger ordered full ahead, to position U-20 in front of the ship, stern-first, so that he could use one of his two stern tubes. At 4:08 P.M. he was ready. The shot was lined up perfectly: a 90-degree angle with the target's course, at a point-blank range of 500 meters, about a third of a mile. "Conditions for our torpedo very favorable," he wrote in his log; "a miss out of the question."

He gave the order to fire. The submarine shivered as the torpedo left its tube. Schwieger waited for the sound of impact.

A long silence followed. As the seconds ticked past, he realized something had gone wrong.

"As periscope is submerged for some time after torpedo had been fired, I am sorry to say that I could not ascertain what kind of a miss it was," he wrote in his log. "The torpedo came out of its tube correctly, and either it did not run at all or at a wrong angle." He doubted that anyone aboard the steamer even noticed.

Schwieger resumed the voyage home. He surfaced to increase speed and recharge his batteries. From atop the conning tower, he saw the smoke trails of at least six large steamers in the distance, inbound and outbound, but made no further effort to attack. As it was, this would prove to be his most successful patrol. In the course of traveling a total of 3,006 miles, 250 under water, he had sunk 42,331 tons of shipping.

THE STEAMER Schwieger had fired upon was a British oil tanker, the *Narragansett*, headed for New Jersey, and contrary to what he imagined, everyone aboard was very much aware of the near miss. The ship's first officer had spotted the periscope, and the captain, Charles Harwood, had ordered a sharp turn and maximum speed.

Harwood reported the encounter by wireless. At the time of the attack he had been responding to an SOS from the *Lusitania*, and had been racing to the scene, but now he suspected the SOS had been faked by the submarine to lure his ship and other would-be rescuers.

His telegram, relayed to the Admiralty's War Room in London, read, "We proceeded with all possible speed 3:45 p.m. sighted submarine about 200 yards on our starboard quarter, submarine fired torpedo which passed ten yards astern of us, maneuvered ship and got all clear; submarine was seen astern 10 minutes later 4 P.M. . . . Saw no sign of *Lusitania* believe call to be a hoax."

Captain Harwood changed heading and fled away from the last reported location of the *Lusitania*.

SEAGULLS

IS LIFE JACKET MADE HIM BUOYANT AND LIFTED HIM from the bridge, but the descending hull pulled him under. "The whole ship seemed to be plucked from my feet by a giant hand," Turner said. When he came back to the surface, he found himself in an archipelago of destruction and death. "Hundreds of bodies were being whirled about among the wreckage," he said. "Men, women and children were drifting between planks, lifeboats and an indescribable litter."

He had done all he could, he believed, and now an instinct to live ignited. He began to swim. He recognized another man nearby, William Pierpoint, the Liverpool police detective. All at once, Pierpoint disappeared. Like newlywed Margaret Gwyer, he was dragged into a funnel. "I thought he had gone," Turner said. But in a burst of steam and hissing air, Pierpoint popped back out, his body coated with a layer of wet black soot that clung to him like enamel. At which point, Turner said, Pierpoint "started swimming for home like ten men, he was so scared."

The ship was still moving at about 4 knots, by Turner's estimate. But as he watched, its bow struck bottom—he was sure of it. "I noticed it because the sinking of the hull stopped for a few seconds with the stern in the air, quivering her whole length of 800 feet, and then down she went."

It was a strange moment for a sea captain. Twenty minutes earlier Turner had stood on the bridge in command of one of the greatest ocean liners ever known. Now, still in uniform, he floated in the place where his ship had been, in a calm sea under a brilliant blue sky, no deck, cabin, or hull in sight, not even the ship's tall masts.

He and Pierpoint swam together. Turner saw the bodies of some of the ship's firemen floating nearby, upside down in their life jackets—he counted forty in all. Seagulls dove among corpses and survivors alike. Turner later told his son, Norman, that he found himself fending off attacks by the birds, which swooped from the sky and pecked at the eyes of floating corpses. Rescuers later reported that wherever they saw spirals of gulls, they knew they would find bodies. Turner's experience left him with such a deep hatred of seagulls, according to Norman, "that until his retirement he used to carry a .22 rifle and shoot every seagull he could."

Turner spent three hours in the water, until he was pulled aboard a lifeboat, and later was transferred to a fishing trawler, the *Bluebell*.

MARGARET MACKWORTH'S first recollection, after having lost consciousness in the sea, was of awakening on the *Bluebell*'s deck, naked under a blanket, her teeth chattering, she wrote, "like castanets."

A sailor appeared above her, and said, "That's better."

She was miffed. "I had a vague idea that something had happened but I thought that I was still on the deck of the *Lusitania*, and I was vaguely annoyed that some unknown sailor should be attending to me instead of my own stewardess."

Her confusion cleared; the sailor brought her tea. With somewhat less chivalry, he told her, "We left you up here to begin with as we thought you were dead, and it did not seem worth while cumbering up the cabin with you."

The sailor and two others helped her below decks, where she found an unexpected giddiness. "The warmth below was delicious," she wrote; "it seemed to make one almost delirious." Everyone around her seemed "a little drunk with the heat and the light and the joy of knowing ourselves to be alive. We were talking at the tops of our voices and laughing a great deal."

She recognized the strangeness of the moment, how it juxtaposed joy and tragedy. Here she was, giddy with delight, and yet she had no idea whether her father was alive or not. Another survivor in the cabin believed her own husband to be dead. "It seemed that his loss probably meant the breaking up of her whole life," Mackworth wrote, "yet at that moment she was full of cheerfulness and laughter."

Captain Turner did not share in the gaiety. He sat quietly by himself, in his sodden uniform.

As Mackworth watched, a woman approached Turner and began telling him about the loss of her child. Her voice was low, almost a monotone. She had placed the boy on a raft, she said. The raft then capsized, and her son was gone. In the same dispassionate manner, she told Turner that her son's death had been unnecessary—that it was caused by the lack of organization and discipline among the crew.

THE RESCUE SHIPS reached Queenstown long after dark. The *Flying Fish* with Charles Lauriat aboard arrived at 9:15, the *Bluebell* at 11:00. The wharf was lit by gas torches that turned the evening mist a pale amber. Soldiers, sailors, and townspeople formed two lines that extended from the gangway into town. They applauded as survivors came ashore. Other soldiers waited in groups of four, with stretchers. Charles Lauriat carried one man on his back—the man with the broken leg, to whom he had spoken so rudely. The man proved to be Leonard McMurray, and this was his second shipwreck. He had survived the 1909 sinking of the White Star Line's *Republic*, after a collision in fog with another liner.

Lauriat's Thackeray drawings and the Dickens *Christmas Carol* were somewhere deep in the Irish Sea. He sent his wife a telegram. "I saved the baby's pictures," he wrote. "They were my mascot."

He closed: "I regret your hours of suspense."

Margaret Mackworth learned upon docking that her father

was alive. She was dressed only in a blanket and asked the *Blue-bell*'s captain for safety pins, but the idea of pins aboard a ship like his made him laugh out loud. A soldier gave her his coat, a "British Warm"; the captain gave her his slippers. She tucked the blanket around her waist to form a makeshift skirt.

She found her father waiting at the end of the gangplank. The relief and joy she felt reminded her of that time a month earlier when she had arrived in New York and seen him on the dock. As one of the first survivors to reach Queenstown, he had waited for hours as boat after boat came in, none carrying his daughter. With each successive arrival, the number of dead on board seemed to increase relative to the number of living souls. A friend said later that for a long time after this the father's face had seemed like that of an elderly man.

Dorothy Conner, the spunky young American who had sat at Mackworth's table and had wanted a "thrill," came to see her the next morning, Saturday. Conner seemed unruffled, Mackworth recalled. "She was still dressed in the neat fawn tweed coat and skirt which she had had on when I saw her step off the deck the day before, and it looked as smart and well tailored as if it had just come out of the shop."

Dwight Harris landed with his engagement ring and other jewelry still hung around his neck, and his money in his pocket. That night he found a shop that had stayed open for survivors and bought an undershirt, socks, slippers, and pajamas. He found a room in a hotel, which he shared with six other men, "and took a huge dose of whiskey before going to bed." On Saturday morning he bought himself a suit, shirt, collar, raincoat, and cap. While doing so he happened to notice a boy of about eighteen who was asking the shopkeeper if he could have some clothes, even though he had no money to pay for them. The boy looked bereft. Harris volunteered to pay. He learned that the boy had lost his mother. "Poor fellow!" Harris wrote to his own mother. "I <u>thank God you</u> weren't with me!!!"

When Theodate Pope's ship, the *Julia*, arrived, a doctor was summoned to come aboard to examine her. Assisted by two soldiers, the doctor helped her down to the wharf and into a motor-car, then accompanied her to a hotel. As she stepped from the car, she collapsed onto the sidewalk. The doctor helped her inside. "I was left on a lounge in a room full of men in all sorts of strange garments while the proprietress hurried to bring me brandy," she wrote. One of the men was the English passenger who at lunch that day had joked about not getting torpedoed before having his ice cream. He was wearing a dressing gown. Pink.

Theodate drank brandy and was helped to a room. Her face was swollen and discolored. She arranged to send her mother a telegram, one word: "Saved."

She tried to sleep. "All night I kept expecting Mr. Friend to appear, looking for me," she wrote. "All night long men kept coming into our rooms, snapping on the lights, bringing children for us to identify, taking telegrams, getting our names for the list of survivors, etc., etc."

But Mr. Friend never did appear, nor did Theodate's maid, Miss Robinson.

TURNER WALKED ashore wrapped in a blanket. He spent the night at the home of a local banker. The next morning, in his uniform, he went for a walk. He had lost his Cunard hat and stopped at a haberdasher's shop to buy something to replace it. A survivor named Beatrice Williams, who had also been aboard the *Bluebell*, saw him and bristled. "You should be worrying about a hat when so many of us have lost everything we own. Why—you ought to be ashamed of yourself!"

A correspondent for the *New York World* also encountered Turner that morning and conducted a brief interview. In a cable to his editor, the reporter wrote that the captain "appeared stunned."

The reporter informed Turner that the bodies of a number of Americans had been recovered, including that of Broadway producer Charles Frohman, with whom Turner had spoken on the morning of the ship's departure. Upon hearing this, Turner seemed to struggle to control his emotions. Tears filled his eyes.

THE LOST

O F THE *LUSITANIA*'S 1,959 PASSENGERS AND CREW, only 764 survived; the total of deaths was 1,195. The 3 German stowaways brought the total to 1,198. Of 33 infants aboard, only 6 survived. Over 600 passengers were never found. Among the dead were 123 Americans.

Families learned of the deaths of kin mostly by telegram, but some knew or sensed their loss even when no telegram brought the news. Husbands and wives had promised to write letters or send cables to announce their safe arrival, but these were never sent. Passengers who had arranged to stay with friends in England and Ireland never showed up. The worst were those situations where a passenger was expected to be on a different ship but for one reason or another had ended up on the *Lusitania*, as was the case with the passengers of the *Cameronia* transferred to the ship at the last minute. The transfers included passengers Margaret and James Shineman, newlyweds from Oil City, Wyoming, who suddenly found themselves aboard the fastest, most luxurious ship in service, for their journey to Scotland to visit Margaret's family. The visit was to be a surprise. Both were killed. Of the forty-two passengers and crew transferred, only thirteen survived, among them Miss Grace French, who breezed through the whole ordeal with aplomb.

There was the usual confusion that follows disasters. For days dozens of cables shot back and forth between Cunard offices in

Liverpool, Queenstown, and New York. These conveyed a sense of both urgency and surprise, as though Cunard had never expected to lose one of its great ships and to actually have to use its passenger records to tally the living and dead.

MAY 10: "DID GUY LEWIN ACTUALLY SAIL LUSITANIA."

MAY 10: "NAME CHARLES WARMEY APPEARS ON SECOND CLASS SHOULD THIS BE CHARLES WARING WHICH DOES NOT APPEAR—REPLY QUICKLY."

MAY 11: "DID F A TWIGG ACTUALLY EMBARK LUSITANIA."

MAY 11: "GIVE US FULL CHRISTIAN NAMES AND CLASSES ALL PASSENGERS NAMED ADAMS WHO SAILED LUSITANIA— VERY URGENT."

A few passengers reported to be dead were in fact alive, but more often those reported alive were dead. "Report of Mr. Bilicke as survivor is erroneous," U.S. consul Frost wrote in a terse telegram to Ambassador Page in London. A five-year-old boy, Dean Winston Hodges, was at first said to be safe, but then came a cable from Cunard to its New York office, "Regret no trace of Master Dean Winston Hodges." His body proved to be among those taken aboard the rescue ship *Flying Fish*. Names of the dead were misspelled, offering moments of false hope. A man identified as Fred Tyn was in fact Fred Tyers, who had died; Teresa Desley was in fact Teresa Feeley, who perished along with her husband, James. There were two Mrs. Hammonds. One lived; the other—Ogden's wife—died. Two waiters were named John Leach. One survived, the other did not. A dead passenger named Greenfield was in fact Greenshields.

Time zones and sluggish communication made it even harder on friends and kin. Those who could afford the cost sent cables to Cunard with detailed descriptions of their loved ones, down to the serial numbers stamped on their watches, but these cables took hours to receive, transcribe, and deliver. In those first days after the disaster, thousands of cables flooded Cunard's offices. Cunard had little information to provide.

The dead collected at Queenstown were placed in three make-shift morgues, including Town Hall, where they were placed side by side on the floor. Whenever possible, children were placed beside their mothers. Survivors moved in slow, sad lines looking for lost kin.

There were reunions of a happier sort as well.

Seaman Leslie Morton spent Friday night looking for his brother Cliff on the lists of survivors and in the hotels of Queenstown but found no trace. Early the next morning he sent a telegram to his father, "Am saved, looking for Cliff." He went to one of the morgues. "Laid out in rows all the way down on both sides were sheeted and shrouded bodies," he wrote, "and a large number of people in varying states of sorrow and distress were going from body to body, turning back the sheets to see if they could identify loved ones who had not yet been found."

He worked his way along, lifting sheets. Just as he was about to pull yet one more, he saw the hand of another searcher reaching for the same sheet. He looked over, and saw his brother. Their reaction was deadpan.

"Hallo, Cliff, glad to see you," Leslie said.

"Am I glad to see you too, Gert," Cliff said. "I think we ought to have a drink on this!"

As it happened, their father had not had to spend very much time worrying. He had received telegrams from both sons, telling him each was looking for the other. The telegrams, Leslie later learned, had arrived five minutes apart, "so that father knew at home that we were both safe before we did."

That night Leslie had his first-ever Guinness. "I cannot say that I thought much of it in those days, but it seemed a good thing in which to celebrate being alive, having got together again and being in Ireland."

—⁂—

THE RESCUE SHIPS brought in many of the bodies, but many others were recovered from the coves and beaches of Ireland, as the sea brought them ashore. One man's body was found on a beach clutching a foot-long fragment of a lifeboat, which later would find its way into the archives of the Hoover Institution at Stanford University, the wood still bearing the brand *Lusitania*.

Consul Frost took responsibility for managing the American dead. The "important" bodies, meaning those in first class, were embalmed at U.S. expense. "There was a curious effacement of social or mental distinction by death, and we often believed a corpse to be important when it turned out to be decidedly the opposite," Frost wrote. "The commonest expression was one of reassured tranquillity, yet with an undertone of puzzlement or aggrievement as though some trusted friend had played a practical joke which the victim did not yet understand." The unimportant bodies were sealed inside lead coffins, "so that they could be returned to America whenever desired."

Cunard went to great lengths to number, photograph, and catalog the recovered bodies. Body No. 1 was that of Catherine Gill, a forty-year-old widow; Body No. 91 was that of chief purser McCubbin, for whom this was to be the last voyage before retirement. Nearly all the dead were photographed in coffins, though one lies in what appears to be a large wheelbarrow, and a toddler rests on a makeshift platform. They still wear their coats, suits, dresses, and jewelry. A mother and tiny daughter, presumably found together, share a coffin. The mother is turned toward her daughter; the child lies with one arm resting across her mother's chest. They look as though they could step from this coffin and resume their lives. Others convey the same restful aspect. A handsome clean-shaven man in his thirties, Body No. 59, lies dressed neatly in white shirt, tweed jacket, polka-dotted bow tie, and dark overcoat. The textures are comforting; the buttons on his overcoat are shiny, like new.

These photographs beg viewers to imagine last moments. Here is Body No. 165, a girl in a white dress with a lacy top. Hair flung back, mouth open as if in a scream, her whole aspect is one of fear and pain. One victim, identified only as Body No. 109, is that of a stout woman who lies naked under a rough blanket, her hair still flecked with sand. Unlike all the other bodies in this collection of photographs, her eyes are squeezed tightly shut. Her cheeks are puffed, her lips are tightly clamped. She looks uncannily as if she were still holding her breath.

The most unsettling image here is that of Body No. 156, a girl of about three, slightly chubby, with curly blond hair, wearing a pullover sweater with overlong sleeves. What is troubling is the child's expression. She looks perturbed. Someone laid flowers across her chest and at her side. But she seems unmollified. She lies on a wood pallet, beside what appears to be a life jacket. Her expression is one of pure fury.

Consul Frost found the sight of so many drowned children difficult to expunge from his thoughts. He had a young daughter of his own. "Several weeks after the disaster, one night out at my home, I went into a bedroom with a lighted match and came unexpectedly upon the sleeping form of my own little daughter," he wrote. For an instant, his mind was jolted back to scenes he had witnessed in the morgues. "I give you my word I recoiled as though I had found a serpent."

The search for bodies still adrift in the sea continued until June, when Cunard suggested to Frost that the time had come to halt the effort. He concurred. The search was suspended on June 4, but bodies continued to wash ashore well into the summer. The later a body was recovered, the higher its assigned number, the worse its condition. Two men came ashore in County Kerry on July 14 and 15, some 200 miles, by sea, from the wreck. One wore a cleric's clothing and had "perfect teeth," according to a report on the find, which noted, "Much of the body was eaten away." The second had no head, arms, or feet, but, like some tentacled sea creature, dragged behind him a full complement of clothing—blue serge trousers, black-and-white-striped flannel shirt, woolen undershirt, undershorts, suspenders, a belt, and a keychain with seven keys.

To encourage reporting of new arrivals, Cunard offered a one-pound reward. Frost offered an additional pound to anyone who recovered a corpse that was demonstrably a U.S. citizen.

On July 11, 1915, one American did come ashore, at Stradbally, Ireland. At first authorities believed him to be a *Lusitania* victim and designated him Body No. 248. He had not been a passenger, however. His name was Leon C. Thrasher, the American who had gone missing on March 28 when the SS *Falaba* was torpedoed and sunk. He had been in the water 106 days.

The people who discovered remains treated them with great respect, despite their often grotesque condition. Such was the case when the body of a middle-aged man was found on Ireland's Dingle Peninsula on July 17, seventy-one days after the disaster. The currents and winds had taken him on a long journey around the southwest rim of Ireland before depositing him at Brandon Bay, a distance of about 250 miles from Queenstown. His body was discovered by a local citizen, who notified the Royal Irish Constabulary in Castlegregory, 6 miles to the east. A sergeant, J. Regan, promptly set out by bicycle, accompanied by a constable, and soon arrived at the scene, an austere but lovely beach. Here they found what little remained of an apparently male corpse. That the man had come from the *Lusitania* was obvious. Part of a life jacket was still attached to the body, and another portion lay nearby, marked *Lusitania*.

There was little question as to his identity. When the officers went through what remained of the man's clothing, they found a watch, with the initials V.O.E.S. stamped on its case, and a knife marked "Victor E. Shields," and a letter addressed to "Mr. Victor Shields, care of steamer Lusitania." The letter was dated April 30, 1915, the day before the ship left New York. In one pocket the officers discovered a copy of an entertainment program from the ship. The documents were soaked. The officers laid them in the sun to dry.

Sergeant Regan noted that the tide was rising quickly, "so I sent for a sheet and placed the body on it and carried it from the tide to a place of safety." He then cycled to a telegraph office and wired the local coroner, who replied that no inquest would be necessary. The police ordered a lead casket and wooden shell, and by evening Shields was placed in a "Swansdown" robe and coffined within. The undertaker took the coffin to a private home, where it remained until the next day, when police buried it in a nearby graveyard. "Everything was done that could be done by the Police," Sergeant Regan wrote in a letter to Consul Frost, "in fact they could do no more for a member of their family, and I on behalf of the Police tender Mrs. Shields our sincere sympathy in her bereavement."

For disbelieving families, struck by grief, it was important to know precisely how their loved ones had died, whether by drowning, exposure, or physical trauma. The Shields family took this to extremes and ordered the body disinterred. The family wanted an autopsy. This was easier asked than achieved. "Needless to say," wrote Frost, "it proved virtually impossible to procure a physician of advanced years and high standing to dissect remains seventy-five days after decease." Frost did manage to find two younger doctors who were willing to take on the task. The character of this endeavor was made clear in the report of one of the physicians, Dr. John Higgins, acting house surgeon of Cork's North Infirmary.

The autopsy began at 2:30, July 23, at the office of an undertaker; the second doctor was to perform his own autopsy the next day. A plumber now opened the lead casket in which Victor Shields lay, and soon the scent of heated lead was joined by another sort of odor. Consul Frost was present for this, but Higgins noted that at a point about halfway through the autopsy he left, "when he was called away."

In life, by Higgins's estimate, Shields had weighed 14 or 15 stone, or roughly 200 pounds. His body was now in "an advanced state of decomposition," Higgins noted. This was an understatement. "The soft parts of his face and head were entirely absent, including the scalp," Higgins wrote. "The majority of the teeth were missing, including all the front teeth. The hands were also absent, and the soft parts of the upper right arm. The back of the calf of the right leg was largely absent, as was a portion of the left calf. The genitals were very much decomposed, virtually missing."

Mr. Shields lay there smiling up at them, but not in an endearing fashion. "I examined the skull," Dr. Higgins wrote. "Externally it was totally bare as far as the lower part of the occipital bone." The occipital forms the bottom rear portion of the skull. "I removed the skull-cap; and found that the brain was too much decomposed for examination, but the membranes were intact." He removed the brain and examined the interior of the skull. He found no evidence of fracture at its base or to the cervical canal. This ruled out death by falling debris or other blunt trauma to the head. Nor did he discover any fractures along the spine, or injury to the back. Shields's internal organs likewise failed to reveal what killed him, but they did provide Dr. Higgins with a look at what remained of the man's last lunch aboard the *Lusitania*. "The stomach contained roughly a pint of a green semi-solid mass, apparently semi-digested food, but contained no water as such."

The lack of a clear cause of death was perplexing. "In my opinion," Higgins wrote, "there is no injury present which would account for death. There is no evidence of drowning; and the probability is that death was brought about as a result of shock or exposure, probably the former. From the contents of the stomach it would appear that death supervened within a very few hours after his last meal, possibly from two to three hours."

After all that, the finding was death with no obvious cause. The other physician reached the same conclusion.

The peripatetic Mr. Shields was returned to his coffin and shipped to America. Consul Frost, in a letter to Washington, praised the effort taken by the police after the discovery of Shields's body. "It would be a most graceful and commendable act if the estate of Mr. Shields should forward from two to five pounds to the sergeant and his colleagues for the excellent spirit in which they discharged their duties."

The mystery as to what killed Shields remained, leaving the family to wonder what horror he had endured. This same fate fell to nearly all the kin of the dead. There can be no doubt that for many passengers death came suddenly and utterly by surprise. The dozens of crewmen who were in the luggage bay at the time of impact were killed instantly by the force of the torpedo blast, but exactly how many and who they were was not known. Passengers were crushed by descending boats. Swimmers were struck by chairs, boxes, potted plants, and other debris falling from the decks high above. And then there were those most ill-starred of passengers, who had put on their life preservers incorrectly and found themselves floating with their heads submerged, legs up, as in some devil's comedy.

One can only imagine the final minutes of the Crompton parents and their children. How do you save a child, let alone six children, especially when one of them is an infant and one is six years old? None of the Cromptons survived. Five of the children were never found. The infant, Master Peter Romilly Crompton, about nine months old, was Body No. 214.

Cunard chairman Booth knew the family well. "My own personal loss is very great," he wrote, in a May 8 letter to Cunard's New York manager, Charles Sumner. "We are all at one in our feelings with regard to this terrible disaster to the 'Lusitania,' and it is quite hopeless to try to put anything in writing." Sumner wrote back that the loss of the ship and so many passengers "is sad beyond expression."

THE MANY unidentified bodies in the three morgues presented Cunard officials with an awkward predicament, and one that needed to be addressed quickly. The bodies—some 140 of them—had begun to decompose, at a rate quickened by the warm spring weather. The company decided on a mass burial. Each body would have its own coffin; mothers and babies would share; but all would be interred together in three separate excavations, lettered A, B, and C, in the Old Church Cemetery on a hillside outside Queenstown.

The date was set for Monday, May 10. All the previous day

and throughout the night, soldiers dug the graves and undertakers coffined the bodies, leaving the lids off as long as possible to encourage last-minute identifications. Owing to a shortage of vehicles, the coffins were transported in shifts beginning early Monday morning, but three coffins were held back for the actual funeral procession, which was to begin in the afternoon.

Trains brought mourners and the curious. Shops closed for the day and pulled their blinds and fastened their shutters. Ship captains ordered flags hung at half-mast. As the procession advanced through Queenstown, a military band played Chopin's "Funeral March." Clerics led the cortege, among them Father Cowley Clark of London, himself a survivor of the disaster. Soldiers and mourners followed. U.S. consul Frost walked as well. Soldiers and citizens lined the entire route, standing bareheaded as a measure of respect. The road they followed passed through hills of vivid green stippled with wildflowers and slashed here and there by the garish yellow of blooming gorse. The sky was clear and without cloud, and in the distant harbor boats dipped and nodded in a light breeze, "a picture of peace," wrote one reporter, "that gave no hint of the recent tragedy."

The procession bearing the three coffins arrived at the cemetery about three o'clock and stopped at the edge of the graves. The many other coffins, each an elongated diamond of elm, had been laid neatly within, arranged in two tiers, the body numbers and locations carefully mapped so that if the photographs and lists of personal effects cataloged by Cunard led to subsequent identifications, the families would at least know the exact whereabouts of their loved ones.

As the three coffins were lowered into the graves, the crowd sang "Abide with Me." Gunfire followed, from a ceremonial guard, and a squad of buglers played "The Last Post," the British military's equivalent of taps. Soldiers converged and began filling the graves. A photograph shows a line of small boys standing on the hillock of excavated soil, watching with avid interest as the soldiers below fill the crevices between coffins.

It was lovely, and dignified, and deeply moving, but this mass burial imposed a psychic cost on kin who learned, belatedly, that their own loved ones were interred within. Cunard's final count found that of these anonymous dead, about half were later identified using personal effects and photographs. For some families the idea of their kin resting alone in that far-off terrain was too hard to bear. The family of Elizabeth A. Seccombe, a thirty-eight-year-old woman from Petersborough, New Hampshire, pleaded with Consul Frost for help in retrieving her and bringing her home. She was the daughter of a Cunard captain who had died some years earlier. Her body was No. 164, buried on May 14 in grave B, sixth row, upper tier.

Frost did what he could. He argued that Seccombe's location in the grave made her coffin particularly easy to locate. Though very much a miser when it came to U.S. funds, he went so far as to offer £100 to cover costs.

The British government was willing, but the local council said no, and its decision held sway. In part, the council was influenced by local superstition—"religious prejudice," Frost called it—but mainly it did not want to set a precedent. At least twenty other families had sought to disinter their loved ones and had been refused. The council's stance, Frost wrote, "is incomprehensible to me."

The greatest burden by far was borne by the relatives of the many passengers and crew whose bodies were never found. Of the 791 passengers designated by Cunard as missing, only 173 bodies, or about 22 percent, were eventually recovered, leaving 618 souls unaccounted for. The percentage for the crew was even more dismal, owing no doubt to the many deaths in the luggage room when the torpedo exploded.

Alice and Elbert Hubbard were never found; nor was Kansas City passenger Theodore Naish. In Queenstown, his wife, Belle, roomed for a time with young Robert Kay, as he recovered from his measles and waited for his grandfather to come and claim him. Joseph Frankum, who had huddled with his family in an unlaunched boat during the *Lusitania*'s last moments, survived, as did one of his sons, but his wife, his baby daughter, and his four-year-old son were lost. Nellie Huston never got to mail that charming diary-like letter in which she confessed that the size of her derrière impeded her access to her berth. The letter was found in a purse floating on the sea. The three members of the Luck family—thirty-four-year-old Charlotte and her two young sons—disappeared as well. Alfred Vanderbilt was never found, despite a $5,000 reward—a fortune—offered by the Vanderbilt family. Charles Lauriat's friend and traveling companion, Lothrop Withington, likewise disappeared.

The absence of so many bodies raised haunting questions for families. Were their loved ones now among the anonymous corpses buried at Queenstown? Were they locked somewhere within the hull, owing to an ill-advised last-minute dash for a personal belonging? Did chivalry do them in, or cowardice? Or did they suffer a fate like that of one unidentified woman, whose body came to rest on Straw Island, off Galway, where she was found by the keeper of the island's lighthouse? She was wearing her Boddy life jacket correctly and had drifted alone for thirty-six days.

Mothers lost children and would be left forever to imagine their final moments or to wonder if somehow, miraculously, their babies had actually been saved and were now in the care of another. Norah Bretherton, the Los Angeles woman who had handed her Betty to a stranger, was spared that brand of haunting. Betty was Body No. 156. Her mother buried her in the graveyard at the Ursuline Convent in Cork. Bretherton's son survived.

For families at home, waiting for news, the absence of a body left them suspended somewhere between hope and grief. One mother set out to learn as much as possible about her lost boy, Preston Prichard. She was aided by her surviving son, Mostyn, who traveled to Queenstown to search the morgues. "The place is alive with miserable creatures like ourselves," he wrote. He found no trace of his brother. "It is bewildering to know what to do."

Mrs. Prichard wrote to dozens of survivors, and, on the basis of information she received, she wrote to dozens more. She sent a flyer with Preston's picture and a detailed description. Among those she contacted was Grace French, Prichard's dining companion, who told Mrs. Prichard that she believed herself to be the last person on the ship to have spoken with him. In one of several letters, French told Mrs. Prichard that she had thought of her son often and of their interrupted excursion to find her double on board. French wrote, "I can see his face so clearly in my mind so sunburned and full of life and ambition."

The many replies offered a fresh view of the voyage and of the trials and sorrows of the last day. The writers recalled fleeting glimpses of Prichard, especially his gregariousness and popularity, and offered their own stories. Mostly, though, survivors tried to offer some small bit of consolation, despite having had only glancing contact with Prichard, or none at all. They assured Mrs. Prichard that her son, given his physical prowess, must surely have been helping women and children up to the last moment.

Theodate Pope, ever true to her spiritualist beliefs, wrote to Mrs. Prichard on February 4, 1916. "I beg of you not to dwell on the thought of what has become of the physical part of the boy you love," she urged. "Can you not constantly keep in mind that whatever has happened to his body has not in any way affected his spirit and that surely lives and will await reunion with you?"

A second-class passenger named Ruth M. Wordsworth, of Salisbury, England, sought to address the disparity between how things actually unfolded on the ship and the nightmarish scenes conjured in the minds of next of kin.

"I know you must be tempted to have most terrible imaginings; may I tell you that although it was very awful, it was not so ghastly as you are sure to imagine it. When the thing really comes, God gives to each the help he needs to live or to die." She described the quiet and the lack of panic among passengers. "They were calm, many of them quite cheerful, and everyone was trying to do the sensible thing, the men were forgetting themselves, and seeing after the women and children. They could not do much, because the list prevented the launching of most of the boats, but they were doing their best and playing the man."

Of the four men in Preston Prichard's cabin, D-90, only one

survived, his friend Arthur Gadsden. Prichard's body was never recovered, yet in the red volume that now contains the beautifully archived replies to Mrs. Prichard's letters there exists a surprisingly vivid sense of him, as though he resided still in the peripheral vision of the world.

PART V

THE SEA OF SECRETS

BLAME

W HAT HAPPENED NEXT CAME AS A SURPRISE TO CAP-
tain Turner. Even though the cause of the disaster was
obvious—an act of war—the Admiralty moved at once
to place the blame on him. Anyone privy to the internal communications, or "minutes," flung between the offices of senior Admiralty officials in the week after the disaster could have had no
doubt as to the zeal with which the Admiralty intended to forge
a case against Turner. In one, Churchill himself wrote, "We sh'd
pursue the Captain without check."

Before the effort could get started, however, the coroner in
Kinsale, Ireland, John J. Horgan, convened an inquest of his own,
much to the Admiralty's displeasure. Horgan claimed the responsibility fell to him because five of the Lusitania's dead had been
landed in his district. The inquest began the day after the sinking, Saturday, May 8. Horgan called Turner as a witness and after
hearing his testimony praised the captain for his courage in staying
with the ship until the last moment. At this, Turner began to cry.
Horgan, in a later memoir, called the captain "a brave but unlucky
man."

On Monday, May 10, the coroner's jury issued its finding: that
the submarine's officers and crew and the emperor of Germany
had committed "willful and wholesale murder."

Half an hour later a message arrived from the Admiralty,

ordering Horgan to block Turner from testifying. Horgan wrote, "That august body were however as belated on this occasion as they had been in protecting the *Lusitania* against attack."

THE ADMIRALTY was far more prompt in laying out the contours of its strategy for assigning fault to Turner. The day after the disaster, Richard Webb, director of the Admiralty's Trade Division, circulated a two-page memorandum, marked "Secret," in which he charged that Turner had ignored the Admiralty's instructions that called for him to zigzag and to "give prominent headlands a wide berth." Instead, Webb wrote, Turner had "proceeded along the usual trade route, at a speed approximately three-quarters of what he was able to get out of this vessel. He thus kept his valuable vessel for an unnecessary length of time in the area where she was most liable to attack, inviting disaster."

Webb made a formal request for an investigation by Britain's Wreck Commission, under Lord Mersey, who had led inquiries into the losses of many ships, including the *Titanic* and the *Empress of Ireland*.

On Wednesday, May 12, Webb intensified his attack on Captain Turner. In a new memorandum, he wrote that Turner "appears to have displayed an almost inconceivable negligence, and one is forced to conclude that he is either utterly incompetent, or that he has been got at by the Germans." In the left-hand margin, First Sea Lord Fisher, in his wild fulminating hand, jotted, "I hope Captain Turner will be arrested <u>immediately</u> after the inquiry <u>whatever</u> the verdict of finding may be."

The Admiralty took the unprecedented step of insisting that key parts of the planned inquiry, especially the examination of Turner, be held in secret.

U.S. CONSUL FROST sensed early on that the Admiralty's soul had hardened against Turner. On Sunday, May 9, Frost paid a call on Admiral Coke, senior naval officer in Queenstown, accompa-

nied by two U.S. military attachés who had just arrived from London to help arrange the return of American dead.

Admiral Coke openly criticized Turner for sailing too close to
shore and too slowly and read aloud the warnings that had been
sent to the *Lusitania* on Friday. But Consul Frost was surprised
at how little detail these messages contained. "Bare facts only,"
Frost noted, later. "No instructions or interpretation. It is true that
Turner should have kept farther out; but to my mind it seemed that
the Admiralty had by no means done their full duty by him."

One of the American attachés, Capt. W. A. Castle, wrote his
own account of the meeting and noted that a particular subject
was glaringly absent from the conversation. "I was struck by the
fact that the Admiral while seeming to be desirous of justifying
the Admiralty in its measures of protection, did not mention the
presence of any destroyers or other Naval vessels." Castle added
that during his train trip back to London he had discussed the subject with a fellow passenger, a Royal Navy lieutenant, "who spoke
quite frankly, although I suppose of course confidentially, and said
that he could not understand nor could his brother officers, why so
many torpedo boats of the old type, which could make 25 knots
an hour without difficulty, and would be just the thing to protect
an incoming steamer, are left at various wharves, instead of being
used for this purpose, and said that had they placed one of these to
starboard, another to port, and another in front of the *Lusitania*,
she could not have been torpedoed."

WHY THE ADMIRALTY would seek to assign fault to Turner de-
fies ready explanation, given that isolating Germany as the sole
offender would do far more to engender global sympathy for Britain and cement animosity toward Germany. By blaming Turner,
however, the Admiralty hoped to divert attention from its own
failure to safeguard the *Lusitania*. (Questioned on the matter in
the House of Commons on May 10, 1915, Churchill had replied,
rather coolly, "Merchant traffic must look after itself.") But there
were other secrets to protect, not just from domestic scrutiny, but

also from German watchers—namely the fact that the Admiralty, through Room 40, had known so much about U-20's travels leading up to the attack. One way to defend those secrets was to draw attention elsewhere.

The Admiralty found added motivation to do so when, on May 12, wireless stations in Britain's listening network intercepted a series of messages from the then homebound U-20, which upon entering the North Sea had resumed communication with its base at Emden. At the Admiralty these messages drew an unusual degree of attention. Room 40 asked all the stations that had intercepted them to confirm that they had transcribed them correctly and to provide signed and certified copies.

In the first message of the series, Schwieger reported: "Have sunk off the South Coast of Ireland, one sailing ship, two steamers, and LUSITANIA. Am steering for the mouth of the Ems."

The Admiralty received it at 9:49 A.M.; the decrypted copy was marked "Most Secret." This message confirmed that the culprit had indeed been U-20, the submarine that Room 40 had been tracking since April 30.

That afternoon, Room 40 received the intercept of a reply sent to Schwieger by the commander of Germany's High Seas Fleet, which read, "My highest appreciation of Commander and crew for the success they have achieved. Am proud of their achievement and express best wishes for their return."

Then came a third message, sent from Schwieger to his base. After detailing the latitude and longitude of his attack on the *Lusitania*, Schwieger noted that he had sunk the ship "by means of one torpedo."

This was a surprise. By now the prevailing view in the world's press was that the *Lusitania* had been sunk by *two* torpedoes and that these accounted for the two major explosions reported by passengers. But now the Room 40 cognoscenti knew without doubt that Schwieger had fired only one torpedo.

And this, they understood, raised sensitive questions: How could a single torpedo sink a ship the size of the *Lusitania*? And if there was no second torpedo, what exactly, caused the second explosion?

They recognized, also, that Schwieger's message had to be kept secret at all costs, for it was precisely this kind of special knowledge that could tip Germany to the existence of Room 40.

BY THE TIME the Mersey inquiry began, on June 15, 1915, the British government had undergone one of its periodic upheavals, amid controversy over the shell shortage on the western front and the failure, at great cost in lives and ships, of Churchill's plan to force the Dardanelles. New men ran the Admiralty. Fisher had resigned, and Churchill had been jettisoned. These changes, however, caused no easing of the campaign against Captain Turner.

After preliminary public testimony from several witnesses, including Turner, who briefly described his experience in the disaster, Lord Mersey convened the first of the secret sessions and again called Turner to the witness box. The Admiralty's lead attorney, Sir Edward Carson, attorney general, questioned the captain in harsh fashion, as if the proceeding were a murder trial with Turner the prime suspect. Carson clearly hoped to prove that Turner had ignored the Admiralty's directives, in particular its instructions to keep to a midchannel course.

Turner testified that by his own standards he *was* in midchannel. Under ordinary circumstances, he said, he passed the Old Head of Kinsale at distances as close as a mile. Indeed, one photograph of the *Lusitania* shows the ship steaming at full speed past the Old Head at the maritime equivalent of a hair's breadth. At the time of the attack, the ship by Turner's reckoning had been a dozen miles off, maybe as many as 15. (Years later a diver would pinpoint the wreck's location at 11¾ miles from Kinsale Head.)

Carson also badgered Turner as to why the *Lusitania* was moving at only 18 knots when it was torpedoed and challenged the wisdom of the captain's plan to reduce speed in order to arrive at the Mersey Bar off Liverpool at a time when he could sail into the harbor without stopping. Carson argued that if Turner had zigzagged at top speed he could have evaded the submarine and, owing to the time consumed by the frequent course changes, would still have made the bar on time. Carson let pass the fact that although Turner was not deliberately zigzagging, his several changes of course that morning to set up his four-point bearing did describe a zigzag pattern, with fatal result: the last starboard turn put him directly in U-20's path.

Turner's own lawyer, Butler Aspinall, Britain's leading expert in maritime law, did his best to sculpt Turner's story into a coherent account of the *Lusitania*'s last morning and to win for him Lord Mersey's sympathy. "I mean to say, we have the very great advantage of knowing so much now which was unknown to him then," Aspinall said; "we are sitting upon the matter in cool judgment, with an opportunity of looking at the charts, and the circumstances under which we are dealing with it were not the circumstances under which the Master would have an opportunity of dealing with it."

In all, Lord Mersey heard testimony from thirty-six witnesses, including passengers, crew, and outside experts. At the conclusion of the inquiry, he defied the Admiralty and absolved Turner of any responsibility for the loss of the *Lusitania*. In his report, Mersey wrote that Turner "exercised his judgment for the best. It was the judgment of a skilled and experienced man, and although others might have acted differently and perhaps more successfully he ought not, in my opinion, to be blamed." Mersey found Cunard's closure of the ship's fourth boiler room to be irrelevant. The resulting reduction in speed, he wrote, "still left the *Lusitania* a considerably faster ship than any other steamer plying across the Atlantic." Mersey laid blame entirely on the U-boat commander.

Turner doubtless was relieved, but, according to his son Norman he also felt he had been unjustly treated. "He was very bitter about the way in which, at the enquiry . . . it was sought to fix the blame on him for the sinking, and particularly to try to condemn him for being on the course he was." Lord Mersey seemed to share this sentiment. Soon afterward, he resigned his post as wreck commissioner, calling the inquiry "a damned dirty business." Cunard retained Turner on its roster of captains.

At no time during the secret portions of the proceeding did the Admiralty ever reveal what it knew about the travels of U-20. Nor did it disclose the measures taken to protect the HMS *Orion* and other military vessels. Moreover, the Admiralty made no effort to correct Lord Mersey's finding that the *Lusitania* had been struck by two torpedoes—this despite the fact that Room 40 knew full well that Schwieger had fired only one.

Nor did the inquiry ever delve into why the *Lusitania* wasn't diverted to the safer North Channel route, and why no naval escort was provided. Indeed, *these* are the great lingering questions of the *Lusitania* affair: Why, given all the information possessed by the Admiralty about U-20; given the Admiralty's past willingness to provide escorts to inbound ships or divert them away from trouble; given that the ship carried a vital cargo of rifle ammunition and artillery shells; given that Room 40's intelligence prompted the obsessive tracking and protection of the HMS *Orion*; given that U-20 had sunk three vessels in the *Lusitania*'s path; given Cunard chairman Booth's panicked Friday morning visit to the navy's Queenstown office; given that the new and safer North Channel route was available; and given that passengers and crew alike had expected to be convoyed to Liverpool by the Royal Navy—the question remains, why *was* the ship left on its own, with a proven killer of men and ships dead ahead in its path?

There is silence on the subject in the records of Room 40 held by the National Archives of the United Kingdom and Churchill College, Cambridge. Nowhere is there even a hint of dismay at missing so clear an opportunity to use the fruits of Room 40's intelligence to save a thousand lives.

The question perplexed at least one prominent naval historian, the late Patrick Beesly, who, during World War II, was himself an officer in British naval intelligence. Britain's secrecy laws prevented him from writing about the subject until the 1970s and 1980s, when he published several books, including one about Room 40, said to be a quasi-official account. There he addressed the controversy only obliquely, stating that if no deliberate plan existed to put the *Lusitania* in danger, "one is left only with an unforgivable cock-up as an explanation."

However, in a later interview, housed in the archives of the Imperial War Museum, London, Beesly was less judicious. "As an Englishman and a lover of the Royal Navy," he said, "I would prefer to attribute this failure to negligence, even gross negligence, rather [than] to a conspiracy deliberately to endanger the ship." But, he said, "on the basis of the considerable volume of information which is now available, I am reluctantly compelled to state that on balance, the most likely explanation is that there was indeed a plot, however imperfect, to endanger the *Lusitania* in order to involve the United States in the war." So much was done for the *Orion* and other warships, he wrote, but nothing for the *Lusitania*. He struggled with this. No matter how he arranged the evidence, he came back to conspiracy. He said, "If that's unacceptable, will someone tell me another explanation to these very very curious circumstances?"

The absence of an escort also surprised Cunard's lawyers. In a lengthy confidential memorandum on the Mersey inquiry, written to help a New York attorney defend the company against dozens of American liability claims, Cunard's London firm wrote, "With regard to the question of convoy, Sir Alfred Booth hoped and expected that the Admiralty would send destroyers to meet & convoy the vessel. There were destroyers at Queenstown and no explanation has been given as to why there was no convoy except Mr. Winston Churchill's statement that it was impossible for the Admiralty to convoy Merchant ships." The memo left unsaid the fact that the Admiralty earlier in the year had in fact made provision to escort merchant ships.

It was a question that also troubled passengers and crew and the citizens of Queenstown. Third Officer Albert Bestic wrote, later, that in light of the German warning in New York and the Admiralty's awareness of new submarine activity, some sort of protective force should have been dispatched. "Even one destroyer encircling the liner as she entered the danger zone would have minimized the danger, if indeed have not rendered the *Lusitania* immune from attack with a resulting loss of lives." One of Cunard's most prominent captains, James Bisset, who had served under Turner and was captain of the HMS *Caronia* when it met the *Lusitania* off New York shortly after departure, wrote in a memoir, "The neglect to provide naval escort for her in the narrow waters as she approached her destination was all the more remarkable as no less than twenty-three British merchant vessels had been torpedoed and sunk by German U-boats near the coasts of Britain and Ireland in the preceding seven days."

As to whether an escort really could have prevented the disaster, Turner himself was ambivalent. "It might," he said, during his testimony at the Kinsale coroner's inquest, "but it is one of those things one never knows. The submarine would have probably torpedoed both of us."

ANOTHER MYSTERY centered on the second explosion within the *Lusitania*. Its cause would be debated for a century to come, with dark talk of exploding munitions and a secret cargo of explosive materials. There may indeed have been a hidden cache of explosives aboard, but if so, it did not cause the second explosion or contribute to the speed at which the ship sank. The myriad accounts left by survivors fail to describe the kind of vivid cataclysm such an explosion would produce. The rifle ammunition was not likely to have been the culprit either. Testing done several years earlier had determined that such ammunition did not explode en masse when exposed to fire, and this prompted the U.S. Department of Commerce and Labor to approve the shipping of such cargoes aboard passenger vessels.

A more plausible theory held that when the torpedo exploded, the concussion shook the ship with such violence that the nearly empty coal bunkers became clouded with explosive coal dust, which then ignited. There is evidence that such a cloud did arise. One fireman, who had been standing in the center of a stokehold, reported hearing the crash of the torpedo and suddenly finding himself engulfed in dust. But this cloud apparently did not ignite: the fireman survived. Here too, survivors' accounts don't depict the kind of fiery convulsion such an ignition would have produced. Subsequent investigation by forensic engineers concluded that the environment in which the ship's coal was stored was too damp, in part from condensation on the hull, to foster the ideal conditions necessary for detonation.

What most likely caused the second event was the rupture of a main steam line, carrying steam under extreme pressure. This was Turner's theory from the beginning. The fracture could have been caused by the direct force of the initial explosion, or by cold seawater entering Boiler Room No. 1 and coming into contact with the superheated pipe or its surrounding fixtures, causing a potentially explosive condition known as thermal shock. The fact is, immediately after the torpedo exploded, steam pressure within the ship plummeted. An engineer in the starboard high-pressure turbine room reported that pressure in the main line dropped "to 50 pounds in a few seconds," roughly a quarter of what it should have been.

IN THE END, Schwieger's attack on the *Lusitania* succeeded because of a chance confluence of forces. Even the tiniest alteration in a single vector could have saved the ship.

Had Captain Turner not had to wait the extra two hours for the transfer of passengers from the *Cameronia*, he likely would have passed Schwieger in the fog, when U-20 was submerged and on its way home. For that matter, even the brief delay caused by the last-minute disembarkation of Turner's niece could have placed the ship in harm's way. More importantly, had Turner not been compelled to shut down the fourth boiler room to save money, he could have sped across the Atlantic at 25 knots, covering an additional 110 miles a day, and been safely to Liverpool before Schwieger even entered the Celtic Sea.

Fog was an important factor too. Had it persisted just a

half hour longer, neither vessel would have seen the other, and Schwieger would have continued on his way.

Then there was the almost miraculous fact that Schwieger's attack even succeeded. Had Captain Turner not made that final turn to starboard, Schwieger would have had no hope of catching up. What's more, the torpedo actually worked. Defying his own experience and the 60 percent failure rate calculated by the German navy, it did exactly what it was supposed to do.

Not only that, it struck precisely the right place in the *Lusitania*'s hull to guarantee disaster, by allowing seawater to fill the starboard longitudinal bunkers and thereby produce a fatal list. No one familiar with ship construction and torpedo dynamics would have guessed that a single torpedo could sink a ship as big as the *Lusitania*, let alone do so in just eighteen minutes. Schwieger's earlier attack on the *Candidate* required a torpedo and multiple shells from his deck gun; his attack later that same day on the *Centurion* required *two* torpedoes. And almost exactly a year later, on May 8, 1916, he would need three torpedoes to sink the White Star liner *Cymric*, which even then stayed afloat for another twenty-eight hours. All three ships were a fraction of the *Lusitania*'s size.

Moreover, Schwieger had overestimated the ship's speed. He calculated 22 knots when in fact the ship was moving at only 18. Had he gauged the speed correctly and timed his shot accordingly, the torpedo would have struck the hull farther back, amidships, possibly with less catastrophic effect and certainly with the result that the many crew members killed instantly in the luggage room would have survived to assist in launching the lifeboats. The steam line might not have failed. If Turner had been able to keep the ship under power, he might have made it to Queenstown, or succeeded in beaching the ship, or even leveraged its extraordinary agility to turn and ram U-20.

However, it also seems likely that if the *Lusitania* had not been so visibly crippled Schwieger might have come back for a second shot.

Really the only good piece of luck that Friday was the weather. The water was preternaturally calm, the day sunny and warm. Even a modest sea would have swept survivors from their floating oars and boxes and planks of wood, and likely swamped overloaded lifeboats. At one point, survivor Ogden Hammond's boat had seventy-five people aboard; its gunnels were only 6 inches above the water. The benign conditions of the day saved scores of lives, if not hundreds.

THE LAST BLUNDER

F OR SEVERAL DAYS AFTER THE SINKING, WILSON SAID nothing about it in public. He stuck to his routines. He golfed on the Saturday morning after the attack, took a drive that afternoon, went to church on Sunday morning. During a conversation in his study, Wilson told his secretary, Joe Tumulty, that he understood his cool response might trouble some people. "If I pondered over those tragic items that daily appear in the newspapers about the *Lusitania*, I should see red in everything and I am afraid that when I am called upon to act with reference to this situation I could not be just to anyone. I dare not act unjustly and cannot indulge my own passionate feelings."

Sensing that Tumulty did not agree, Wilson said, "I suppose you think I am cold and indifferent and little less than human, but my dear fellow, you are mistaken, for I have spent many sleepless hours thinking about this tragedy. It has hung over me like a terrible nightmare. In God's name, how could any nation calling itself civilized purpose so horrible a thing."

Wilson believed that if he went then to Congress to ask for a declaration of war, he would likely get it. But he did not think the nation was truly ready for that kind of commitment. He told Tumulty, "Were I to advise radical action now, we should have nothing, I am afraid, but regrets and heartbreaks."

In fact, apart from a noisy pro-war faction led by former

president Teddy Roosevelt, much of America seemed to share Wilson's reluctance. There was anger, yes, but no clear call to war, not even from such historically pugnacious newspapers as the *Louisville Courier-Journal* and *Chicago Tribune*. In Indiana, newspapers serving smaller communities urged restraint and support for the president, according to one historian's study of Indiana's reaction to the disaster. The state's "six- and eight-page dailies and the weekly journals were practically of one mind in their hope for peace." Petitions arrived at the White House counseling caution. The Tennessee State Assembly voted a resolution expressing confidence in Wilson and urging the state's residents "to refrain from any intemperate acts or utterances." The Louisiana Legislature voted its support as well and warned that the crisis at hand "calls for coolness, deliberation, firmness and precision of mind on the part of those entrusted with the power of administration." The students of Rush Medical College in Chicago weighed in, all signing a petition expressing "confidence in the sagacity and patience of our President" and urging him to continue his policy of neutrality. Dental students at the University of Illinois took time out to do likewise.

German popular reaction to the sinking of the *Lusitania* was exultant. A Berlin newspaper declared May 7 "the day which marked the end of the epoch of English supremacy of the seas" and proclaimed: "The English can no longer protect trade and transport in their own coastal waters; its largest, prettiest and fastest liner has been sunk." Germany's military attaché in Washington told reporters that the deaths of the Americans aboard would at last show the nation the true nature of the war. "America does not know what conditions are," he said. "You read of thousands [of] Russians or Germans being killed and pass it over without qualm. This will bring it home to you."

WILSON KEPT SILENT until Monday evening, May 10, when he traveled to Philadelphia to give a previously scheduled speech before four thousand newly minted citizens. He had seen Edith that afternoon, and by the time he reached Philadelphia was still roiled in the emotional after-sea of that encounter. In his speech he talked of the importance of America as a force for instilling peace in the world and of the need for the nation to stand firm even in the face of the *Lusitania* tragedy. He used an outline, not a fixed text, and improvised as he went along, not the best approach given his emotional state. "There is such a thing as a man being too proud to fight," he told his audience. "There is such a thing as a nation being so right that it does not need to convince others by force that it is right."

These were lofty sentiments, but that phrase "too proud to fight" struck a dull chord. America did not want to go to war, but being too proud to fight had nothing to do with it. A pro-war Republican, Sen. Henry Cabot Lodge, called it "probably the most unfortunate phrase that [Wilson] had ever coined."

Wilson told Edith he had spoken while in an emotional haze caused by his love for her. In a letter composed Tuesday morning, he wrote, "I do not know just what I said at Philadelphia (as I rode along the street in the dusk I found myself a little confused as to whether I was in Philadelphia or New York!) because my heart was in such a whirl from that wonderful interview of yesterday and the poignant appeal and sweetness of the little note you left with me; but many other things have grown clear in my mind."

All that Tuesday, Wilson worked on a protest he planned to send to Germany about the *Lusitania*. Typing on his Hammond portable, he sought to find the right tone—firm and direct, but not bellicose. By Wednesday evening, he was done. He wrote to Edith, "I have just put the final touches on our note to Germany and now turn—with what joy!—to talk to you. I am sure you have been by my side all evening, for a strange sense of peace and love has been on me as I worked."

Wilson sent the note over the objection of Secretary of State Bryan, who felt that to be truly fair and neutral, the United States should also send a protest to Britain, condemning its interference in trade. Wilson declined to do so. In his note he mentioned not just the *Lusitania* but also the *Falaba* and the death of Leon

Thrasher, the bombing of the *Cushing*, and the attack on the *Gulflight*. Citing what he called "the sacred freedom of the seas," he described how submarines, when used against merchant vessels, were by their nature weapons that violated "many sacred principles of justice and humanity." He asked Germany to disavow the attacks, to make necessary reparations, and to take steps to ensure that such things did not happen in the future. But he was careful also to note the "special ties of friendship" that had long existed between America and Germany.

Wilson's protest—the so-called First *Lusitania* Note—was the initial salvo in what would become a two-year war of paper, filled with U.S. protests and German replies, made against a backdrop of new attacks against neutral ships and revelations that German spies were at work in America. Wilson did all he could to keep America neutral in action and in spirit, but Secretary Bryan did not think he tried hard enough, and resigned on June 8, 1915. His resignation brought universal condemnation, with editors comparing him to Judas Iscariot and Benedict Arnold. The Goshen, Indiana, *News-Times* said, "The Kaiser has awarded the Iron Cross for less valuable service than that rendered by Mr. Bryan." In a letter to Edith Galt, Wilson himself described Bryan as a "traitor." He replaced him with the department's number two man, Undersecretary Robert Lansing, who by this time had come to long for war.

Wilson had cause for cheer, however. In a letter dated June 29, 1915, Edith at last agreed to marry him. They wed on December 18, 1915, in a simple ceremony at the White House. Late that night the couple set out on their honeymoon, traveling by private railcar to Hot Springs, Virginia. They had chicken salad for a late supper. As the train pulled into the station early the next morning, Wilson's Secret Service man Edmund Starling happened to look into the railcar's sitting room and, as Starling later wrote, saw "a figure in top hat, tailcoat, and gray morning trousers, standing with his back to me, hands in his pockets, happily dancing a jig."

As Starling watched, Wilson, still oblivious to his presence, clicked his heels in the air, and sang, "Oh, you beautiful doll! You great big beautiful doll!"

GERMANY'S U-BOAT campaign waxed and waned, in step with the rising and falling influence of factions within its government that favored and opposed submarine warfare against merchant ships. Kaiser Wilhelm himself expressed a certain repugnance for attacks on passenger liners. In February 1916, he told fleet commander Admiral Scheer, "Were I the Captain of a U-boat I would never torpedo a ship if I knew that women and children were aboard." The next month, Germany's most senior advocate of unrestricted warfare, State Secretary Alfred von Tirpitz, resigned, in frustration. This brought a sympathy note from an odd quarter—Britain's former First Sea Lord, Jacky Fisher. "Dear Old Tirps," he wrote. He urged Tirpitz to "cheer up" and told him, "You're the one German sailor who understands War! Kill your enemy without being killed yourself. *I don't blame you for the submarine business*. I'd have done the same myself, only our idiots in England wouldn't believe it when I told 'em. Well! So long!"

He signed off with his usual closing, "Yours till hell freezes, Fisher."

That June, 1916, the Kaiser issued an order forbidding attacks against all large passenger ships, even those that were obviously British. He went on to order so many restrictions on how and when U-boat commanders could attack ships that the German navy, in protest, suspended all operations against merchant vessels in British waters.

But the *Lusitania* remained a point of conflict. President Wilson's protests failed to generate a response he deemed satisfactory—much to the delight of Britain's director of naval intelligence, Blinker Hall, who argued that any delay in resolving the *Lusitania* situation was "advantageous to the Allied cause."

Kapitänleutnant Schwieger did his part to worsen relations between America and Germany. On September 4, 1915, in the midst

334 / ERIK LARSON

of a patrol during which he sank ten steamships and one four-masted bark, he torpedoed the passenger liner *Hesperian*, killing thirty-two passengers and crew.

The *Hesperian* was clearly outbound, on its way to New York, and thus unlikely to be carrying munitions or other contraband. Among its cargo was the corpse of a *Lusitania* victim, Frances Stephens, a wealthy Canadian at last being transported home to Montreal.

WILSON WON reelection in 1916. He played golf nearly every day, often with the new Mrs. Wilson. They even played in snow: Secret Service man Starling painted the golf balls red to improve visibility. They routinely took drives through the countryside, a pastime Wilson adored. Marriage buoyed his spirits and eased his loneliness. Like the previous Mrs. Wilson, Edith became a trusted counselor, who listened to drafts of his speeches, critiqued his various notes to Germany, and now and then offered advice.

Outside the White House, Wilson's many notes to Germany and their replies became the target of wry humor, as when one editor wrote: "Dear Kaiser: In spite of previous correspondence on the subject another ship with American citizens on board has been sunk. Under the circumstances we feel constrained to inform you, in a spirit of utmost friendliness, that a repetition of the incident will of necessity require the dispatch of another note to your majesty's most estimable and peace-loving government."

As late as December 1916, Wilson believed he could still keep America neutral and, further, that he might himself be able to serve as a mediator to bring about a peace accord. He was heartened, therefore, when that winter Germany stated it might consider seeking peace with Britain, under certain conditions. Britain dismissed the overture out of hand, describing it as a German attempt to declare victory, but to Wilson it offered at least the hope that future negotiations could take place. Germany's ambassador to America, Count Johann-Heinrich von Bernstorff, reinforced Wilson's optimism, signaling that Germany was indeed willing to engage in discussions toward peace.

But Bernstorff tended to be more optimistic than facts warranted and possessed only a limited grasp of a new and dramatic change in his own government's thinking.

In Germany, a paradoxical shift was under way. Even as its leaders seemed to be maneuvering toward peace, the camp within the government that favored all-out submarine warfare gained ground. These were military officials who now sought authority to sink *all* merchant ships entering the war zone, neutral or otherwise—even American vessels. The shift was driven in part by the enthusiasm of the German public, who, dismayed by the carnage of the trenches, had come to see the U-boat as a miracle weapon—a *Wunderwaffe*—that if deployed for total war would quickly force Britain to her knees. This coincided with a fundamental change in German naval thinking, in which Schwieger and U-20 played an important role.

Throughout the fall of 1916, Schwieger had continued his exemplary performance as a submarine commander, sinking ship after ship, but early that November he ran into trouble. While returning from a three-week patrol in the Western Approaches, his boat ran aground, in fog, about 20 feet from the Danish shore. He radioed for assistance. The response was overwhelming. Admiral Scheer ordered destroyers to the scene, to attempt to pull U-20 loose, and dispatched an entire battle squadron—cruisers and battleships—to provide protection. Still U-20 remained mired. Schwieger was ordered to destroy the boat to keep it from falling into enemy hands. He exploded two torpedoes in the bow. If his intent was to obliterate the boat, he failed. The bow was mangled, but the rest of the boat, and its gun, remained intact, embedded in the sand to a depth of about 15 feet, and fully visible from the shore.

Meanwhile, in London, Room 40 began receiving wireless

intercepts that indicated something extraordinary was taking place. The Room 40 log noted, "Great excitement & activity." The Admiralty dispatched a submarine to the scene, whose commander found four battleships and managed to torpedo two of them, damaging both, sinking neither.

The episode proved to have a crystallizing effect on German naval strategy. At first, Kaiser Wilhelm upbraided Admiral Scheer for putting so many ships at risk on behalf of one submarine. But Scheer countered that the U-boat force had supplanted the High Seas Fleet as the primary offensive weapon of the German navy. The fleet, hiding in its bases while ostensibly waiting for the great battle, had achieved nothing. Henceforth, Scheer told Wilhelm, the fleet "will have to devote itself to one task—to get the U-boats safely out to sea and bring them safely home again." Scheer argued that U-20 was especially important, because if the Royal Navy had been allowed to destroy or capture the U-boat that had sunk the *Lusitania*, "this would be glad tidings for the British Government."

He told Wilhelm that if submarine crews were to maintain their daring—their "ardor"—they needed full assurance that they would not be abandoned if they encountered difficulties. "To us," Scheer declared, "every U-boat is of such importance, that it is worth risking the whole available Fleet to afford it assistance and support."

By this point, Germany's U-boat fleet had achieved a level of strength that at last gave it the potential to become a truly imposing force. Where in May 1915 the navy had only thirty U-boats, by 1917 it had more than one hundred, many larger and more powerful than Schwieger's U-20 and carrying more torpedoes. With this robust new fleet now ready, the pressure to deploy it to the fullest grew steadily.

A German admiral, Henning von Holtzendorff, came up with a plan so irresistible it succeeded in bringing agreement between supporters and opponents of unrestricted warfare. By turning Germany's U-boats loose, and allowing their captains to sink *every* vessel that entered the "war zone," Holtzendorff proposed to end the war in six months. Not five, not seven, but six. He calculated that for the plan to succeed, it had to begin on February 1, 1917, not a day later. Whether or not the campaign drew America into the war didn't matter, he argued, for the war would be over before American forces could be mobilized. The plan, like its territorial equivalent, the Schlieffen plan, was a model of methodical German thinking, though no one seemed to recognize that it too embodied a large measure of self-delusion. Holtzendorff bragged, "I guarantee upon my word as a naval officer that no American will set foot on the Continent!"

Germany's top civilian and military leaders converged on Kaiser Wilhelm's castle at Pless on January 8, 1917, to consider the plan, and the next evening Wilhelm, in his role as supreme military commander, signed an order to put it into action, a decision that would prove one of the most fateful of the war. On January 16, the German Foreign Office sent an announcement of the new campaign to Ambassador Bernstorff in Washington, with instructions that he deliver it to Secretary Lansing on January 31, the day before the new campaign was to begin. The timing was an affront to Wilson: it left no opportunity for protest or negotiation and came even as Bernstorff was promoting the idea that Germany really did want peace.

Wilson was outraged but chose not to see the declaration itself as sufficient justification for war. What he did not yet know was that there was a second, very secret message appended to the telegram Bernstorff had received and that both telegrams had been intercepted and relayed to Blinker Hall's intelligence division in the Old Admiralty Building in London, which by now oversaw a second, and singularly sensitive, component of Room 40's operations—the interception of diplomatic communications, both German and, incidentally, American.

THE FIRST OF Hall's men to grasp the importance of the second telegram was one of his top code breakers, Lt. Cdr. Nigel de Grey.

On the morning of January 17, 1917, a Wednesday, Hall and another colleague were attending to routine matters, when de Grey walked into the office.

"D.I.D.," he began—using the acronym for Director of Intelligence Division—"d'you want to bring America into the war?"

"Yes, my boy," Hall answered. "Why?"

De Grey told him that a message had come in that was "rather astonishing." It had been intercepted the day before, and de Grey had not yet managed to read the entire text, but what he had deciphered thus far seemed almost too far-fetched to be plausible.

Hall read the partial decrypt three or four times, in silence. "I do not remember a time when I was more excited," he wrote.

But just as quickly, he realized that the remarkable nature of the message presented a challenge. To disclose the text right away would not only put the secret of Room 40 at risk but also raise questions about the credibility of the message, for what it proposed was certain to raise skepticism.

The telegram was from Germany's foreign secretary, Arthur Zimmermann, written in a new code that was unfamiliar to Room 40. The process of rendering its text in coherent English was slow and difficult, but gradually the essential elements of the message came into view, like a photograph in a darkroom bath. It instructed Germany's ambassador in Mexico to offer Mexican president Venustiano Carranza an alliance, to take effect if the new submarine campaign drew America into the war. "Make war together," Zimmermann proposed. "Make peace together." In return, Germany would take measures to help Mexico seize previously held lands—"lost territory"—in Texas, New Mexico, and Arizona.

Hall had no doubt as to the telegram's importance. "This may be a very big thing," he told de Grey, "possibly the biggest thing of the war. For the present not a soul outside this room is to be told anything at all." And that included even Hall's superiors in the Admiralty.

Hall hoped he could avoid revealing the telegram altogether. There was a chance that Germany's declaration of unrestricted U-boat warfare by itself would persuade President Wilson that the time for war had come. Hall's hopes soared on February 3, 1917, when Wilson broke off diplomatic relations with Germany and ordered Ambassador Bernstorff to leave. But Wilson stopped short of calling for war. In a speech that day, Wilson stated that he could not believe Germany really intended to attack every ship that entered the war zone and added, "Only actual overt acts on their part can make me believe it even now."

Hall realized the time for action had come—that he had to get the telegram into American hands but at the same time protect the secret of Room 40. Through a bit of skulduggery, Hall managed to acquire a copy of the telegram as it had been received in Mexico, from an employee of the Mexican telegraph office, thereby allowing Britain to claim that it had obtained the telegram using conventional espionage techniques. On February 24, 1917, Britain's foreign secretary formally presented a fully translated copy of the telegram to U.S. ambassador Page.

WILSON WANTED to release the text immediately, but Secretary Lansing counseled against it, urging that they first confirm beyond doubt that the message was real. Wilson agreed to wait.

That same day, the news broke that a Cunard passenger liner, the *Laconia*, had been sunk off the coast of Ireland, after being struck by two torpedoes. Among the dead were a mother and daughter from Chicago. Edith Galt Wilson had known them both.

WILSON AND LANSING resolved to leak the telegram to the Associated Press, and on the morning of March 1, 1917, America's newspapers made it front-page news. Skeptics immediately proclaimed the telegram to be a forgery concocted by the British, just as Lansing and Captain Hall had feared would happen. Lansing expected Zimmermann to deny the message, thereby forcing the United States either to disclose the source or to stand mute and insist that the nation trust the president.

But Zimmermann surprised him. On Friday, March 2, during

a press conference, Zimmermann himself confirmed that he had sent the telegram. "By admitting the truth," Lansing wrote, "he blundered in a most astounding manner for a man engaged in international intrigue. Of course the message itself was a stupid piece of business, but admitting it was far worse."

THE REVELATION that Germany hoped to enlist Mexico in an alliance, with the promise of U.S. territory as a reward, was galvanizing by itself, but it was followed on Sunday, March 18, by news that German submarines had sunk three more American ships, without warning. (To add to the sense of global cataclysm, a popular rebellion sweeping Russia—the so-called February Revolution—had caused the abdication on March 15 of Tsar Nicholas and filled the next day's papers with news of violence in the streets of Russia's then capital, Petrograd.) A tectonic shift occurred in the nation's mood. The press now called for war. As historian Barbara Tuchman put it: "All these papers had been ardently neutral until Zimmermann shot an arrow in the air and brought down neutrality like a dead duck."

Secretary Lansing was elated. "The American people are at last ready to make war on Germany, thank God," he wrote in a personal memorandum, in which he revealed a certain bloodlust. "It may take two or three years," Lansing wrote. "It may even take five years. It may cost a million Americans; it may cost five million. However long it may take, however many men it costs we must go through with it. I hope and believe that the President will see it in this light."

Wilson gathered his cabinet on March 20, 1917, and asked each member to state his views. One by one each weighed in. All said the time for war had come; most agreed that in effect a state of war already existed between America and Germany. "I must have spoken with vehemence," Lansing wrote, "because the President asked me to lower my voice so that no one in the corridor could hear."

Once all had spoken, Wilson thanked them but gave no hint as to what course he would take.

The next day, he sent a request to Congress to convene a special session on April 2. He prepared his speech, again typing on his Hammond portable. Ike Hoover, the White House usher, told another member of the staff that judging by Wilson's mood, "Germany is going to get Hell in the address to Congress. I never knew him to be more peevish. He's out of sorts, doesn't feel well, and has a headache."

To prevent leaks, Wilson asked Hoover to bring the speech to the printing office in person, on the morning of April 2. That same day, news arrived that a German submarine had sunk yet another American ship, the *Aztec*, killing twenty-eight U.S. citizens. Wilson hoped to speak that afternoon, but various congressional processes intervened, and he was not called until the evening. He left the White House at 8:20 P.M.; Edith had set off for the Capitol ten minutes earlier.

A spring rain fell, soft and fragrant; the streets gleamed from the ornate lamps along Pennsylvania Avenue. The dome of the Capitol was lit for the first time in the building's history. Wilson's Treasury secretary and son-in-law, William McAdoo, would later recall how the illuminated dome "stood in solemn splendor against the dark wet sky." Despite the rain, hundreds of men and women lined the avenue. They removed their hats and watched with somber expressions as the president passed slowly in his car, surrounded by soldiers on horseback, as clear a sign as any of what was to come. Hooves beat steadily against the street and gave the procession the air of a state funeral.

Wilson arrived at the Capitol at 8:30, to find it heavily guarded by additional cavalry, the Secret Service, post office inspectors, and city police. Three minutes later, the Speaker announced, "The President of the United States." The vast chamber exploded with cheers and applause. Small American flags fluttered everywhere, like birds' wings. The tumult continued for two minutes, before settling to allow Wilson to begin.

He spoke in the direct and cool manner that had become familiar to the nation and that listeners often described as professorial. His voice betrayed no hint of what he was now prepared to ask of

Congress. At first he kept his eyes on his text, but as he progressed he now and then looked up to underscore a point.

He described Germany's behavior as constituting "in effect nothing less than war against the government and people of the United States." He outlined Germany's past efforts at espionage and alluded to the Zimmermann telegram, and he cast America's coming fight in lofty terms. "The world," he said, "must be made safe for democracy."

At this there rose the sound of one man's applause, slow and loud. Sen. John Sharp Williams, a Mississippi Democrat, brought his hands together "gravely, emphatically," according to a reporter for the *New York Times*. In the next moment, the idea that this was the centerpiece of Wilson's speech, and that it encapsulated all that America might hope to achieve, suddenly dawned on the rest of the senators and representatives, and a great roar filled the room.

Wilson's remarks gained force and momentum. Warning of "many months of fiery trial and sacrifice ahead," he declared that America's fight was a fight on behalf of all nations.

"To such a task we can dedicate our lives and our fortunes, everything that we are and everything that we have, with the pride of those who know that the day has come when America is privileged to spend her blood and her might for the principles that gave her birth and happiness and the peace which she has treasured. God helping her, she can do no other."

Now came pandemonium. Everyone rose at once. Flags waved. Men cheered, whistled, shouted, cried. Wilson had spoken for thirty-six minutes; he never mentioned the *Lusitania* by name. He quickly walked from the chamber.

Four days passed before both houses of Congress approved a resolution for war. During this period, as if deliberately seeking to ensure that no American had last-minute doubts, U-boats sank two American merchant ships, killing at least eleven U.S. citizens. Congress took so long not because there was any question whether the resolution would pass but because every senator and representative understood this to be a moment of great significance and wanted to have his remarks locked forever in the embrace of history. Wilson signed the resolution at 1:18 P.M. on April 6, 1917.

To Winston Churchill, it was long overdue. In his memoir-like history *The World Crisis, 1916–1918*, he said of Wilson, "What he did in April, 1917, could have been done in May, 1915. And if done then what abridgment of the slaughter; what sparing of the agony; what ruin, what catastrophes would have been prevented; in how many million homes would an empty chair be occupied today; how different would be the shattered world in which victors and vanquished alike are condemned to live!"

As it happened, America joined the war just in time. Germany's new campaign of unrestricted submarine warfare had succeeded to an alarming degree, although this had been kept secret by British officials. An American admiral, William S. Sims, learned the truth when he traveled to England to meet with British naval leaders to plan America's participation in the war at sea. What Sims discovered shocked him. German U-boats were sinking ships at such a high rate that Admiralty officials secretly predicted Britain would be forced to capitulate by November 1, 1917. During the worst month, April, any ship leaving Britain had a one-in-four chance of being sunk. In Queenstown, U.S. consul Frost saw striking corroboration of the new campaign's effect: in a single twenty-four-hour period, the crews of six torpedoed ships came ashore. Admiral Sims reported to Washington, "Briefly stated, I consider that at the present moment we are losing the war."

Just ten days later, the U.S. Navy dispatched a squadron of destroyers. They set off from Boston on April 24. Not many of them. Just six. But the significance of their departure was lost on no one.

ON THE MORNING of May 4, 1917, anyone standing atop the Old Head of Kinsale would have seen an extraordinary sight. First there appeared six plumes of dark smoke, far off on the horizon. The day was unusually clear, the sea a deep blue, the hills emerald, very much like a certain day two years earlier. The ships became steadily more distinct. Wasplike with their long slender hulls, these were ships not seen in these waters before. They approached in a line, each flying a large American flag. To the hundreds of onlookers by now gathered on shore, many also carrying American flags, it would be a sight they would never forget and into which they read great meaning. These were the descendants of the colonials returning now at Britain's hour of need, the moment captured in an immediately famous painting by Bernard Gribble, *The Return of the Mayflower*. American flags hung from homes and public buildings. A British destroyer, the *Mary Rose*, sailed out to meet the inbound warships, and signaled, "Welcome to the American colors." To which the American commander answered, "Thank you, I am glad of your company."

On May 8, the destroyers began their first patrols, just a day beyond the two-year anniversary of the sinking of the *Lusitania*.

PERSONAL EFFECTS

O NE HOT DAY IN JULY 1916, A HARBOR PILOT WALKED into the ship-news office in Battery Park in Manhattan and invited a group of reporters to accompany him on a brief voyage, by tugboat, up the Hudson River to Yonkers, north of Manhattan, where he was to "fetch out" a ship, that is, guide it downriver to the wider and safer waters of New York Harbor. Ordinarily this was not a voyage the reporters would be inclined to make, but the day was stifling and the pilot said the fresh air would do them all good. The reporters, among them the *Evening Mail*'s Jack Lawrence, also brought along a good deal of alcohol, or, as Lawrence put it, "liquid sustenance." As their tugboat approached the Yonkers wharf, the reporters saw that the ship was an old Cunard ocean liner, the *Ultonia*, docked there to pick up a load of horses for the war. It was a small ship, with one funnel. "She looked so smeared and dirty and utterly woebegone that we hardly recognized her," Lawrence wrote. The ship's black hull had been painted gray, in haphazard fashion. "Much of this had chipped off, giving her a peculiar, spotted appearance."

The day was languid, the river calm, and yet the ship moved with a peculiar side-to-side motion. Lawrence had never seen such a thing and found it "almost uncanny." This rolling, the pilot explained, was caused by the hundreds of horses within the ship. Sensing movement, all the horses roped to one side of the hull would suddenly rear backward in alarm, causing a slight roll. This in turn would startle the horses anew and cause those on the opposite side to step back. The side-to-side roll became more pronounced with each cycle, to the point where the ship looked as if it were being buffeted by a heavy sea. This, the pilot explained, was called a "horse storm," and under certain conditions it could bang a ship against its wharf and damage deck rails and boats.

As the tugboat pulled up alongside the *Ultonia*, the ship's cargo doors swung open to admit the pilot. The sun blazed. Inside the darkened hold stood one man, shaded by the overhead door. He looked down at the pilot and reporters. He did not smile. Lawrence recognized him at once: Capt. William Thomas Turner. "His old blue uniform was soiled and wrinkled," Lawrence wrote, but "his cap, bearing the Cunard Line insignia, was still at the familiar jaunty angle. The figure of the man was still erect and commanding."

The pilot climbed into the ship.

"Glad to see you aboard, sir," Turner told him. "We'll get under way immediately. These horses are raising hell."

Turner had been given command of the ship in November 1915, after its regular captain had fallen ill during a stop in France. He had been the only captain available to replace him. Just before Turner left Liverpool to take over command, Cunard's chairman Alfred Booth asked him into his office. Booth began to apologize about assigning Turner to such a modest vessel, but the captain stopped him. "I told him there were no regrets on my part," Turner said. "I would go to sea on a barge if necessary to get afloat again, as I was tired of being idle and on shore while everyone else was away at sea."

In December 1916, Cunard reassigned Turner and put him in command of the *Ivernia*, another passenger ship recommissioned for war duty, though this one carried troops, not horses. Turner was not its master for long. On January 1, 1917, while in the Mediterranean off the island of Crete, the ship was torpedoed and sunk, killing 153 soldiers and crew. Turner survived. The ship had been zigzagging at the time of the attack.

Cunard made Turner a relief captain and put him back in charge of the *Mauretania*, but this was a thin expression of confidence, for the ship was in dry dock.

In 1918, Turner was once again compelled to relive the *Lusitania* disaster when a federal judge in New York opened a trial to determine whether Cunard was liable for the ship's loss. The proceeding combined seventy lawsuits filed by American survivors and next of kin. Here too the judge ruled that the sole cause of the disaster was Schwieger's attack and that he had fired two torpedoes.

The final humiliation for Turner came later, with publication of Winston Churchill's book, in which Churchill persisted in blaming Turner for the disaster and, despite possessing clear knowledge to the contrary, reasserted that the ship had been hit by two torpedoes.

The old captain—"this great little man," as his friend George Ball put it—had survived the sinking of the *Lusitania* with his pride intact; he'd survived the sinking of the *Ivernia*; but this new affront hurt him. At sixty-four, when Cunard required captains to retire, Turner left the company and traveled to Australia to try to mend things with his estranged family but found that life there did not suit him. He returned to England and retired to his home in Great Crosby, outside Liverpool, to be looked after by his longtime companion, Mabel Every. He kept bees in half a dozen hives that he had built in his yard and harvested the honey they produced. Often in conversation he would absentmindedly pick stingers from his arms and shins.

Turner was said to be a fundamentally happy man who liked a good pipe now and then. He told stories of the sea, but never the one most people wanted to hear. "Capt. Turner felt the loss of the *Lusitania* very much, and seldom mentioned it to anyone," wrote Miss Every. It was this silence that told his friends how heavily the disaster weighed on him. In a reply to a sympathetic female friend in Boston, Turner wrote, "I grieve for all the poor innocent people that lost their lives and for those that are left to mourn their dear ones lost." But that was all he was willing to say on the subject, he told her. "Please excuse me saying more, because I hate to think or speak of it."

At the same time, he was not haunted by the disaster; nor did it leave him depressed and broken, as popular conception might have held. Wrote George Ball, "He was far too strong a character to brood over a matter that was beyond rectification and allow it to worry him to the point of melancholy—a characteristic he never at any time displayed." Turner himself said, in an interview with the *New York Times*, "I am satisfied that every precaution was taken, and that nothing was left undone that might have helped to save human lives that day."

Turner retained his good humor, according to George Ball. "Merriment and humor were always prominently observable in his company and never was he unable to keep all his associates interested and amused." This became more difficult when, in his seventies, cancer infiltrated his colon. "The poor fellow did suffer great agony in the last year of his life," Ball wrote.

Turner died on June 24, 1933, at the age of seventy-six. "He died as he had lived," Ball wrote, "full of courage and spirit and without complaint. So passed to the great beyond one of the hardy and able sailors of the old hard school."

Turner's niece, Mercedes Desmore, attended the funeral. The captain was buried at a cemetery in Birkenhead, across the Mersey from the Liverpool docks. His name was engraved at the bottom of the family tombstone, along with a brief reference to the *Lusitania*.

A new war came, and on September 16, 1941, a Nazi U-boat torpedoed and sank a British ship, the *Jedmoor*, off the Outer Hebrides, killing thirty-one of its thirty-six crew. Among the lost was a fifty-five-year-old able seaman named Percy Wilfred Turner—Captain Turner's youngest son.

IN APRIL 1917, Kptlt. Walther Schwieger was given command of a new submarine, U-88, larger than U-20, and with twice the number of torpedoes. A few months later, on July 30, he received the German navy's highest award, a pretty blue cross with a French name, Pour le Mérite, nicknamed the Blue Max. At the time he was only the eighth U-boat commander to receive one, his reward for having sunk 190,000 gross tons of shipping. The *Lusitania* alone accounted for 16 percent of the total.

In London, in the Old Admiralty Building, Room 40 tracked Schwieger and his new boat through four cruises, one of which lasted nineteen days. The fourth cruise began on September 5, 1917, and proved to be considerably shorter. Soon after entering the North Sea, Schwieger encountered a British Q-ship, the HMS *Stonecrop*, one of a class of so-called mystery ships that outwardly looked like vulnerable freighters but were in fact heavily armed. While trying to escape, Schwieger steered his boat into a British minefield. Neither he nor his crew survived, and the submarine was never found. Room 40 recorded the loss with a small notation in red: "Sunk."

In Denmark, coastal residents continued to visit the shore where his previous boat, U-20, had run aground, and now and then would climb upon the wreckage, until in 1925 the Danish navy demolished the remains with a spectacular explosion. By then, the conning tower, deck gun, and other components had been removed. They reside today in a seaside museum in Thorsminde, Denmark, on an austere stretch of North Sea coastline. Severed from its base and laced with rust, the conning tower sits on the museum's front lawn with all the majesty of a discarded refrigerator, a forlorn ghost of the terrifying vessel that once hunted the seas and changed history.

CAPT. REGINALD "BLINKER" HALL was knighted in 1918 for his work with Room 40, though the work itself was kept secret for decades. He went on to win election to the House of Commons as a Conservative member and remained active in politics through the 1920s. At one point, during a general strike in 1926, the Conservative party established a temporary newspaper, the *British Gazette*, and put Hall in charge of personnel. The editor in chief was his old boss, Winston Churchill. Circulation soared to one million copies a day before the strike ended. Hall retired from politics in 1929 and moved to a home in the New Forest, a lovely terrain of pasture and woods in southern England.

He set out to publish a book about Room 40 and his exploits as intelligence chief, but in August 1933 the Admiralty and Foreign Office, sensing a new dark tilt in the world, made clear their displeasure and their wish that the story remain secret. Hall withdrew the manuscript, though his notes and a number of completed chapters reside today in the Churchill Archives in Cambridge, England. In one notation Hall exults, "How simple is intelligence!"

Hall believed that new trouble was indeed soon to come in Europe. He visited Germany and Austria in 1934. Ever the intelligence man, he reported his observations about the National Socialist movement to the government. He also described his experience to a friend in America. "All the young are in the net," he wrote, "anyone who tried to keep out of being a Nazi is hazed till they change their mind; a form of mass cruelty which exists only in such a country." He added, "It will, some time soon, be the duty of HUMAN BEINGS to deal with a mad dog; when that time comes your people will have to take their share."

When the next war did begin, Hall joined Britain's Home Guard. He became its chief of intelligence. His health, never good, declined as the war progressed. In July 1943 one of his former code breakers, Claude Serocold, by that point a director of Claridge's Hotel, put him up in one of the hotel's suites so that he could spend his last days in comfort. At one point a plumber arrived to deal with a problem in the bathroom. In keeping with the dignified character of the hotel, the plumber was dressed in a black suit. Hall said, "If you're the undertaker, my man, you're too early." He died on October 22, 1943.

AMONG THE PASSENGERS who survived—all of whom received from Cunard a lifetime discount of 25 percent—there were marriages, lifelong friendships forged, and at least two suicides. Rita Jolivet's sister, Inez, a renowned violinist, was not herself a passenger, but her husband was among the lost. She decided she could not live without him and in late July 1915 shot herself to death. At least two young men who had survived the sinking were subsequently killed in the war.

Margaret Mackworth experienced a complex suite of after-effects. Her ordeal had the perverse result of eliminating her long-standing fear of water and substituting an exaggerated terror of being trapped in an enclosure *under* water. This fear came to her primarily when she took the train that passed through the Severn Tunnel, under the Severn River. It was a journey she had to take often, and every time, she wrote, "I insistently pictured the tunnel giving way, the water rushing in, and the passengers being caught and suffocated and drowned like rats in a trap in the little boxes of carriages."

Overall, though, she believed the disaster had made her a better person. She had a new confidence. "If anyone had asked me whether I should behave as I ought in a shipwreck I should have had the gravest doubts," she wrote. "And here I had got through this test without disgracing myself." She also found, to her surprise, that the experience had eliminated a deep horror of death that she had harbored since childhood. "I do not quite understand how or why it did this," she wrote. "The only explanation I can give is that when I was lying back in that sunlit water I was, and I knew it, very near to death." The prospect had not frightened her, she wrote: "Rather, somehow, one had a protected feeling, as if it were a kindly thing."

Her friend and tablemate, Dorothy Conner, went on to join the war effort, working in a canteen in France close to the front. In honor of her help and bravery, the French awarded her the Croix de Guerre.

Young Dwight Harris presented his engagement ring to his betrothed, Miss Aileen Cavendish Foster, and they were married on July 2, 1915, in London. The little boy he saved, Percy Richards, reached the age of forty, but killed himself on June 24, 1949.

George Kessler, the Champagne King, made good on a pledge he had made during his time in the water—that if he survived he would devote himself to the care of victims of the war. He established a foundation to help soldiers and sailors blinded in battle. Helen Keller became a trustee and later gave her name to the organization, which operates today as Helen Keller International.

Five months after the disaster, Charles Lauriat wrote a book about his experience, entitled *The Lusitania's Last Voyage*. It became a bestseller. He continued to sell books, manuscripts, and works of art, and in 1922 filed a claim against Germany with the U.S. Mixed Claims Commission for the value of the lost Thackeray drawings and the Dickens *Carol*. He wanted $51,399.31, which included interest; the commission awarded him $10,000. He died on December 28, 1937, at the age of sixty-three. His obituary in the *Boston Globe* noted the fact that over the years he had made sixty voyages to London and Europe. A succession of new owners built the Lauriat company into an empire of 120 "Lauriat's" stores, but this expansion came too quickly, at too great a cost, just as bookstores came under pressure from national chains and online sellers. The company filed for bankruptcy protection in 1998 and a year later closed for good.

Belle Naish, the Kansas City passenger who lost her husband, found that long after the disaster she could not look at a clear blue sky without feeling a deep sense of foreboding. Theodate Pope put Mrs. Naish in her will as thanks for that moment on the deck of the rescue ship *Julia* when Naish realized that Theodate was not in fact dead and called for help.

Theodate's recovery took time. Her spiritualist friends rallied and arranged for her to stay in a private home in Cork. She arrived with her face still battered and vividly hued, wearing a mélange of clothing that she had selected from a collection donated by Queenstown residents. Her host family placed her in a guest room with white walls, tulips in window boxes, and a lively coal fire. Until this point she had existed in a kind of emotional trance, unable to feel much of anything. But now, suddenly, in this cozy home, she felt safe. "I dropped into a chair and, for the first time, cried my heart out." She received letters of consolation. Mary Cassatt wrote, "If you were saved it is because you have still something to do in this world."

To complete her recovery, Theodate moved on to London, to the Hyde Park Hotel. Henry James was a regular visitor. Theodate described herself as being "in such a state of exhaustion and shock" that she would drift off to sleep in his presence, but each time she awoke, he was there, "his folded hands on the top of his cane, so motionless that he looked like a mezzotint." Though she had adored England on her past visits, she now found it utterly changed. "You can have no idea of the war atmosphere here," she wrote to her mother. "It is suffocating, it is so—not depressing—but so constantly in the thoughts and on the lips of everyone." She returned to her beloved house, Hill-Stead. For long afterward she endured severe insomnia, and nightmares in which she searched for her young companion of the *Lusitania*, Edwin Friend. On the worst nights a cousin would walk her through her house until she had calmed enough to return to bed.

She eventually adopted the "gold collar" and married a former U.S. ambassador to Russia, John Wallace Riddle. She achieved her goal of creating a progressive boys' school as a memorial to her late father. She built it in Avon, Connecticut, and called it Avon Old Farms School, which exists today.

Her companion, Edwin Friend, had indeed been lost but was reported by members of the reconstituted American Society for Psychical Research to have paid the group several visits.

SOURCES AND ACKNOWLEDGMENTS

The Gun in the Museum

IN THE DUSTY TIMELINE of world events installed in my brain back in high school, the *Lusitania* affair constituted the skimpiest of entries, tucked somewhere between the Civil War and Pearl Harbor. I always had the impression, shared I suspect by many, that the sinking immediately drove President Woodrow Wilson to declare war on Germany, when in fact America did not enter World War I for another two years—half the span of the entire war. But that was just one of the many aspects of the episode that took me by surprise. As I began reading into the subject, and digging into archives in America and Britain, I found myself intrigued, charmed, and moved.

What especially drew me was the rich array of materials available to help tell the story in as vivid a manner as possible—such archival treasures as telegrams, intercepted wireless messages, survivor depositions, secret intelligence ledgers, Kapitänleutnant Schwieger's actual war log, Edith Galt's love letters, and even a film of the *Lusitania*'s final departure from New York. Together these made a palette of the richest colors. I can only hope I used them to best effect.

Finding these things was half the fun. Every book is an expedition into unfamiliar realms, with both an intellectual and a physical component. The intellectual journey takes you deep into a subject, to the point where you achieve a level of expertise. A *focused* expertise, however. Am I an expert on World War I? No. Do I know a lot now about the *Lusitania* and World War I–era U-boats? Yes. Will I ever write another book about a sinking ship or submarine warfare? Most likely not.

The physical journey proved especially compelling, in ways I had not anticipated. At one point I found myself aboard Cunard's *Queen Mary 2* in a Force 10 gale during a winter crossing from New York to Southampton. At another, I wound up horribly lost in Hamburg with a German-speaking GPS system that unbeknownst to me had been tuned to a different city but gamely tried to direct me to my hotel all the same. I felt like a character in the *Bourne Identity*, taking wild turns down alleys and into cul-de-sacs, until I realized no GPS system would ever send a driver the wrong way down a one-way street. My travels took me as far north as Thorsminde, Denmark (in February no less); as far south as Christopher Newport University in Newport News, Virginia; as far west as the Hoover Library at Stanford University; and to various points east, including the always amazing Library of Congress and the U.S. National Archives, and equally enticing archives in London, Liverpool, and Cambridge. There will always be an England, and I am so very glad.

Along the way came quiet moments of revelation where past and present for an instant joined and history became a tactile thing. I live for these moments. No sooner did I sit down to work at the Hoover Library at Stanford University than an archivist brought me, unbidden, a fragment of planking from a lifeboat stamped with the name *Lusitania*, originally found beside the corpse of a passenger who had washed ashore. In the Strandingsmuseum St. George, in Thorsminde, Denmark, I was able to stand beside and touch the deck gun of U-20—the actual gun that had sunk the *Earl of Lathom*—adopting poses that my wife assured me were beyond dorky. At the National Archives of the United Kingdom, in Kew— well guarded by swans—I opened one file box to find the actual codebook, the SKM, or *Signalbuch der Kaiserlichen Marine*, that had been retrieved by the Russians and given to Room 40 in 1914. One of the most powerful moments came when I was given permission by the University of Liverpool, repository of the Cunard Archive, to view morgue photos of *Lusitania* victims. The effect of such moments is like sticking a finger in a mildly charged electric socket. It is always reassuring, because no matter how deeply I immerse myself in a subject, I still like having actual, physical proof that the events I'm writing about really did occur.

Strangely, in the week before I sent my initial draft to my editor, the Korean ferry *Sewol* sank in the Yellow Sea, subjecting hundreds of schoolchildren to an experience very close to that of the passengers on the *Lusitania*. One morning I finished rewriting a passage dealing with the *Lusitania*'s severe list and how it impaired the launching of lifeboats, only to visit CNN's website a few minutes later to read about exactly the same phenomenon occurring with the *Sewol*.

My voyage on the *Queen Mary 2*—a beautiful and gracious ship, by the way—brought me invaluable insights into the nature of transoceanic travel. Even today, when you are in the middle of the Atlantic you are very much alone, and far from rescue if something cataclysmic were to occur. Unlike the passengers of the *Lusitania*, before we left New York we all were required to try on our life jackets. No one was exempted, regardless of how many voyages he or she had already made. This was serious business and, frankly, a bit scary, for putting on a life jacket forces you to imagine the unimaginable.

When writing about the *Lusitania*, one has to be very careful to sift and weigh the things that appear in books already published on the subject. There are falsehoods and false facts, and these, once dropped into the scholarly stream, appear over and over again, with footnotes always leading back to the same culprits. Fortunately, I had a guide to help me through all this, Mike Poirier of Pawtucket, Rhode Island, an amateur historian who very likely knows more about the ship and its passengers than any other living soul, and who read my manuscript for things that might cause *Lusitania* buffs to howl with laughter. One gets the sense that Mike cares about the "Lucy's" passengers as if they were his nephews and nieces. His help was invaluable. I was aided as well by another *Lusitania* aficionado, Geoffrey Whitfield, who gave me a tour of modern-day Liverpool. I must assert, however, that if any errors persist in this book, the fault is solely my own.

For evaluations of pace and narrative integrity—whether the book worked or not—I relied on my trusted cadre of advance readers, my great friends Carrie Dolan and Penny Simon, my friend and agent David Black, and my secret weapon, my wife, Christine Gleason, whose margin notations—smiley faces, tear-streamed eyes, down arrows, and long rows of zzzzzs—as always provided excellent markers as to where I went wrong and what I did right. My editor at Crown Publishing, Amanda Cook, wrote me an eleven-page letter that provided a brilliant road map to tweaking the narrative. She proved a master at the art of offering praise, while at the same time shoving tiny knives under each of my fingernails, propelling me into a month of narrative renovation that was probably the most intense writing experience of my life. Thanks as well to copy editor Elisabeth Magnus for saving me from having one character engage in the decidedly dangerous practice of dressing with "flare," and from having passengers go "clamoring" aboard. I must of course thank the three Superheroes—my term—of Crown, Maya Mavjee, Molly Stern, and David Drake, who I confess are far more adept at managing martinis than I. Thanks also to Chris Brand and Darren Haggar for a truly excellent cover. And finally cheers to the *real* heroes, Emma Berry and Sarah Smith.

In the course of my research, I sought whenever possible to rely on archival materials, but I did find certain secondary works to be of particular value: Arthur S. Link's monumental multivolume biography of Woodrow Wilson, titled, well, *Wilson*—the most valuable volume being, for me, *The Struggle for Neutrality, 1914–1915*; A. Scott Berg's more recent *Wilson*; John Keegan's wrenching *The First World War*; Martin Gilbert's *The First World War*; Gerhard Ritter's *The Schlieffen Plan*; Lowell Thomas's 1928 book about World War I U-boats and their crews, *Raiders of the Deep*; Reinhard Scheer's *Germany's High Sea Fleet in the World War*;

Churchill's *The World Crisis, 1911–1918*; Paul Kennedy's *The War Plans of the Great Powers, 1880–1914*; and R. H. Gibson and Maurice Prendergast's primer, *The German Submarine War, 1914–1918*.

I especially enjoyed the many works of intimate history—memoirs, autobiographies, diaries—that I came across along the way, though these of course must be treated with special care, owing to fading memories and covert agendas. Their greatest value lies in the little details they offer about life as once lived. These works include *Starling of the White House*, by one of Wilson's Secret Service men, Edmund W. Starling ("as told to" Thomas Sugrue), who took me aboard Wilson's honeymoon train; *Woodrow Wilson: An Intimate Memoir*, by Wilson's physician, Cary T. Grayson; *My Memoir*, by Edith Bolling Wilson; *Commodore*, by James Bisset; *Voyage of the Deutschland*, by Paul Koenig; *The Journal of Submarine Commander von Forstner*, by Georg-Gunther Freiherr von Forstner; *The Lusitania's Last Voyage*, by Charles E. Lauriat Jr.; *This Was My World*, by Margaret Mackworth (Viscountess Rhondda); and *When the Ships Came In*, by Jack Lawrence. Another such intimate work, valuable for grounding me in British high society before the war, was *Lantern Slides: The Diaries and Letters of Violet Bonham Carter, 1904–1914*, edited by Mark Bonham Carter and Mark Pottle, which I found utterly charming. I confess to having fallen a little in love with Violet, the daughter of British prime minister Herbert Henry Asquith.

THE FOLLOWING LIST of citations is by no means exhaustive: to cite every fact would require a companion volume and would be tedious in the extreme. I cite all quoted material and anything else that for one reason or another requires noting or amplification or that might cause a *Lusitania* buff to burn a lifeboat on my lawn. Throughout I have included small stories that I could not fit into the main narrative but that struck me as worth telling all the same for the oblique insights they offer but also for the best reason of all: just because.

NOTES

ABBREVIATIONS USED IN NOTES

Foreign Relations
U.S. Department of State, *Papers Relating to the Foreign Relations of the United States*. 1915, Supplement, The World War, University of Wisconsin Digital Collections, http://digital.library.wisc.edu/1711.dl/FRUS.FRUS1915Supp.

"Investigation"
"Investigation into the Loss of the Steamship 'Lusitania,'" Proceedings Before the Right Hon. Lord Mersey, Wreck Commissioner of the United Kingdom, June 15–July 1, 1915, National Archives UK.

Lauriat, Claim
Charles E. Lauriat Jr., Claim, Lauriat vs. Germany, Docket 40, Mixed Claims Commission: United States and Germany, Aug. 10, 1922. U.S. National Archives and Records Administration at College Park, MD.

Merseyside
Maritime Archives, Merseyside Maritime Museum.

Schwieger, War Log
Walther Schwieger, War Log. Bailey/Ryan Collection, Hoover Institution Archives, Stanford University, Stanford, CA.

U.S. National Archives–College Park
U.S. National Archives and Records Administration at College Park, MD.

U.S. National Archives–New York
U.S. National Archives and Records Administration at New York City.

A WORD FROM THE CAPTAIN

2   "vessels flying the flag": See *New York Times*, May 1, 1915. An article about the warning appears on p. 3, the ad itself on p. 19.

2   "thinking, dreaming, sleeping": *Liverpool Weekly Mercury*, May 15, 1915.

2   He assured the audience: Preston, *Lusitania*, 172.

2   "The truth is": Bailey and Ryan, *Lusitania Disaster*, 82.

2   on two previous occasions: Ibid., 65; Beesly, *Room 40*, 93; Ramsay, *Lusitania*, 50, 51.

3   "You could see the shape": Testimony, Thomas M. Taylor, Petition of the Cunard Steamship Company, April 15, 1918, U.S. National Archives–New York, 913.

PART I: "BLOODY MONKEYS"

LUSITANIA: THE OLD SAILORMAN

7   Despite the war in Europe: "General Analysis of Passengers and Crew," R.M.S. Lusitania: Record of Passengers & Crew, SAS/29/6/18, Merseyside.

7   This was . . . the greatest number: *New York Times*, May 2, 1915.

8   During an early trial voyage: *Cunard Daily Bulletin*, July 19, 1907, Merseyside.

8   "a vote of censure": Ibid.

8   "for I calculate that there is room": Ibid.

8   "Please deliver me": Ibid.

8   "The inhabitants were warlike": "*Lusitania*," D42/S9/5/1, Cunard Archives.

9   "Rule, Britannia!": The title of this song is often written and said incorrectly, as if it were a declaration. The title, however, is meant to be an exhortation, as in "Go Britain!"

9   "You do not get any idea": Letter, C. R. Minnitt to Mrs. E. M. Poole, July 9, 1907, DX/2284, Merseyside.

9   The ship's lightbulbs: Minutes, Cunard Board of Directors, July 10, 1912, D42/B4/38, Cunard Archives; Fox, *Transatlantic*, 404.

10   He found it "very gratifying": Letter, W. Dranfield to W. T. Turner, Jan. 20, 1911, D42/C1/2/44, Cunard Archives; Letter, W. T. Turner to Alfred A. Booth, Feb. 6, 1911, D42/C1/2/44, Cunard Archives.

10   Its 300 stokers: Bisset, *Commodore*, 32.

11   Cunard barred crew members: The company called the permissible matches "Lucifer matches," though in fact that name harked back to a decidedly unsafe early precursor that lit with a pop and sent embers flying.

12   "counteract, as far as possible": "Cunard Liner *Lusitania*," 941.

12   The guns were never installed: Strangely, this remained a point of con-

troversy for decades, reinforced by reports by at least one diver who reported seeing the barrel of a naval gun protruding from the wreckage. But no passenger ever spoke of seeing a gun aboard, and a film of the ship's departure shows clearly that no guns were mounted. Also, a search by Customs in New York found no evidence of armament.

12   "devil-dodger": Hoehling and Hoehling, *Last Voyage*, 42.

12   "Had it been stormy": *Hobart Mercury*, March 8, 1864.

12   "I was the quickest man": Hoehliing and Hoehling, *Last Voyage*, 42.

13   "never, at any time": Letter, George Ball to Adolf Hoehling, July 22, 1955, Hoehling Papers.

14   "On the ships": Letter, Mabel Every to Adolf Hoehling, May 4, 1955, Hoehling Papers.

14   "a load of bloody monkeys": Preston, *Lusitania*, 108; also see "William Thomas Turner," Lusitania Online, http://www.lusitania.net/turner.htm.

14   On one voyage: "Captain's Report, Oct. 15, 1904," Minutes, Cunard Executive Committee, Oct. 20, 1904, D42/B4/22, Merseyside.

15   "Madam, do you think": Letter, George Ball to Adolf Hoehling, July 22, 1955, Hoehling Papers.

15   more "clubbable": Preston, *Lusitania*, 108.

15   "He was a good, and conscientious skipper": Letter, R. Barnes (dictated to K. Simpson) to Mary Hoehling, July 14, 1955, Hoehling Papers.

15   "Captain's compliments": Albert Bestic to Adolf Hoehling, June 10, 1955, Hoehling Papers.

16   "one of the bravest": Letter, Thomas Mahoney to Adolf Hoehling, May 14, 1955, Hoehling Papers.

17   "The wave," Turner said: *New York Times*, Jan. 16, 1910.

17   The Cunard manual: The manual was an exhibit in the New York limit-of-liability proceedings. Cunard Steamship Company, "Rules to Be Observed in the Company's Service," Liverpool, March 1913, Admiralty Case Files: Limited Liability Claims for the Lusitania, Box 1, U.S. National Archives–New York.

18   The dangers of fog: Larson, *Thunderstruck*, 376.

18   "to keep the ship sweet": Cunard Steamship Company, "Rules," 54.

18   "The utmost courtesy": Ibid., 43.

18   "much to the amusement": *New York Times*, May 23 and 24, 1908.

19   "should not be made a market place": Minutes, Sept. 1910 [day illegible], D42/B4/32, Cunard Archives.

There were other sorts of complaints. On a couple of voyages in September 1914 third-class passengers "of a very superior type" complained about the fact that Cunard did not supply them with sheets, unlike other less exalted steamship lines, according to a report by the chief third-class steward. He wrote, "They did not quite understand why sheets should not be supplied on vessels like the LUSITANIA and MAURETANIA where higher rates were charged." The company studied the matter and found that it could supply two thousand sheets and one thousand quilts at a cost of £358 per voyage. Memoranda, General Manager to Superintendent of Furnishing Department, Sept. 30, 1914, and Oct. 2, 1914, D42/PR13/3/24-28, Cunard Archives.

19 "When you have it on": Lauriat, *Lusitania's Last Voyage*, 21.

20 "to be severely reprimanded": Captain's Record: William Thomas Turner, D42/GM/V6/1, Cunard Archives.

21 "tired and really ill": Preston, *Lusitania*, 110; Ramsay, *Lusitania*, 49.

WASHINGTON: THE LONELY PLACE

22 The train carrying the body: Schachtman, *Edith and Woodrow*, 41; G. Smith, *When the Cheering Stopped*, 11; *New York Times*, Aug. 12, 1914.

23 just a year and a half: In 1913, Inauguration Day came in March.

23 "For several days": Schachtman, *Edith and Woodrow*, 72.

23 "felt like a machine": Ibid., 48. Harlakenden House was owned by an American author named Winston Churchill, whose books were, at the time, very popular—enough so that he and the other Winston exchanged correspondence and the latter resolved that in all his writings he would insert a middle initial, S, for Spencer. His full and formal name was Winston Leonard Spencer-Churchill.

23 The South in particular suffered: Berg, *Wilson*, 341–42.

24 The lead story: *New York Times*, June 27, 1914.

24 In Europe, kings and high officials: Keegan, *First World War*, 53–54, 55, 57, 58; Thomson, *Twelve Days*, 89.

25 In England, the lay public: Thomson, *Twelve Days*, 186. When Shackleton read a report in the press that Britain was soon to mobilize, he rather chivalrously volunteered to cancel his expedition and offered his ship and services to the war effort. Churchill telegraphed back: "Proceed."

25 "These pistols": Ibid., 64, 65, 67, 97.

25 Far from a clamor for war: Keegan, *First World War*, 10, 12, 15.

25 the Ford Motor Company: *New York Times*, June 27, 1914.

25 But old tensions and enmities persisted: Devlin, *Too Proud to Fight*, 220; Keegan, *First World War*, 17, 18, 19, 38, 42–43.

26 "Europe had too many frontiers": Thomson, *Twelve Days*, 23.

26 As early as 1912: Tuchman, *Zimmermann Telegram*, 11.

26 In Germany, meanwhile, generals tinkered: Keegan, *First World War*, 29, 30, 32–33.

27 "It's incredible—incredible": Berg, *Wilson*, 334.

27 "We must be impartial": Ibid., 337, 774.

Britain resented American neutrality. On December 20, 1914, First Sea Lord Jacky Fisher wrote, "The time will come when the United States will be d—d sorry they were neutral. . . . We shall win all right.

I am only VERY *sorry*" (Marder, *Fear God*, 3:99). In the same letter Fisher made reference to a widely published poem, popular in Britain, by William Watson, entitled "To America Concerning England." Watson asks:

> . . . *The tiger from his den*
> *Springs at thy mother's throat, and canst thou now*
> *Watch with a stranger's gaze?*

27   "The United States is remote": Brooks, "United States," 237–38.

28   Louvain: Keegan, *First World War*, 82–83; Link, *Wilson: Struggle*, 51; *New York Times*, Oct. 4, 1914.

28   "felt deeply the destruction": Link, *Wilson: Struggle*, 51.

28   The German toll: Keegan, *First World War*, 135–36.

28   By year's end: Ibid., 176.

29   For Wilson, already suffering depression: Berg, *Wilson*, 337.

29   "I feel the burden": Link, *Wilson: Struggle*, 50.

29   "The whole thing": Ibid., 52.

29   There was at least one moment: Berg, *Wilson*, 339–40; Devlin, *Too Proud to Fight*, 227; Schachtman, *Edith and Woodrow*, 52.

29   "We are at peace": Berg, *Wilson*, 352.

30   On entering waters: Doerries, *Imperial Challenge*, 94. Wilson wrote to House, later: "Such use of flags plays directly in the hands of Germany in her extraordinary plan to destroy commerce" (290).

And indeed, news of the *Lusitania* flag episode incensed the German press and public, as reported by America's ambassador to Germany, James Watson Gerard. "The hate campaign here against America has assumed grave proportions," he cabled to Secretary Bryan, on Feb. 10, 1915. "People much excited by published report that *Lusitania* by order of British Admiralty hoisted American flag in Irish Channel and so entered Liverpool." Telegram, Gerard to Bryan, Feb. 10, 1915, *Foreign Relations*.

30   At the beginning of the war: Germany's first U-boat sortie seemed to affirm the German navy's initial skepticism about the value of submarines. On Aug. 6, 1914, after receiving reports that English battleships had entered the North Sea, Germany dispatched ten U-boats to hunt for them. The boats set out from their base on Germany's North Sea coast, with authority to sail as far as the northern tip of Scotland, a distance no German submarine had hitherto traveled. One boat experienced problems with its diesel engines and had to return to base. Two others were lost. One was surprised by a British cruiser, the HMS *Birmingham*, which rammed and sank it, killing all aboard. The fate of the other missing boat was never discovered. The remaining submarines returned to base having sunk nothing. "Not encouraging," one officer wrote. Thomas, *Raiders*, 16; see also Halpern, *Naval History*, 29; Scheer, *Germany's High Sea Fleet*, 34–35.

30   "this strange form of warfare": Churchill, *World Crisis*, 723.

30 Only a few prescient souls: See Doyle, "Danger!" throughout.

31 Doyle's forecast: *New York Times*, Nov. 16, 1917.

32 "The essence of war": Memorandum, Jan. 1914, Jellicoe Papers.

32 "abhorrent": Churchill, *World Crisis*, 409. In British eyes the sinking of a civilian ship was an atrocity. "To sink her incontinently was odious," Churchill wrote; "to sink her without providing for the safety of the crew, to leave that crew to perish in open boats or drown amid the waves was in the eyes of all seafaring peoples a grisly act, which hitherto had never been practiced deliberately except by pirates" (672).

32 "if some ghastly novelty": Ibid., 144, 145.

32 German strategists, on the other hand: Breemer, *Defeating the U-Boat*, 12; Frothingham, *Naval History*, 57; Scheer, *Germany's High Sea Fleet*, 25, 88. The German term for "approximate parity" in naval strength was *Kräfteausgleich*. Breemer, *Defeating the U-Boat*, 12.

32 "So we waited": Churchill, *World Crisis*, 146; Scheer, *Germany's High Sea Fleet*, 11. This stalemate did not sit well with either side. Both navies hoped to distinguish themselves in the war and chafed at the lack of definitive, glory-yielding action. German sailors had to bear mockery by German soldiers, who taunted, "Dear Fatherland rest calmly, the fleet sleeps safely in port." On the British side, there was the Admiralty's long heritage of naval success that had to be protected. As one senior officer put it, "Nelson would turn in his grave."

Jellicoe was sensitive to how so defensive a strategy would sit with his fellow navy men, current and former. In an Oct. 30, 1914, letter to the Admiralty he confessed to fearing that they would find the strategy "repugnant."

He wrote, "I feel that such tactics, if not understood, may bring odium upon me." Nonetheless, he wrote, he intended to stick to the strategy, "without regard to uninstructed opinion or criticism." Koerver, *German Submarine Warfare*, xxviii, xv; see Jellicoe's letter in Frothingham, *Naval History*, 317.

32 "In those early days": Hook Papers.

33 He was soon to learn otherwise: Breemer, *Defeating the U-Boat*, 17; Churchill, *World Crisis*, 197–98; Marder, *From the Dreadnought*, 57. Breemer states that more than 2,500 sailors died in the incident.

33 "the live-bait squadron": When Churchill first heard the nickname "live-bait squadron" during a visit to the fleet, he investigated and grew concerned enough that on Friday, September 18, 1914, he sent a note to his then second in command, Prince Louis of Battenberg (soon to be forced from the job because of his German heritage), urging him to remove the ships. The prince agreed and issued orders to his chief of staff to send the cruisers elsewhere. "With this I was content," Churchill wrote, "and I dismissed the matter from my mind, being sure that the orders given would be complied with at the earliest moment."

But four days later the ships were still in place, and in a state even more exposed than usual. Ordinarily a group of destroyers kept watch over them, but over the next several days the weather became so rough that it forced the destroyers to return to their home port. By Tuesday, September 22, the sea had calmed, and the destroyers began making their way back to the patrol zone. Weddigen got there first. Churchill, *World Crisis*, 197–98.

33 "my first sight of men struggling": The ship heeled over far enough that part of its bottom was exposed, as was its "bilge keel." Hook saw "hundreds of men's heads bobbing" in the water, "while a continuous stream of very scantily-clad men appeared from the upper deck and started tobogganing down the ship's side, stopping suddenly when they came to the bilge keel, climbing over it, and continuing their slide until they reached the water with a splash. I remember wondering whether they hurt themselves when they started traveling over the barnacles below the water line." Hook Papers.

35 This posed a particularly acute threat: The two-thirds figure comes from Black, *Great War*, 50.

35 "doom the entire population": Telegram, Count Johann-Heinrich von Bernstorff to William Jennings Bryan, Feb. 7, 1915, and see enclosure "Memorandum of the German Government," *Foreign Relations*.

35 "Does it really make any difference": Scheer, *Germany's High Sea Fleet*, 218.

Admiral Scheer had a rather cool view of the human costs of war and the role of U-boats in advancing Germany's goals. "The more vigorously the war is prosecuted the sooner will it come to an end, and countless human beings and treasure will be saved if the duration of the war is curtailed," he wrote. "Consequently a U-boat cannot spare the crews of steamers, but must send them to the bottom with their ship." He added, "The gravity of the situation demands that we should free ourselves from all scruples which certainly no longer have justification."

This logic, he argued, also required that the submarine be used to its fullest advantage. "You do not demand of an aeroplane that it should attack the enemy on its wheels," Scheer wrote. Failure to make maximum use of the submarine's ability to attack by surprise, he wrote, "would be nonsensical and unmilitary."

And besides, Scheer argued, in delineating a war zone and warning ships to stay out, Germany had made its intentions clear. Therefore, if a submarine sank merchant ships, "including their crews and any passengers," it was the fault of the victims, "who despised our warnings and, open-eyed, ran the risk of being torpedoed" (220, 221, 222–23, 228).

35 "to a strict accountability": Telegram, William Jennings Bryan to German Foreign Office, via James W. Gerard, Feb. 10, 1915, *Foreign Relations*.

36 Chancellor Theobald von Bethmann Hollweg: Bethmann was something of a humanist—he was an expert pianist and classicist, able to read Plato in Greek. Thomson, *Twelve Days*, 119.

36 "Unhappily, it depends": Devlin, *Too Proud to Fight*, 322; Gibson and Prendergast, *German Submarine War*, 105.

37 "If in spite of the exercise": Scheer, *Germany's High Sea Fleet*, 231.
"Who is that beautiful lady?": Cooper, *Woodrow Wilson*, 282; Grayson, *Woodrow Wilson*, 50; Levin, *Edith and Woodrow*, 52.

38 "I had no experience": Wilson, *My Memoir*, 22; Cooper, *Woodrow Wilson*, 282.

38 "taken for a tramp": Wilson, *My Memoir*, 56; Cooper, *Woodrow Wilson*, 281.

38 "There is not a soul here": Wilson, *My Memoir*, 56; Link, *Wilson: Confusions*, 1–2.

38 "This was the accidental meeting": Wilson, *My Memoir*, 56; Cooper, *Woodrow Wilson*, 281; Levin, *Edith and Woodrow*, 53.
Ever since the death of Ellen Wilson, there had been little laughter in the White House. During this first encounter between Galt and the president, Helen Bones heard Wilson laugh twice. "I can't say that I foresaw in the first minute what was going to happen," she recalled. "It may have taken ten minutes." G. Smith, *When the Cheering Stopped*, 14.

39 "He is perfectly charming": Schachtman, *Edith and Woodrow*, 74; Link, *Wilson: Confusions*, 1–2.

39 "and all sorts of interesting conversation": Link, *Wilson: Confusions*, 1–2.

39 "impressive widow": Levin, *Edith and Woodrow*, 51.

39 He had little time to dwell: Mersey, *Report*, throughout. One newspaper called it an act of "shocking bloodthirstiness." At least one witness aboard the ship reported that the U-boat's crew had laughed and jeered at survivors struggling in the water. A report telegraphed from the U.S. Embassy in London quoted another witness as stating that if the submarine had allowed just ten or fifteen more minutes before firing, "all might have been saved." A subsequent investigation by Britain's wreck commission was headed by Lord Mersey, who three years earlier had presided over an inquiry into the sinking of the *Titanic*. Mersey decried the amount of time Forstner had given the passengers, calling it "so grossly insufficient . . . that I am driven to the conclusion that the Captain of the submarine desired and designed not merely to sink the ship but, in doing so, also to sacrifice the lives of the passengers and crew." As to the evidence of laughing and jeering, Mersey said, "I prefer to keep silence on this matter in the hope that the witness was mistaken." Mersey, *Report*, 5; see also Link, *Wilson: Struggle*, 359; Walker, *Four Thousand Lives Lost*, 80, 81; telegram, U.S. Consul General, London, to William Jennings Bryan, April 7, 1915, *Foreign Relations*.

40   "I do not like this case": Cooper, *Woodrow Wilson*, 277.

40   "Perhaps it is not necessary": Link, *Wilson: Struggle*, 365.

LUSITANIA: SUCKING TUBES AND THACKERAY

41   "Thousands of sweltering, uncomfortable men": *New York Times*, April 28, 1915.

42   "The public," he complained: Ibid.

42   "All men are young": *New York Times*, April 29, 1915.

42   a record trade surplus: *New York Times*, Dec. 9, 1915.

42   There were extravagant displays: *New York Times*, May 1, 1915.

43   On Thursday, April 29: *New York Times*, April 30, 1915.

43   "A surprise," he said: *New York Times*, May 1, 1915.

43   "after a thorough search": Ibid.

43   "Space is left": Ibid.

43   The *Lusitania*'s roster: "Summary of Passengers' Nationality," R.M.S. Lusitania: Record of Passengers & Crew, SAS/29/6/18, Merseyside. Passengers' addresses, including hotels and other temporary addresses in New York, may be found in Public Record Office Papers, PRO 22/71, National Archives UK.

43   The American complement: Here I use Cunard's official tally. But other sources offer varying totals, one as high as 218. "Summary of Passengers' Nationality," R.M.S. Lusitania: Record of Passengers & Crew, SAS/29/6/18, Merseyside; "List of American Passengers Believed to Have Sailed on the Lusitania," U.S. National Archives–College Park.

44   They brought their best clothes: The items that follow, alas, were what Cunard cataloged from some of the dead whose bodies were recovered but not identified. "Unidentified Remains," R.M.S. Lusitania: Record of Passengers & Crew, SAS/29/6/18, Merseyside.

45   Ian Holbourn, the famed writer: Holbourn was known widely as "the Laird of Foula," for his ownership of an island in the Shetlands. The island, Foula, was a haven for all manner of birdlife, bearing storybook names coined by Foula's past inhabitants: the cra', of course—the crow, but also the rochie, the maa and maallie, and the tammie norie, wulkie, bonxie, ebb-pickie, snipoch, and the Allen Richardson, or Scootie Allen, or just plain Allen, this last the Arctic skua. For these and other charming details, certain to set alight the imaginations of birders everywhere, please see Holbourn's own *The Isle of Foula*, throughout.

45   "the golden age": Bolze, "From Private Passion," 415.

45   "born boat sailor": *Boston Daily Globe*, May 11, 1915.

45   Something of a celebrity: Szefel, "Beauty," 565–66.

46   "as much a debating society": Bullard et al., "Where History and Theory," 93.

46   "guide, counselor and friend": Sargent, *Lauriat's*, 10.

46   "homeness": *Publishers' Weekly*, Feb. 21, 1920, 551.

46 The store was long and narrow: For these and myriad other details about "Lauriat's," see text and photographs, Sargent, *Lauriat's*, 39–46.

46 "great gems": Ibid., 46.

46 "through the breaking up": Ibid.

47 One acquisition, of a Bible: *New York Times*, Sept. 28, 1895. For background on "Breeches" Bibles, see *Daily Mirror*, Dec. 3, 2013.

47 "for the risk . . . is practically nil": In a lengthy filing with the Mixed Claims Commission, convened after the war to levy compensation from Germany to various claimants, Lauriat provides a great many details about his journey and the things he carried with him. He filed his claim on April 6, 1923. All details mined from the proceeding will be cited as Lauriat, Claim. His remark about the safety of transporting things by ocean liner can be found in his filings at "Affidavit, March 12, 1925, or Charles Lauriat Jr."

47 "convoyed through the war zone": Lauriat, *Lusitania's Last Voyage*, 6.

47 "but this year": Ibid., 69.

48 He packed: "Exhibit in Support of Answer to Question 1," Lauriat, Claim.

49 "In 1915, to come out": Mackworth, *This Was My World*, 239.

49 "In the evenings": Ibid., 240.

49 "I have always been grateful": Ibid.

51 "Certainly not": "Deposition of William Thomas Turner," April 30, 1915, Petition of the Cunard Steamship Company, April 15, 1918, U.S. National Archives–New York.

U-20: THE HAPPIEST U-BOAT

53 That same day, Friday: Details of Schwieger's voyage, here and in following chapters, come from his War Log, a translation of which appears in the Bailey/Ryan Collection at the Hoover Institution Archives. The log proved invaluable in helping me reconstruct, in detail, U-20's journey to the Irish Sea and back. Hereafter, where necessary, I'll cite it simply as Schwieger, War Log.

54 "A particularly fine-looking fellow": Thomas, *Raiders*, 91.

54 At routine cruising speeds: Gibson and Prendergast, *German Submarine War*, 356–57.

55 Schwieger noted in his log: Koerver states that the "normal" wireless range for submarines was "several hundred miles." Schwieger's log indicates that for U-20, at least, the range was far shorter. Koerver, *German Submarine Warfare*, xix. Jan Breemer states that early in 1915 "reliable" communications between submarines and shore stations at distances of "up to 140 nautical miles were possible." Breemer, *Defeating the U-Boat*, 15.

55 "I want to stress": Edgar von Spiegel interview, *Lusitania*, Catalog No. 4232, Imperial War Museum, London.

55 "a splendid, dapple-gray horse": Spiegel, *Adventures*, 20.

56 "It was a very hard task": Edgar von Spiegel interview, *Lusitania*, Catalog No. 4232, Imperial War Museum, London.

56 Such authority could be thrilling: As German captain Paul Koenig put it, "The master of no ship is so lonely, so forced to depend entirely upon himself as the master of a submarine" (*Voyage*, 76).

56 When on patrol: According to Hans Koerver, by May 1915 Germany had only an average of fifteen U-boats available for long-range service each day. At any one time, typically only two patrolled the British Isles. Koerver, *German Submarine Warfare*, xxi, xxiii.

56 "on the fastest possible route": Bailey, "Sinking," 54.

57 The submarine as a weapon: Compton-Hall, *Submarine Boats*, 14, 21, 36, 38–39, 99, 102, 109; Fontenoy, *Submarines*, 8, 10.

58 Schwieger's boat was 210 feet long: Rössler, *U-Boat*, 14; von Trapp, *To the Last Salute*, 32–33; Neureuther and Bergen, *U-Boat Stories*, 173.

58 "More dials and gauges": Thomas, *Raiders*, 82.

59 Even his superiors seemed surprised: Ledger: U-20, Feb. 6, 1915, Ministry of Defence Papers, DEFE/69/270, National Archives UK.

59 "She was a jolly boat": Thomas, *Raiders*, 81, 91.

60 "He was a wonderful man": Edgar von Spiegel interview, *Lusitania*, Catalog No. 4232, Imperial War Museum, London.

60 "Apparently the enemy was at home": Thomas, *Raiders*, 83.

60 It was the one time: Spiegel, *Adventures*, 12.

60 "And now," Schwieger said: For details about this Christmas scene, see Thomas, *Raiders*, 83–85.

61 at least one dog aboard: Hoehling and Hoehling, *Last Voyage*, 4; Thomas, *Raiders*, 90–91. Supposedly one commander once transported a juvenile camel.

62 That Schwieger was able to conjure: Forstner, *Journal*, 56–57; Neureuther and Bergen, *U-Boat Stories*, 189; Thomas, *Raiders*, 86.

62 "And now," said Zentner: Thomas, *Raiders*, 86.

63 "U-boat sweat": Spiegel, *Adventures*, 15.

64 "You can have no conception": Koenig, *Voyage*, 116.

64 "The first breath of fresh air": Niemöller, *From U-Boat to Pulpit*, 1.

64 It was early in the war: Zentner tells this story in Thomas's *Raiders*, 87–89.

The literature on U-boats is full of stories that can only make you wonder why on earth any young man would ever join Germany's submarine service. Case in point: One boat, U-18, attempted an attack on Britain's main fleet based in Scapa Flow, off northern Scotland, but was spotted and rammed by a patrol vessel, a trawler. The collision damaged the boat's periscope and the horizontal rudders—the hydroplanes—that controlled its ascent and descent. The captain ordered an emergency dive, but the boat plunged to the bottom, then shot back up to the surface, out of control. There it was rammed a second time, now by a destroyer. The U-boat sank but struggled back to the surface, where it drifted, disabled. The captain signaled surrender. The destroyer managed to rescue all but one member of the crew.

On another U-boat, during a practice dive, the commander dashed from the conning tower at the last minute and slammed the hatch behind him. It didn't close. As the boat went below the surface, water surged in and quickly began flooding the interior. The boat sank 90 feet. The water rose so quickly that for some crew it was soon at neck level. It was then that one crewman, himself nearly submerged, thought to engage the boat's compressed-air apparatus, which blew water from its diving tanks. The boat shot to the surface. The crew engaged its internal pumps, and the water quickly disappeared. "But suddenly," recalled Leading Seaman Karl Stoltz, "the whole interior was filled with a greenish choking vapor—chlorine gas from the water that had flooded the electric battery." The captain ordered all the men out on deck, except for an engine-room mechanic and the helmsman. Fresh air flowing through the hatch thinned the gas.

The cause was a simple error by the captain. The hatch, once closed, was supposed to be sealed in place using a wheel that operated a series of clamps, but before the dive the captain had mistakenly turned the wheel the wrong way, setting the clamps in their sealed position, thus blocking the hatch from closing. Stoltz estimated that the crew had been just seconds away from being drowned.

Even the stealth of U-boats, their main asset, could work against them. On January 21, a U-boat of the same class as Schwieger's U-20 was on patrol off the coast of Holland when its crew spotted another submarine. Presuming at first that this was another German boat, they tried twice to hail it but got no answer. The U-boat's captain, Bruno Hoppe, now decided the other submarine must be British and launched an attack. He sank it with one torpedo, then moved close to attempt to rescue survivors. There was only one, who now informed him the boat he had just destroyed was in fact the German navy's own U-7, under the command of Hoppe's closest friend. "The two men had been inseparable for years," according to U-boat captain Baron von Spiegel, who knew them both.

For these and other stories, see Gibson and Prendergast, *German Submarine War*, 17–18, 20; Neureuther and Bergen, *U-Boat Stories*, 154–57; Thomas, *Raiders*, 171–72.

65 Depth charges did not yet exist: Depth charges were first deployed in January 1916 but initially were not very effective. They would not become a significant threat to U-boat commanders for another year. Sonar—the source of the iconic "ping" in submarine movies—would not be introduced until after World War I. Breemer, *Defeating the U-Boat*, 34; Marder, *From the Dreadnought*, 350.

66 This was a strenuous maneuver: Forstner, *Journal*, 14–15.

66   oil-laced water: Neureuther and Bergen, *U-Boat Stories*, 25.

67   Throughout Friday: Schwieger, War Log.

LUSITANIA: MENAGERIE

68   That Friday, Charles Lauriat: Lauriat, Claim.

69   At Pier 54, on Friday morning: Letter, Albert E. Laslett to Principal Officer, Liverpool District, June 8, 1915, Ministry of Transport Papers, MT 9/1326, National Archives UK. That this drill did take place is documented by various references in the Admiralty Papers at the National Archives UK. For example, see "'*Lusitania*'— American Proceedings," Admiralty Papers, ADM 1/8451/56, National Archives UK.

69   Taken together: Answers of Petitioner to Interrogatories Propounded by Hunt, Hill & Betts, Petition of the Cunard Steamship Company, April 15, 1918, U.S. National Archives–New York.

70   For the Friday drill: Testimony, Andrew Chalmers, April 18, 1918, Petition of the Cunard Steamship Company, April 15, 1918, U.S. National Archives–New York, 20.

70   It was Turner's belief: Deposition, William Thomas Turner, April 30, 1915, Petition of the Oceanic Steam Navigation Co. Limited, for Limitation of Its Liability as Owner of the S.S. *Titanic*, U.S. National Archives–NY.

70   What made raising a crew even harder: "Cunard Liner," 939.

70   He noted "the awkward way": Walker, *Four Thousand Lives Lost*, 169.

70   Baker idled away: Baker Papers.

70   "The old-fashioned able seaman": *New York Times*, Nov. 21, 1915.

71   "They are competent enough": Testimony, William Thomas Turner, June 15, 1915, "Investigation," 7.

71   He also had two tattoos: These details were listed in Morton's "Ordinary Apprentice's Indenture," a four-year contract that obligated Morton to obey the commands of his captain and the captain's associates "and keep his and their secrets." It stipulated further that the apprentice could not "frequent Taverns or Alehouses . . . nor play at unlawful games." Above all, each apprentice agreed not to "absent himself . . . without leave." In return, apprentices received an annual salary of £5 in the first year, which increased to slightly more than £10 in the last year. They were also guaranteed room and board and "Medicine and Medical and Surgical Assistance." Each got ten shillings to do his wash. "Ordinary Apprentice's Indenture," Morton Papers, DX/2313, Merseyside; "Continuous Certificate of Discharge," Morton Papers, DX/2313, Merseyside.

71   "We were still looking upon war": Morton, *Long Wake*, 97.

72   "What a sight": Ibid., 98.

72   "What are you boys looking at?": Ibid., 99.

73   Malone was said to be a dead ringer: Bailey and Ryan, *Lusitania Disaster*, 108.

73 For German spies and saboteurs:

Some British officials even had concerns about the loyalty of the men employed by Cunard in its New York office, which was run by Charles P. Sumner, manager of all the company's operations in America. Cunard's own Captain Dow was said to distrust Sumner "on the score of intimacy with Germans," according to a telegram from Britain's consul general in New York, Sir Courtenay Bennett. Sir Courtenay too was convinced the office was under the sway of Germany. He saw proof of this in the number of employees with German-sounding last names, such as Fecke, Falck, Buiswitz, Reichhold, Brauer, Breitenbach, and Muller. Sir Courtenay's countryman Sir Arthur Herbert, a former diplomat, believed likewise. Their repeated inquiries made these already tense times all the more trying for Sumner, a skilled manager who kept Cunard's ships sailing on schedule and had the full confidence, verging on friendship, of Cunard's chairman, Alfred A. Booth.

Sir Arthur was so convinced that something sinister was afoot within Cunard's New York operations that he hired a private detective to investigate without telling Sumner. The detective lacked subtlety and behaved in a manner that caused Cunard's employees to suspect that *he* might be a spy. As Sumner recalled, "This man excited my suspicions so much that I put our Dock Detective on to the work of watching Sir Arthur Herbert's detective." Sumner sent a report to Sir Arthur about the private eye's odd behavior, thinking he would be interested. "Instead of being pleased at what I had done," Sumner wrote, "he [Sir Arthur] flew into a terrible passion and said that he had never been so insulted in his life." Sir Arthur went so far as to accuse Sumner of spying on *him* and seemed so distressed that Sumner began to wonder if the ex-diplomat might in fact be harboring secrets of his own. Sumner wrote, "It really excited some suspicions in my mind that something might be disclosed by watching his movements."

"Confidentially," Sumner wrote, "I think I may safely express the opinion that Sir Arthur Herbert is a little 'peculiar.' "

On that point at least, even Sumner's other antagonist, Sir Courtenay Bennett, seemed to agree. On one occasion Sir Arthur paid a call on Sir Courtenay. An altercation arose, Sumner wrote, during which Sir Courtenay told his visitor to " 'go home and teach his mother how to suck eggs.' "

Sumner wrote, "While I cannot help thinking this was a somewhat undignified procedure . . . it affords the only funny incident that I have experienced in all my dealings with the two men."

Telegram, C. Bennett to Alfred Booth, Nov. 30, 1914, D42/C1/1/66, Part 2 of 4, Cunard Archives; "Salaries of New York Office Staff," D42/C1/1/66, Part 3 of 4, Cunard Archives; letter, Charles P. Sumner to D. Mearns, Dec. 29, 1914, D42/C1/2/44, Cunard Archives; letter,

Charles P. Sumner to Alfred A. Booth, Aug. 4, 1915, D42/C1/1/66, Part 3 of 4, Cunard Archives; telegram, Richard Webb to Cecil Spring-Rice, May 11, 1915, "Lusitania Various Papers," Admiralty Papers, ADM 137/1058, National Archives UK.

73 "The crew of the *Lusitania*": Telegram, April 27, 1915, Box 2, Bailey/Ryan Collection.

74 "You're not going to get back": Francis Burrows, interview, *Lusitania*, BBC Written Archives Centre.

74 "began doing something we shouldn't": Robert James Clark, interview, *Lusitania*, BBC Written Archives Centre.

74 In fact, exactly one year earlier: Memorandum, May 7, 1914, D42/PR13/3/14-17, Cunard Archives.

75 He made his way to Broadway: Preston, *Lusitania*, 110; Ramsay, *Lusitania*, 51; *New York Times*, March 30, 1915.

75 He went to Lüchow's: Preston, *Lusitania*, 110.

75 That evening, back at his sister's apartment: Lauriat, Claim.

76 Elsewhere in the city: See the website Lusitania Resource, www .RMSLusitania.info, which presents an easily searchable database about the ship and its passengers.

ROOM 40: "THE MYSTERY"

77 In London, two blocks from the Thames: My description of Room 40 and its operations is derived from documents held by the Churchill Archives, Churchill College, Cambridge, and the National Archives of the United Kingdom, at Kew, in its Admiralty Papers. For further reading, see Beesly, *Room 40*; Gannon, *Inside Room 40*; Adm. William James, *Code Breakers*; and Ramsay, *"Blinker" Hall*.

78 By far the most important: I cannot tell you how delighted I was when during one of my visits to the National Archives of the United Kingdom I was able to examine the actual codebook. It came to me like a gift, wrapped in paper with a cloth tie, in a large box. Touching it, and opening it, and turning its pages—gently—gave me one of those moments where the past comes briefly, physically alive. This very book had been on a German destroyer, sunk by the Russians in the early days of World War I. *Signalbuch der Kaiserlichen Marine*, Berlin, 1913, Admiralty Papers, ADM 137/4156, National Archives UK; see also Beesly, *Room 40*, 4–5, 22–23; Halpern, *Naval History*, 36; Adm. William James, *Code Breakers*, 29; Grant, *U-Boat Intelligence*, 10.

78 The Russians in fact recovered *three* copies: For varying accounts of the recovery of the codebook, see Churchill, *World Crisis*, 255; Halpern, *Naval History*, 36–37; and Tuchman, *Zimmermann Telegram*, 14–15.

79 "chiefly remarkable for his spats": History of Room 40, CLKE 3, Clarke Papers.

79   "It was the best of jobs": Ibid.

79   said to be obsessed: Halpern, *Naval History*, 37; Beesly, *Room 40*, 310–11.

80   "I shall never meet another man like him": Adm. William James, *Code Breakers*, xvii.

Even before the war, while then in command of a cruiser, the HMS *Cornwall*, Hall distinguished himself with an intelligence coup. The year was 1909, and his ship was to be among other British vessels paying a ceremonial visit to Kiel, Germany, home of the German fleet. The Admiralty asked Hall for help in gathering precise information about the configuration of ship-construction slips in the harbor, which were kept from view by a cordon of patrol vessels.

An idea came to Hall. The Duke of Westminster was present for the regatta and had brought along his speedboat, the *Ursula*, to show off. German sailors loved the boat and cheered every time they saw it. Hall asked the duke if he could borrow it for a couple of hours. The next day, two of Hall's men went aboard the *Ursula* disguised as civilian engine-room hands. The boat then put on a display of speed, racing out to sea and tearing back through the harbor. The yacht roared through the line of patrol boats, drawing cheers from their crews. But then, something unfortunate happened. The *Ursula*'s engines broke down, right in front of the Germany navy's shipbuilding facilities. As the boat's crew made a show of trying to start the engines, Hall's men took photograph after photograph of the shipyard. One of the patrol vessels ended up towing the boat back to its moorage. "The Germans were delighted to get such a close view of her," Hall wrote, "but they were hardly less delighted than I was, for one of the 'engineers' had secured the most perfect photographs of the slips and obtained all the information we wanted." "The Nature of Intelligence Work," Hall 3/1, Hall Papers.

80   The Machiavelli side: Adm. William James, *Code Breakers*, 202.

81   the empire's first defeat: Gilbert, *First World War*, 102.

81   British warships nearby: Gibson and Prendergast, *German Submarine War*, 19; Gilbert, *First World War*, 124.

82   And then came April 22: Clark, *Donkeys*, 74; Gilbert, *First World War*, 144–45; Keegan, *First World War*, 198–99.

83   "I saw some hundred poor fellows": Clark, *Donkeys*, 74.

83   The Admiralty also harbored: Frothingham, *Naval History*, 66, 75.

83   "no major movement": History of Room 40, CLKE 3, Clarke Papers.

83   "the risk of compromising the codes": Memorandum, Henry Francis Oliver, CLKE 1, Clarke Papers.

84   "Had we been called upon": History of Room 40, "Narrative of Capt. Hope," CLKE 3, Clarke Papers.

84   "shook the nerve": History of Room 40, CLKE 3, Clarke Papers.

85   "soul-destroying . . . object of hatred": Ibid.

85 "Watch this carefully": Beesly, *Room 40*, 92.

85 "Any messages which were not according to routine": History of Room 40, CLKE 3, Clarke Papers.

85 "The final note": Memorandum, Herbert Hope to Director of Operations Division, April 18, 1915, "Captain Hope's Memos to Operations Division," Admiralty Papers, ADM 137/4689, National Archives UK.

85 "Whenever any of their vessels": History of Room 40, CLKE 3, Clarke Papers.

85 a sense of the flesh-and-blood men: Reports derived from interrogations of captured U-boat officers and crew yield a sense of U-boat life far richer than that provided by any other published memoir or book. Admiralty Papers, ADM 137/4126, National Archives UK. Specifically, see interrogations involving crew from U-48, U-103, UC-65, U-64, and UB-109; see also Grant, *U-Boat Intelligence*, 21.

86 They used their wireless systems incessantly: Beesly, *Room 40*, 30.

86 "extreme garrulity": History of Room 40, CLKE 3, Clarke Papers; Beesly, *Room 40*, 30.

86 "I fooled 'em that time": *New York Times*, May 8, 1915.

86 Room 40 had long followed: "Capt. Hope's Diary," Admiralty Papers, ADM 137/4169, National Archives UK.

87 Addressed to all German warships: Record of Telegrams, March 3, 1915, Norddeich Naval Intelligence Center, Admiralty Papers, ADM 137/4177, National Archives UK.

87 "Four submarines sailed": Intercepted telegrams, April 28 and 29, 1915, Admiralty Papers, ADM 137/3956, National Archives UK. Anyone examining these files will note, to his or her pleasure, that these are the actual handwritten decodes.

88 "that of mystifying and misleading the enemy": "A Little Information for the Enemy," Hall 3/4, Hall Papers.

   Hall loved the surprise of intelligence work and loved knowing the real stories behind events reported in the news, which often were censored. For example, Room 40 learned the real fate of a German submarine, U-28, that had attacked a ship carrying trucks on its main deck. One shell fired by the U-boat's gun crew blew up a load of high explosives stored in the ship, and suddenly "the air was full of motor-lorries describing unusual parabolas," Hall wrote. Officially, the U-boat was lost because of explosion. But Hall and Room 40 knew the truth: one of the flying trucks had landed on the submarine's foredeck, penetrating its hull and sinking it instantly. "In point of actual fact," wrote Hall, "U-28 was sunk by a motor-lorry!"

   As strange as such stories were, Hall wrote, "I am sometimes inclined to think that perhaps the strangest thing of all was the intelligence Division itself. For it was like nothing else that had ever existed." "The Nature of Intelligence Work," Hall 3/1, Hall Papers.

LUSITANIA: A CAVALCADE OF PASSENGERS

89 All these things were captured on film: The film, *SS Lusitania on Her Final Departure from New York City, During World War I*, can be viewed at CriticalPast.com (www.criticalpast.com/video/65675040085 _SS-Lusitania_passengers-arrive-at-the-dock_passengers-aboard-SS-Lusitania_author-Elbert-Hubert). An agent for the Justice Department's Bureau of Investigation (not yet the *Federal* Bureau of Investigation) watched this film twice in succession during a private showing at a theater in Philadelphia. The agent, Frank Garbarino, was struck by the detail it captured and believed it would provide all the information necessary to confirm that the film was not a fake. "It will be easy to identify many of the persons who were aboard the steamer by those who knew them intimately," he wrote. "Furthermore we were able to distinguish the numbers of the license on three taxicabs which drove up to the pier with passengers and the features of the passengers as they emerged from the taxicabs are very clear. The license numbers of the taxicabs were 21011, 21017, 25225. It will be easy to ascertain what taxicab company has these licenses and they will probably have a record of the persons they took to the Cunard pier that morning." Letter, Bruce Bielaski to Attorney General, June 27, 1915, Bailey/Ryan Collection.

90 Here came Charles Frohman: For details about Frohman and his life, see Marcosson and Frohman, *Charles Frohman*, throughout; also *New York Times*, May 16, 1915; Lawrence, *When the Ships Come In*, 126.

91 Another arrival was George Kessler: For an overview of Kessler's flamboyant life as the "Champagne King," see "Compliments of George Kessler," *American Menu*, April 14, 2012 (courtesy of Mike Poirier); for the Gondola Party, see Tony Rennell, "How Wealthy Guests Turned the Savoy into the World's Most Decadent Hotel," *Daily Mail*, Dec. 17, 2007, www.dailymail.co.uk/news/article-502756/How-wealthy-guests-turned-Savoy-worlds-decadent-hotel-shuts-100m-refit.html, and "The Savoy: London's Most Famous Hotel," Savoy Theatre, www.savoytheatre.org /the-savoy-londons-most-famous-hotel/ For reference to "freak dinners," see *Lexington Herald*, May 16, 1915.

According to one account, Kessler had brought with him cash and securities valued at $2 million. Preston, *Lusitania*, 137.

91 "misconducting himself": *New York Times*, May 26, 1908, and June 11, 1909.

91 "Just Missed It" club: "Titanic's 'Just Missed It Club' an Elite Group," *Pittsburgh Post-Gazette*, April 16, 2012, www.post-gazette.com/life /lifestyle/2012/04/15/Titanic-s-Just-Missed-It-Club-an-elite-group /stories/201204150209.

92 "Ships do have personalities": Jack Lawrence's memoir, *When the Ships Came In*, to which I was directed by *Lusitania* ace Mike Poirier, is really very charming and conveys a sense of New York's vibrant maritime days in compelling fashion, to the point where a reader has to long for

those days when dozens of ships nuzzled Manhattan's Hudson River shoreline. Lawrence, *When the Ships Came In*; 116, see also 15, 16, and 117.

92 "to give satisfaction": Cunard Steamship Company, "Rules to Be Observed in the Company's Service," Liverpool, March 1913, Admiralty Case Files: Limited Liability Claims for the Lusitania, Box 1, U.S. National Archives–New York, 73.

93 "I'm about to become": Lawrence, *When the Ships Came In*, 119–21.

93 "Alfred Vanderbilt may have been a riot": Ibid., 124.

93 "The *Lusitania* is doomed": Ibid., 125.

93 Lawrence came across Elbert Hubbard: Ibid., 123.

94 "When I showed it to him": Ibid.

94 "When you are getting ready to sail": Ibid., 122.

95 "A feeling grew upon me": See "Not on Board," under "People," at Lusitania Resource, www.rmslusitania.info/people/not-on-board/.

95 A few others canceled: Ibid., and *New Zealand Herald*, June 26, 1915.

95 "From the very first": Letter, A. B. Cross, published June 12, 1915, in *Malay Mail*, Doc. 1730, Imperial War Museum.

96 "there is a general system": *New York Times*, May 1, 1915.

96 "Perfectly safe; safer than the trolley cars": Testimony, Ogden Hammond, Petition of the Cunard Steamship Company, April 15, 1918, U.S. National Archives–New York, 166. For details about trolley accidents, see *New York Times*, Jan. 3, 1915; May 3, 1916; July 9, 1916.

96 "Of course we heard rumors": May Walker, interview transcript, BBC Radio Merseyside, 1984, Imperial War Museum (with permission, BBC Radio Merseyside).

97 "looked personally after their comfort": Letter, Charles P. Sumner to Alfred A. Booth, May 26, 1915, D42/C1/1/66, Part 2 of 4, Cunard Archives.

98 Theodate Pope: I came across several worthy accounts of Pope's life and work. See Cunningham, *My Godmother*; Katz, *Dearest*; Paine, *Avon Old Farms School*; and S. Smith, *Theodate Pope Riddle*.

98 "You never act as other girls do": Katz, *Dearest*, 25.

98 "the momentary effect": Quoted in Cunningham, *My Godmother*, 53–54, and Katz, *Dearest*, 54.

99 "I have no memory at all": Quoted in S. Smith, *Theodate Pope Riddle*, ch. 1, p. 3 (each chapter paginated separately).

100 "the greatest blot": Ibid., ch. 2, p. 4.

100 "As it is my plan": Ibid., ch. 4, p. 2; see full letter at Appendix B.

100 "I have wrung my soul dry": Ibid., ch. 5, p. 1.

101 One incident in particular underscored: Katz, *Dearest*, 1.

101 "I am having such persistent insomnia": S. Smith, *Theodate Pope Riddle*, ch. 6, p. 7.

101 "There is nothing like the diversion": Katz, *Dearest*, 75.

102 "I was surprised": Lauriat, *Lusitania's Last Voyage*, 65–66.

102 Chandler joked: Lauriat, Claim.
103 "A thousand thanks": Letter, Harris to "Gram and Gramp," May 1, 1915, Harris Papers.
103 "was of that brand": Lawrence, *When the Ships Came In*, 129.
104 "When a British skipper knows": Ibid., 130.

ROOM 40: BLINKER'S RUSE

105 "An untried agent": Record of Telegrams, April 24, 1915, Antwerp to Bruges, Antwerp Naval Intelligence Center, Admiralty Papers, ADM 137/4177, National Archives UK.
106 "So that's what war looks like!": von Trapp, *To the Last Salute*, 24.
107 At some point that day: Bailey and Ryan, *Lusitania Disaster*, 73, 83.

WASHINGTON: LOST

108 "I hope it will give": Letter, Wilson to Galt, April 28, 1915, Wilson Papers.
108 "fill my goblet": Letter, Galt to Wilson, April 28, 1915, Wilson Papers.
109 It had been particularly welcome: Levin, *Edith and Woodrow*, 58.
109 "Such a pledge of friendship": Letter, Galt to Wilson, April 28, 1915, Wilson Papers.
109 "It's a great privilege": Letter, Wilson to Galt, April 30, 1915, Wilson Papers.
109 "a heaven—haven—sanctuary": Levin, *Edith and Woodrow*, 55.
109 "From the first": Wilson, *My Memoir*, 58.
109 "perhaps the weal or woe of a country": Levin, *Edith and Woodrow*, 57.
110 "In order to fit yourself": Ibid.; for a variation, see Wilson, *My Memoir*, 55.
110 "life giving": Letter, Galt to Wilson, April 28, 1915, Wilson Papers.
110 She had never met a man: Schachtman, *Edith and Woodrow*, 78.
110 "no mean man in love-making": Levin, *Edith and Woodrow*, 74.
110 "He's a goner": Starling, *Starling*, 44.
110 On Saturday, May 1: Gilbert, *First World War*, 154.
110 "In Flanders fields": Quoted in ibid., 156.
110 By the end of the month: Ibid., 164.
111 "We are still in our old positions": Ibid., 126.
111 Elsewhere, wholly a new front: Ibid., 121, 135–36; Keegan, *First World War*, 238, 239.
111 a systematic slaughter: Gilbert, *First World War*, 142–43.
111 "It is difficult, if not impossible": Lansing, Private Memoranda, April 15, 1915, Lansing Papers.
112 "A neutral in time of international war": Ibid., April 29, 1915.
112 "German naval policy": Link, *Wilson: Struggle*, 366.
112 "It was not thought in official quarters": *New York Times*, May 2, 1915.

113   The ship remained afloat: Ledger, Messages Received, Admiralty Papers, ADM 137/4101, National Archives UK.

113   "lids": *Washington Herald*, May 1 and 2, 1915.

113   "cool and clean": *New York Times*, May 7, 1915.

LUSITANIA: UNDER WAY

115   "Dark brown hair": Poster, "Lusitania Disaster. Information Wanted," Prichard Papers.

115   "a most interesting face": Letter, Theodate Pope to Mrs. Prichard, Feb. 4, 1916, Prichard Papers.

115   "rather dull": Letter, Thomas Sumner to Mrs. Prichard, Oct. 28, 1915, Prichard Papers.

116   "He was a great favorite": Letter, Henry Needham to Mrs. Prichard, May 20, 1915, Prichard Papers.

116   "counting the time": Letter, Arthur Gadsden to Mrs. Prichard, July 4, 1915, Prichard Papers.

116   "Do you think all these people": Hoehling and Hoehling, *Last Voyage*, 21; see also *New York Times*, May 6, 1915.

117   "Captain Turner . . . neglected his duty": Letter, Oliver Bernard to Mrs. Prichard, Aug. 15, 1915, Prichard Papers.

118   While moving downriver: I culled these details of New York Harbor from a variety of sources, held at the New York Public Library main branch. These include Map of New York and Harbor, A. R. Ohman Map Co., 1910; Sea Chart, New York Bay and Harbor, 1910; Map of Depths, New York Bay and Harbor, U.S. Coast and Geodetic Survey, May 1914; Map, Manhattan, G. W. Bromley & Co., 1916, Plate 38; Map, New York City, 1910, Section 2, Plate 10, 1911. Interestingly, the last map makes a reference to "Sir Peter Warren Farm," just above Fourteenth Street in Manhattan, once a vast tract of open land acquired in the eighteenth century by Warren, a British sea captain. May I offer a pointless observation: there is no farm in that location today.

119   Governors Island: In the interests of filling the reader's mind with yet more useless knowledge, I'd like to note, here, that the 1960s comedy duo the Smothers Brothers—Tom and Dick—were born on Governors Island.

120   This being wartime: Preston, *Lusitania*, 136. There is scant information about these mysterious gentlemen. I was unable to find any source that identified them by name. It is also unclear exactly where they were held aboard ship, as the *Lusitania* had no formal "brig," but all reports agree they were confined behind locked doors.

120   Alta Piper: See "Not on Board," under "People," at Lusitania Resource, www.rmslusitania.info/people/not-on-board/.

U-20: TOWARD FAIR ISLE

121   The boat's ventilators: Spiegel, *Adventures*, 3.

121   "here and there rain and fog": Schwieger, War Log. All references in this chapter to course, weather, wave heights, and so forth come from this log.

121   Men served as ballast: Neureuther and Bergen, *U-Boat Stories*, 126, 186, 195.

122   One boat, U-3: Rössler, *U-Boat*, 25.

123   "The scratches on the steel walls": Neureuther and Bergen, *U-Boat Stories*, 145.

LUSITANIA: RENDEZVOUS

125   Its walls were covered: See details in "Saloon (First Class) Accommodations," under "Lusitania Accommodations," at Lusitania Resource, www.rmslusitania.info/lusitania/accommodations/saloon.

126   Theodate found a copy: Letter, Pope to Ada Brooks Pope, June 28, 1915, Riddle Papers. Pope's letter provides one of the most detailed accounts of shipboard life and the sinking that I was able to locate.

126   The paper devoted: *New York Sun*, May 1, 1915.

127   "The President was entirely unaware": Ibid.; see also Berg, *Wilson*, 347–49.

127   A German drive: *New York Sun*, May 1, 1915.

127   "Whatever else could they expect": Katz, *Dearest*, 103.

127   "Under no circumstances": Ibid.

127   "Passengers are informed": Ibid., 109.

128   "to head off American travel": *New York Sun*, May 1, 1915.

128   "That means of course": Letter, Pope to Ada Brooks Pope, June 28, 1915, Riddle Papers.

128   "My! . . . The mail I got today": Letter, Huston to "Ruth," May 1, 1915. This compelling bit of *Lusitania* arcana was provided to me by Geoffrey Whitfield. The letter is published in Kalafus, Poirier et al., *Lest We Forget*.

129   "swirling mist-veils": Bisset, *Commodore*, 45.

130   Turner was under orders: "Answers of the Petitioner to the Interrogatories Propounded by May Davies Hopkins," Petition of the Cunard Steamship Company, April 15, 1918, U.S. National Archives–New York, 3, 9; Memorandum, " 'Lusitania'—American Proceedings," Admiralty Papers, ADM 1/8451/56, National Archives UK; minute, Nov. 19, 1914, Cunard Archives.

ROOM 40: CADENCE

131   Intercepted Position Reports: Minute Sheet: U-20, Ministry of Defence Papers, DEFE/69/270, National Archives UK.

PART II: JUMP ROPE AND CAVIAR

U-20: "THE BLIND MOMENT"

135   By 8:25 A.M., Sunday: Schwieger, War Log.

135   Simple enough in concept: For additional details about diving, see Forstner, *Journal*, 20–27; Koenig, *Voyage*, 51–58; Neureuther and Bergen, *U-Boat Stories*, 174.

135   as little as seventy-five seconds: Bailey and Ryan, *Lusitania Disaster*, 120.

136   Certain older boats: Koerver says that boats built before U-20, numbered U-5 to U-18, all powered by gasoline, took "several minutes" to dive (*German Submarine Warfare*, xxxvii). Breemer says, "By 1914 a diving time of five minutes or less had become standard for a boat when fully surfaced, about one minute from an awash condition" (*Defeating the U-Boat*, 14).

136   "suicide boats": Koerver, *German Submarine Warfare*, xxxvii.

136   Commander Paul Koenig recalled: Koenig, *Voyage*, 51–58.

137   a reddish light: Spiegel, *Adventures*, 15.

137   "Well, we seem to have arrived": Koenig, *Voyage*, 54.

138   To speed the process: Thomas, *Raiders*, 33.

138   with an angry growl: Koenig, *Voyage*, 27. He calls it a "furious" growl.

139   "the blind moment": Ibid., 31; Forstner, *Journal*, 75.

139   "some of the most nerve-racking": Neureuther and Bergen, *U-Boat Stories*, 118.

140   U-20 emerged: Schwieger, War Log.

LUSITANIA: A SUNDAY AT SEA

141   the "long course": *New York Times*, Sept. 12, 1909.

141   Timing was crucial: "Answers of the Petitioner to the Interrogatories Propounded by May Davies Hopkins," Petition of the Cunard Steamship Company, April 15, 1918, U.S. National Archives–New York, 4; Ramsay, *Lusitania*, 227.

142   Theodate Pope awoke: Letter, Pope to Ada Brooks Pope, June 28, 1915, Riddle Papers.

142   Second-class passenger William Uno Meriheina: Meriheina's letter was reprinted in an unidentified news article "Saves 15 Lusitania Passengers, Then Writes to Wife from Raft," held by the New-York Historical Society, New York, NY. It is excerpted as well in Kalafus et al., *Lest We Forget*.

143   "A braver man": Kalafus et al., "William Meriheina: An Inventive Survivor," *Encyclopedia Titanica*, March 29, 2014, www.encyclopedia-titanica.org/documents/William-meriheina-an-inventive-survivor.pdf.

143   "We have passed": "Saves 15 Lusitania Passengers, Then Writes to Wife from Raft," unidentified news article, New-York Historical Society, New York, NY.

144 into the crow's nest: Testimony, Charles E. Lauriat Jr, Petition of the Cunard Steamship Company, April 15, 1918, U.S. National Archives–New York, 87.

144 On Sunday, the ship's first full day: Lauriat, *Lusitania's Last Voyage*, 3.

144 "At this rate": Quoted in "Mr. Charles Emelius Lauriat, Jr.," under "People," "Saloon (First Class) Passenger List," at Lusitania Resource, www.rmslusitania.info/people/saloon/charles-lauriat.

144 He looked them over: Lauriat, Claim. Lauriat's claim before the Mixed Claims Commission numbers hundreds of pages and contains many details about his journey, down to the number of bags he brought with him and where he stored them. His claim also provides insights into his dealings with Thackeray's daughter and granddaughter.

145 "absolutely necessary": "Answers of Petitioner to Interrogatories Propounded by Hunt, Hill & Betts," Petition of the Cunard Steamship Company. April 15, 1918, U.S. National Archives–New York, 58.

145 expressly prohibited from "gossiping": Memorandum, to Captain and Staff Captain, *Lusitania*, Nov. 21, 1914, Cunard Archives, GM 22/1/1.

145 "*Ships should give*": "Answers of the Petitioner to the Interrogatories Propounded by May Davies Hopkins," Petition of the Cunard Steamship Company, April 15, 1918, U.S. National Archives–New York, 5; "Memorandum as to Master's Actions," Admiralty Papers, ADM 1/8451/56, National Archives UK.

145 "in a place where it can be destroyed": "Instructions for Owners and Masters," Admiralty Papers, ADM 1/8451/56, National Archives UK. A May 1915 Admiralty memorandum entitled "Notes on Mines and Torpedoes" instructs ship captains on how to treat a torpedo found floating in the sea. The first, and possibly wisest, bit of advice: "Do not hit it on the nose." Bailey/Ryan Collection.

146 This was an effective maneuver: Telegram, Adm. John Jellicoe to Admiralty, March 23, 1915, Churchill Papers, CHAR 13/62/83. In his telegram, Jellicoe recounts the sinking of U-29 and praises the "seamanlike handling" of the *Dreadnought*, but nonetheless urges that the sinking be kept secret. In telegraphic prose, he writes: "It must be very disconcerting to the enemy when submarine disappeared and cause of loss not known."

146 "It is not in any way dishonorable": "Instructions for Owners and Masters," Admiralty Papers, ADM 1/8451/56, National Archives UK.

146 "No ocean-going British merchant vessel": Ibid.

146 "War experience has shown": Confidential Memorandum, April 16, 1915. Admiralty Papers, ADM 1/8451/56, National Archives UK; "Answers of the Petitioner to the Interrogatories Propounded by May Davies Hopkins," Petition of the Cunard Steamship Company, April 15, 1918, U.S. National Archives–New York, 5–6.

146 Cunard's lawyers later would hedge: "Answers of Petitioner to Inter-

rogatories Propounded by Hunt, Hill & Betts," Petition of the Cunard Steamship Company, April 15, 1918, U.S. National Archives–New York, 4.

147   little impression: *Lusitania* seaman Leslie Morton, for example, wrote in a letter to the Associated Press that "zig-zagging for merchant ships had not at that time been introduced, also a ship traveling at sixteen knots or over was considered by practice and precedent to be safe from submarine attack." Morton to Associated Press, May 15, 1962, Morton Papers, DX/2313, Merseyside.

During Cunard's limit-of-liability trial in New York, Thomas Taylor, a Cunard captain, testified that merchant captains did not begin zigzagging until five months *after* the sinking of the *Lusitania*. Asked whether he would have considered doing so before the disaster, he said, "No, we would not have done it. We never thought of it up to that time." Testimony of Thomas M. Taylor, Petition of the Cunard Steamship Company, April 15, 1918, U.S. National Archives–New York, 907, 911, 915.

147   "I took a look around": Letter, Dwight Harris to Mother, May 10, 1915, Harris Papers.

ROOM 40; QUEENSTOWN; LONDON: PROTECTING ORION

148   "There will be less moon": Telegram, Henry Francis Oliver to Jacky Fisher, May 2, 1915, Admiralty Papers, ADM 137/112, National Archives UK.

148   "in view of the submarine menace": Telegram, Henry Francis Oliver to Adm. John Jellicoe, May 2, 1915, Admiralty Papers, ADM 137/112, National Archives UK.

148   Oliver would send explicit warnings: Beesly, *Room 40*, 100; Ramsay, *Lusitania*, 246.

148   declared it clear on April 15: Beesly, *Room 40*, 96–97.

149   Admiral Oliver issued orders: Ibid., 100.

149   That Sunday: Ibid.

149   the Admiralty also tracked: Telegram, St. Marys Scilly to Admiralty, May 2, 1915, 4:05 P.M., Admiralty Papers, ADM 137/112, National Archives UK; telegram, St. Marys Scilly to Admiralty, May 2, 1915, 6:07 P.M., Admiralty Papers, ADM 137/112, National Archives UK; Telegram, Admiral, Devonport to Admiralty, May 2, 1915, 10:22 P.M. Admiralty Papers, ADM 137/112, National Archives UK; ledger, "Subs," May 2, 1915, 10:27 A.M., 4:05 P.M., and 6:07 P.M., Admiralty Papers, ADM 137/4101, National Archives UK.

149   "The reference to the *Lusitania*": Frost, *German Submarine Warfare*, 186.

150   In fact, Wilson had by now: Link, *Wilson: Struggle*, 48, 120–22;
       Devlin, *Too Proud to Fight*, 318–19.

150   "The blowing up of a liner": Cooper, *Walter Hines Page*, 306.

U-20: A PERILOUS LINE

151   At 12:30 p.m. Sunday: All details in this chapter come from Schwieger,
       War Log.

LUSITANIA: HALIBUT

155   to "see that everything was clean": Testimony, John I. Lewis, Petition
       of the Cunard Steamship Company, April 15, 1918, U.S. National Ar-
       chives–New York, 598.

155   "I remember putting an eye splice in": Morton, *Long Wake*, 101.

155   The *Washington Times*: *Washington Times*, May 3, 1915.

156   "a very dyspeptic sort of fellow": Letter, Grace French to Prichard,
       Sept. 10, 1915, Prichard Papers.

156   On one voyage the menu: Menus, SAS/33D/2/13b, Merseyside.

157   The company laid in a supply: All from Cunard Archives, D42/B4/45:
       Minutes, Feb. 18, 1915; March 10, 1915; April 21, 1915; May 5, 1915.

157   Michael Byrne: Letter, Michael Byrne to William Jennings Bryan. June
       8, 1915, Lusitania Papers, Microcopy 580, Roll, 197, U.S. National Ar-
       chives–College Park.

157   "war, and submarines": Harold Smethurst, "Hand-Written Account,"
       DX/2085, Merseyside.

157   "over consciousness": S. Smith, *Theodate Pope Riddle*, ch. 1, p. 3.

157   "Tears come": Katz, *Dearest*, 20.

157   "Cheer up": Ibid., 19.

158   Mitchell's solution: Ibid., 22.

158   "At first, and in some cases": Mitchell, *Fat and Blood*, 42.

158   "would do far better": Mitchell, *Wear and Tear*, 47.

158   "I am always happy": Katz, *Dearest*, 22.

158   "Live as domestic a life": Knight, "All the Facts," 277.

158   "Never touch pen": Ibid.

159   "who so nearly drove me mad": Ibid., 259. Although Gilman's story
       dampened Mitchell's popularity, it did not stop Woodrow Wilson,
       shortly after his 1912 election to the presidency, from undergoing an
       examination at Mitchell's clinic. For over a decade Wilson had suffered
       small strokes and other events associated with an undiagnosed cerebral-
       vascular disorder, including one jarring moment in 1906 when, while
       president of Princeton, he temporarily lost vision in his left eye. Dr.
       Mitchell offered the prognosis that Wilson would not survive his first
       term. He recommended rest, exercise, and a healthy diet and advised
       the president to keep stress to a minimum. Link, "Dr. Grayson's Predic-
       ament," 488–89.

159 "I find that my material world": S. Smith, *Theodate Pope Riddle*, ch. 5, p. 1.

159 "Pictures have been dead": Ibid.

159 "My interest in architecture": Ibid.

159 "tired of seeing": Ibid.

160 "I truly believe": Letter, Pope to Ada Brooks Pope, June 28, 1915, Riddle Papers.

160 "I can't help hoping": Mackworth, *This Was My World*, 242.

160 "We noticed this with much surprise": Ibid., 241–42.

160 "one very smart navy blue serge": Letter, Grace French to Mrs. Prichard, Nov. 12, 1915, Prichard Papers.

160 "very short": Letter, Grace French to Mrs. Prichard, Nov. 20, 1915, Prichard Papers. Mike Poirier contends this woman was Irish.

161 "A party of us": Letter, Olive North to Mrs. Prichard, Sept. 11, 1915, Prichard Papers.

161 "I never saw him again": Ibid.

161 "There were so many on the ship": letter, Gertrude Adams to Mrs. Prichard, undated, Prichard Papers.

161 In the evening: Ramsay, *Lusitania*, 50.

U-20: THE TROUBLE WITH TORPEDOES

162 "Very beautiful weather": Schwieger, War Log.

163 Another indicator of velocity: At night, fast ships with all lights doused betrayed themselves by the glow of the white wake climbing their bows. The problem became acute when a ship passed through waters prone to the phosphorescence caused by certain marine organisms. Some U-boat men reported feeling a sense of awe upon seeing the bow wakes raised by speeding destroyers, even though destroyers were their most lethal opponents. One crewman called this "a lovely sight." U-boat commander Georg von Trapp wrote that at such moments it seemed as though the destroyers were "wearing white mustaches." Von Trapp, *To the Last Salute*, 75; Neureuther and Bergen, *U-Boat Stories*, 112, 199.

163 According to a German tally: Translation notes, Arno Spindler, *Der Handelskrieg mit U-Booten*, Box 2, Bailey/Ryan Collection; Preston, *Lusitania*, 165; Richard Wagner, "Lusitania's Last Voyage," *Log*, Spring 2005, www.beyondships.com/files/hLUSITANIAarticler.pdf, 3.

164 One U-boat experienced three torpedo failures: "U-58: Interrogation of Survivors," Admiralty Papers, ADM 137/4126, National Archives UK, 5.

164 Another submarine: "Report of Interrogation of Survivors of 'U.B. 109,'" Admiralty Papers, ADM 137/4126, National Archives UK, 7.

164 Schwieger's target: Schwieger, War Log.

LUSITANIA: SUNSHINE AND HAPPINESS

166 "Tuesday—Resumption": "Saves 15 Lusitania Passengers, Then Writes to Wife from Raft," unidentified news article, New-York Historical Society, New York, NY.

166 "Tuesday: I didn't write": Letter, Huston to "Ruth," May 1, 1915, Kalafus et al., *Lest We Forget*.

166 "I think a happier company": "Narrative of Mrs. J. MacFarquhar," Lusitania Papers, Microcopy 580, Roll 197, U.S. National Archives–College Park.

167 "As the days passed": Lauriat, *Last Voyage*, 69.

167 "I'd never seen": Conner account, quoted in Kalafus et al., *Lest We Forget*.

ROOM 40: THE ORION SAILS

168 Admiral Oliver ordered the ship to depart: Telegram, Admiralty to C.-in-C. Devonport, May 4, 1915, and telegram, Stockton to Admiralty, May 5, 1915, both in "Home Waters: General Operation Telegrams," May 1–5, 1915, Admiralty Papers, ADM 137/112, National Archives UK.

168 A succession of reports: Telegram, Admiralty to C.-in-C., May 4, 1915, telegram, Naval Center Devonport to Admiralty, May 4, 1915, telegram, Stockton to Admiralty, May 5, 1915, telegram, *Orion* (via Pembroke) to Admiralty, May 5, 1915, and telegram, C.-in-C. Home Fleet to Admiralty, May 5, 1915, all in "Home Waters: General Operations Telegrams," May 1–5, 1915, Admiralty Papers, ADM 137/112, National Archives UK.

168 On the morning of Sunday: Ledger, "Subs," May 2, 1915, 10:30 A.M., and May 3, 2:30 A.M., Admiralty Papers, ADM 137/4101, National Archives UK; *New York Times*, May 3, 1915.

169 "large sheet of flame": Ledger, "Subs," May 4, 1915, 3:32 A.M., Admiralty Papers, ADM 137/4101, National Archives UK.

U-20: FRUSTRATION

170 At 7:40 P.M., Tuesday: Schwieger, War Log.

LONDON: BERLIN: WASHINGTON: COMFORT DENIED

173 "The situation is curious": Marder, *From the Dreadnought*, 266.

Even their schedules clashed. Fisher's best hours were the early morning, between 4:00 A.M. and breakfast; he also went to bed early, by nine at night. Churchill began work at eight in the morning, while still in his bed, and continued until 1:00 A.M. As Rear Adm. Sir Douglas Brownrigg recalled: "He presented a most extraordinary spectacle, perched up in a huge bed, with the whole of the counterpane littered with dispatch boxes, red and all colors, and a stenographer sitting at the foot—Mr. Churchill himself with an enormous Corona Corona in his mouth, a glass of warm water on the table by his side and a writing-pad on his knee!" (267).

173 Churchill's "energy and capacity": "Lord Fisher and Mr. Churchill," Hall 3/5, Hall Papers.

Violet Asquith, daughter of Prime Minister Herbert Asquith, was a keen observer of her time and the men she encountered, including Churchill and Fisher.

She quotes Churchill as saying, "I think a curse should rest on me because I am so happy. I know this war is smashing and shattering the lives of thousands every moment—and yet—I cannot help it—I enjoy every second I live" (quoted in Hough, *Winston and Clementine*, 286).

She also has some choice observations to offer about Fisher. "I said both to my father and Winston that though I did not doubt Lord Fisher's genius I thought him dangerous because I believed him to be mad" (quoted in Hough, *Winston and Clementine*, 284). On another occasion, she remarked, "What a strange man he is!" (quoted in Hough, *Winston and Clementine*, 306).

One of her close friends, Archie Gordon, happened to take a voyage on the *Lusitania* in December 1908. He experienced something of a letdown. "I had hoped for novel sensations, experiences & acquaintances," he wrote in a letter to her. "Instead, something closely resembling a hyper-dull hotel with the doors & windows shut." The crossing was rough and uncomfortable at first, then improved. "The sea calmed, the sun came out, & people hitherto undreamt of came out like rabbits" (Carter and Pottle, *Lantern Slides*, 172).

173 "Gradually we in the Admiralty": "Lord Fisher and Mr. Churchill," Hall 3/5, Hall Papers.

173 "The state of affairs at Head Quarters": Letter, Jellicoe to Sir Frederick Hamilton, April 26, 1915, Jellicoe Papers.

173 "But he was seventy-four years old": Churchill, *World Crisis*, 230.

174 "I took him because I knew": Hough, *Winston and Clementine*, 270.

174 "great nervous exhaustion": Churchill, *World Crisis*, 443.

174 "He had evinced unconcealed distress": Ibid.

174 "Just look after 'the old boy' ": Soames, *Clementine Churchill*, 157–58; Hough, *Winston and Clementine*, 270.

174 "the constant bombardment": Marder, *Fear God*, 209.

175 "it has repeatedly occurred": Telegram, James Gerard to William Jennings Bryan, May 6, 1915, *Foreign Relations*.

175 "creamy lace": Wilson, *My Memoir*, 61.

176 "Cousin Woodrow looks really ill": Ibid., 61–62.

176 She nicknamed him "Tiger": Ibid., 67.

177 "Just as I thought": Ibid., 61–62.

177 "I don't think he believed her": Ibid., 62.

177 "playing with fire": Ibid.

178 "an almost unqualified denial": Telegram, William Jennings Bryan to Edward Grey, via Walter Hines Page, March 30, 1915, *Foreign Relations*; Link, *Winston: Struggle*, 347.

178 the prompt release of an automobile: William Jennings Bryan to U.S. Consul General, London, May 3, 1915, *Foreign Relations*.

178 "In the life and death struggle": Link, *Winston: Struggle*, 119.

178 "Together England and Germany are likely": Ibid., 348.

178 "No formal diplomatic action": *New York Times*, May 5, 1915.

179 "a sharp note": Seymour, *Intimate Papers*, 1:432.

LUSITANIA: THE MANIFEST

180 "I shall never forget": Hart, *Gallipoli*, 244.

181 "I got back into the trench": Ibid.

181 "They crept right up": Ibid., 210.

181 By the time the Allied invading force: Keegan, *First World War*, 248.

181 "The scene . . . was tragically macabre": Hart, *Gallipoli*, 37.

182 Here were muskrat skins: "Supplemental Manifest," Bailey/Ryan Collection. For the insurance value of Hugh Lane's paintings, see "Sir Hugh Percy Lane," under "People," "Saloon (First Class) Passenger List," at Lusitania Resource, www.rmslusitania.info/people/saloon/hugh-lane/.

182 "The army in France": Churchill, *World Crisis*, 421, 447.

182 The shrapnel shells were essentially inert: Wood et al., "Sinking," 179–80.

U-20: AT LAST

184 Throughout the morning: Schwieger, War Log.

SIGHTING

187 "Small boat containing": Telegram, Head of Kinsale to Admiralty, May 5, 1915, "Home Waters: General Operation Telegrams," May 1–5, 1915, Admiralty Papers, ADM 137/112, National Archives UK.

ROOM 40: SCHWIEGER REVEALED

188 gunfire in the fog: Telegram, Naval Center to Admiralty, May 5, 1915, Lusitania Various Papers. Admiralty Papers, ADM 137/1058, National Archives UK. This spooky telegram reads: "Old Head Kinsale reports five forty three sounds of gunfire south, foggy, Brow Head."

188 The new message: Telegram, Head of Kinsale to Admiralty, May 5, 1915, "Home Waters: General Operation Telegrams," May 1–5, 1915, Admiralty Papers, ADM 137/112, National Archives UK.

188 The captain of a British ship: Telegram, Naval Center Queenstown

to Admiralty, May 5, 1915, "Home Waters: General Operation Telegrams," May 1–5, 1915, Admiralty Papers, ADM 137/112, National Archives UK.

188 Now came a fourth message: Telegram, Naval Center Queenstown to Admiralty, May 5, 1915 (9:51 P.M.), "Home Waters: General Operations Telegrams," May 1–5, 1915, Admiralty Papers, ADM 137/112, National Archives UK.

189 A detailed record: Ledger, Ministry of Defence Papers, DEFE/69/270, National Archives UK.

189 They accompanied the dreadnought: Telegram, *Orion* (via Pembroke) to Admiralty, May 5, 1915, "Home Waters: General Operation Telegrams," May 1–5, 1915, Admiralty Papers, ADM 137/112, National Archives UK.

189 The *Orion* continued: Ibid.

190 "most important to attract neutral shipping": Beesly, *Room 40*, 90; Ramsay, *Lusitania*, 202.

LUSITANIA: HELPFUL YOUNG LADIES

191 "wakened by shouts": Letter, Pope to Ada Brooks Pope, June 28, 1915, Riddle Papers.

191 "we mustered the cooks": Testimony, John I. Lewis, Petition of the Cunard Steamship Company, April 15, 1918, U.S. National Archives–New York, 587.

192 "The men were not efficient": Myers account, quoted in Kalafus et al., *Lest We Forget.*

192 "On Thursday morning": "Narrative of Mrs. J. MacFarquhar," Lusitania Papers, Microcopy 580, Roll 197, U.S. National Archives–College Park.

193 "We were not issued with paint brushes": Morton, *Long Wake*, 101. Mike Poirier contends Morton may in fact have encountered two Crompton girls.

194 A boy named Robert Kay: Robert Kay Account, courtesy of Mike Poirier. Special thanks also to Robert Kay.

195 "It's alright drilling": *New York Times*, May 10, 1915.

U-20: SPECTACLE

196 Thursday morning, May 6: Schwieger, War Log.

196 St. George's Channel: Anyone interested in getting a better sense of where all these places and bodies of water are in relation to one another need only type the names into a Google search box.

LUSITANIA: LIFE AFTER DEATH

200   Theodate too was a member: For more on the Society for Psychical Research and on spiritualism at the end of the nineteenth century and the start of the twentieth, please see my own *Thunderstruck*, 386–87.

201   "If you wish to upset the law": Ibid., 11, 13, 401.

201   Theodate claimed her own turban levitated: S. Smith, *Theodate Pope Riddle*, Notes, 8.

201   In 1907, the year Theodate turned forty: Katz, *Dearest*, 69.

201   Though only in his twenties: Ibid., 103; S. Smith, *Theodate Pope Riddle*, ch. 8, p. 1.

202   "There were passages that illustrated": Letter, Pope to Ada Brooks Pope, June 28, 1915, Riddle Papers.

202   "All around us": Quoted in "The Story of the Sinking of the *Lusitania*," by Deborah Nicholson Lines Davison. Courtesy of Ms. Davison.

203   As of noon Thursday: Memorandum, " 'Lusitania'—American Proceedings," Admiralty Papers, ADM 1/8451/56, National Archives UK.

U-20: CHANGE OF PLAN

204   On Thursday afternoon: Schwieger, War Log.

LUSITANIA: MESSAGES

206   "Submarines active": Telegram, Censor, Valencia to Admiralty, May 7, 1915, Lusitania Various Papers, Admiralty Papers, ADM 137/1058, National Archives UK.

206   "Submarines off Fastnet": Ibid.

207   After dinner, Preston Prichard: Letter, Guy R. Cockburn to Mrs. Prichard, Sept. 6, 1915, Prichard Papers.

207   On past voyages: "Programme in Aid of Seamen's Charities," R.M.S. *Lusitania*, Sept. 21, 1912, DX/728, Merseyside; "Programme of Entertainment," April 21 and 22, 1915, D42/PR3/8/25, Cunard Archive.

208   "I was keenly interested": Lauriat, *Lusitania's Last Voyage*, 5.

208   Under certain conditions: Ramsay, *Lusitania*, 164.

208   "that no suggestion would be made": "Statement of Mr. A. J. Mitchell," May 14, 1915, Lusitania Papers, Microcopy 580, Roll 197, U.S. National Archives–College Park.

209   "She was only too happy": Josephine Brandell Account, quoted in Kalafus et al., *Lest We Forget*.

209   "Hope you have a safe crossing": Record of Wireless Signals, May 6, 1915, "Lusitania Various Papers," Admiralty Papers, ADM 137/1058, National Archives UK.

LONDON; WASHINGTON; BERLIN: TENSION

210 "in sight for five minutes": Telegram, Naval Center Queenstown to Admiralty, May 6, 1915, "Home Waters: General Operation Telegrams," May 6–10, 1915, Admiralty Papers, ADM 137/113, National Archives UK.

211 "heart failure, accelerated by shock": *New York Times*, May 6, 1915; *Washington Times*, May 5, 1915.

211 "running amok": *Washington Times*, May 5, 1915.

211 "There are some things": Wilson to Galt, May 5, 1915, Wilson Papers.

211 "I can hardly see": Wilson to Galt, May 6, 1915, Wilson Papers.

212 "There was the fear": Wilson, *My Memoir*, 66–67.

212 "Oh, so many things swarmed": Ibid., 67.

212 "all the problems which confronted him": Ibid.

212 "unwelcome publicity": Ibid.

213 "This fact is eminently bound not only to alter our good relations": Link, *Wilson: Struggle*, 398.

213 That evening: *Washington Times*, May 6, 1915.

213 At midnight that Thursday: Intercepted telegram, "Norddeich to all Ships," Admiralty Papers, ADM 137/3959. Here's the actual text:

> MAY 6, 1915
> NORDDEICH TO ALL SHIPS
> NO. 48
> S.S. LUSITANIA LEAVES LIVERPOOL FOR NEW YORK ON MAY 15TH. S.S. TUSCANIA LEAVES GLASGOW ON MAY 7TH FOR NEW YORK VIA LIVERPOOL. S.S. CAMERONIA 11,000 TONS LEAVES ON MAY 15TH FOR NEW YORK.

U-20: FOG

214 Schwieger and his crew: Schwieger, War Log.

PART III: DEAD WAKE

THE IRISH SEA: ENGINES ABOVE

217 Early Friday morning a number of passengers: "Statement of Mrs. Theodore Naish," Lusitania Papers, Microcopy 580, Roll 187, U.S. National Archives–College Park; "Statement of Maude R. Thompson," Lusitania Papers, Microcopy 580, Roll 187, U.S. National Archives–College Park; Ramsay, *Lusitania*, 77.

217 "We had been told": "Statement of Mrs. Theodore Naish," Lusitania Papers, Microcopy 580, Roll 187, U.S. National Archives–College Park.

218 "I do not like this": Ibid.

218 "As the horn was blowing": Lauriat, *Lusitania's Last Voyage*, 5, 69–70.

219 "just the loom of the land": Testimony, Leo Thompson, Petition of the

Cunard Steamship Company, April 15, 1918, U.S. National Archives–New York, 673.

219 "Number and directions": Telegram, Kilrane to Director Naval Intelligence, London, May 7, 1915, "Home Waters: General Operation Telegrams," May 6–10, 1915, Admiralty Papers, ADM 137/113, National Archives UK.

219 Booth quit breakfast: Testimony, Alfred Booth, "Investigation," Lines 262–65, 276–77; "Answers of Petitioner to Interrogatories Propounded by Hunt, Hill & Betts," Petition of the Cunard Steamship Company, April 15, 1918, U.S. National Archives–New York, 1, 3.

220 "Submarines active": Telegram, May 7, 1915, 11:25 A.M., cited in "Answers of the Petitioner to the Interrogatories Propounded by May Davies Hopkins," Petition of the Cunard Steamship Company, April 15, 1918, U.S. National Archives–New York, 8.

221 "It was a beautiful day": Lauriat, *Lusitania's Last Voyage*, 70.

222 "just flat as a billiard table": Francis Burrows, interview, *Lusitania*, BBC Written Archives Centre.

222 "The view was grand": "Narrative of Mrs. J. MacFarquhar," Lusitania Papers, Microcopy 580, Roll 197, U.S. National Archives–College Park.

222 "All of a sudden": Schwieger, War Log.

223 A seven-year-old girl: As you perhaps have guessed, these and other details that follow also come from lists of belongings recovered from the unidentified dead of the *Lusitania*. "Unidentified Remains," R.M.S. Lusitania: Record of Passengers & Crew, SAS/29/6/18, Merseyside; "Lusitania: Effects of Unidentified Bodies," in Wesley Frost to William Jennings Bryan, June 4, 1915, decimal file 341.111L97/37, U.S. National Archives–College Park.

224 "I pinned the big diamond brooch": Letter, Dwight Harris to Mother, May 10, 1915, Harris Papers.

224 "I replied that his word": "Statement of Mrs. Theodore Naish," Lusitania Papers, Microcopy 580, Roll 187, U.S. National Archives–College Park.

225 "Submarines 5 miles south": "Memorandum as to Master's Actions," Admiralty Papers, ADM 1/8451/56, National Archives UK.

225 At his periscope: Schwieger, War Log.

226 "After I was through swearing": Thomas, *Raiders*, 96.

226 "Unusually good visibility": Schwieger, War Log.

LONDON; WASHINGTON: THE KING'S QUESTION

227 "We spoke of the probability": Seymour, *Intimate Papers*, 1:432; also in Ramsay, *Lusitania*, 77–78.

227 "Suppose they should sink": Seymour, *Intimate Papers*, 1:432; Cooper, *Walter Hines Page*, 306; Ramsay, *Lusitania*, 78.

228 severe shortage of artillery shells: Keegan, *First World War*, 199; Churchill, *World Crisis*, 437.

228   "incurring unjustifiable risks": Churchill, *World Crisis*, 437.
228   "Without actually taking part": Ibid.
228   "suffering from every form of horrible injury": Ibid., 438.
228   "In this clear morning air": Letter, Wilson to Galt, May 7, 1915, Wilson Papers.

THE IRISH SEA: FUNNELS ON THE HORIZON

229   U-20 moved: Schwieger, War Log.
229   "At first I thought": Thomas, *Raiders*, 97.
229   "Ahead and to starboard": Schwieger, War Log.
231   At about 1:30 P.M.: Bailey and Ryan, *Lusitania Disaster*, 143.
232   But as he watched: Robert Kay Account, courtesy of Mike Poirier.
232   "I suggested that the passengers": Kessler, quoted in Kalafus et al., *Lest We Forget*.
232   Just as Pilot Lanz arrived: Schwieger, War Log.
233   That the ship "was not sent": Ibid.
233   Charles Lauriat went to lunch: Lauriat, *Lusitania's Last Voyage*, 73.
234   "A young Englishman at our table": Letter, Pope to Ada Brooks Pope, June 28, 1915, Riddle Papers.
235   "While at table": Letter, Dwight Harris to Mother, May 10, 1915, Harris Papers.
235   "talking about Submarines": Letter, Gadsden to Mrs. Prichard, July 4, 1915, Prichard Papers.
235   "volunteered to point her out": Letter, Grace French to Mrs. Prichard, Sept. 10, 1915, Prichard Papers.
236   "I replied that Mr. Prichard": Letter, Grace French to Mrs. Prichard, Sept. 19, 1915, Prichard Papers.
236   They joked as they hunted: Ibid.
236   Schwieger estimated: Schwieger, War Log.

LUSITANIA: BEAUTY

237   "At five minutes to four bells": Morton, *Long Wake*, 103.
238   "All lookouts had been warned": Letter, Thomas Mahoney to Adolf Hoehling, May 14, 1955, Hoehling Papers.
238   "trick at the wheel": Hugh Johnston, interview, Lusitania, BBC Written Archives Centre.
238   "We carried on": Ibid.
238   "seeing a dozen things": Morton, *Long Wake*, 102–3.
238   A group of children: John Brennan, interview, *Lusitania*, BBC Written Archives Centre.
239   "At ten minutes past two": Leslie Morton, testimony, June 16, 1915, 16, "Investigation."
239   "10 points on the port bow": Hugh Johnston, testimony, June 16, 1915, 19, "Investigation."

239 "Here is a torpedo coming": Ibid.

239 "a *real walk*": Lauriat, *Lusitania's Last Voyage*, 7.

240 "a piece of vitriolic English": Ibid., 7–8.

240 "which was a marvelous blue": Letter, Pope to Ada Brooks Pope, June 28, 1915, Riddle Papers.

240 "a streak of froth": *Liverpool Weekly Mercury*, May 15, 1915.

240 "That isn't a torpedo, is it?": Ibid.

240 "I did not think that anybody": Ibid.

240 That first turmoil: Ballard, *Exploring the Lusitania*, 84–85; *New York Times*, May 10, 1915; Preston, *Lusitania*, 441–42; Testimony, Casey B. Morgan, Petition of the Cunard Steamship Company, April 15, 1918, U.S. National Archives–New York, 714, 715; testimony, Lawrence Y. Spear, Petition, 766, 767. Anyone interested in more detail about torpedoes, and German U-boats generally, would do well to visit uboat.net, a well-monitored and authoritative website on German submarine warfare in both world wars. See especially "Selected Technical Data of Imperial German U-Boats and Their Torpedoes," www.uboat .net/history/wwi/part7.htm. See also www.navweaps.com/Weapons /WTGER_PreWWII.htm.

241 "I saw the torpedo coming!": Letter, Dwight Harris to Mother, May 10, 1915, Harris Papers.

242 "It was a beautiful sight": James A. Brooks, quoted in unidentified, undated news clipping, Hoehling Papers.

242 In just two months, another Cunard captain: Bisset, *Commodore*, 65.

U-20: "TREFF!"

243 "Torpedo hits starboard": Schwieger, War Log.

PART IV: THE BLACK SOUL

LUSITANIA: IMPACT

247 "I saw it disappear": Quoted in telegram, Pitney to Tribune, New York, May 9, 1915, "Lusitania Various Papers," Admiralty Papers, ADM 137/1058, National Archives UK.

247 "The side of the ship is nothing": Testimony, Gregory C. Davison, Petition of the Cunard Steamship Company, April 15, 1918, U.S. National Archives–New York, 837.

247 "was blown to atoms": Deposition, Thomas Quinn, May 15, 1915, Admiralty Papers, ADM 137/1058, National Archives UK; Preston, *Lusitania*, 453.

248 Just inside the hull: See Garzke et al., *Titanic*, and Wood, et al., "Sinking," throughout.

248 "forced flooding": Wood et al., "Sinking," 177.

248 Captain Turner was standing: Deposition, William Thomas Turner, May 15, 1915, Admiralty Papers, ADM 137/1058, National Archives UK; Preston, 453.

249 "Well, that wasn't so bad": Ballard, *Exploring the Lusitania*, 87.

249 "Water, bits of coal": Letter, Dwight Harris to Mother, May 10, 1915, Harris Papers.

249 "The ship listed so much": Letter, Grace French to Mrs. Prichard, Sept. 10, 1915, Prichard Papers.

249 "I timed everything": Testimony, William McMillan Adams, Petition of the Cunard Steamship Company, April 15, 1918, U.S. National Archives–New York, 24.

249 Charles Lauriat checked his stem-winding wristwatch: Lauriat, *Lusitania's Last Voyage*, 9.

250 "You could feel the two separate motions": Ibid., 72.

250 "more like an explosion of a boiler": Testimony, Charles E. Lauriat Jr., Petition of the Cunard Steamship Company, April 15, 1918, U.S. National Archives–New York, 92, 104.

250 "I think we might stay up": Mackworth, *This Was My World*, 242.

250 "wasted a minute or so": Ibid., 243.

251 "I always thought": Ibid., 244.

251 "Mr. Hubbard stayed by the rail": Lauriat, *Lusitania's Last Voyage*, 9.

251 "If you don't care to come": Ibid., 73.

251 Norah Bretherton: Statement of Norah Bretherton (n.d.), Lusitania Papers, Microcopy 580, Roll 197, U.S. National Archives–College Park.

252 On entering the bridge: Deposition, Hugh Johnston, Admiralty Papers, ADM 137/1058, National Archives UK.

252 "All right, boy": All dialogue here is as reported by Johnston in Ibid.

254 "every step was an effort": Robert Kay Account, courtesy of Mike Poirier.

254 "In their hurry, they put them on": Lauriat, *Lusitania's Last Voyage*, 11.

254 "Captain, what do you wish us to do": Ibid., 11.

255 "The Captain says the boat will not sink": Letter, Henry Needham to Mrs. Prichard, July 9, 1915, Prichard Papers.

255 "I don't know what possessed me": *New York Times*, June 2, 1915.

256 "I left my coffee and nuts": Testimony, Frederic J. Gauntlett, Petition of the Cunard Steamship Company, April 15, 1918, U.S. National Archives–New York, 115.

257 The two first-class elevators: There is debate as to exactly what happened in these two elevators. Preston quotes one of the ship's bellboys as saying, "We could hear their screams coming up—they knew they were trapped." She also quotes a passenger's statement that the elevators were "filled with passengers screaming." Certainly, the loss of electric power would have stopped the elevators and would have provided a truly terrifying moment for passengers within. But *Lusitania* expert

Mike Poirier questions whether anyone was in fact trapped or killed in the elevators. He bases his skepticism on the absence of additional corroborating accounts in the scores of statements made by passengers after the disaster. The debate, however, cannot be settled in any definitive way. Preston, *Lusitania*, 210.

257 The scores of men: There is, however, no debate about what happened with this elevator, and in the luggage room.

257 "rush of water": Ramsay, *Lusitania*, 214.

257 By one estimate, at least 70 portholes: Ibid., 215.

257 "A strange silence prevailed": *Irish Independent*, May 7, 1955.

FIRST WORD

258 "'LUSITANIA' in distress": "Copies of Telegrams Relative to Sinking of S.S. *Lusitania*," Lusitania Various Papers, Admiralty Papers, ADM 137/1058, National Archives UK.

258 "'Lusitania' S.E. 10 miles sinking": Telegram, Galley Head to Admiralty, May 7, 1915, Churchill Papers, CHAR 13/64.

258 "'Lusitania' torpedoed": Telegram, Naval Center Queenstown to Admiralty, May 7, 1915, Churchill Papers, CHAR 13/64; also, Ledger, "Subs," Admiralty Papers, ADM 137/4101, National Archives UK.

LUSITANIA: DECISIONS

259 Ogden Hammond: Testimony, Ogden H. Hammond, Petition of the Cunard Steamship Company, April 15, 1918, U.S. National Archives-New York, 171–78; letter, Ogden H. Hammond to Joseph F. Tumulty, May 21, 1915, Lusitania Papers, Microcopy 580, Roll 197, U.S. National Archives–College Park.

260 The boat contained: Testimony, Leslie Morton, June 16, 1915, 17, "Investigation"; James H. Brooks, "Statement or Story on the Sinking of the Lusitania," Lusitania Papers, Microcopy 580, Roll 197, U.S. National Archives–College Park; testimony, Isaac Lehmann, Petition of the Cunard Steamship Company, April 15, 1918, U.S. National Archives–New York, 297.

260 "It is the captain's orders": This segment of dialogue was reported by Isaac Lehmann in Ibid., 297–98.

261 "I took a look at things": Letter, Dwight Harris to Mother, May 10, 1915, Harris Papers.

262 "The deck suddenly looked very strange": Letter, Pope to Ada Brooks Pope, June 28, 1915, Riddle Papers.

262 "We walked close together": Ibid.

263 "Come Robinson": Ibid.

263 another readout of the spirit gauge: Testimony, Hugh Robert Johnston, June 16, 1915, 19, "Investigation."

263 "My God": Hugh Johnston, interview, *Lusitania*, BBC Written Archives Centre.

263 "Save yourself": Hugh Johnston, interview, *Lusitania*, BBC Written Archives Centre; testimony, Hugh Robert Johnston, June 16, 1915, 19, "Investigation."

U-20: SCHWIEGER'S VIEW

264 "I took my position": Thomas, *Raiders*, 97.

264 "It would have been impossible": This sentence seems so unlike something Schwieger would write that it has prompted some *Lusitania* scholars to wonder whether he, or someone else, altered his log after the fact. But, as it is in the log, and I am in no position to know for certain whether he did in fact touch up the log to improve his future stature in the eyes of history, I quote it here. Schwieger, War Log.

LUSITANIA: THE LITTLE ARMY

265 The floor was canted: Lauriat, *Lusitania's Last Voyage*, 14, 78.

266 "The steamer was all the time rapidly settling": Ibid., 17.

266 "Never could one realize": Statement of Mr. A. J. Mitchell, May 14, 1915, Lusitania Papers, Microcopy 580, Roll 197, U.S. National Archives–College Park.

266 Lauriat stood on a seat: Lauriat, *Lusitania's Last Voyage*, 82–83.

267 "Please will you show me": Newspaper account, "Knox Describes Lusitania's End," provided by Mike Poirier, quoted in Kalafus et al., *Lest We Forget*.

267 Norah Bretherton: Statement of Norah Bretherton (n.d.), Lusitania Papers, Microcopy 580, Roll 197, U.S. National Archives–College Park.

267 "I opened my eyes": Letter, Pope to Ada Brooks Pope, June 28, 1915, Riddle Papers.

268 "The gulls were flying overhead": Kalafus et al., *Lest We Forget*.

269 "It got blacker and blacker": Grace French Account, *Lennox Herald*, May 1975, courtesy of Mike Poirier.

269 "I had no feeling of fear": Letter, Dwight Harris to Mother, May 10, 1915, Harris Papers.

269 For the family of Joseph Frankum: *Liverpool Weekly Mercury*, May 15, 1915.

270 "I clung to my wife": Ibid.

270 "gently and vaguely": Mackworth, *This Was My World*, 244.

270 "Well, you've had your thrill": Ibid.

270 "One gets very close in three minutes": Dorothy Conner Account, courtesy of Mike Poirier.

271 "She's all right": "Statement of Mrs. Theodore Naish," Lusitania Papers, Microcopy 580, Roll 187, U.S. National Archives–College Park, 2.

271 "I thought about how wondrously beautiful": Ibid., 3.

271 The sinking crowned a troubled period: This detail provided by Mike Poirier.

272 After helping to launch: Testimony, Leslie Morton, June 16, 1915, "Investigation," line 495. Morton writes that this boat was No. 13, but *Lusitania* expert Mike Poirier suggests that he may have erred, that the boat was actually No. 9.

272 "If you had to jump": Morton, *Long Wake*, 105.

272 "to waste in either horror or sympathy": Ibid., 106.

272 "in some mistaken belief": Ibid., 107.

273 "The time for heroics": Ibid.

273 "but seeing the turmoil": Ibid.

273 Lauriat swam clear: Lauriat, *Lusitania's Last Voyage*, 18.

274 "An all-swallowing wave": *The Irish Independent*, May 7, 1955.

274 As measles-poxed Robert Kay: Robert Kay Account, courtesy of Mike Poirier.

274 "I couldn't imagine what was landing on me": Lauriat, *Lusitania's Last Voyage*, 20–21, 85.

TELEGRAM

275 "S.O.S. from 'Lusitania'": Ledger, "Subs," May 7, 1915, 2:26 P.M., Admiralty Papers, ADM 137/4101, National Archives UK; also in Churchill Papers, CHAR 13/64.

LUSITANIA: A QUEEN'S END

276 One woman, Margaret Gwyer: Morton, *Long Wake*, 108.

276 Two other passengers: Ramsay, *Lusitania*, 87; Morton, *Long Wake*, 108.

277 "a slow, almost stately, dive": Morton, *Long Wake*, 108; For depth, see Ballard, *Exploring the Lusitania*, 10.

277 "plunged forward like a knife blade": Letter, Dwight Harris to Mother, May 10, 1915, Harris Papers.

277 "As she went under": Lauriat, *Lusitania's Last Voyage*, 85–87.

278 "never met anyone as 'cool'": Letter, Hugh Johnston to Adolf Hoehling, Sept. 25, 1955, Hoehling Papers.

278 "'Lusitania' sunk": Telegram, Head of Kinsale to Admiralty, May 7, 1915, Churchill Papers, CHAR 13/64.

ALL POINTS: RUMOR

279 Frost walked to the windows: I decided to footnote this because it is precisely the kind of detail that is likely to cause a reader to pause a moment and ask him- or herself, Hmmm, how do you *know* he walked to

his windows? Answer: because he tells us so. Frost, *German Submarine Warfare*, 187.

279 "I hear there is some sort of street rumor": Ibid., 188.

280 After hanging up, Frost paced his office: Again, we know this because Frost tells us, "I must have spent ten or fifteen minutes pacing the floor of the office." Ibid.

280 "Urgent: Recall *Juno*": Telegram, Admiralty to S.N.O. Queenstown, May 7, 1915, Churchill Papers, CHAR 13/64.

280 "I then received a telegram": Letter, Vice-Admiral C. H. Coke to Admiralty, May 9, 1915, Admiralty Papers, ADM 137/1058, National Archives UK.

281 Each call brought fresh reports: Hendrick, *Life and Letters*, 2:1–2.

281 "We shall be at war": Ibid., 2:2.

281 That morning, in New York: Jack Lawrence's account, including dialogue, appears at Lawrence, *When the Ships Came In*, 134–39.

283 "I was pacing the streets": Cooper, *Woodrow Wilson*, 286.

283 "Astern in the distance": Schwieger, War Log.

LUSITANIA: ADRIFT

284 "I saw myself hundreds": Letter, E. S. Heighway to Mrs. Prichard, June 25, 1915, Prichard Papers.

284 the killer was hypothermia: For a primer on hypothermia, see Weinberg, "Hypothermia."

285 "The most frightful thing": Letter, Dwight Harris to Mother, May 10, 1915, Harris Papers.

285 "The cries for help": Ibid.

286 "When I came to the surface": Mackworth, *This Was My World*, 246.

286 "a little dazed": Ibid., 247.

286 "so that one could inhale it": Ibid., 248.

286 "an oasis in a desert of bodies": Morton, *Long Wake*, 108

286 "We were picking people out of the water": Testimony, Frederic J. Gauntlett, Petition of the Cunard Steamship Company, April 15, 1918, U.S. National Archives–New York, 123.

287 "Never have I heard": Lauriat, *Lusitania's Last Voyage*, 25.

287 "I would, old chap": How delightful, frankly, that people actually did once upon a time use the phrase "old chap." Ibid., 40.

287 Seaman Morton swam to get her: Morton, *Long Wake*, 108–9.

287 "The clothes were almost blown off": Lauriat, *Lusitania's Last Voyage*, 29.

287 "I heard a woman's voice say": Ibid.

288 "Come, Holy Ghost": Henry Wood Simpson's account in "Saved from the *Lusitania*," *Church Family*, May 14, 1915, courtesy of Mike Poirier.

289 "I was fully expecting the submarine": Mersey, *Report*, 1, account of George Bilbrough.

289   Here were the *Brock*: See a list of boats that participated in the rescue effort, enclosed within letter, Vice-Admiral C. H. Coke to Admiralty, May 9, 1915, Admiralty Papers, ADM 137/1058, National Archives UK.

289   "No news could be had": Frost, *German Submarine Warfare*, 191.

290   "We did everything we could": Ramsay, *Lusitania*, 25–26.

290   As they approached the vessel: Lauriat, *Lusitania's Last Voyage*, 34.

290   "songs were being sung": "Statement of Mr. A. J. Mitchell," May 14, 1915, Lusitania Papers, Microcopy 580, Roll 197, U.S. National Archives–College Park.

291   "She's conscious": Letter, Pope to Ada Brooks Pope, June 28, 1915, Riddle Papers.

U-20: PARTING SHOT

292   "All we thought of": Hayden Talbot, "The Truth About the Lusitania," *Answers*, Nov. 8, 1919, in "Lusitania Various Papers," Admiralty Papers, ADM 137/1058, National Archives UK.

292   "Of course he couldn't hear anything": This is the phrase that makes her account seem credible. It is a subtle point that only submariners understood—the silence, even though what they see through their periscopes is fire and death.

293   Just five minutes: Schwieger, War Log.

293   The steamer Schwieger had fired upon: Hoehling and Hoehling, *Last Voyage*, 85, 147–48.

294   "We proceeded with all possible speed": Telegram, Lands End Wireless Station to Chief Censor, May 7, 1915, Churchill Papers, CHAR 13/64.

LUSITANIA: SEAGULLS

295   "The whole ship": Ramsay, *Lusitiana*, 274.

295   "I thought he had gone": *New York Times*, Nov. 21, 1915.

295   "I noticed it because": Ibid.

296   "he used to carry a .22 rifle": Letter, Norman H. Turner to Adolf Hoehling, Sept. 18, 1955, Hoehling Papers.

296   "That's better": The dialogue here is as reported by Mackworth, *This Was My World*, 248–49.

297   They applauded: Letter, Dwight Harris to Mother, May 10, 1915, Harris Papers.

297   Charles Lauriat carried one man: Lauriat, *Lusitania's Last Voyage*, 41. Mike Poirier provided McMurray's identity.

297   "I saved the baby's pictures": *Boston Daily Globe*, May 11, 1915.

298   She found her father waiting: Mackworth, *This Was My World*, 251.

298   "She was still dressed in the neat fawn tweed": Ibid., 254.

298   "and took a huge dose of whiskey": Letter, Dwight Harris to Mother, May 10, 1915, Harris Papers.

299   "I was left on a lounge": Letter, Pope to Ada Brooks Pope, June 28, 1915, Riddle Papers.

299   She arranged to send: Katz, *Dearest*, 120.

299   "All night I kept expecting Mr. Friend": Letter, Pope to Ada Brooks Pope, June 28, 1915, Riddle Papers.

299   "You should be worrying": Hoehling and Hoehling, *Last Voyage*, 161.

299   "appeared stunned": Telegram, Tuchy, London to *New York World*, New York, May 9, 1915, Churchill Papers, CHAR 13/64.

299   Tears filled his eyes: Ibid.

QUEENSTOWN: THE LOST

300   Of the Lusitania's 1,959 passengers and crew: As on so many points involving the *Lusitania*, there is disagreement as to just how many passengers and crew were aboard, how many died, and how many of the passengers were American. Here I'm using Cunard's official tally. See "General Analysis of Passengers and Crew" and "Summary of Passengers' Nationality," both in R.M.S. Lusitania: Record of Passengers & Crew, SAS/29/6/18, Merseyside.

300   For days dozens of cables: Letter, Charles P. Sumner to General Manager's Office, Cunard, May 18, 1915, D42/PR13/32, Cunard Archive. This letter alone provides a jarring portrait of the dimension of the disaster. Running thirteen pages, single-spaced, it lists scores of cables sent between Cunard's headquarters and its New York office.

302   "Am saved, looking for Cliff": Details of Leslie Morton's search for his brother, including dialogue, are from Morton, *Long Wake*, 112–13.

303   One man's body: The fragment of lifeboat resides at the Hoover Institution, Stanford University.

303   "There was a curious effacement": Frost, *German Submarine Warfare*, 226–28.

303   The unimportant bodies: Ibid., 226.

303   Body No. 1: "Identified Remains, South Coast List," R.M.S. Lusitania: Record of Passengers & Crew, SAS/29/6/18, Merseyside.

304   "Several weeks after the disaster": Frost, *German Submarine Warfare*, 228.

304   "Much of the body was eaten away": Telegram, July 15, 1915, "Male body washed ashore," D42/PR13/1/226–250, Cunard Archives.

305   Frost offered an additional pound: Telegram, Wesley Frost to William Jennings Bryan, May 13, 1915, decimal file 341.111L97/16, U.S. National Archives–College Park.

305   His name was Leon C. Thrasher: Telegram, U.S. Consul General, London, to William Jennings Bryan, April 7, 1915, *Foreign Relations*.

       Thrasher is sometimes identified in news accounts as Thresher. I've chosen to use "Thrasher" because it is the spelling used in official U.S. diplomatic correspondence included in the *Foreign Relations* series.

305 Such was the case: Letter, Sgt. J. Regan to U.S. Consul Wesley Frost, Aug. 20, 1915, decimal file 341.111L97/105, U.S. National Archives–College Park.

306 "Needless to say": Details of the Shields autopsy may be found in letter, Wesley Frost to U.S. Secretary of State, July 27, 1915, and enclosure, "Autopsy on Remains of Victor E. Shields," decimal file 341.111. L97/87, U.S. National Archives–College Park.

308 "My own personal loss": Letter, Alfred A. Booth to Charles P. Sumner, May 8, 1915, D42/C1/1/66, Part 2 of 4, Cunard Archives.

308 "is sad beyond expression": Letter, Charles P. Sumner to Alfred A. Booth, May 14, 1915, D42/C1/1/66, Part 2 of 4, Cunard Archives.

309 "a picture of peace": *Washington Times*, May 10, 1915.

310 The family of Elizabeth A. Seccombe: "Identified Remains," R.M.S. Lusitania: Record of Passengers & Crew, SAS/29/6/18, Merseyside; letter, Wesley Frost to U.S. Secretary of State, Sept. 17, 1915, decimal file 341.111L97/123-124, U.S. National Archives–College Park.

310 Of the 791 passengers: I computed these numbers on the basis of data provided in R.M.S. Lusitania: Record of Passengers & Crew, SAS/29/6/18, Merseyside.

311 "The place is alive": Preston, *Lusitania*, 297.

312 "I can see his face": Letter, Grace French to Mrs. Prichard, Sept. 10, 1915, Prichard Papers.

312 "I beg of you": Letter, Theodate Pope to Mrs. Prichard, Feb. 4, 1916, Prichard Papers.

312 "I know you must be tempted": Letter, Ruth M. Wordsworth to Prichard, July 9, 1915, Prichard Papers.

PART V: THE SEA OF SECRETS

LONDON: BLAME

317 "We sh'd pursue the Captain": Annotation to telegram, Richard Webb to Cecil Spring-Rice, May 11, 1915, "Lusitania Various Papers," Admiralty Papers, ADM 137/1058, National Archives UK.

317 "a brave but unlucky man": Horgan, *Parnell to Pearse*, 274.

317 "willful and wholesale murder": Ibid., 273.

318 "That august body": Ibid., 275.

318 "proceeded along the usual trade route": "Memorandum as to Master's Actions," May 8, 1915, Admiralty Papers, ADM 1/8451/56, National Archives UK.

318 "appears to have displayed": Telegram, Richard Webb to Cecil Spring-Rice, May 11, 1915, "Lusitania Various Papers," Admiralty Papers, ADM 137/1058, National Archives UK.

319 "Bare facts only": Letter, Wesley Frost to William Jennings Bryan, May

11, 1915, Lusitania Papers, Microcopy 580, Roll 197, U.S. National Archives–College Park.

319 "I was struck by the fact": Memorandum, "Statement of Captain W. A. Castle," May 14, 1915, Lusitania Papers, Microcopy 580, Roll 197, U.S. National Archives–College Park.

319 "Merchant traffic must look after itself": *Independent*, May 24, 1915.

320 "Have sunk off the South Coast of Ireland": Images of the actual hand-written decodes may be found in the papers of the Ministry of Defence, DEFE/69/270, National Archives UK.

320 "My highest appreciation": Ibid.

320 "by means of one torpedo": Ibid.

321 Turner testified that by his own standards: Testimony, William Thomas Turner, June 15, 1915, 4, "Investigation."

322 Carson let pass the fact: Bailey and Ryan, *Lusitania Disaster*, 143; telegram, Wesley Frost to William Jennings Bryan, May 9, 1915, *Foreign Relations*. In his telegram, Frost quotes a passenger's statement, which began, "At 12 noon ship began to zigzag . . . off Irish coast."

322 "I mean to say, we have the very great advantage": Testimony, William Thomas Turner, June 15, 1915, 15, "Investigation."

322 "exercised his judgment for the best": Annex to the Report, Ministry of Transport Papers, MT 9/1326, "Investigation," 9.

322 "still left the *Lusitania* a considerably faster ship": Ibid., 7.

322 "He was very bitter": Letter, Norman H. Turner to Adolf Hoehling, Sept. 18, 1955, Hoehling Papers.

323 "a damned dirty business": Memorandum, Head of Naval Historical Branch, Oct. 25, 1972, Ministry of Defence Papers, DEFE/69/270, National Archives UK.

324 "one is left only with an unforgivable cock-up": Beesly, *Room 40*, 121.

324 "As an Englishman": Article and associated interview, Patrick Beesly, Misc. 162, Item 2491, Imperial War Museum.

324 "With regard to the question of convoy": Memorandum, "'Lusitania'—American Proceedings," Admiralty Papers, ADM 1/8451/56, National Archives UK.

324 "Even one destroyer encircling the liner": *Irish Independent*, May 7, 1955.

325 "The neglect to provide naval escort": Bisset, *Commodore*, 46.

325 "It might . . . but it is one of those things one never knows": *Liverpool Weekly Mercury*, May 15, 1915.

325 Testing done several years earlier: Bailey and Ryan, *Lusitania Disaster*, 101; Wood et al., "Sinking," 179–80.

325 A more plausible theory: Ballard, *Exploring the Lusitania*, 194–95. Ballard's book, by the way, has many compelling photographs (152–91) of what remains of the *Lusitania* at the bottom of the sea, taken during his exploration of the wreck in 1993.

326 Subsequent investigation by forensic engineers: Garzke et al., *Titanic*,

260–61; Wood et al., "Sinking," 181–83, 187. Also see Annex to the Report, Ministry of Transportation Papers, MT 9/1326, "Investigation."

326   This was Turner's theory: Preston, *Lusitania*, 453.

326   "to 50 pounds in a few seconds": Deposition, George Little, May 15, 1915, "Depositions Removed from Trade Division Papers," Admiralty Papers, ADM 137/1058, National Archives UK; Preston, *Lusitania*, 453.

327   Not only that, it struck precisely the right place: Garzke et al., *Titanic*, 256–60, 263–67; Wood et al., "Sinking," 174–78, 186, 188.

WASHINGTON; BERLIN; LONDON: THE LAST BLUNDER

329   "If I pondered": *New York Times*, Nov. 15, 1921.

329   In fact, apart from a noisy pro-war faction: Resolution, May 16, 1915; Rush Medical College, Resolution, May 16, 1915; College of Dentistry, University of Illinois, Resolution, May 11, 1915; and Tennessee State Assembly, Resolution all in Lusitania Papers, Microcopy 580, Roll 197, U.S. National Archives–College Park; Cooper, *Vanity of Power*, 33–34; Cummins, "Indiana's Reaction," 13, 15, 17.

And may I just say how refreshing it was to read the state of Louisiana's resolution, in light of the rancor in American politics that prevailed at the time I completed this book:

"Such a crisis as now confronts our country calls for coolness, deliberation, firmness and precision of mind on the part of those entrusted with the power of administration.

"Under the providence of God this country has such a leader in Woodrow Wilson . . . who with his advisers has so signally shown the temper and courage and great humanity that reflects the sentiment of his loyal countrymen." Resolution, May 20, 1915, Louisiana Legislature, Lusitania Papers, Microcopy 580, Roll 197, U.S. National Archives–College Park.

330   "the day which marked the end": *Neue Preussische Zeitung*, May 10, 1915, translation, Foreign and German Press Analysis, Box 2, Bailey/Ryan Collection.

330   "America does not know what conditions are": Telegram, Heer[illegible], New York, to *Evening News*, London, May 8, 1915, Churchill Papers, CHAR 13/64.

331   "There is such a thing": Berg, *Wilson*, 364; Link, *Wilson: Struggle*, 382. Newspaper editor Oswald Garrison Villard, in his autobiography *Fighting Years*, claimed it was he who had planted the phrase "too proud to fight" in the president's mind. He did so inadvertently, he wrote. He had discussed the concept with Wilson's personal secretary, Tumulty, never thinking that Tumulty would pass it along to Wilson. Villard, *Fighting Years*, 256–57.

331 "probably the most unfortunate phrase": Berg, *Wilson*, 364.

331 "I do not know just what I said": Wilson to Galt, May 11, 1915, Wilson Papers.

331 "I have just put the final touches": Wilson to Galt, May 12, 1915, Wilson Papers.

Wilson understood that diplomatic notes were likely to have little effect in the short term but believed them valuable all the same. "They alter no facts," he wrote, in a letter to Galt, dated Aug. 8, 1915; "they change no plans or purposes; they accomplish nothing immediate; but they <u>may</u> convey some thoughts that will, if only unconsciously, affect opinion, and set up a counter current. At least such is my hope; and it is also the only hope for these distracted English!"

332 "the sacred freedom of the seas": Telegram, William Jennings Bryan to German Foreign Office, via U.S. Amb. James Gerard, May 13, 1915, *Foreign Relations*, 394; Berg, *Wilson*, 365–66.

332 "The Kaiser has awarded the Iron Cross": Cummins, "Indiana's Reaction," 24.

332 Wilson himself described Bryan as a "traitor": Wilson to Galt [undated], Wilson Papers. Wilson wrote: "For he <u>is</u> a traitor, though I can say so, as yet, only to you."

Bryan's defection caused Wilson deep hurt. In a letter to Galt dated June 9, 1915, he wrote, "The impression upon my mind of Mr. Bryan's retirement is a very painful one <u>now</u>. It is always painful to feel that any thinking man of disinterested motive, who has been your comrade and confidant, has turned away from you and set his hand against you; and it is hard to be fair and not think that the motive is something sinister."

To which Galt replied, "Hurrah! Old Bryan is out!"

332 "a figure in top hat, tailcoat": Starling, *Starling*, 62.

333 "Were I the Captain of a U-boat": Halpern, *Naval History*, 306.

333 "Dear Old Tirps": Bailey and Ryan, *Lusitania Disaster*, 36.

333 "advantageous to the Allied cause": Hall, Minute, Dec. 27, 1915, "Lusitania Various Papers," Admiralty Papers, ADM 137/1058, National Archives UK.

333 Kapitänleutnant Schwieger did his part: *New York Times*, Sept. 9, 1915; "List of Tonnage Sunk by U-88," Box 2, Bailey/Ryan Collection.

334 "Dear Kaiser: In spite of previous correspondence": Cummins, "Indiana's Reaction," 30.

336 "Great excitement & activity": "Capt. Hope's Diary," Nov. 5, 1916, Admiralty Papers, ADM 137/4169, National Archives UK.

336 "will have to devote itself to one task": Scheer, *Germany's High Sea Fleet*, 194.

336 "every U-boat is of such importance": Ibid.

337 "I guarantee upon my word": Tuchman, *Zimmermann Telegram*, 141; Birnbaum, *Peace Moves*, 277. Tuchman notes that Holtzendorff's memorandum, which ran to two hundred pages, included such fine-grained

details as the number of calories in a typical English breakfast and the amount of wool in skirts worn by Englishwomen.

Koerver reports another example of delusional thinking within the German navy. Adm. Edouard von Capelle said, on Feb. 1, 1917, "From a military point of view I rate the effect of America coming on the side of our enemies as nil." Tuchman, *Zimmermann Telegram*, 139; Koerver, *German Submarine Warfare*, xxxiii.

338   "d'you want to bring America into the war?": The dialogue in this chapter is as reported by Hall in ch. 25, "Draft D," of his unpublished autobiography, Hall Papers.

338   "Make war together": Ibid.; Boghardt, *Zimmermann Telegram*, 106–7; Link, *Wilson: Campaigns*, 343.

338   "This may be a very big thing": Hall, "Draft D.," ch. 25, Hall Papers.

339   "Only actual overt acts on their part": Tuchman, *Zimmermann Telegram*, 151.

339   Hall realized the time for action had come: Boghardt, *Zimmermann Telegram*, 78, 101, 105. My account here is necessarily abbreviated, for one could write an entire volume just on the Zimmermann telegram—as indeed other authors have done. For further reading, turn first to Tuchman, mainly for the sheer panache with which she tells the story. For the most up-to-date scholarship, however, see Boghardt's *Zimmermann Telegram* (2012) and Gannon's *Inside Room 40* (2010).

340   "By admitting the truth": Beesly, *Room 40*, 223.

340   "All these papers had been ardently neutral": Tuchman, *Zimmermann Telegram*, 185.

340   "The American people are at last ready": Lansing, Private Memoranda, March 19, 1917, Lansing Papers.

340   "I must have spoken with vehemence": Ibid., March 20, 1917.

341   "Germany is going to get Hell": Link, *Wilson: Campaigns*, 421.

341   "stood in solemn splendor": Sullivan, *Our Time*, 272–73.

342   "in effect nothing less than war": The *New York Times* of April 3, 1917, published Wilson's entire speech on the front page. See also Link, *Wilson: Campaigns*, 422–26.

342   "gravely, emphatically": *New York Times*, April 3, 1917.

343   "What he did in April, 1917": Churchill, *World Crisis*, 682–83. One early-twentieth-century British diarist, Lady Alice Thompson, did not think very highly of America's restraint. On Feb. 27, 1917, after the sinking of a Cunard liner, the *Laconia*, she wrote, "The <u>contemptible</u> President of the U.S. may yet be '<u>kicked</u>' into taking notice of this fresh German outrage. He is still masquerading at 'considering the matter'—"

After another sinking she wrote, on March 24, 1917: "I suspect Wilson will write <u>another</u> <u>note</u>!! & then this new act of Barbarity will sink into oblivion. They are a wonderful nation of Big talk & little action—I leave them at that." Diaries of Lady Alice Thompson, vols. 2 and 3, Doc. 15282, Imperial War Museum.

343   In Queenstown, U.S. consul Frost: Frost, *German Submarine Warfare*, 5.

343   "Briefly stated, I consider": Sims, *Victory at Sea*, 43.

344   "Welcome to the American colors": Ibid., 51.

344   On May 8, the destroyers: Halpern, *Naval History*, 359.

EPILOGUE: PERSONAL EFFECTS

345   "She looked so smeared and dirty": Lawrence, *When the Ships Came In*, 131–32.

346   "horse storm": Ibid., 132.

346   "His old blue uniform": Ibid., 133.

346   "I told him there were no regrets": *New York Times*, Nov. 21, 1915.

346   On January 1, 1917: Ramsay, *Lusitania*, 161; Hoehling and Hoehling, *Last Voyage*, 172.

347   "this great little man": Letter, George Ball to Adolf Hoehling, July 22, 1955, Hoehling Papers.

347   "Capt. Turner felt the loss": Letter, Mabel Every to Adolf Hoehling, May [4], 1955, Hoehling Papers; Ramsay, *Lusitania*, 161; letter, George Ball to Adolf Hoehling, July 22, 1955, Hoehling Papers.

347   "I grieve for all the poor innocent people": Letter, William Thomas Turner to Miss Brayton, June 10, 1915, D42/PR13/29, Cunard Archive.

348   "He was far too strong a character": Letter, George Ball to Adolf Hoehling, July 22, 1955, Hoehling Papers.

348   "I am satisfied that every precaution was taken": *New York Times*, Nov. 21, 1915.

348   "Merriment and humor": Letter, Geroge Ball to Adolf Hoehling, July 22, 1955, Hoehling Papers.

348   "He died as he had lived": Ibid.

349   Room 40 recorded the loss: Ledger, Tactical Formation of Submarines: Summary of Submarine Cruises, Entry: Sept. 5, 1917, Admiralty Papers, ADM 137/4128, National Archives UK; Grant, *U-Boat Intelligence*, 73, 185.

349   They reside today: The museum is the Strandingsmuseum St. George, Thorsminde, Denmark, just a brief stroll from the North Sea. U-20's conning tower stands on a lawn out front, stripped of all hatches and apparatus. Schwieger's deck gun, once so accurate and deadly, stands inside the museum, opposite a cabinet that displays other pieces of the submarine. For more on the museum, see its website at www.strandingsmuseet.dk/about-us

350   "How simple is intelligence!": "Rough Notes," Hall 2/1, Hall Papers.

350   "All the young are in the net": Letter, Hall to Percy Madeira, Oct. 6, 1934, Hall 1/6, Hall Papers.

350   "If you're the undertaker, my man": Ramsay, *"Blinker" Hall*, 299.

351   "I insistently pictured the tunnel giving way": Mackworth, *This Was My World*, 262.

351   "If anyone had asked me": Ibid., 259.

351   "I do not quite understand": Ibid., 260.

352   He established a foundation: "Compliments of George Kessler," *American Menu*, April 14, 2012, 12.

352   A succession of new owners: For the more recent history of Lauriat's, see the *Boston Globe*, Oct. 1, 1972, and May 19 and June 13, 1999.

352   a clear blue sky: *Kansas City Star*, June 15, 1919. Courtesy of Mike Poirier.

352   "I dropped into a chair": Katz, *Dearest*, 121.

353   "If you were saved": Cunningham, *My Godmother*, 51.

353   "in such a state of exhaustion": Katz, *Dearest*, 122.

353   "You can have no idea": Ibid., 125.

353   Her companion, Edwin Friend: Hoehling and Hoehling, *Last Voyage*, 171.

BIBLIOGRAPHY

ARCHIVAL COLLECTIONS

Baker, James. Papers. Imperial War Museum, London.

BBC Written Archives Centre. Caversham, Reading, England.

Bailey, Thomas Andrew, and Paul B. Ryan Collection. Hoover Institution Archives, Stanford University. Stanford, CA.

Bruford, Walter Horace. Papers. Churchill Archives, Churchill College, Cambridge, England.

Bryan, William Jennings. Papers. Library of Congress Manuscript Division. Washington, D.C.

Churchill, Winston. Papers. Churchill Archives, Churchill College, Cambridge, England.

Clarke, William F. Papers. Churchill Archives, Churchill College, Cambridge, England.

Cunard Archives ("Records of the Cunard Steamship Co."), Sydney Jones Library, University of Liverpool, England. Courtesy of the University of Liverpool Library.

Denniston, Alexander Guthrie. Papers. Churchill Archives, Churchill College, Cambridge, England.

Fisher, Jacky. Papers. Churchill Archives, Churchill College, Cambridge, England.

Hall, William Reginald. Papers. Churchill Archives, Churchill College, Cambridge, England.

Harris, Dwight. Papers. New-York Historical Society. New York, N.Y. (File: BV Lusitania, MS 1757.) Courtesy of the New-York Historical Society.

Hoehling, Adolf, and Mary Hoehling. Papers. RMS Lusitania Collection. Mariners' Museum and Library. Christopher Newport University, Newport News, VA.

Hook, Hereward. Papers. Imperial War Museum, London.

Jellicoe, John. Papers. Churchill Archives, Churchill College, Cambridge, England.

Kell, Vernon. Papers. Imperial War Museum, London.

Lansing, Robert. Papers. Library of Congress Manuscript Division. Washington, DC (Desk Diaries and Private Memoranda).

Lorimer, D. Papers. Imperial War Museum, London.

Maritime Archives. Merseyside Maritime Museum. Liverpool, England.

McAdoo, William Gibbs. Papers. Library of Congress Manuscript Division. Washington, DC.

National Archives of the United Kingdom, Kew, England. Material cited in accord with Britain's Open Government License.

Prichard, Mrs. G. S. Papers. Imperial War Museum, London.

Riddle, Theodate Pope. Papers. Hill-Stead Museum, Farmington, CT.

U.S. Department of State. *Papers Relating to the Foreign Relations of the United States.* 1915. Supplement, The World War. University of Wisconsin Digital Collections.

U.S. National Archives and Records Administration, College Park, MD.

U.S. National Archives and Records Administration at New York City. New York, NY.

Wilson, Woodrow. Papers. Library of Congress Manuscript Division. Washington, DC.

BOOKS AND JOURNAL ARTICLES

Albertini, Luigi. *The Origins of the War of 1914.* Translated by Isabella M. Massey. London: Oxford University Press, 1953.

Bailey, Thomas A. "German Documents Relating to the '*Lusitania.*'" *Journal of Modern History* 8, no. 3 (September 1936): 320–37.

———. "The Sinking of the Lusitania." *American Historical Review* 41, no. 1 (Oct. 1935): 54–73.

Bailey, Thomas A., and Paul B. Ryan. *The Lusitania Disaster: An Episode in Modern Warfare and Diplomacy.* New York: Free Press, 1975.

Ballard, Robert, with Spencer Dunmore. *Exploring the Lusitania: Probing the Mysteries of the Sinking That Changed History.* Toronto: Warner/Madison Press, 1995.

Beesly, Patrick. Interview. "Sinking of the *Lusitania.*" Imperial War Museum, London.

———. *Room 40: British Naval Intelligence, 1914–18.* London, Hamish Hamilton, 1982.

Berg, A. Scott. *Wilson.* New York: G. P. Putnam's Sons, 2013.

Bernstorff, Count Johann-Heinrich von. *My Three Years in America.* New York: Scribner's Sons, 1920.

Birnbaum, Karl E. *Peace Moves and U-Boat Warfare.* Stockholm: Almqvist and Wiksell, 1958.

Bisset, James. *Commodore: War, Peace and Big Ships.* London: Angus and Robertson, 1961.

Bixler, Julius Seelye. "William James and Immortality." *Journal of Religion* 5, no. 4 (July 1925): 378–96.

Black, Jeremy. *The Great War and the Making of the Modern World.* New York: Continuum, 2011.

Boghardt, Thomas. *The Zimmermann Telegram: Intelligence, Diplomacy, and America's Entry into World War I.* Annapolis, MD: Naval Institute Press, 2012.

Bolze, Thomas A. "From Private Passion to Public Virtue: Thomas B. Lockwood and the Making of a Cultural Philanthropist, 1895–1935." *Libraries and the Cultural Record* 45, no. 4 (2010): 414–41.

Breemer, Jan S. *Defeating the U-Boat: Inventing Antisubmarine Warfare.* Newport, RI: Naval War College Press, 2010.

Brooks, Sydney. "The United States and the War: A British View." *North American Review* 201, no. 711 (Feb. 1915): 231–40.

Broomfield, Andrea. "The Night the Good Ship Went Down." *Gastronomica* 9, no. 4 (Fall 2009): 32–42.

Bullard, Melissa Meriam, S. R. Epstein, Benjamin G. Kohl, and Susan Mosher Stuard. "Where History and Theory Interact: Frederic C. Lane on the Emergence of Capitalism." *Speculum* 79, no. 1 (Jan. 2004): 88–119.

Carter, Mark Bonham, and Mark Pottle, eds. *Lantern Slides: The Diaries and Letters of Violet Bonham Carter, 1904–1914.* London: Weidenfeld and Nicolson, 1996.

Churchill, Winston S. *The World Crisis, 1911–1918.* 1923. Reprint, London: Thornton Butterworth, 1931.

Clark, Alan. *The Donkeys.* London: Pimlico, 1961.

Clements, Kendrick A. "Woodrow Wilson and World War I." *Presidential Studies Quarterly* 34, no. 1 (March 2004): 62–82.

Compton-Hall, Richard. *Submarine Boats.* New York: Arco, 1983.

Cooper, John Milton, Jr. *The Vanity of Power: American Isolationism and the First World War, 1914–1917.* Westport, CT: Greenwood, 1969.

———. *Walter Hines Page: The Southerner as American, 1855–1918.* Chapel Hill: University of North Carolina Press, 1977.

———. *Woodrow Wilson.* New York: Knopf, 2009.

Crow, Duncan. *A Man of Push and Go: The Life of George Macaulay Booth.* London: Rupert Hart-Davis, 1965.

Cullen, Fintan. "The Lane Bequest." *Field Day Review* 4 (2008): 187–201.

Cummins, Cedric C. "Indiana's Reaction to the Submarine Controversy of 1915." *Indiana Magazine of History* 40, no. 1 (March 1944): 1–32.

"The Cunard Liner *Lusitania.*" *Journal of the American Society for Naval Engineers* 19, no. 4 (Nov. 1907): 933–83.

Cunningham, Phyllis Fenn. *My Godmother: Theodate Pope Riddle.* Canaan, NH: Phoenix, 1983.

Devlin, Patrick. *Too Proud to Fight: Woodrow Wilson's Neutrality.* New York: Oxford University Press, 1975.

Directory of Directors. City of Boston. Boston: Bankers' Service Co., 1905.

Doerries, Reinhard R. *Imperial Challenge: Ambassador Count Bernstorff and German-American Relations, 1908–1917*. Translated by Christa D. Shannon. Chapel Hill: University of North Carolina Press, 1989.

Doyle, Arthur Conan. "Danger!" In *Danger! and Other Stories*. London: John Murray, 1918.

Egan, Timothy. *Short Nights of the Shadow Catcher*. Boston: Houghton Mifflin, 2013.

Figueiredo, Peter de. "Symbols of Empire: The Buildings of the Liverpool Waterfront." *Architectural History* 46 (2003): 229–54.

Fontenoy, Paul. *Submarines: An Illustrated History of Their Impact*. Weapons and Warfare. Santa Barbara, CA: ABC-CLIO, 2007.

Forstner, Georg-Gunther Freiherr von. *The Journal of Submarine Commander von Forstner*. Translated by Mrs. Russell Codman. Boston: Houghton Mifflin, 1917.

Fox, Stephen. *Transatlantic: Samuel Cunard, Isambard Brunel, and the Great Atlantic Steamships*. New York: HarperCollins, 2003.

Frost, Wesley. *German Submarine Warfare: A Study of Its Methods and Spirit*. New York: D. Appleton, 1918.

Frothingham, Thomas G. *The Naval History of the World War*. Vol. 1. Cambridge, MA: Harvard University Press, 1925.

Gannon, Paul. *Inside Room 40: The Codebreakers of World War I*. Hersham, Surrey, UK: Ian Allan, 2010.

Garzke, William H., Jr., D. K. Brown, A. D. Sandiford, J. Woodward, and P. K. Hsu. "The *Titanic* and *Lusitania*: A Final Forensic Analysis." *Marine Technology* 33, no. 4 (Oct. 1996): 241–89.

Gibson, R. H., and Maurice Prendergast. *The German Submarine War 1914–1918*. 1931. Reprint, Uckfield, East Sussex: Naval and Military Press, 2003.

Gilbert, Martin. *The First World War*. New York: Henry Holt, 1994.

Grant, Robert M. *U-Boat Intelligence, 1914–1918*. North Haven, CT: Archon Books, 1969.

Grayson, Cary T. *Woodrow Wilson: An Intimate Memoir*. 1960. Reprint, Washington, DC: Potomac Books, 1977.

Halpern, Paul G. *A Naval History of World War I*. Annapolis, MD: Naval Institute Press, 2012.

Hart, Peter. *Gallipoli*. New York: Oxford University Press, 2011.

Hazen, David W. *Giants and Ghosts of Central Europe*. Portland, OR: Metropolitan Press, 1933.

Hendrick, Burton J. *The Life and Letters of Walter H. Page*. Vols. 1–3. Garden City, NY: Doubleday, Page, 1922.

Hoehling, Adolf A., and Mary Hoehling. *The Last Voyage of the Lusitania*. London: Longmans, Green, 1957.

Holbourn, Ian B. Stoughton. *The Isle of Foula*. 1938. Reprint, Edinburgh: Birlinn, 2001.

Horgan, John J. *Parnell to Pearse: Some Recollections and Reflections.* 1949. Reprint, Dublin: University College Press, 2009.

Hough, Richard. *Winston and Clementine.* London: Transworld, 1990.

Houston, David F. *Eight Years with Wilson's Cabinet, 1913 to 1920.* New York: Doubleday, Page, 1926.

James, Adm. William. *The Code Breakers of Room 40.* New York: St. Martin's Press, 1956.

James, William. "Address of the President Before the Society for Psychical Research." *Science,* n.s., 3, no. 77 (June 19, 1896): 881–88.

Kahn, David. *The Codebreakers: The Story of Secret Writing.* New York: Macmillan, 1967.

Kalafus, Jim, Michael Poirier, Cliff Barry, and Peter Kelly. *Lest We Forget: The Lusitania.* Published online, May 7, 2013. www.encyclopedia-titanica .org/lest-we-forget-the-lusitania.html.

Katz, Sandra L. *Dearest of Geniuses: A Life of Theodate Pope.* Windsor, CT: Tide-Mark Press, 2003.

Keegan, John. *The First World War.* New York: Vintage Books, 1998.

Kennedy, Paul M. *The War Plans of the Great Powers, 1880–1914.* London: George Allen and Unwin, 1979.

Kilgour, Raymond L. *Estes and Lauriat: A History, 1872–1898.* Ann Arbor: University of Michigan Press, 1957.

Knight, Denise D. "'All the Facts of the Case': Gilman's Lost Letter to Dr. S. Weir Mitchell." *American Literary Realism* 37, no. 3 (Spring 2005): 259–77.

Koenig, Paul. *Voyage of the Deutschland.* New York: Hearst's International Library, 1917.

Koerver, Hans Joachim. *German Submarine Warfare 1914–1918 in the Eyes of British Intelligence.* Steinbach, Austria: LIS Reinisch, 2012. http://germannavalwarfare.info/01gnw/subm/jpg/subm.pdf.

Lambert, Nicholas. *The Submarine Service, 1900–1918.* London: Ashgate, 2001.

Lamont, Peter. "Spiritualism and a Mid-Victorian Crisis of Evidence." *Historical Journal* 47, no. 4 (2004): 897–920.

Lane, Anne Wintermute, and Louise Herrick Wall, eds. *The Letters of Franklin K. Lane.* Boston: Houghton Mifflin, 1922.

Larson, Erik. *Thunderstruck.* New York: Crown, 2006.

Lauriat, Charles E., Jr. *The Lusitania's Last Voyage.* Boston: Houghton Mifflin, 1915.

Lawrence, Jack. *When the Ships Came In.* New York: Farrar and Rinehart, 1940.

Levin, Phyllis Lee. *Edith and Woodrow.* New York: Scribner, 2001.

Link, Arthur S. "Dr. Grayson's Predicament." *Proceedings of the American Philosophical Society* 138, no. 4 (Dec. 1994): 487–94.

———. *Wilson: Campaigns for Progressivism and Peace, 1916–1917.* Princeton, NJ: Princeton University Press, 1965.

———. *Wilson: Confusions and Crises, 1915–1916*. Princeton, NJ: Princeton University Press, 1964.

———. *Wilson: The Struggle for Neutrality, 1914–1915*. Princeton, NJ: Princeton University Press, 1960.

Lord, Walter. *A Night to Remember*. New York: Henry Holt, 1955.

Mackworth, Margaret. *This Was My World*. London: Macmillan, 1933.

Marcosson, Isaac F., and Danniel Frohman. *Charles Frohman: Manager and Man*. New York: Harper and Brothers, 1916.

Marder, Arthur J. *Fear God and Dread Nought: The Correspondence of Admiral of the Fleet Lord Fisher of Kilverstone*. Vols. 2 and 3. London: Jonathan Cape, 1959.

———. *From the Dreadnought to Scapa Flow: The Royal Navy in the Fisher Era, 1904–1919*. Vol. 2. London: Oxford University Press, 1965.

Mellown, Muriel. "Lady Rhondda and the Changing Faces of British Feminism." *Frontiers* 9, no. 2 (1987): 7–13.

Mersey, Lord (John Charles Bingham). *Report on the Loss of the "Falaba."* London: H. M. Stationery Office, 1915.

Messimer, Dwight R. *The Merchant U-Boat*. Annapolis, MD: Naval Institute Press, 1988.

Mitchell, S. Weir. *Doctor and Patient*. Philadelphia: J. B. Lippincott, 1888.

———. *Fat and Blood: And How to Make Them*. Philadelphia: J. B . Lippincott, 1877.

———. *Wear and Tear or Hints for the Overworked*. Philadelphia: J. B. Lippincott, 1897.

Morton, Leslie. *The Long Wake*. London: Routledge and Kegan Paul, 1968.

Neureuther, Karl, and Claus Bergen, eds. *U-Boat Stories*. Uckfield, East Sussex, UK: Naval and Military Press, 2005.

Niemöller, Martin. *From U-Boat to Pulpit*. Chicago: Willett, Clark, 1937.

Paine, Judith. "Avon Old Farms School: The Architecture of Theodate Pope Riddle." *Perspecta* 18 (1982): 42–48.

Preston, Diana. *Lusitania: An Epic Tragedy*. New York: Walker, 2002.

Ramsay, David. *"Blinker" Hall: Spymaster*. Gloucestershire, UK: History Press, 2009.

———. *Lusitania: Saga and Myth*. New York: W. W. Norton, 2002.

Rintelen, Franz von. *The Dark Invader: Wartime Reminiscences of a German Naval Officer*. New York: Penguin, 1939.

Ritter, Gerhard. *The Schlieffen Plan*. Translated by Andrew and Eva Wilson. New York: Frederick A. Praeger, 1958.

Rössler, Eberhard. *The U-Boat*. Translated by Harold Erenberg. London: Arms and Armour Press, 1981.

Rossano, Geoffrey L. *Stalking the U-Boat: U.S. Naval Aviation in Europe During World War I*. Gainesville: University Press of Florida, 2010.

Sargent, George H. *Lauriat's, 1872–1922*. Boston: privately printed, 1922.

Schachtman, Tom. *Edith and Woodrow*. New York: G. P. Putnam's Sons, 1981.

Scheer, Reinhard. *Germany's High Sea Fleet in the World War.* 1919. Reprint, New York: Peter Smith, 1934.

Seymour, Charles. *The Intimate Papers of Colonel House.* Vols. 1 and 2. Boston: Houghton Mifflin, 1926.

Sims, William Sowden. *The Victory at Sea.* 1920. Reprint, Annapolis: Naval Institute Press, 1984.

Smith, Gene. *When the Cheering Stopped: The Last Years of Woodrow Wilson.* New York: William Morrow, 1964.

Smith, Sharon Dunlap. *Theodate Pope Riddle: Her Life and Architecture.* 2002. www.valinet.com/~smithash/theodate/.

Soames, Mary. *Clementine Churchill: The Biography of a Marriage.* Boston: Houghton Mifflin, 1979.

Spiegel, Edgar von. *The Adventures of the U-202.* New York: Century, 1917. Google Book.

Starling, Edmund W. (as told to Thomas Sugrue). *Starling of the White House.* 1916..Reprint, Chicago: People's Book Club, 1946.

Steinberg, Jonathan. *Yesterday's Deterrent: Tirpitz and the Birth of the German Battle Fleet.* New York: Macmillan, 1965.

Sullivan, Mark. *Our Times, 1900–1925.* New York: Charles Scribner's Sons, 1936.

Szefel, Lisa. "Beauty and William Braithwaite." *Callaloo* 29, no. 2 (Spring 2006): 560–86.

Thomas, Lowell. *Raiders of the Deep.* Garden City, NY: Garden City Publishing, 1928.

Thomson, George Malcolm. *The Twelve Days: 24 July to 4 August 1914.* London: Hutchinson, 1964.

Trapp, Georg von. *To the Last Salute: Memories of an Austrian U-Boat Commander.* Translated by Elizabeth M. Campbell. Lincoln: University of Nebraska Press, 2007.

Trommler, Frank. "The *Lusitania* Effect: America's Mobilization Against Germany in World War I." *German Studies Review* 32, no. 2 (May 2009): 241–66.

Tuchman, Barbara W. *The Zimmermann Telegram.* 1958. Reprint, New York: MacMillan, 1966.

"The Use of Neutral Flags on Merchant Vessels of Belligerents." *American Journal of International Law* 9, no. 2 (April 1915): 471–73.

U.S. Navy Department. *German Submarine Activities on the Atlantic Coast of the United States and Canada.* Washington, DC: GPO, 1920.

Valentiner, Max. *La terreur des mers: Mes aventures en sous-marin, 1914–1918.* Paris: Payot, 1931.

Villard, Oswald Garrison. *Fighting Years: Memoirs of a Liberal Editor.* New York: Harcourt, Brace, 1939.

Walker, Alastair. *Four Thousand Lives Lost: The Inquiries of Lord Mersey into the Sinkings of the Titanic, the Empress of Ireland, the Falaba, and the Lusitania.* Stroud, Gloucestershire, UK: History Press, 2012.

Ward, Maisie. *Father Maturin.* London: Longmans, Green, 1920.

Weinberg, Andrew D. "Hypothermia." *Annals of Emergency Medicine* 22, pt. 2 (Feb. 1993): 370–77.

Weir, Gary E. *Building the Kaiser's Navy.* Annapolis, MD: Naval Institute Press, 1992.

Weizsäcker, Ernst von. *Memoirs of Ernst von Weizsäcker.* London: Victor Gollancz, 1951.

Wilson, Edith Bolling. *My Memoir.* 1938. Reprint, New York: Bobbs-Merrill, 1939.

Wood, M. G., D. I. Smith, and M. R. Hayns. "The Sinking of the *Lusitania*: Reviewing the Evidence." *Science and Justice* 42, no. 3 (2002): 173–88.

INDEX

The Devil in the White City

Erik Larson

One man built a heaven on earth. Another built hell beside it.

The Chicago World's Fair of 1893 was one of the great wonders of
the world. This is the extraordinary story of its realization, and
of two men whose fates it linked: one was an architect, the other a
serial killer . . .

The architect was Daniel H. Burnham. He created the 'White
City', a massive, visionary landscape of white buildings set in an
incandescent wonderland of canals and gardens. The killer was
H. H. Holmes, a handsome doctor with intense blue eyes, who
used the attraction of the great fair and his own devilish charms to
lure scores, perhaps hundreds, of young women to their deaths.
And while Burnham overcame politics, infighting, personality
clashes and Chicago's infamous weather to transform the swamps
of Jackson Park into the greatest show on Earth, Holmes built his
own edifice. He called it the World's Fair Hotel. In reality it was a
torture palace, a gas chamber, a crematorium.

These two disparate yet driven men together with a remarkable
supporting cast, including Buffalo Bill, George Ferris and Thomas
Edison, are brought to life in this mesmerizing, murderous tale of
the spectacle that transformed America and set it on course for the
20th century.

In the Garden of Beasts
Erik Larson

'A stunning work of history'
NEWSWEEK

Berlin, 1933. William E. Dodd is America's first ambassador to Hitler's Germany and is about to witness a turning point in history.

A mild-mannered academic, Dodd brings his family with him, including his vivacious daughter, Martha. At first, Martha is captivated by the pomp, the parties and the handsome young men of the Third Reich whose enthusiasm for restoring Germany to world prominence proves infectious.

But then evidence of Jewish persecution mounts, drafts of frightening new laws begin to circulate, the press is censored and Dodd telegraphs his growing concerns to a largely indifferent U.S. State Department. As this tumultuous year unfolds, Dodd's disillusion deepens and a time of excitement and romance is transformed into one of intrigue, fear and – ultimately – horror when a climactic spasm of violence and murder revealed Hitler's true character and ruthless ambition.

'Larson writes history like a novelist. He presents a familiar story through fresh eyes, conveying quite wonderfully the electrically charged atmosphere of a whole society turning towards the stormy dark'
SUNDAY TELEGRAPH

'Larson's best and most enthralling work . . .
a transportingly true story'
NEW YORK TIMES

'Reads like an elegant thriller . . . utterly compelling'
PHILIP KERR